The Bassoon

Also available in the series

The Flute
Ardal Powell

Timpani and Percussion
Jeremy Montagu

The Oboe
Geoffrey Burgess and Bruce Haynes

The Trombone
Trevor Herbert

The Clarinet
Eric Hoeprich

The Trumpet
John Wallace and Alexander McGrattan

THE YALE MUSICAL INSTRUMENT SERIES

The Bassoon

James B. Kopp

Yale University Press
New Haven and London
Published in Association with the William Waterhouse Estate

Published with assistance from Furthermore: a program of the J.M. Kaplan Fund

For information about this and other Yale University Press publications please contact:
U.S. Office: sales.press@yale.edu   yalebooks.com
Europe Office: sales@yaleup.co.uk   www.yalebooks.co.uk

Set in Columbus MT by IDSUK (DataConnection) Ltd

Printed in Great Britain by TJ International Ltd, Padstow, Cornwall

Library of Congress Cataloging-in-Publication Data

Kopp, James B.
  The bassoon / James B. Kopp.
    p. cm.
  ISBN 978-0-300-11829-2 (cl : alk. paper)
1. Bassoon—History. I. Title.
  ML950K66 2012
  788.5'819—dc23

                                                        2012013715

A catalogue record for this book is available from the British Library.

10 9 8 7 6 5 4 3 2 1

To Elisabeth Waterhouse, a pianist who has long championed the bassoon

Contents

Illustrations

Music examples

Preface

This is a book about the history of the bassoon idea. Why did this mystifying instrument arise? How and why did it evolve, and what traits persisted through its long history? Why did it not disappear from use, like so many other instruments of the sixteenth century? Why was the bassoon an instrument of choice in the ensembles of kings, nobles, and military commanders? What sort of life did a bassoonist lead in a given century? Answers to these and other questions are attempted in the following chapters.

If I say that Chopin, Donizetti, or Stravinsky 'chose' the bassoon, specific sound images will spring to the minds of many readers. Each composer opted for the bassoon, among all orchestral instruments, to present one of his most memorable melodic ideas. A list might easily continue with examples from Bach, Rameau, Beethoven, Tchaikovsky, and Shostakovich. Probing the 'why' of their choices is a bottomless question, but I hope to advance the discussion by identifying some of the 'wheres'. Before the true orchestra arose during the baroque era, the early bassoon played unique roles inside churches and in the open air. It later played a nearly ubiquitous supporting role in creating the 'Viennese classical' texture, which echoes in much music of the present. My music examples and discussions of repertory represent in a highly selective way the place of the bassoon in the consciousness and output of composers.

The historical record of the bassoon is made up of surviving instruments, images, and several types of writing: musical staff notation, tablature, and prose. Before about 1700, we have images of early bassoons and writing about early bassoons, but not always both together. The bassoon is thus in frequent danger of being confused with other wind instruments current during its early years. The untangling of these confusing references is a worthy goal, only partly realized here.

As I look over these chapters, I see five persistent themes – the instrument, its makers, its players, its repertory, and its audiences. Because relatively little of prior writing about the bassoon has been devoted to its acoustical design and behavior, many noteworthy issues have gone unraised. In budgeting my words and space, I have chosen to give first priority to the instrument itself.

A short introduction to the Bibliography identifies various books, articles, and web sites that cover broad categories of information of interest to the bassoon-minded reader. Specifics of repertory, performers, makers, surviving instruments, etc., are already available in great detail, and I am pleased to point the way. The trees, so to speak, are closely examined in these cited sources; this book is about the forest.

Acknowledgements

This book owes a debt to the writings and research materials of Lyndesay G. Langwill and William Waterhouse, two lifelong advocates of the bassoon.[1] Langwill, an amateur bassoonist and avid collector, in 1941 distributed a typescript listing of early wood-wind (and brasswind) instrument makers, which he had compiled from tireless global correspondence with collectors and museum curators, beginning in 1930.[2] Periodic revisions of this list by 1960 took the form of a book, which went through six self-published editions by 1980. Langwill, entering his ninth decade, invited Waterhouse to edit the next edition. An eminent professional bassoonist and a researcher of related topics, Waterhouse put the new edition on a solid scholarly footing, supported by much library and museum research and correspondence with colleagues on several continents. The resulting volume, called *The New Langwill Index: A Dictionary of Musical Wind-Instrument Makers and Inventors*, is still the pre-eminent reference work in its field.[3]

Langwill, always curious and desirous of correcting obvious errors (he was a chartered accountant by profession), also wrote articles, then a small monograph, and finally a substantial book, *The Bassoon and Contrabassoon*.[4] Virtually all the research files he accumulated during this lifetime of scholarship passed to Waterhouse as life trustee, who continued to add new information from his own reading and correspondence. It came as no surprise that Waterhouse was himself invited to write books about his instrument. *Bassoon*, his contribution to the Yehudi Menuhin Guides, is a practical guide for the aspiring or accomplished bassoonist, lucidly written and full of original insights.[5] I recommend it without reservation to readers.

Waterhouse also signed a contract in 1997 to write the present book for Yale University Press. It was understood by both parties that the long-delayed Menuhin Guide would take priority. Meanwhile Waterhouse continued a busy schedule of performing, teaching, adjudicating, lecturing, and writing, including the 14,000-word 'Bassoon' article in the *New Grove Dictionary of Music and Musicians* (2001). The Grove article, which reflected much original research, was a foretaste of the historically oriented book he might have written for Yale University Press. Doubtless he had many more insights tucked away in his fabled memory, but he did not put them down on paper (or into computer memory, I should say). In July 2007, with his time in demand by the broad public of bassoonists and organologists and his health beginning to threaten, Waterhouse invited me to join him as co-author of the present book, and his publisher agreed. We exchanged initial thoughts about the subject and our collaboration, but in early November 2007 he died a sudden and premature death.

Aside from the incomparable Langwill-Waterhouse archive described above, he left only a detailed table of contents for the Yale book. I found his organizational scheme to be well suited to the task and largely followed it, although I filled in many blank spaces, as we two co-authors had already agreed to do. But all the words that follow (except quoted passages, of course) are my own, as are the judgements, interpretations, and opinions. His name appears on the title page in appreciation of the research materials put at my disposal by Elisabeth Waterhouse, his widow, who has been an advocate of bassoonists' interests during most of her life.

Many correspondents who contributed to Waterhouse's archive are already mentioned as authors in the Bibliography. Some others figure among those persons who helped me personally: Richard Abel, Meyrick Alexander, Margaret Downey Banks, Cliff Bevan, Tony Bingham, Geoffrey Burgess, Benjamin Coelho, Carlo Colombo, Allan Comstock, the late Gerald Corey, Mathew Dart, Jean-François Dupont-Danican, Michael Finkelman, Alan Fox, Heike Fricke, Alberto Grazzi, Roger Hellyer, Herbert Heyde, Larry Ibisch, Bruno Kampmann, Thomas Kiefer, Maggie Kilbey, Kenneth Kreitner, Luc Loubry, Bård Lyngnes, Holden McAleer, David McGill, Renato Meucci, Tim Milner, Richard Moore, Louis Nolemi, Elvira Ortiz, Janet Page, Jimena Palacios Uribe, David Rachor, Ricardo Rapoport, Edith Reiter, Albert Rice, Leslie Ross, Andrew Schwartz, Marlow Sigal, Bradley Strauchen-Scherer, Orum Stringer, Dominic Teresi, Marc Vallon, Václac Vonášek, Andrew Watts, Sebastian Werr, Robert Wiemken, and Yanhui Xu. All have my sincere gratitude. My wife Joanne, a former oboe player, was a cheerful source of patience and good judgment throughout this project. Particular thanks are due to Robert Baldock, Malcolm Gerratt, and Steve Kent of Yale University Press, and to Furthermore: a program of the J.M. Kaplan Fund, which provided support for the publication of this book.

Author's note

Pitch notation

Pitches are described by the American Standard System, in which the piano's middle C is C4, and A 440 is A4. Accordingly, the lowest note of the bassoon is B♭1, the next C is C2, and the highest C is C5. The lowest note of the modern contrabassoon is A0, B♭0, or C1, according to the bell configuration; contrabassoon parts normally sound an octave lower than notated.

Describing the bassoon

The familiar modern bassoon is assembled from four wooden pieces, via socket-and-tenon connections (Ill. 1a). In English, these pieces are called the **tenor or wing joint**, the **boot or butt joint**, the **long or bass joint**, and the **bell**. Inserted into the **receiver** socket atop the wing joint is a **crook or bocal**, a conical metal tube that comprises the top part of the bassoon's internal cavity or **bore**. The **reed**, made of cane formed into the requisite shape, has two vibrating **blades** connected to the crook by a **tube** portion. The vibrations of the reed set up a standing wave of vibration in the air column, which is defined by the bassoon's internal cavity. The effective acoustical length of the air column is shortened or lengthened by the opening or closing of **tone holes**, which lead from the outer circumference of the bassoon to the central bore. Among these are five **finger holes**, which are covered directly by the player's fingertips. Other tone holes are covered by **key cups**, controlled by **spatulas** or **touches**; the key cups may be open-standing or closed-standing. On the wing and boot joints, the deep, narrow tone holes are sometimes called chimneys (Ill. 1b). The tone-hole cavities, whether open or closed, are part of the bassoon's bore. When the player assumes a given fingering, the highest tone hole left open is called the primary vent for that pitch. Two or three of the several spatulas operated by the player's left thumb act on holes of small diameter called **register vents** or **speaker keys**. Their different function is to persuade the air column to 'overblow' – to vibrate in a higher mode of resonance, like a singer's falsetto. Pitches up to F3 are produced by first-mode vibrations; pitches from F#3 to D4 by second-mode vibrations; E♭4 to A4 by third-mode vibrations; and higher pitches by fourth- or higher-mode vibrations. Trained bassoonists are currently expected to produce pitches as high as E5, which is written in some twentieth-century repertory, always the subject of much preparation by the

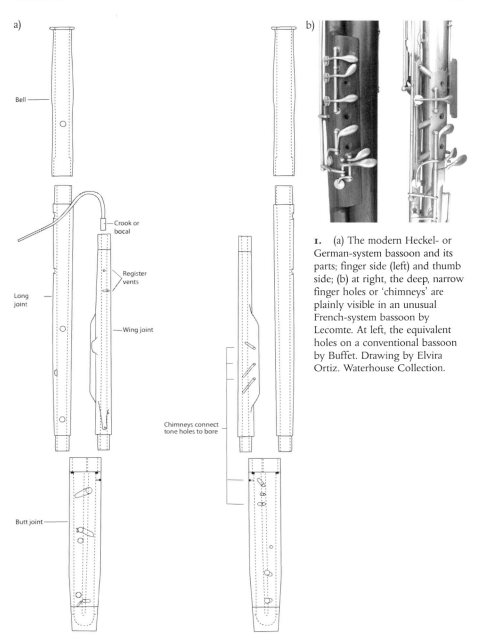

a)

Bell

Long joint

Butt joint

Crook or bocal

Register vents

Wing joint

Chimneys connect tone holes to bore

b)

I. (a) The modern Heckel- or German-system bassoon and its parts; finger side (left) and thumb side; (b) at right, the deep, narrow finger holes or 'chimneys' are plainly visible in an unusual French-system bassoon by Lecomte. At left, the equivalent holes on a conventional bassoon by Buffet. Drawing by Elvira Ortiz. Waterhouse Collection.

bassoonist. Student bassoonists are often more comfortable with an upper limit of C5, beyond which fingerings become increasingly idiosyncratic and response less dependable. Virtuosos can sometimes reach F5 and higher.

I refer to the player's fingers using the following abbreviations: **LT** (left thumb), **L1** (left index finger), **L2** (left middle finger), **L3** (left ring finger), **L4** (left little finger), and **RT, R1, R2, R3,** and **R4** in similar fashion. In some instances, these abbreviations can also refer to the corresponding tone hole.

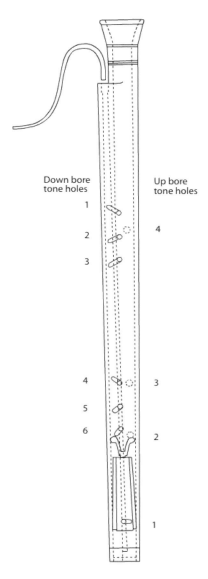

Down bore
tone holes

Up bore
tone holes

1

2   4

3

4   3

5

6   2

1

2. The bore and tone holes of a dulcian,
the earliest form of bassoon. Drawing by
Elvira Ortiz.

The earliest bassoon was called the dulcian (Ill. 2). Its smooth skin and concealed keys show little family resemblance to the twenty-first century bassoon, which is bedecked with an elaborate and glittering key mechanism. But during five centuries of existence, the bassoon has been marked by certain consistent principles of design. The dulcian included a **down bore** (descending from the crook to the butt) containing six diatonic finger holes, and an **up bore** (ascending from the butt to the bell) containing four diatonic tone holes. The ten tone holes plus the bell opening allowed it to produce eleven diatonic pitches.

This acoustical information is the very essence of the bassoon idea. It can be expressed in a long sentence, or it can be expressed in a short formula like the following: **6 down + 4 up** (that is, a down bore containing six diatonic fingerholes, leading to an up bore containing four diatonic finger-holes). The + represents a fold in the bore; the crook and bell opening are taken for granted.

A major shift in the bassoon's design schema came when the lower range was extended from C 1 to B♭; the new layout of **6 down + 5 up** is the shared design of mainstream bassoons made between about 1700 and the current day. (For the sake of comparisons, none of the vents later added to produce chromatic pitches are shown in the formula.) Bassoons built at different nominal pitches – a tenoroon, a standard-size bassoon, and a contrabassoon, for example – may nevertheless share a basic design. The octave contra of the baroque era was simply a bassoon (6 down + 5 up) of larger size, sounding an octave lower. A quart-bassoon (a semi-contra, sounding only a fourth below the standard bassoon) had the same design schema and the same formula, even though similar fingerings produced different pitches. By the classical era, the octave contra was truncated for portability, extending only to sounding D1, with a resulting schema of **6 down + 3 up**.

Several early instruments related to the bassoon are explored in chapters 1 and 3. Many of the subtle differences among these mostly obscure instruments are schematically summarized by the formula. In the romantic era, after rod-axle key technology freed makers to introduce new folds into the contra's bore, a rich variety of models appeared in quick succession. These also had numerous chromatic keys, creating a picture bewildering to most viewers. But the formula quickly sorts out the commonalities and peculiarities of competing designs. For example, the following models had three folds; the first tube, leading downward but containing no diatonic finger holes, is shown in brackets here, but omitted from the formula in chapters of this book:

1851   Haseneier   Contrabassophon   [o down +] **3 up + 5 down + 2 up**
1877   Stritter patent   Contrabassoon   [o down +] **5 up + 3 down + 2 up**
1905   Evette & Schaeffer Contrabassoon   [o down +] **3 up + 4 down + 4 up**

(These or similar instruments are shown in Ills. 62, 59, and 60.)

Abbreviations

The letter 'a' before a date stands for 'ante' (before); 'p' stands for 'post' (after).

AmZ	*Allgemeine musikalische Zeitung*
BzMw	*Beiträge zur Musikwissenschaft*
BJbHMp	*Basler Jarbuch für historische Musikpraxis*
DR	*The Double Reed*
DRN	*Double Reed News*
EM	*Early Music*
EPM	*Encyclopedia of Popular Music*, ed. Colin Larkin, accessed through *GMO*
FoMRHIQ	*Fellowship of Makers and Researchers of Historical Instruments Quarterly*
GMO	*Grove Music Online*
GSJ	*Galpin Society Journal*
HBSJ	*Historic Brass Society Journal*
JAMS	*Journal of the American Musicological Society*
JAMIS	*Journal of the American Musical Instrument Society*
JIDRS	*Journal of the International Double Reed Society*
Larigot	*Larigot: Bulletin de l'Association des Collectioneurs d'Instruments de Musique à Vent*
MGG 1	*Die Musik in Geschichte und Gegenwart*
MGG 2	*Die Musik in Geschichte und Gegenwart*, second edition
MI	*Das Musikinstrument*
MII	*Musique Images Instruments*
NAMIS	*Newsletter of the American Musical Instrument Society*
NGDJ	*New Grove Dictionary of Jazz* (accessed through *GMO*)
NGDMM 2	*New Grove Dictionary of Music and Musicians*, second edition
NGDO	*New Grove Dictionary of Opera* (accessed through *GMO*)
QMMR	*Quarterly Musical Magazine & Record*
Rm	*Revue musicale*
TWB	*To the World's Bassoonists*
ZfI	*Zeitschrift für Instrumentenbau*

Introduction

Among musical instruments, the bassoon is a happy accident, a biotechnical work-around that quickly became an archetype. A double-reed woodwind instrument that plays the bass register with robust volume has to have a substantial bore length – something approaching the nominal eight feet of its original lowest note, C2. This being too long for easy management by a human player, some unidentified maker, probably an Italian of the early sixteenth century, conceived the idea of folding the bore in half for convenience of carrying, fingering, and manufacture. The first seven diatonic tone holes, analogous to the first seven of the oboe, are fingered much like the oboe, using the six longest fingers plus one little finger. But the remaining tone holes, called the bore extension, were a new challenge. With seven digits already committed to other finger holes, how could the three added holes be controlled? The palms, the upper little finger, and some middle phalanges of the fingers were employed on a few experimental woodwinds (see chapter 3), but it was the two thumbs that entered permanent service.

The finger holes of the dulcian were drilled at oblique angles to bring them within convenient reach of a human hand span; the resulting finger holes, much deeper than they are wide, are called chimneys. Together, the chimneys and the bore extension enclose a larger and more complicated acoustical space than on other woodwinds; in simple terms, this unusual cavity helps make the bassoon a more stringent filter of sound emissions. The filtering is not a simple matter of suppressing the instrument's loudness – the low register of the bassoon has been quite assertive throughout its long history. The filtering is more a matter of timbre, and is highly selective, resulting in a mordant lower register, paired with a gentler, universally blending upper register, which listeners have often noted. More than once, commentators have invoked the words 'chiaroscuro' and 'mysterious' in descriptions. It may be accidental, it may be peculiar, but the bassoon's tone quality is irreplaceable. No one knows this more than composers, who have for centuries exploited it as a unique tone color.

The bassoon of the sixteenth century, called the dulcian, had ten chimneys. After a major revision of the archetype, the baroque bassoon of the late seventeenth century had eight chimneys and three shallower tone holes. Since then, the essential archetype of the instrument has endured, despite subtle alterations of the bore and tone-hole lattice, and the addition of numerous tone holes for chromatic and high-register pitches.[1]

Later attempts at fundamental redesign during the bassoon's five-century history were short-lived. Since the early nineteenth century, critics and reformers of the bassoon have been influenced by acoustical science, as they understood it. In early, short-sighted pronouncements, various savants declared that tone holes should be wide, relatively shallow, and drilled in scientifically determined locations. Even Theobald Boehm (the best-known of these reformers, though not the earliest) eventually admitted that the oboe and bassoon were not susceptible to the same design principles as the flute (because of the influence of the double reed). But critics and would-be reformers were not easily deterred; they wished to discard the centuries-old archetype of the bassoon in a macro-level reform. The resulting instruments – experimental models in limited production – were less stringent filters of timbre; they lacked the complex, 'nut-like' flavor that the bassoon's admirers have often praised.

Meanwhile, mainstream bassoons underwent a much-diluted reform. Many tone holes were enlarged, the bore extension was lengthened, and chromatic keys were added. Yet the mainstream makers retained chimneys, traditional tone-hole spacing (more or less), and sometimes a choke in the bell portion of the bore. As a result, the traditional timbre underwent a gradual evolution. By the twentieth century, two patterns (French and German types) were broadly accepted, both of them extensions of the baroque and classical archetype, and both of them 'mathematically imperfect' in the view of Boehm-minded reformers. Most subsequent research and testing focused on micro-level issues: bore perturbations, tone-hole shapes, and what might be called boundary issues (crook design, joint conditions, tone-hole borders, pads, and bore surfaces).

Bassoon players

The earliest bassoon emerged only when there was a musical need for bass-register voices and instruments. From Italy, the early bassoon spread during the sixteenth century to most corners of Europe. Broadly speaking, it also was exported to wherever the European powers had colonies, including the Americas and the South and East of Asia. By the early seventeenth century, regional makers and a few regional variations in design were seen. The bassoon evolved thereafter in response to musical requirements, undergoing an archetypal revision in the late seventeenth century, and a continuing refraction into regional styles, which peaked in the nineteenth century. The twentieth century saw a consolidation of the regional styles of making and playing the bassoon, as a complex result of improved communications.

Bassoonists before the twentieth century were often generalists, able to play not just other woodwinds, but often brass, string, or keyboard instruments as well. Early players evidently struggled with many concerns that are familiar to players of the twenty-first century: shifting standards of tuning, instruments that needed repairs, a never-ending need for new and serviceable reeds, and efforts to increase one's income.

The bassoon, like many wind instruments, was typically a man's instrument before the twentieth century. Men made up the choirs that most church bassoonists accompanied, and many new players were maturing choirboys. As soldiers, men were bassoon players in military bands, sometimes well into the twentieth century. Losses of lives, capital, and equilibrium during wartime always had a noticeable effect on bassoon playing and making. Meanwhile, however, Spanish nuns played the dulcian or *bajón* (sometimes in the smaller *bajoncillo* version) by the early seventeenth century, but they did so outside the public eye. This was partly social (puffing out the cheeks was considered ill-becoming for women, and to some extent also for men), and partly physical. The physical spacing of finger holes for a simple-system woodwind in the bass size sometimes precluded its use by players with very small hands. During the nineteenth century, the adoption of Boehm-inspired rod-axle key systems allowed makers to address this obstacle. But even today, players with small hands, including some men and some women, complain of uncomfortable stretches for the hand, unless modifications to the standard keys are made.

From player to bassoon to listener

Whenever a live bassoonist is heard, a player, an instrument, and a listener are present. The reed is also involved, as is the hall or other acoustical environment in which the instrument is heard. These acoustical elements combine to give the bassoon its essential character. Some also give the individual bassoonist his or her 'personal sound', at least in the realm of timbre. How does a player's physiognomy influence his or her tone production? Does a good bassoonist have all the same expressive possibilities as, say, a good cellist? Why are some individual instruments hailed as great bassoons, while most are thought adequate to good? Many of the answers to these questions lie in the acoustical facts of bassoon playing.

The **player** has ten fingers, an 'ear', and an embouchure. In the following discussion, the embouchure is defined broadly as comprising the lips, the tongue, the oral cavity, the larynx, and the breathing muscles. The lips serve to couple the vibrations of the reed to the player's body. Since they vibrate along with the reed blades, the lips' shape, size and application will influence the individual player's sound. The tongue is the main source of articulation – the starting of individual tones. It also helps modulate the shape of the oral cavity. The larynx helps focus the air stream of an artistic player. Artistic tone production has much to do with this focus, which results in part from a tightening of the glottal aperture, which functions much like the nozzle of a hose.[2] The oral cavity makes various resonances available to the vibrating system (only some of which are used at any one time). The expert player, who produces a fuller, rounder tone than the beginner, does so partly by marshalling additional body resonances.

While the fingers are responsible for basic pitch distinctions, finer pitch distinctions demand 'a good ear' – pitch and timbre perception. The fine intonation is then regulated mostly by the embouchure: the player is able, within limits, to vary the lips' engagement with the reed, and to vary the shape of the oral cavity in ways that affect intonation. The adjustments made are not linear and observable, like those of a violin player, but instead invisible, non-linear, and largely intuitive.

The function of the **reed** is to excite the bassoon's air cavity into vibration, using the air stream provided by the player. When blown, the aperture (the opening at the reed's tip) cycles open and shut, creating a standing wave bounded by the bassoon's bore. The rear portions of the two blades are the reed's interface with the player's lips, which perform an acoustical function known as damping – they encourage the persistence of certain vibrations, while discouraging others.

The **bassoon** itself allows the performer to choose various standing waves, enough to produce the audible three-and-a-half octaves of musical sounds. The uppermost two octaves are obtained by 'overblowing' – eliciting the second or higher modes of the air cavity's vibration. The bassoon does not always overblow according to a harmonic ratio; its second mode is a fairly in-tune octave of the fundamental, but the higher modes of vibration are increasingly sharp of harmonic ratios. This stretched resonance curve is ultimately responsible for (1) contrasting timbres from the bass register to the tenor, and (2) fingering irregularity in higher modes of vibration.[3]

The primary function of the tone holes is to adjust the length of the air column. But players often open or close finger holes beyond those of the charted or simple fingering in order to improve tuning or resonance. Writers of bassoon methods and finger charts (Ozi, Fröhlich, Jancourt, etc.) documented this practice from early times. The bassoon's long extension bore has an effect even on pitches that vent high on the bore, like open F3. The 'bore beyond opening' functions as both a resonator and a filter; the particular patterns of overtones filtered out leave behind the distinctive timbres of the bassoon's various registers.

As the bassoon underwent further development, the increased number and diameter of open holes made for a more open tone-hole lattice. An open-standing key and tone hole were added to the bell of German-system bassoons in the early nineteenth century in order to provide a dependable B1. But this sizeable open-standing vent also affected the tuning and quality of other notes. Later, other existing open-standing vents on the bore of the bassoon were enlarged and moved lower on the air column. This trend was helpful in evening out the timbre and increasing the instrument's power, but it was not without side effects. The more open lattice destabilized E3; this problem could be cured by using smaller reeds. The smaller reeds, however, made the old, simple fingering for G3 sound too high on the Heckel-system bassoon; nowadays this problem is often corrected by opening the low E♭2 key. With the smaller reed, many traditional cross-fingerings ceased to function. These complications, like the modern bassoon's complicated finger technique, are the price paid for a bassoon producing a wide dynamic range and forty chromatic half-steps of pitch.

During more than three centuries of its long life, the bassoon often fulfilled an outdoor and/or military role. But louder bass wind instruments – the saxophones and tubas – arose, gradually displacing the bassoon and contrabassoon for most outdoor use. The increasing retreat of the bassoon to indoor **listening spaces** led makers and players toward refinement of tone, and away from an emphasis on raw volume. The bassoon's fundamental, in the lowest octave of its range, is weaker than the next several overtones within the sounding pitch. Yet the listener's 'ear' – in reality, the prefrontal cortex of the brain – interprets this array of harmonically arranged overtones as representing the fundamental, weak though it is. So the instrument is perceived as having a powerful bass register.

Chapter 1

Early names; precursors; the bassoon idea; the founding myth

The rich array of historical names for different sizes of bassoons falls into four families, which overstep national boundaries of language. One refers to its shortened aspect:

Curtal, curtail, storta, stortito, Stört, sztort, etc.

Another refers to its supposedly gentle sound:

Dulcian, *Dulzian, dolziana, dulcin,* etc.

A third refers to its archetypical bass register (even when made in other, non-bass sizes):

Bassoon, *basson, bassono, basoncico, bajón, vajon, bajoncillo, bajica,* etc.

The fourth refers to its supposed resemblance to a bundle of sticks:

Fagot, Fagott, fagotto, Vagot, Fagoth, facotto, fagottino, fagotilho, etc.

But ambiguities abounded. *Storto* was a common name for the crumhorn, yet 'eine vergülte Stortte oder Dulcian' was purchased in Danzig in 1594. Meanwhile, the dulcina or dulzaina was apparently a cylindrical or 'still' shawm, as discussed below. Seemingly synonymous names sometimes connoted different sizes. Praetorius equated the terms Fagotten and Dolzianen, but added that 'some people would have it that the true Dolzian is the instrument called the *zingel Korthol'*, that is, the tenor curtal or dulcian.[1] Pietro Flaccomio scored for 'basoncico alias fagotto piccolo' in 1611.[2] In inventories of the Leipzig Hofkapelle, four different names were seen in less than thirty years, all seeming to refer to dulcians.[3]

Some known traps await the modern reader. For example, a 1678 inventory of instruments of the Leipzig Thomaskirche included an *Octave-bombard.* In the strictest usage, bombard means *Pommer* (a four-keyed large shawm), but here it denoted a dulcian (one of the two *Octav Bomhart* purchased from Johannes Bohlmann in 1668 and 1671).[4] In a similar usage, Brossard in 1703 defined *bombardo* as 'our basson'.[5]

To take a second example, the words *basun* in Danish and *bassun* in Norwegian usage during the seventeenth and eighteenth centuries meant 'trombone'. The word dulcian or *dultsian* in both languages during these centuries meant 'dulcian', but later it meant 'baroque bassoon'. A third trap waits in Latin America: not to be confused with *bajones* – dulcians – are *bajunes*, parallel arrays of palm-leaf trumpets formerly played in northern Chile.

The first goal of the following discussion is to identify – it is possible in a few instances – exactly which non-bassoon was meant by some of these terms. Later, a few demonstrable misconceptions about the bassoon's origin, still seen in reference books of our day, are briefly traced back through history.

Double reeds in antiquity

In cultures where playing was generally monophonic, deep bass instruments were rare and the idea of folding the instrument's bore was unneeded. Thus the bassoon had no precise ancestor in classical antiquity. But the *aulos* and *tibia* (Greek and Roman reed-pipes, the precursors of oboes) often had an extension bore below the finger holes, drilled with holes which could be opened or closed by means of movable sleeves or rings. The result was a complicated tone-hole lattice, analogous in a rough way to the cylindrical still shawm or dulcina (described below). The aulos of ancient Greece was cylindrical in bore, but conical tibiae were known in the Etruscan culture and throughout the Roman world. Much less is known about medieval instruments than about antique ones, although some archaeological remains have been found.

Post-classical writers in Latin, including Tinctoris, Mersenne, and Kircher, often used 'tibia' as a generic term for a woodwind instrument. Classical associations were tenacious enough to cause the birth of some renaissance instruments, and to discourage the use of others, at least at times.

> Plato and Aristotle had considered winds to be less noble than strings, and the tradition is carried straight through to the renaissance in two closely connected myths dear to the nobility of the late quattrocento. These are the tales of two musical contests, one between Apollo and Pan, and the other between Apollo and Marsyas. In both, Apollo's lyre is deemed superior to the wind instruments of his competitors. [In the second tale,] Pallas Athena invents the pipes, but throws them away because her fellow gods have ridiculed her because of her puffed cheeks while playing the instrument.[6]

Given their age-old martial uses and their frequently phallic shapes, wind instruments had come to be associated with males and the cult of Dionysus.[7] Yet classical influences were occasionally favorable to the development of wind instruments. The phagotum, discussed below, was seen as a successor to the double pipes, or auloi, of the mythical Greek musicians Hyagnis and Marsyas. A century later, Lully added the oboe (among other wind instruments) to his opera orchestra, a radical innovation at the time, in order to invoke the varied associations – shepherding and war – that the aulos had under Virgil and other writers of eclogues. The bassoon, considered the bass of the oboe family, shared these attributes and likewise joined the baroque orchestra.

The dulcina, dolzaine, and dolzaina

A large cloud of variants surrounds the term 'dulcina' (also dulzina, dolzaina, douçaine, etc.), frequently used in the fourteenth to seventeenth centuries to refer to musical instruments. At one edge of the spectrum, some of the variants (dolziana, dulcin) can refer to the dulcian, at least in some sizes and locales.[8] Yet the terms dulcina and dolzaina, at least, can be linked to other instruments; these instruments, liable to be confused with the dulcian, are discussed here.

In Naples, c.1481–3, Johannes Tinctoris contrasted the *celimela* (shawm) with the dulcina:

> On the other hand that tibia called the dulcina, on account of the softness of its sound, has seven holes in front and one behind, like a fistula (recorder). Since not every kind of piece can be played on it, it is considered to be imperfect.[9]

No picture was present, but the thumb hole and soft sound imply that Tinctoris's dulcina had a cylindrical bore; its 'imperfection' was presumably its narrow range – a ninth. It is widely assumed that Tinctoris's dulcina did not overblow. (A cylindrical woodwind would overblow at the twelfth; obtaining a full diatonic scale would require upper-extension keys, which were not present.) Tinctoris did not give the pitch level of the dulcina. But other instruments with similar names seem to have been pitched in the tenor or bass ranges (thus inviting confusion with the dulcian). Another theorist, Ludovico Zacconi, in 1592 gave the range of the dolzaine (again unpictured) as nine tones (C3 to D4) or, with keys, eleven tones. In its unkeyed version, then, the Zacconi dolzaine had a range as wide as that of the Tinctoris dulcina.[10] The keys of the eleven-tone instrument may have been for an upper extension or for a lower extension. Boydell concluded that the dolzaina was primarily associated with North Italy. He also noted the loose usage of the time: Praetorius gave dolzaine/Fagotto as Italian terms for Dulcian/Fagott, and also used the following variants of dulcian without comment: dolcian, dolcesuono, dolzian.[11]

Significant new evidence has come from a rediscovered instrument. In 1980 a cylindrical shawm was brought up from the wreck of the *Mary Rose*, flagship of Henry VIII of England, which had sunk off the south coast of England in 1545. The instrument, which has been studied and reproduced, is now thought to be the sole surviving example of the still shawm, mentioned in England in 1509–66.[12] With two keys for the lower hand, in addition to seven finger holes and a thumbhole, the *Mary Rose* shawm was not identical to the Tinctoris dulcina. Foster argued, however, that it was an effort to correct the 'imperfection' Tinctoris had noted in the dulcina: the limited range. A replica, which overblows at the twelfth, has a gapped diatonic range extending from F2 to D4, plus C2 at the bottom[13] (Ill. 3).

Some dolzaine possibly resembled the *Mary Rose* shawm. But the somewhat divergent information provided by Tinctoris and Zacconi makes clear that such instruments were variable in form. The following table surveys possible evidence of this sort of cylindrical, unfolded instrument.

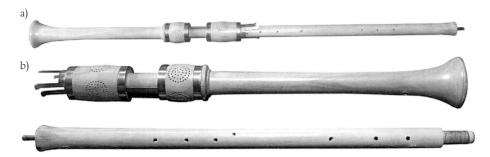

3. (a) Reproduction of a cylindrical shawm from the *Mary Rose*. (b) The same instrument disassembled. Photos by the maker, Charles Foster.

Selected occurrences of the terms dulcina, dolzaina, *etc.*

Date	Place	Notes
1481/3	Naples	Dulcina described by Tinctoris; 7 finger holes + thumb hole
1520	North Italy	Dolzaina in death inventory of Ippolito d'Este[14]
1529	Ferrara	Dolzaina as 'contrabasso secondo'[15]
1539	Florence	Dolzaina in Corteccia's 'Sacro et Santo Hymeneo'[16]
1565/8	Florence	Dolzaina played in two works by Corteccia[17]; five dolzaine doubled tenor and bass voices in a work by Striggio[18]
1565	Ferrara or Modena	A dolzaina had a bent brass crook[19]
1568	Munich	Dolzaina and fagoto played together[20]
1586	Florence	Dolziani played in a work of Bardi[21]
1589	Florence	Dolzaine and fagotti played in a work of Malvezzi[22]
1592	Venice	Zacconi described both fagotto and dolzaina
1598	Ferrara/Venice	Ducal music of Ferrara included dolzaine[23]
1617	Modena	Dolzaina listed in an Estense court inventory[24]
1628	Verona	Inventory included nine dolzaine with brass crooks 'for the bass'[25]
1636	Venice	Buonamente, Canzon à 2 for dolzaina and violin; range D_2 to C_4[26]

Under liberal interpretations of the examples cited above, instruments called dulcina, dolzaina, dolzaine, or still shawm (possibly related to one another, but distinct from the dulcian) seem to have been known in England and northern Italy during more than a century (1481–1592 or later). These instruments may have shared such characteristics as a double reed and a cylindrical bore, but there is no evidence that they were identical in form. Except in lacking a windcap, the morphology of the dulcina is comparable to that of the *Baβet*, illustrated by Praetorius in 1619[27] (Ill. 4).

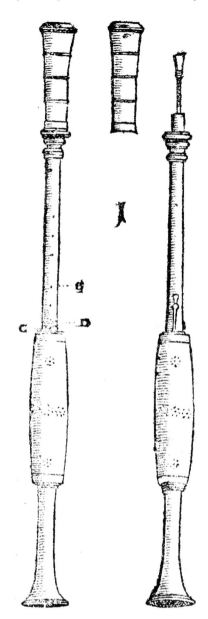

4. The *Baßet-Nicolo*, a cylindrical shawm. Praetorius, *Syntagma Musicum II: De Organographia* (Wolfenbüttel, 1618–20).

Related terms shade from slight respellings into distant variants: duçayna, dulzan, Dolzian, baszdulzani, Tolzanae, etc.[28] I have made an arbitrary decision to group all the occurrences of dolzaina, together with the helpful but incomplete evidence offered by Tinctoris, Zacconi, and the *Mary Rose* shawm, into this chapter. 'Dulcian' and other variants are treated in chapter 2.

The trombone

The trombone, known by the fifteenth century, shared two important virtues with the bassoon: it could play diatonically (and even chromatically) in the bass register, and it could be used while marching, thanks to its folded bore. It is not a woodwind instrument, but early players and makers of the trombone were often players of the earliest bassoons. The trombone's influence as a model is difficult to prove, but impossible to exclude.

The phagotum

The ambiguity surrounding the term dulcina/dolzaina is fully matched by the ambiguity surrounding the term fagotto. The *phagotum*, a bagpipe, is known largely from a description with woodcut illustration published in 1539.[29] It had almost nothing in common with the dulcian or bassoon. It has frequently been cited as an early source of the name fagotto (originally meaning a bundle of sticks) for a musical instrument; this assertion is not without problems, as described below. By the early nineteenth century the term phagotum had been detached, in the writings of historians and bassoon teachers, from the picture that had once accompanied it. As a result, writers who had never seen the picture began to assert that the phagotum of 1539 was an early bassoon. This is demonstrably untrue.

The phagotum was in use in Italy from 1522 to 1565 and possibly a few years earlier (Ill. 5). Its two chanters were wooden cylinders, each having three connected bores and a metal single reed. As on many other double-chanter bagpipes, the cylinders were inserted into a stock, a manifold that concealed the reeds and supplied air from the bag and bellows. In this instance, however, the decorative stock was elaborate to the point of visual distraction, and was not sewn into the bag, but rather connected by a flexible air duct. Each of these chanters (essentially a sort of one-hand racket) had a thumb hole and three finger holes, plus various keys for the thumb, palm, and little finger, giving a range of a tenth. According to a fingering chart dating from 1565, the left-hand chanter had a range from G2 to F3, using one lower-extension key and one upper-extension key; the right-hand chanter had a range from C3 to E4, using four upper-extension keys. On a simplified reconstruction by Cocks, the layouts of the chanters were 1 + 3 + 3 (left chanter) and 1 + 3 + 2 (right chanter).[30]

The invention of the phagotum has for centuries been attributed to Canon Afranio degli Albonesi.[31] But the earliest source, described below, said only that Afranio's prototype phagotum was brought to Italy after 1521. In the absence of a clarifying illustration, period references to the term phagotum are not easy to distinguish from the term fagot or fagotto. Three references from northern Italy during the years 1516–18 may (or may not) refer to the bagpipe phagotum.

> In [Ferrara in] 1516 the Frenchman Gerardo, 'sonator de fagoth', employed by Ippolito d'Este I, was paid for 'a faghotto da sonare with silver key'. . . . And in 1517 a further payment was made . . . 'for the fagotto played by Janes de pre Michele'. [In nearby Mantua in 1518] the lutenist Giovanni Angelo Testagrosse wrote to Isabella d'Este and her husband Francesco Gonzaga II, Marquis of Mantua. He offered them a gift if they would re-employ him: '. . . a handsome case of recorders and another of storte, [and a] fagot [which is said to be] a very beautiful thing'.[32]

The three references of 1516–18 are important evidence in one of two ways: any or all may refer to the phagotum, or alternatively, any or all may refer to an early dulcian.

Afranio, arriving in Ferrara in or after 1521, approached Giovanni Battista Ravilio, an artisan at the court, for help with his prototype. If a phagotum – in the sense of Afranio's bagpipe – already existed there, then Ravilio was possibly its inventor or an experienced maker of such instruments. Ravilio's contributions to Afranio's instruments were, respectively, metal reeds, silver ferrules, a trumpet-shaped brass extension to the bore, and keys.[33] He possibly deserves credit as co-inventor of Afranio's phagotum, at least in the version shown in the 1536/9 woodcuts.[34]

If Afranio was not necessarily the inventor of the phagotum bagpipe, he was the only identifiable player. He reportedly played solos on 'il suo fagoto' at Este family banquets in 1529 and 1532.[35] In 1539, Teseo Ambrogio, the nephew of Afranio, illustrated and described the phagotum. The plates included were reportedly at least three years old at the time of publication. Thus the most familiar image of the phagotum, though published in 1539, can be properly dated 1536 or earlier.[36] In another early source – a painting of the Ferrara school – a clearly detailed phagotum

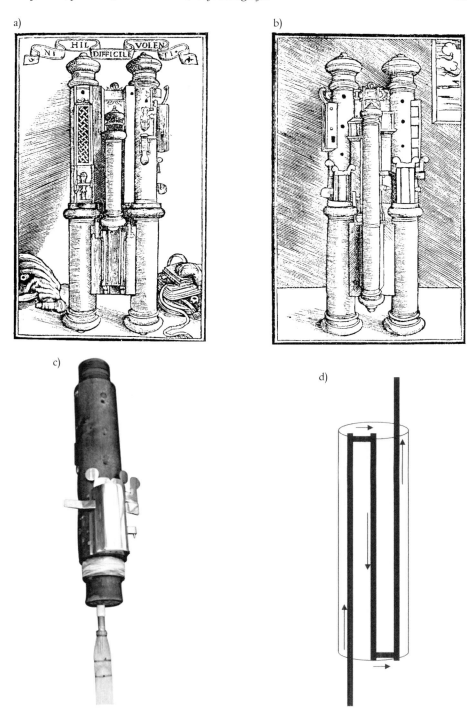

5. (a) Phagotum, thumb side. (b) phagotum, finger side. (c) chanter detached from a reproduction phagotum by Eric Moulder and Tony Millyard. (d) schematic drawing showing the folded bore within the chanter. Ambrogio, *Introductio in Chaldaicam linguam* (Pavia, 1535). Photo by Tony Millyard.

is seen. Its design differs slightly from that pictured by Ambrogio. The painting, *Jacob and Rachel at the Well* by the Master of the Twelve Apostles, has been dated to 1530–40.

Ambrogio saw the double pipes of the phagotum as a successor to the double auloi of antiquity, invoking two mythical players:

> He [Afranio or another player] would appear able to rival Hyagnis (the father of Marsyas), who was the first to hold his hands apart in playing (as on the double pipes), the first to fill two pipes with one breath. . . . If that upstart Marsyas had in olden day used this Phagotum against Apollo, I could easily believe that he would not have met with the disgrace inflicted by the Muses.[37]

A fingering chart and other instructions for playing the instrument, handwritten after Afranio's death by Ambrogio, is inscribed '1565'.[38]

The bassoon idea

One essential part of the bassoon idea is the folded bore. If we seek the origin of the name fagotto, or if we ask if other woodwinds were related to the earliest bassoons, we come to grips with this seemingly straightforward idea. Canon Galpin cited Afranio's phagotum as the 'earliest known use of the doubled-back bore'. He noted that the idea might have been borrowed from the medieval trumpet.[39]

Folded or multi-drilled woodwinds earlier than the 1536/9 woodcut of Afranio's phagotum have not been positively identified. Yet they almost certainly existed. The diary of Johannes Spießhaimer, for example, contains an entry referring to some sort of folded-bore musical instrument. Spießhaimer, also known as Cuspinian, was physician at the court of Emperor Maximilian I in Vienna. In a diary entry of 22 July 1515, describing new musical instruments recently invented or produced at court, he wrote:

> And yet still more wonderful, that was recently invented by a monk, that has no pipes, but certain cavities, cut into a broad piece of wood in a serpentine fashion, which gives true musical pleasure.[40]

This may be early evidence of some unspecified folded-bore woodwind.

There are other possibilities beyond the phagotum and the Spießheimer instrument. The stock of a bagpipe is a wooden socket or receptacle, typically sewn into the bag, into which the reed end of the drone or chanter was inserted. Bagpipes sometimes had two chanters, or two or more drones; multi-drilled stocks for multiple drones or chanters were known by the sixteenth century. Some traditional stocks were quite deep (perhaps 15 cm or so), as on the Hümmelchen and Dudey illustrated by Praetorius in 1619. Some hypothetical bagpipe maker, engaged in the design and fabrication of deep, multi-drilled stocks, may have opted to connect some of the parallel bores end to end. This would have saved the considerable time, labor, and material of boring and turning a straight drone of many centimeters in length. Such a drone (or chanter) might have been the first folded-bore woodwind. A depiction of a 'racket drone' dating from 1551 is known (see chapter 3), and there were doubtless earlier attempts.

Anthony Baines offered yet another hypothesis about the 'embryo' of the bassoon concept, citing a triple-drilled 'box' that shortens the drone of an early Polish or Bohemian bellows-blown bagpipe: 'Such doubling back of the tube is quite common in bagpipes, and the idea may well have originated in them. During the sixteenth century it came to be employed in various cylindrical-bore instruments. . . .'[41] Indeed, this triple drilling is seen in each of the chanters in Afranio's phagotum. The finger holes of Afranio's chanters, moreover, make each chanter roughly analogous to a one-hand racket (speaking hypothetically; the normal two-hand racket, known by the 1560s, is discussed in chapter 3).

Among conical woodwinds, however, there is no earlier evidence of a folded bore than the dulcian. It appears to predate even some of the longer multi-drilled cylindrical woodwinds like the sordun, courtaut, and doppioni. Few of these instruments can be dated precisely, but earliest evidence places them later in the sixteenth century; they are discussed in chapter 3.

The meaning of fagotto

Neither Afranio nor his nephew Ambrogio claimed that the phagotum resembled a bundle of sticks – this etymology was given by Mersenne in 1636 (see below). Afranio left no writings, while Ambrogio called the instrument a phagotum; its two individual chanters he called *columnae*. The anonymous recipient of the 1565 manuscript, apparently an associate of Ambrogio, used the word more liberally. In an annotation, he used phagotum to refer to the overall bagpipe, but also to each individual chanter (which looks, of course, like a stick, not a bundle of sticks). Curiously, Mersenne in his *Harmonie universelle* (1636) also referred to each individual chanter as a fagot (and also as a basson).[42] This extended usage of phagotum or basson can relate to the 'bundle of sticks' idea only if the viewer has a sort of X-ray vision, able to see multiple cavities 'bundled' within the unrevealing exterior.

This is all worth noting when we come to discuss the name fagotto as a label for the dulcian. By whatever logic, the term 'fagot' by 1565 could refer to smooth-skinned folded woodwinds, including the phagotum chanter and the fagotto or dulcian.[43] It is possible and perhaps likely that an earlier chapter of the phagotum/fagotto/fagot etymology has been lost.

The origin myth of the bassoon

A myth sometimes arises to justify the origin or attributes of some revered object, person, or society. The myths of Orpheus, Apollo, Amphion, Marsyas, and Dionysus explained the origins and qualities of the lyre and aulos to the ancient Greeks. In post-classical times, the origins of the trombone were long clouded by the mistranslation of a passage from the biblical Book of Daniel. Beginning with the Geneva translation (1560) of the Vulgate Bible, the word 'sambuca' was rendered as 'sackbut'. In the resulting myth, this immediate ancestor of the modern trombone was considered to have originated in pre-Christian times. In fact, the sambuca was 'a type of Greco-Roman angle harp', while the trombone can be traced back only to the fifteenth century.[44] In recent years, Powell explored the creation myth of the baroque flute, and Cheape refuted the mythic origin ascribed to the Highland bagpipes.[45]

The bassoon has its own origin myth, compounded of several tropes or themes that arose in the seventeenth to nineteenth centuries. These tropes, loosely derived from historical persons and instruments, addressed various aspects of the bassoon's name, invention, structure, personality, or history. Two central tropes, often combined, derived the fagotto name from the 'bundle of sticks' etymology, and cited the phagotum and its supposed inventor, Canon Afranio, as evidence. A third trope, drawing a contrast between the dulcian and shawm, sprang from Praetorius's comments about the Dolzian (dulcian) in 1619. A fourth, added in 1703, drew the bassoon into the already confused history of the cromorne. A fifth, added c.1814, inserted Sigmund Schnitzer, a sixteenth-century maker of shawms, into the existing phagotum trope. Later historians and authors of bassoon methods cited the tropes as evidence for statements – sometimes fanciful – about the bassoon's origin. They connected the tropes in ever-evolving patterns, improvising when necessary to make the mythic web fit their purposes.

Through repetition and rich variation over several centuries, these five mythic tropes have taken root in our culture and literature, persisting in some reference books that are now in print. They merit discussion here, both for an overdue comparison with documented evidence, and as an example of a long-lived literary culture inspired by the bassoon idea.

The phagotum and Afranio tropes

The phagotum, having two main columns (left- and right-hand chanters) and two additional shorter columns (mostly decorative) mounted front and rear, looked plausibly like a bundle of short sticks (fagotto, fagot, or phagotum). This is true in all surviving pictures – Ambrogio's woodcuts and the painting of Rachel and Jacob at the Well. Marin Mersenne introduced the phagotum and Afranio tropes, launching the bassoon's origin myth into printed circulation. In a 'corollary' following proposition 33 he linked the term phagotum to the *fagots* depicted there:

> [O]ne can say that it is taken from our French usage Fagot, because it contains two or more bores or billets [flûtes] bound or fagotted together, as is seen in the two preceding [fagots or proto-bassoons, shown on page 298], which I have explained and illustrated.[46]

Mersenne understood that the phagotum was a bagpipe; he cited the page number of the illustration in Ambrogio's treatise, as well as the page of the description.[47] This awareness did not hinder Mersenne, however, from likening the two-reed, polyphonic bagpipe to the one-reed, monophonic fagot or basson.[48] Pandora's box now lay open,

Mersenne's words flying out to stir readers' imaginations, while Ambrogio's woodcut of the phagotum remained stubbornly hidden inside. Not having seen Ambrogio's picture, the myth-makers imagined that the phagotum somehow resembled a dulcian or bassoon.[49]

The conventional dulcian looked nothing like a bundle of sticks, even to initiates who understood that two bores were contained within the smooth, unrevealing body. But Zaccaria Tevo, a Franciscan monk and dulcian player, asserted in 1706 that 'Afiano Pavese trovò il Fagotto'.[50] This information, misspelling included, was reproduced in the influential *Musikalisches Lexikon* of J. G. Walther (1732).[51] Ernst Ludwig Gerber, the German lexicographer, may have been the first, c.1814, to make an explicit identification of Afranio's phagotum with the bassoon:

> Canon Afranio of Ferrara, born in Pavia, lived in the year 1539, in which year he invented our beloved Fagott. At least the learned canon [Ambrogio] Albonese attributed this to him in his treatise on oriental languages, in which on page 179 a description and depiction are supplied of the Fagott of Afranio's invention. Walther named him as inventor of this instrument, following Tevo, chapter 12, page 12.[52]

After Fétis in 1828 repeated the Afranio trope,[53] other writers picked up on the story. The bassoon method of Willent-Bordogni (1844), a protégé of Fétis, presented a woodcut from Mersenne showing a courtaut and two proto-bassoons (though without their labels or most of their finger holes) as an example of 'Afranio's bassoon', 'formed of several pieces, a little like the current basson'.[54] W. H. Stone in the first edition of Grove's *Dictionary of Music and Musicians* cited Willent-Bordogni as a source for the history of the early bassoon.[55]

The Schnitzer trope

This trope arose in 1730, in a reference to the Nuremberg maker Sigmund Schnitzer I:

> Neudorfer praised him [Schnitzer] in 1547 as the best woodwind instrument maker of his time, noting his manufacture of large out-size 'Pfeifen' which were also being played in Roma, elsewhere in Italy and in France; Doppelmayer (1730), misquoting this, credited Schnitzer with the making of extraordinarily large bassoons rather than Pommers, and apparently confused him with his son.[56]

Gerber in 1812/14 cited Doppelmayer in his article on Sigmund Schnitzer. He concluded (without reference here to Afranio): 'Since the Fagott had reached such a degree of perfection by 1550, it may be reckoned among the oldest instruments, with an origin of c.1450.'[57] The date of 1450 was apparently Gerber's conjecture. This new trope was grafted onto the older phagotum trope, possibly first by Schneider in 1834. He repeated and blended the Afranio and Schnitzer tropes, attributing both to Gerber. Other German writers quickly echoed Schneider's words.[58]

The myth of the bassoon's origin had sunk such deep roots that other well-informed writers could be misled. Wasielewski realised that Afranio had invented a bagpipe; he even published a re-engraved (and incomplete) version of Ambrogio's woodcut in 1878.[59] But he wrote credulously of the transformation of the 'phagotum into the Fagott'. He attributed this transformation to the maker Schnitzer, citing Gerber's authority. The same year Lavoix expanded on the Schnitzer trope in a fresh attempt to justify the bassoon's existence. His misspelling was echoed by many later writers:

> About thirty years after Afranio, Sigismond Scheltzer [*sic*] improved the bassoon. He freed it from the skins that encumbered it and, joining the two tubes of the instrument, made of it really the bassoon that we have until today.[60]

Langwill noted that Gandolfi in 1887 and Vittorioso in 1913 had taken up the 'Scheltzer' variant of the Schnitzer trope.[61] Its later occurrences are too numerous to count.

The Dolzian trope

Praetorius provided the germ of an important trope describing the supposed nature of the 'Dolzian'; it had a 'softer, sweeter sound' than the shawms and Pommers, he said. I leave his spelling unchanged here as a distinguishing label for this trope.

> Fagotten and Dolzianen (Italis *fagotto, dolcesouno* [*sic*]) are to all intents synonymous terms. . . . In register and tone-quality they resemble the basset shawm, although the sound of the dolzians and Fagotten is softer than that of shawms. Thus – on account of this softer, sweeter sound, perhaps – they are known as Dolzianen – dulcisonantes. The reason for the difference is that whereas in shawms the bore passes straight through the body and has the same length – the lower end being completely open – in curtals [Fagotten] the bore is doubled back on itself, and the sound-exit is at the top. Sometimes it is left completely open, sometimes it is covered with a perforated lid. . . . A dulcian so covered sounds much more gentle and pleasant than otherwise.[62]

As Klitz noted, references to the dolzaina (of whatever construction) 'are found much earlier than the Fagott (Dolzian) is known to have existed', undercutting the etymology that Praetorius offered.[63] Yet the perforated lid (gedackt cap), illustrated in Praetorius's plate, was a device any reader could comprehend, even if both Praetorius and his readers possibly over-estimated its effect. During later centuries, in which few listeners had heard the sound of a dulcian, gedackt or open, the idea of a softer, sweeter instrument took wing, and a new trope went forth into the world.

Valdrighi, who had rediscovered the 1565 instructions written by Ambrogio and annotated by the recipient, was not immune to the pull of the ancient myth. He in 1884 repeated the phagotum, Afranio and Schnitzer tropes, seemingly translating at times directly from Lavoix, before adding the Dolzian trope:

... the phagotum of Afranio ... whose organ-like nature was transformed thirty years later by Sigismund Scheltzer, who freed it from the leather bags of the bagpipe, and uniting its two tubes, gave to the fagotto [bassoon] nearly the distinctive form it has today, conserving the gentleness of its sound, for which reason it is called dolcisuono (or dolcino or dolzaina) among the Latin races.[64]

In a side effect, the originally mild comparison by Praetorius made the bass shawm (or Pommer or hautbois) into a target for unfavorable comparisons by later writers.

The cromorne trope

The cromorne, a type of contrabass oboe, is the subject of a durable trope in the bassoon's mythology. This trope does not account for the bassoon's origin, but it has for centuries blurred the identities of the cromorne and the bassoon. The trope arose in 1703, when Sébastian de Brossard included the following definition in his *Dictionnaire de musique*: 'Fagotto. Instrument a vent, qui répond à notre basson, ou Basse de Chromorne'. As Brossard wrote this, the basse de cromorne was still in use in the French royal chapel in Versailles, and yet the confusion is not altogether surprising. Like the bassoon, the basse de cromorne played the bass line. Moreover, the cromorne at times (and especially outside the royal chapel) went under a different name, like basse de hautbois or contrebasse de hautbois.

Brossard's misidentification of the basse de cromorne with the bassoon was echoed by Mattheson (1713), Majer (1732), and Adlung (1758). Walther (1732) dropped the qualifier 'basse de', so that any cromorne was now equated with a bassoon. The spellings of the term eventually included such remote variants as 'nomhorne'.[65] Although a clearly labeled illustration of the cromorne was published in 1760, and despite scholarly attention to the cromorne in the late twentieth century, the 2001 edition of the New Grove Dictionary of Music still stated that 'the cromorne therefore appears to have been a type of bassoon'.[66]

Critics of the myth

The bassoon's creation myth, made up of these several tropes, was functional and satisfying, as long as readers were unaware of conflicting evidence. It justified the bassoon's existence (portability and suave tone quality), and it accounted for two of the instrument's early names (fagotto and Dolzian). But researchers began to note contradictions. Euting and Kleefeld both noted that the phagotum had 'nothing in common with the Fagott'.[67] Forsyth was a vigorous critic of the phagotum trope:

This instrument had no connection whatever either technical or historical with the bassoon. However, a continental historian and theorist of the last century, misled by the name and by an imperfect acquaintance with its mechanism, hailed it as the first attempt to cut up the long pipe of the old Bass-Pommer into two parts, in fact as the original bassoon. Naturally this claim has been repeated over and over again by subsequent writers until it has almost acquired the sanctity of truth. It may be found, mechanically copied with the original theorist's orthographical mistakes, even in our most recent musical works of reference.[68]

Forsyth devoted four pages, in an appendix to his manual of orchestration, to reproducing Ambrogio's woodcuts of the phagotum and explaining its workings, based on his reading of Ambrogio's orginal text. Galpin, another perceptive student of the phagotum, recognized the problems that had arisen from Mersenne's un-illustrated words comparing the phagotum and fagot:

> The suggestion that the bassoon received the name because it was divided into parts for ease of carriage, making as it were a small fagot, is absurd, as such a method did not obtain until well into the seventeenth century.[69]

Langwill, finding in the literature about musical instruments 'the monotonous repetition of a few dubious statements about the origin of the bassoon', was spurred to write articles and ultimately a book on the bassoon's history.[70]

Chapter 2

The dulcian family

Few laymen, let alone bassoon players, would have trouble distinguishing a one-piece dulcian from a four-piece baroque bassoon. But verbal mentions are often unaccompanied by pictures, and thus an abundance of different historical names, most of them carried over from dulcian to baroque bassoon, has led to much verbal ambiguity over the two types. In this chapter, therefore, original terminology – fagotto, fagot, dulzian, curtal, bajón, etc. – is reproduced faithfully, and some possible variations in meaning are noted. In quoted passages, 'bassoon' refers to the one-piece dulcian, unless otherwise noted.

Physical description

The typical dulcian was probably made by drilling a cylindrical hole in a long billet of wood, then reaming the cylinder to create a long conical cavity. Once this was achieved, the maker drilled another hole alongside and reamed it from the opposite end. The septum between two bores was cut or drilled away near the end of the billet, connecting the two bores to create a continuously expanding cone. Beneath this cavity, wooden or cork plugs sealed the bores, creating an air-tight U-shaped linkage. The exterior of the body was planed to an oval cross-section.

A crook of brass is inserted into the dulcian's receiver, which is side-by-side with the bell opening, or nearly so. The bell may continue the existing bore angle, or it may flare abruptly; the bell may be open or have a perforated cover (gedackt, as Praetorius termed it).[1] One side of a typical dulcian is drilled with six holes covered by the player's fingers; these finger holes connect to the down bore (Ill. 6). Under an open-standing key on the finger side, a seventh tone hole connects to the up bore. These seven holes correspond to those of the early alto shawm or oboe, and thus far the dulcian's fingerings are only slightly different. On the other side of the body, however, are three holes controlled by the player's two thumbs; one of the lower two is controlled by an open-standing key. The extension bore is vented by the last two holes and bell; the layout may be expressed as 6 + 4.[2] With all tone holes closed, the bass instrument sounds C2; the first register extends to F3. (The Spanish bajón has a different tuning, discussed below.) Higher notes are produced by overblowing (using the second and third modes of vibration). Except on late Spanish bajones, which were provided with additional keys, chromatic pitches on dulcians were available only by half-covering a tone hole, or by cross-fingering.

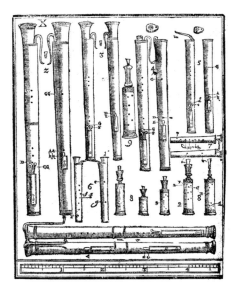

6.   *Sorduen-Bas* (no.1); dulcians in five sizes (nos. 2–7); rackets in four sizes (nos. 8–9). Praetorius, *Syntagma Musicum II: De Organographia* (Wolfenbüttel, 1618–20).

Religious processions, civic processions, royal entries, and military parades – among the centuries-old uses of wind music – demanded portable instruments.[3] The trombone had arisen by the fifteenth century, providing a diatonic scale in the bass register; thanks to its two bore reversals, it was easily carried. The dulcian, with one bore reversal, was similarly portable, while its ten tone holes gave the player technical facility down to C2, even lower than the trombone's E2 or D2. As Kolneder and Waterhouse noted, the dulcian is louder than the bass recorder, handier than the Pommer, and more agile than the trombone.[4] Castello's Sonata 9 (Venice, 1629), which shows the dulcian in a virtuosic light, might easily have been conceived as an anti-trombone showpiece (Ex. 2.1). The fourth movement ends with a fourteen-measure Presto in which continuous sixteenth notes predominate, ending with flourishes of thirty-seconds and then a sixteenth-note arpeggio down to low C2. All of these elements would have been difficult or impossible on the early trombone, which had existed for perhaps two centuries before Castello composed the Presto.

It is tempting to regard the bass dulcian as a folded bass shawm (or Pommer) – the two instruments have a similar compass, conical bore, and similar key technology. Even aside from the Pommer's large flared bell, however, there is another important acoustical difference: all ten of the dulcian's tone holes have a much greater depth-to-diameter ratio. Such tone holes, called chimneys, give the dulcian its characteristic timbre. None of the shawm's tone holes have such a great depth-to-diameter ratio. Nor is the notion of the dulcian as a folded shawm provable in a chronological sense, as a bass dulcian is documented by 1546 at the latest, not significantly later than the earliest securely documented bass shawms. The two instruments may truly be cousins, rather than ancestor and descendant – the historical record is too bare to say more at present.

Ex. 2.1. Castello, Sonata 9, fourth movement, final cadenza (1629).

Whichever arose first, the dulcian was a compact alternative to the bass shawm, being both shorter and lighter. Its design made control of the extension bore simpler for the player, and simplified production for the maker. Underneath the Pommer's key cover or fontanelle – which required much effort to hollow out – the four keys were mounted on a flat table, which required more excavation; the two longer key flaps and levers protruding from the fontanelle were protected by an additional brass key cover. In contrast, the dulcian required only two shorter keys and their respective key covers. If present, the bell of the dulcian required a smaller billet of wood than the massive bell of the shawm.[5] Perhaps for these reasons, the dulcian was often cheaper to make and purchase: in 1559, one maker charged 37 lire, 4 soldi for bass shawms, but 24 lire, 16 piccoli for 'bassoni curti' (dulcians).[6] The typical wood was maple or sycamore.[7]

The control of the bass dulcian's lowest three tone holes by the two thumbs was an incremental improvement over shawm fingerings, in which the lower little finger controlled two keys, and the lower thumb controlled two more. Open tone holes could be shaded by the thumbs for fine tuning, as Praetorius later commented. Meanwhile, the overlapped pairs of keys on the bass shawm did not lend themselves to certain rapid technical passages.[8]

The dulcian's narrower bell supposedly gave it a gentler tone than the bass shawm. It is traditional to note that the name 'dulcian' implies sweetness or gentleness, as Praetorius wrote:

[T]he Fagotten are quieter and have a smoother tone than the shawms. Perhaps it is because of their softness that they are called Dolzianen – from Dulcisonantes.[9]

Yet this softness has probably been exaggerated by writers. Some dulcians were made in a version Praetorius called 'gedackt' ('covered') – a perforated cap was installed over the bell opening, in an effort to soften the tone, especially on the lowest pitches. Spanish bajones were sometimes specified as 'tapado' or 'con sordino', that is, 'with mute'. The need for such a cap or mute, together with surviving complaints against a few loud Spanish players, makes clear that the dulcian or bajón was not always as quiet as was desired.[10]

Several features distinguish Spanish bajones from other European dulcians. (Bajoncillos, the smaller sizes, do not always share these features; see below.) The *estrangul* (literally 'choke') is a metal insert that extends into the uppermost bore of many Spanish instruments, down to about the first finger hole. This insert was an original design feature in some new instruments, though it was other times an addition or replacement, as shown in invoices from 1613 and 1622 by Antonio de Selma.[11] The keys of bajones are typically mounted on bands that girdle the instrument's exterior, rather than in saddles. All surviving Spanish bajones in the bass size have a regionally peculiar tuning and fingering in D Dorian, rather than the customary C Major.[12] This is discussed below.

A Nuremberg maker in 1625 provided a strap of some sort for a great bass dulcian (see below).[13] For smaller sizes, however, the player's hands supported the instrument, possibly unassisted. Praetorius recommended the baritone clef for the bass dulcian, and said that 'even though some players can go up to G4 on this Chorist-Fagotten . . . only a few can do this. Everyone else has to stop at D4 on the Fagotten.'[14] Daniel Speer's fingering chart of 1697 extended to F4, but few surviving works scored specifically for dulcian exceed D4.[15]

Sizes and consort use

'Corista' in Italian means 'tuning pitch'; one of the dulcian's functions was to support a singer or chorus in Gregorian chant, lending both volume and a stable tuning. The bass size of dulcian came to be called the *fagotto corista, Choristfagott,* or *bajón corista.* In this function, the dulcian might be used as the only bass, or in combination with the organ, or to double the men's bass voices. In convents, it was a convenient substitute for male singers. It also replaced the bass voice in soprano/alto/tenor choral music in several Spanish cathedrals.

The fullest enumeration of sizes was given by Praetorius in 1619. Besides the bass, Praetorius pictured sizes a fourth lower (Quartbassfagot) and a fifth lower (Quintbassfagot), and he referred to an Octavbassfagot, supposedly under development by Hans Schreiber of Berlin.[16] He also pictured sizes a fifth higher than the bass (baßet or tenor; lowest note G2), a ninth higher (alto; lowest note D3), and a thirteenth higher (diskant or exilent; lowest note A3). Recent research has made it clear, however, that other consort schemes and sizes existed. Instead of the successive fifths Praetorius described, surviving Spanish dulcians fit into a recursive scheme: D2 bass, A2 tenor, D3 alto, A3 soprano.[17] Many other musical establishments in Europe and Latin America would manage with only a few sizes, most commonly the bass or Choristfagott, the tenor or Hochquint, and one smaller or larger size.

According to the Praetorian scheme, a consort of four dulcians would be made up of two of equal size, plus one larger and one smaller, with an interval of a perfect fifth between sizes.[18] For example, an inventory of the ducal chapel of Styria made in 1577 listed 'a set of dolzani, including a bass, two tenors and a little descant' (the 'descant' may have been equivalent to alto). But inventories often included additional dulcians in adjacent sizes, suggesting that various instrumentations or transpositions were available.[19] At his death in Cracow, 1599, the estate of the instrument maker Bartlomiej Kiejcher included two 'consorts of sztort', each comprising seven items.[20] 'Consort' in this sense meant instrumentarium; not all seven were necessarily used at once.

Musicians of the time often played an assigned part in consort music, doubling on instruments of various families. Hamburg's Kantor, Thomas Selle, in 1642 'demanded five members of the Ratsmusik to be present at Sunday services, with all the instruments they play [including] one player of a string bass who must also have a bass curtal [dulcian] and a bass trombone, to use *pro variatione*'.[21]

Early evidence from Italy

The status quo of European secular music c.1470 was three vocal or instrumental parts. For purely instrumental music, the only written part was sometimes the tenor (or cantus firmus), over which cantus (soprano) and alto voices were improvised within a framework of conventional counterpoint.[22] Bass parts were generally not required, nor were bass instruments.[23]

In Italy, however, compositional style began to evolve at a noticeable pace. By 1480, imitation between voices became a common feature, and the combined range of voices expanded to two octaves and a fifth. By 1490, imitation between voices was a consistent feature, and four-voice texture became common. The first contratenor instrument added to the *alta banda* or shawm consort, by about 1480, was usually the tenor sackbut or trombone. With the subsequent expansion to five- and six-voice textures, the overall range of pitches expanded to three octaves, including a bass voice.[24]

The dulcian seems to have originated in Italy, spreading to much of Europe and Latin America before 1600. Exactly where and when the dulcian emerged is unclear, partly because terms such as fagotto, storto, and dolzana were spelled and used

7. Early dulcian in an alabaster relief by Antonius von Zerun, 1563. Freiberg Cathedral.
Photograph by Günter Angerhöfer.

loosely. The earliest known pictorial evidence for the instrument is 'a monument showing a dulcian player, carved in Antwerp . . . installed in Freiberg, Lower Saxony, in 1563'[25] (Ill. 7). References from Ferrara and Modena to a faghotto, fagoth, fagott, and fagot in the years 1516–18 were cited in chapter 1. These instruments may have been dulcians, or they may have been phagotum bagpipes. A record from the Accademia Filarmonica, Verona, dated March 1546, tells that

> . . . it was decided to buy a fagoto and a dolzana of . . . Alvise soldato for an honest price, and the price was fixed between 10 and 12 ducati. Item, not having done so, it was decided to go to Venice in order to buy a fagoto and two basonj below the fagoto of the pitch of the nine crumhorns.[26]

In this reference, the dolzana was possibly a dulcian of a particular size, or it may have been a dolzaina, as described in chapter 1. The fagoto was probably a dulcian, as the phagotum bagpipe is not known to have existed in Venice. The basonj (plural of bassono) were possibly dulcians of a different pitch, but they may have been bass shawms (see below).

The earliest identifiable surviving dulcians are signed 'HIERO.S', a mark associated with the famed Bassano family of Venetian wind instrument makers, several of whom immigrated to England. A history of the town of Bassano del Grappa, written in 1577, credited one member of the family, Maestro Gieronymo (Jeronimo, d. c.1545), also known as Piva, with the invention of an unspecified bass instrument.[27] A source from 1741, giving no evidence but citing a date, claimed that Gerolamo Piva invented 'uno strumento di basso da fiato' (a bass wind instrument) in 1503.[28] In any event, the Bassanos were making dulcians by 1559, an earlier date than any other identifiable maker. In that year the makers Jacomo Bassano (son of the late Jeronimo Bassano) and Santo Gritti (son-in-law of Jacomo) contracted to make woodwind instruments for three of the Doge's pifferi in Venice. In the contract, the category of 'shawms' included four sizes (soprano, tenori, bassetti, bassoni), as well as 'bassoni curti'. At least one of the three pifferi – Paulo Vergeli, Paulo de Laudis, and Francesco Ceneda – was presumably a player of the bassono curto. Context suggests that the bassono curto could be used in place of the bass shawm, especially in processions, as Ongaro noted.[29]

Early repertory

During the first era of the dulcian's existence, little music was written expressly for it. Many early uses involved either (1) non-written music – memorized or improvised compositions – or (2) written compositions not expressly for dulcian. An early example of written music is Susato's *Het derde musyck boexken (The Third Music Book;* Antwerp, 1551), in which popular melodies are arranged as dances in four parts, and no instrument is specified.[30] Written or not, much of the early repertory was based on vocal composition, as pictures, archival clues, and literary references suggest.

In musical function, the dulcian was the younger brother of the early trombone, increasingly matching the trombone's role as a portable and forceful bass instrument.[31] Some trombonists also played the dulcian, and the dulcian was sometimes present among 'the trombones'.[32] (A striking correlation is visible between the spread of the trombone and the spread of the dulcian through Italy, Austria, Germany, and Spain.) A dulcian was often used as the bass voice in cornetto or recorder consorts, or to play various voices of more thoroughly mixed consorts. Examples are given below.

By the early seventeenth century, a specific repertory for the dulcian began to emerge in Italy. Arcangelo Crotti's first book of sacred concertos (Venice, 1608) called for fagotto in one concerto.[33] In 1611 Mikolai Zielenski scored for dulcian as middle voice in two- and three-part instrumental fantasies.[34] A solo composition for dulcian – the earliest one known – was published (among other non-dulcian solos) in a 1638 work by Bartolomeo Selma y Salaverde. Giovanni Antonio Bertoli published a set of sonatas devoted entirely to the dulcian (plus continuo) in Venice, 1645. This was, according to Newman, the first known collection devoted to solo sonatas published for any instrument, and the first to contain the word 'solo' rather than *a due* in the title.[35]

The dulcian exported from Italy

Power and status are conveyed when even a small squad of men (soldiers, policemen, musicians) is deployed in files or ranks, outfitted in matching or coordinated costumes. Smart-looking weapons or musical instruments, adding to the splendor, quickly became symbols of status and power themselves. Several dulcians now in the collection of the Kunsthistorischesmuseum, Vienna, came from the Obizzi collection of arms and armour at Catajo Castle, near Padua.[36] Technologically advanced, of cultivated visual design, instruments were often made in consorts that appealed to the eye as well as the ear. Large musical instruments often borrowed the names of weapons.[37]

Hans Jakob Fugger in 1571 described an 'instrument chest which the Bassani [Bassano] brothers have made, together with the absolutely beautiful and excellent instruments *as would befit any eminent lord or potentate*'. Besides cornetts, a fife, crum-horns, and recorders, the chest included eleven unnamed instruments that seem to have been treble, tenor, bass and great bass dulcians, the smallest of which are described as being 'more beautiful than any precious stone'.[38] Generations later, in 1653, Johann Georg II wrote to his father Johann Georg I, elector of Saxony, advising him that if 'two good cornet players and six sackbut players and if the violinists and fagot and bombard players were also appointed . . . then certainly your Grace would have a perfect ensemble *in the eyes of all potentates*'.[39] One surviving dulcian by J. C. Denner is decorated with heavily engraved silver bands, analogous to the decora-tions applied to trumpets and trombones by Nuremberg makers. While some other dulcians by other makers are decorated with such engravings and bosses,[40] many more have decorative turnings or carvings that are more idiomatic in wood. Spanish bajones have their own style of decoration, discussed below.

During the sixteenth century, the grand ducal Medici family of Tuscany, wealthy through banking enterprises, consolidated political power through marriages. In its family weddings – extravagant demonstrations of wealth and social connections – theater and music mingled in lavish productions that included the most recently developed wind instruments. A similar concern for projecting wealth and power preoccupied the Fuggers, a merchant family closely associated with the Habsburg emperors. Raymund Fugger II amassed in Augsburg 'the largest documented collec-tion of musical instruments in the sixteenth century', including more than a dozen dulcians.[41] The Fugger family had a depot and a sumptuous residence in Venice, as well as depots in Antwerp, Berlin, Breslau, Danzig, Frankfurt-am-Main, Hamburg, Helsingor, Innsbruck, Leipzig, Lisbon, London, Lübeck, Madrid, Munich, Nuremberg, and Vienna. All these cities later showed abundant evidence of dulcian use. It appears that the Fuggers (perhaps among others) exported this symbolic Venetian instrument to many corners of the Habsburg empire, where it served as a model for local makers.

The middle of this chapter is organized by country or region, roughly according to earliest documentation of dulcian use, beginning with Italy. Dulcian use was docu-mented in the Netherlands and Spain by 1556, in Latin America by 1568, in Portugal by 1570, in England by 1574, in the Philippines by 1598, in France by 1602, in Denmark by 1632, in Sweden by 1682, and in China by 1699. Doubtless the earliest use often predated the earliest clear documentation, as in England.

Dulcian use in Italy

As noted in chapter 1, instruments called dolzaina or dolzaine were recorded at Florentine wedding celebrations and festivals between 1539 and 1589. Any of these mentions could have referred to dulcians, although we cannot be certain. Similar events continued into the seventeenth century, spreading to other Italian courts and cities. A 'dolzana' was heard at a festival in Florence, 1574.[42] In Turin, 1618, a dramatic ballo included music of 'cornetts and dulcian'.[43]

Dulcians had been used in Venice by the Doge's pifferi from 1559, as noted above. From 1576, this group included Giovanni Bassano, a second cousin of the woodwind maker Geronimo Bassano. In 1601, Giovanni became head of the instrumental ensemble at the basilica of San Marco, 'relaying the beat of the maestro di cappella from the floor of the basilica' to the ensemble, stationed in the organ loft.[44] His appointment was likely a factor in bringing the dulcian to the basilica, where it was documented by 1602.[45] Throughout the century, the dulcian played a notable role at San Marco, where the composers Giovanni Gabrieli, Monteverdi, Cavalli, and Legrenzi, among others, served as directors of music. One of the first fagotto players, documented 1602–5, was Nicolò Mosto, employed as a trombonist since 1593.[46] The virtuoso Giovanni Sansoni (c.1593–1648), who played dulcian, cornett, and trombone, is variously reported to have been at San Marco or in an archducal chapel in Graz from 1614 until c.1619.[47] The basilica's orchestra sometimes included two bassoonists, according to payroll records between 1642 and 1652. Fagotto players were recorded by name from 1602 until 1696, when budget pressures and papal injunctions led to the elimination of the post.[48] Several of these players eventually dispersed to Vienna and other European courts, carrying with them a Venetian tradition of instrumental virtuosity.

Dozens of sacred concertos (works combining voices and instruments) from San Marco include fagotto parts.[49] Selfridge-Field reported that a bassoon was required in the 'Jubilate Deo' of Gabrieli's *Symphoniae Sacrae* (1615).[50] Surviving Venetian sacred scores typically call for only one fagotto, although the actual practice was sometimes otherwise. At a vespers service in 1620, 'Monteverdi directed the music, which included four theorboes, two cornetti, two bassoons, two violins, and "a bass viol of monstrous dimensions"'.[51] Monteverdi's psalm *Laetatus sum* (SV 198; 1649/50) calls for fagotto in the accompaniment.[52]

Some of the fagotto players at San Marco taught at the Ospedale dei Mendicanti, as a record shows in 1669. In five inventories of the Ospedale's instruments made from 1661/2 to 1673, one fagotto is listed, but none in later inventories.[53] After Legrenzi reformed the Saint Mark's orchestra in 1685, one dulcian was included, along with twenty-eight string instruments, two cornetts, and three trombones.[54]

Purely instrumental music at San Marco sometimes called for the dulcian, among other instruments. 'Church sonatas', forerunners of the secular instrumental sonata of the eighteenth century, were often written as a substitute for the gradual and communion of the Roman Catholic Mass, or for the psalm antiphons at vespers services.[55] These were scored, naturally enough, for the same instruments that accompanied the vocal works: some combination of violins, cornetti, trombones, viols, and dulcian. During this period, Venice was the European center of publication for both instrumental and concerted works, although reprints were sometimes issued in Antwerp and Bologna.[56] Non-Italian composers like Selma y Salaverde and Zielenski, employed in other corners of the Habsburg empire, also chose to publish their works for dulcian in Venice.

The chiaroscuro lent by the dulcian's rich tone delighted the seventeenth-century ear. In Venice it was the bass instrument of choice in trio sonatas with violins. Across Europe, it was specified in countless ensemble sonatas and sacred concertos alongside trombones, or sometimes in their stead. In some printed collections – a conspicuous example is Schutz's *Symphoniae sacrae* (Venice, 1629) – a given sonata calls for one or more fagotti, while the next sonata calls for one or more trombones instead. The dulcian was thus, like its peer the trombone, a recognized tone color on composers's palettes.

Beginning with Biagio Marini's Op. 1 sonata 'La Aguzzona' (1618), the agile dulcian was frequently specified as a bass to the newly popular violin.[57] Sonatas for two dulcians plus upper voices were also written.[58] The *Compositioni armoniche* (1619) of Gabriel Sponga detto Usper includes examples of both.[59] In a canzona by G. B. Riccio (1620), the flautino and fagotto imitate a stringed instrument's tremolo by rapidly tonguing through a series of chromatically shifting tenths. The publication's title, 'La Grimaneta con il tremolo', suggests that the effect was celebrated at the time.[60] Among the sixty-eight works in Marini's op. 8 (Venice, 1626) are two sonatas specifying two dulcians and continuo. Marini's writing included G#3, a pitch obtainable by half-holing or by a 'long' cross-fingering.

Many obbligato parts for fagotto in canzonas, fantasias, or sonatas seem written as showcases for its technical facility: arabesque clusters of thirty-second notes, profuse sequences of trills, rapid arpeggios, and rapid staccato tonguing. Some of these effects were difficult or impossible on the trombone. Even before the sonatas of Selma and Bertoli (and the bassoon concertos of Vivaldi), Dario Castello established a tradition of virtuosic writing for dulcian. The closing Presto of his Sonata no. 9 for two violins and bassoon (Book I, 1621), mentioned above, is a celebration of the dulcian's idiom. In this sonata (and Sonata no. 7), Castello frequently called for C2, a pitch too low for the trombone.

The same vein of improvisational-sounding virtuosity is again notated in the *Canzoni, Fantasie et Correnti* of Bartolomeo Selma y Salaverde, a Spanish-born Augustinian monk. Selma, who had served at one minor Habsburg court in Innsbruck, dedicated the publication (Venice, 1638) to another Habsburg noble in Breslau. Selma's canzona (no. 10 in C major), titled 'per fagotto solo', is full of rapid runs and wide leaps. After a harmonically tame first section, the second section veers unexpectedly into arpeggios on Eb2 and Bb1; the latter note lies outside the standard range of the dulcian.[61] (Of sonatas 5 through 9, labeled 'per il basso', three more descend to Bb1.)

The strain of virtuosity continued in Giovanni Antonio Bertoli's nine sonatas for dulcian and continuo (Venice, 1645), written in a restless, ostentatious style that includes syncopations, wide leaps, and rapid scalar passages. In these one-movement works, phrases are repeated with steadily increasing rhythmic difficulty and melodic complexity, becoming in effect a proto-variation form. Most of the works present contrasting melodic materials and a shift into triple meter.[62]

In string sonatas by Massimiliano Neri (Op. 1, 1644, and Op. 2, 1655) and Cavalli (*Musiche sacre*, 1656), the dulcian was named as an optional substitute for the violone.[63] (Cavalli's will, written in 1675, specified a bassoon among the forces for his funeral Mass, to be performed in the basilica.[64]) A sonata in Giovanni Legrenzi's op. 8 (1663) opposed a wind choir (cornetti and dulcian) to a string choir (violins and cello). [65]

The dulcian was occasionally heard in Venetian opera. In stereotyped roles it represented the underworld or sea monsters (a motif arising from Venice's mastery of the seas). One early example, cited by Selfridge-Field, was a short piece for five bassoons in Act I of the anonymous opera *Il Pio Enea* (1641).[66] (This sort of role probably inspired the Tartölt and Anciuti's contrabassoon, both described below.)

The Netherlands

Mary of Austria, Queen of Hungary (to give her full Habsburg name), was governor of the Spanish Netherlands in Brussels from 1530. When she set sail from Ghent in 1556, intending to retire in Castile (Tordesillas, Spain), an inventory of her possessions included 'two contrabass musical instruments, which are called fagots, which are kept in two round cases [and] one contralto fagot'.[67] Even if the size designations may need interpretation, it is clear that dulcians of two sizes were present in the governor's household in Brussels.

Brussels was one terminal of the 'Spanish Road', an important trade route that stretched northward from Milan (both cities were possessions of the Spanish line of the Habsburgs). Dulcians, artworks showing dulcians, and dulcian makers moved fluidly along the road. In 1563, an altarpiece showing a dulcian among other wind instruments was installed in Freiberg, Lower Saxony; this had been carved in Antwerp by Antonius van Zerun.[68] The Nuremberg *Stadtpfeifer* in 1575 received a dulcian made in Antwerp. Melchior Billingkheim, reportedly a Dutchman, was employed as an instrument maker at the Stuttgart court 1586–8; a tenor dulcian by him was listed in a 1589 inventory there.[69] Brussels, Amsterdam, and Antwerp also pursued maritime trade with Baltic and Mediterranean ports, including Venice. The maker Richard Haka of Amsterdam supplied six bass dulcians to the Swedish navy in 1685.[70]

Philippe van Ranst (c.1541–1628) served in the royal chapel and chamber of the Netherlands from 1583 as 'instrumentist', and during 1605–19 as 'musicien fagotiste'.[71] A town wait in Bruges, 1588, was expected to play the fagote.[72] Jan Meulepas played fagot by 1589 with the Antwerp *staadspeelieden*.[73] By 1605 he had replaced his fagot with one of his own making. In 1615, Meulepas entered the service of the archduke of Brussels, becoming the court's third fagot, a newly created position.

8. Dulcian player in a religious procession, Antwerp, 1616. Detail of Denis van Alsloot, *Procession to Mary at the Zavel in Brussels*. Museo del Prado, Madrid.

A well-known painting shows a bass dulcian player, together with a cornett, three shawms, and a sackbut, leading a religious procession in Antwerp[74] (Ill. 8). Spiessens suggested that the dulcian player depicted was Anthony van den Steen, a *staadspeelman* since 1585, and successor to Meulepas in 1608.[75] The dulcian was sometimes used to accompany singing; it was shown with cornetto, trumpet and singers in a painting by van der Horst, 'The Pilgrimage of the Infanta Isabelle to Laken in 1622'.[76]

In 1621 Lambert Du Mont entered the choir school of Onze-Lieve-Vrouwkerk, Maastricht, along with his brother Henry, later a composer in the royal chapel of France. While in the choir school, Lambert studied bassoon.[77] Nicolaus à Kempis published three collections of ensemble sonatas that specify fagotto.[78] Jehan Henry's *Symphonia* for three cornetti and dulcino is published in Kircher's *Musurgia universalis* (1650). Benedictus a Sancto Josepho, a Dutch Carmelite monk, specified dulcian in his sacred concertos, opp. 1–7, published at Antwerp 1666–93. Certain works of the Fleming Lambert Pietkin are scored for dulcian.[79]

The two-key bajón in Spain

The dulcians of Mary of Austria, brought from Brussels to Tordesillas in 1556, may or may not have been the first dulcians in Spain.[80] In the next few years, however, use of the dulcian or bajón spread to cathedrals and churches in Palencia (by 1560), Madrid (1562), the monastery El Escorial (1563), Valencia (1564), Avila (1565), Granada (1566), Segovia (1566), Valladolid (1566), and more than a dozen other cities by 1600.[81] By 1590 a workshop for instruments was attached to Madrid cathedral's Capilla Real. The dynasty of bajón makers there included Juan de Perpignan (1590–98), Francisco de Olivera (1603–7), Bartolmé de Selma (1612–16; also active at Cuenca, 1593–1612), Antonio de Selma (1616–43), Pedro Aldao (1643–69), and Melchor Rodríguez (1669–1701). The workshop was abolished in 1701. Other early makers in Spain included Felix Diaz (fl. Madrid, 1617) and Jerónimo de Medina (fl. Seville, 1590). Two other marks appear on surviving instruments: MTNZ (possibly Martinez) and MR°MER (possibly Romero). Makers of the eighteenth century included Joseph Estrella (fl. Madrid, 1786) and Fernando Llop (Madrid). In the early nineteenth century, Claret was a bajón maker in Madrid, followed by J. E. Sanchez (Spain, late nineteenth century).

The Spanish bajón was a distinct physical subtype of the dulcian, as described above (Ill. 9). It also had a variant tuning in D-Dorian, rather than the normal European C major. The D aspect is mostly conceptual – the lowest note of the instrument was considered as being D2, customarily the lowest note of a bass singer's voice. But the Dorian aspect called for a physical difference – holes 1 and 2 of the bajón corista were small and widely separated, as were holes 4 and 5; hole 9 was also smaller than on non-Spanish instruments. Starting with all fingers closed, then opening the finger holes one at a time, resulted in the scale D, E, F, G, A, B, C, D – a modal scale called Dorian. This modal tuning is also implicit in the arrangement of thumb keys on later three-piece bajones, described below.

Josip Borràs i Roca in 2008 offered a definition of the distinctive Spanish bajón, citing both physical characteristics and early theoretical sources.[82] Among the latter, Pere Rabassa's 'Guía para los principiantes' (c.1724) classified the bajón among the old

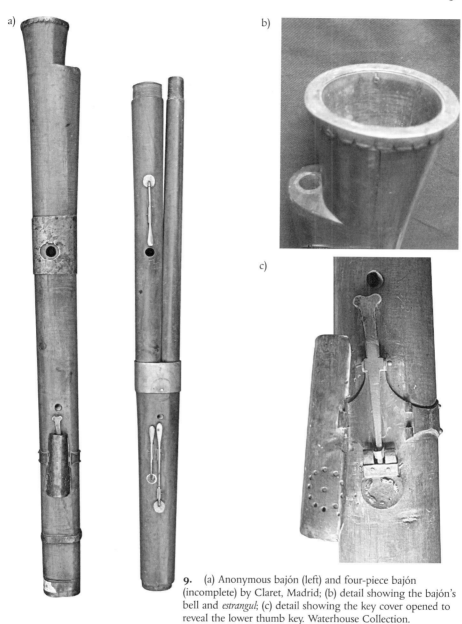

9. (a) Anonymous bajón (left) and four-piece bajón (incomplete) by Claret, Madrid; (b) detail showing the bajón's bell and *estrangul*; (c) detail showing the key cover opened to reveal the lower thumb key. Waterhouse Collection.

ministriles (instruments associated with the choir); the new baroque bassoon was classified among the orchestral instruments.[83] Both Rabassa and an anonymous method from 1810 (Ms, Roncesvalles, Navarre) described the bajón's lowest pitch as D. An anonymous fingering table conserved in the parochial archive of Xàtiva (Valencia), dating from c.1800, shows two chromatic octaves of fingerings. Among these are some 'long' cross fingerings, in which more than one tone hole is closed beneath the primary vent. According to the chart, the effect of closing a remote tone hole is sometimes to raise the pitch, sometimes to lower it[84] (Ill. 10).

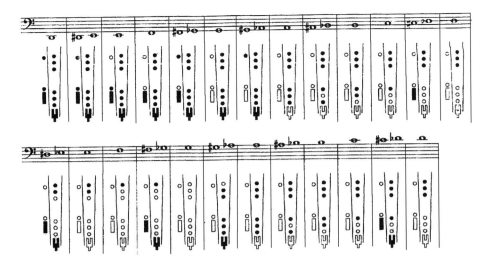

10.   Fingering chart for bajón, c.1800. Iglesia Collegial de Santa Maria de Xàtiva (Valencia). Transcription by Josep Borràs i Roca.

Surviving bajones in the corista size show a high degree of conformity in their dimensions, including a relatively short bell.[85] Yet the characteristic design of the bajones was only occasionally carried through to the smaller sizes. Most of the eight surviving bajoncillos lack the four brass girdles and crown characteristic of the bajones. Only one bajoncillo, a tenor, has an estrangul.

The bajón had a key role in the Spanish liturgy. In at least some Spanish cathedrals, the bajonista was engaged years earlier than other ministrel (non-organ) instruments, often on a more permanent basis. A document from Palencia cathedral, dated 1598, specified the services of the liturgical calendar when the bajón was required. Kenyon de Pascual gave details of the bajón's elaborate role there in the special feast of Corpus Christi in 1627, while Kilbey outlined the routine there during the church year, as reflected in records from 1643.[86]

> Bajonistas were expected to be versatile and hard-working: at audition they not only had to sight-read virtuoso music, but also improvise at sight and transpose by any required interval. . . . . Many new recruits were found among the boy choristers who were about to receive their valediction, and it was a standard duty of the bajonista to teach them . . .[87]

One of the earliest functions of the bajón corista, of course, was to support the singing of Gregorian chant. Singers and the bajonista read from a single large chant book, a practice called *facistol*. Even after polyphonic sections were added to the liturgy, they were sometimes interspersed with sections of chant. The document from Palencia cathedral, entitled 'Obligations of the Minstrel Bajón when Assisting the Choir by Himself', describes a specific alternatim practice in which the bajón alone accompanied a vocal soloist in half-verses, lending pitch stability until the organ and choir joined in each remaining half-verse. Among the earliest datable scorings to specify bajón are works by (Juan) Ginés Peréz de la Parra (1548–1600; choirmaster at the cathedrals of Orihuela and Valencia) and Alonso Lobo (1555–1617; maestro de capilla at the cathedrals of Toledo and Seville). Kilbey noted 'a huge repertoire' of Spanish sacred music calling for the bajón, much of it still uncatalogued and unpublished.[88] Certain works by José de Vaquedano, maestro de capilla at the Cathedral of Santiago de Compostela from 1681 to 1711, used the bajón to replace the bass voice in soprano/alto/tenor choral music. This practice, apparently peculiar to Spanish composers, was later seen in the works of his successors at Santiago, and at Avila Cathedral. Another regional peculiarity was the use of muted instruments (bajones tapados) in pieces by Francisco Pascual (fl. Palencia, 1723–43), Melchor López Jimenez (1750–1822), and Agapito Sancho (fl. Zamora, nineteenth century).[89]

The bajón was sometimes used in polyphonic music along with shawms, as in works by Vaquedano, by Ramos (Avila), and by Arquimbau (fl. Seville, 1803). More often than shawms, however, bajoncillos played or doubled the upper voices (see chapter 11). Kenyon noted in Spanish church music of the seventeenth century a preference for double reeds (shawms, bajoncillos, and bajones) and opposition to the introduction of violins.[90] Sizes larger than corista were probably known in Spain; Kilbey cited evidence from Plasencia cathedral, 1573, and Madrid, 1602 and 1620.[91]

By 1596, in the (female) Monasterio de Constantinople, Madrid, a nun was being taught to play a bajón.[92] Three bajoncillos were purchased in 1614 by the Duke of Lerma for the nuns at the Monasterio de San Blas.[93] Two bajoncillos were purchased for Santa Isabel de los Reyes by 1620; the community bought another bajoncillo around 1638 and a new bajón around 1643. Nuns often received financial rewards for their musical contributions to the religious community.[94] But not every female monastery trained nuns to play; at the Monasterio de las Descalzas Reales in seventeenth-century Madrid, the chapel was composed of hired male musicians.[95]

Within ecclesiastical circles the bajón was sometimes used as an obbligato voice, and in later times in combination with baroque oboes or bassoons. Use of the bajón was occasionally documented in Spanish secular music. Fr. Anselm Viola (1738–98) composed a concerto with 'baixó obligat'.[96] Miguel de Lope wrote a sonata para bajón as an audition piece for the Madrid Capilla Real, 1791, as did Miguel Sánche García (sonatina, 1819). José Vinyals Gali (1771–1825) wrote six works for a harmonie ensemble: two oboes, two horns and bajón.

German-speaking lands adopt the dulcian

During the centuries of Habsburg dominance, German was spoken by many within the boundaries of today's Germany, Austria, Switzerland, Czech Republic, Hungary, Poland, Russia, and the Baltic countries. The Spanish Road, the Fugger network of business interests, and the Hanseatic League facilitated communication, trade, and work transfers among the musical community. German-speaking courts fervently embraced the Venetian musical style, importing composers, performers, and instruments, while sending German-born composers to study in Venice.[97] By 1566,

Raymond Fugger of Augsburg owned more than a dozen fagotti, as well as a 'small doltzana made in Venice'.[98] The Graz Hofkapelle of Archduke Karl of Styria purchased 'dulzeine' from Venice in 1570; between 1577 and 1590, the court owned dulcians in at least five sizes, from quintbass to 'little descant'.[99] Resident makers of dulcians are recorded at some German-speaking courts from the 1570s and 1580s (see below).[100]

Among the emigrants from Italy was Orlando di Lasso, who served the duke of Bavaria. The duke's wedding in Munich, 1568, echoed the elaborate festivities of the Medici weddings; a picture shows 'a pageant of Diana and nymphs and a band of satyrs playing shawm, fagoto, two crumhorns, and cornetto'.[101] Lasso in 1588 ordered a Venetian 'Vagott' for Munich.[102]

Hundreds of early Latin or German sacred concertos are known, a large number of them calling for dulcian.[103] Among the German emigrants to Venice was Heinrich Schütz, who studied composition with Giovanni Gabrieli at San Marco during 1609–13. Two Schütz works are scored for multiple dulcians: SWV 476 and SWV 49.[104] Kilbey believed that Schütz brought bassanelli (an invention of the Bassano family) and dulcians from Venice to the Kassel court c.1613.[105] These may have been the instruments that Praetorius depicted in 1619–20. Schütz moved to the court Kapelle in Dresden in 1614. He returned to Italy in 1628 or 1629, studying with Monteverdi in Florence, and sending instruments to Dresden from Italy.[106]

Other Germanic chapels also craved the sound of dulcians, and the more the better. Between 1613 and 1658, multiple dulcians were required in sacred concertos published or performed in Vienna, Stuttgart, Wolfenbüttel, Mainz, Nuremberg, Salzburg, Halle, and Mühlhausen.[107] Buxtehude, working at Lübeck from 1668 to 1707, scored dulcian parts in twenty-three sacred works, including one (BuxWV 72) for three fagotten.[108]

Purely instrumental sonatas or suites were written and often published in the German-speaking countries, including Zielenski's two fantasies of 1611, combining one fagotto with one or two violins. Among the most prolific writers of such instrumental works was Johann Christoph Pezel, a Stadtpfeifer in various towns, who published five sets of suites between 1669 and 1686. The four surviving collections include dozens of sonatas and suites for mixed ensembles, often including dulcian. Some of these were reprinted numerous times. During the century, many analogous works were published by composers working within the German-speaking lands. Sometimes neither their names nor the places of publication were German.[109]

The opus 4 of Philip Friedrich Buchner (Frankfurt, 1662) includes a sonata for two dulcians and continuo; it contains close imitation for the two dulcians and makes free use of rapid arpeggios. As in Italy, however, the solo sonata for dulcian and basso continuo was a rarity. An exception was Philipp Friedrich Böddecker's *Sonata sopra La Monica* (Strasbourg, 1651), based on a popular tune, 'Madre, non mi far monaca'.

A symphonia in Staden and Harsdörfer's *Seelewig* (Nuremberg, 1644) called for 'Pomparten or Fagotten' in three sizes, the earliest documented use of dulcian in the German theatre.[110] Sonatas sometimes accompanied dining; the titles of two collections of ensemble sonatas by Daniel Speer suggest the merriment of some Tafelmusik: *Neugebachene Taffel-Schnitz* (freshly baked slices, 1685) and *Musicalisch-Türkisch Eulenspiegel* ('musical jokes', including ethnic dances, 1688).[111]

The civic office of town pipers or Stadtpfeifer, a common institution in German-speaking lands, supported the culture of the dulcian between about 1570 and 1660, as Kilbey noted: 'many Stadtpfeifer were also dulcian makers, for example Hans Drebs and Konrad Rude of Leipzig'.[112] The German military was yet another employer of dulcian players: 'Towards the end of the Thirty Years War (1646) the Brandenburg Dragoon Guards had a band of shawms (two treble and one tenor, with a dulcian for the bass) and drums.'[113] Both civic and military musicians might have marched in religious or civic processions. In Dresden, Spagnoli noted, 'the great processions of the sixteenth century were held out of doors; during the seventeenth century, however, they were moved indoors, where they became connected with the development of the ballet'.[114]

German-speaking courts and cities

The Augsburg Stadtpfeifer owned dulcians bearing the Bassano mark (see above), but local makers were documented by the early seventeenth century, including Messenhauser and MH (two distinct marks). The maker Martin Reiff of Prague supplied both Fagotten and rackets to the Württemberg court (Stuttgart and Ludwigsburg) in 1578–9. By 1581, however, a court instrument maker was installed: Hans Thanner, whose shop inventory included a small dulcian.[115] He was succeeded by Melchior Billigkheim, known as the Dutchman, who also served as a court instrumentalist, during the years 1586 to 1588.[116]

The Württemberg court eventually employed a single maker of both armor and instruments (mutually emblematic of the local potentate's status and power). Father Samuel Baisch held this post until 1593, supplying 'Fagottes, bombards, and armor'. He was succeeded by Daniel Schorndorfer, whose shop was within the armory. Schorndorfer, a player and the stepson of Thanner, had already made two dulcians by 1590.[117] Ludwig Daser, Kapellmeister at the court from 1572 to 1589, composed a motet for eight voices, four Vagotten and four bombards. It was revived in 1616, long after the composer's death, for a court baptism ceremony.[118] Johann Michael Nicolai, a member of the court Kapelle, included obbligato bassoon parts in his ensemble sonatas (1675) and arias. He was on friendly terms with P. F. Böddecker (1607–83), the local organist and dulcian player mentioned above. Daniel Speer, a member of the Stuttgart town band in the mid-1660s, drew on his experiences for autobiographical novels.[119] Speer published a set of twelve ensemble sonatas in 1685, including two for two violins and fagotto. In 1697 he published two sonatas scored for three dulcians, as well as the earliest known fingering chart for the instrument[120] (Ill. 11).

Konrad Rude, a Leipzig Stadtpfeifer and probably a maker, supplied a dulcian to the Bremen Stadtpfeifer in 1577.[121] Hans Drebs, a Leipzig Stadtpfeifer in 1598, was a documented maker of cornets, flutes, dulcians, and shawms. He was succeeded by his son Christian, who was active until about 1667.[122] Near Leipzig, Johann Beer (1655–1700) was Kapellmeister at the court of Saxe-Weissenfels. In chapter 27 of his novel *Musicalische Discurse* (Nuremberg, 1719), a narrator mediates a wager between a trombonist and a Fagottist about whose instrument is superior. In a battle

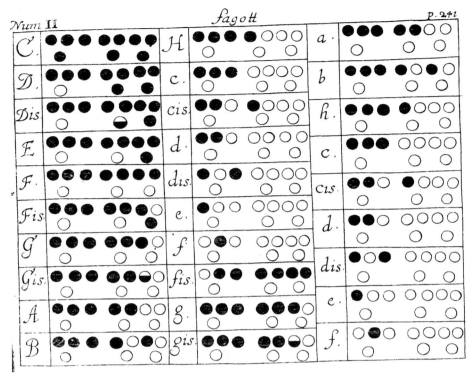

11.   Fingering chart for dulcian from Daniel Speer, *Grund-richtiger . . . Unterricht* (Ulm, 1697).

of boasts, the Fagottist claims he can be heard buzzing from twenty feet outside the church door, while the trombone can hardly be heard by a listener inside the church.[123]

Jörg Haas made or supplied dulcians to the Nuremberg Stadtpfeifer and Frauenkirche in the period 1596–1609. Johannes Höffler, a dealer, supplied dulcians to buyers as far away as Frankfurt am Main, c.1625–6. Nuremberg's particular fondness for the dulcian is illustrated by the work of Andreas Hußgatt, a third maker, who supplied and repaired dulcians between 1616 and 1635 for several of the Nuremberg churches. In 1626 Hußgatt charged the Stadtpfeifer for cleaning several dulcians, making replacement parts and reeds, and 'in order to have a more complete set of instruments', he supplied two more 'tenore dulcianen' and one alto dulcian. These new instruments were in addition to 'one octavebass, two quartbasses, seven ordinary basses and one tenor quint'. In 1629 Hussgatt supplied another dulcian, and in 1630 the council ordered still another quartbass, another bass, and a tenor.[124] Some of these instruments presumably were used at a ceremonial banquet held at the Nuremberg Rathaus in 1649, celebrating the end of the Thirty Years War. Among four spatially separated choirs, the fourth included three singers, a loud regal, a bass dulcin, a Quart Fagot, and a 'Contra and Octav-Fagott'. The program included two grand works, David Schedlich's 'Herr Gott, dich loben wir' à 23 and Sigmund Staden's setting of Psalm 150.[125] The rich orchestration was motivated by the occasion and the text of the psalm.

Among the latest surviving dulcians made in Nuremberg are four by J. C. Denner (fl. 1678–1707).[126]

A collection assembled by Karl of Styria by 1596 included 'one new Doltana, bought from Venice'. The collection, kept at Ruhelust Castle near Innsbruck, also included 'Tolzanae, eight of them, namely two bass, four tenor, four treble; also accompanied by a bass Dolcima bought from Hheronimos Geroldi's successors'.[127] Karl's son, Archduke Leopold of Austria, employed the dulcian player and composer Selma y Salaverde at Innsbruck from 1628 until 1630.[128]

The Polish and Baltic courts had a tradition of dulcian usage, as yet little explored. In 1587, the musician Jonas Depensee from Stralsund wrote to the town of Reval (now Talinn, Estonia), stating that he was able to play a wide variety of instruments. In his will, dated 1607, Depensee left to his son entire consorts of dulcians, sackbuts and cornets, shawms, large cornets, crumhorns, flutes, recorders, and violins, 'so that he can change between eight kinds of instrument'.[129]

A Polish-language poem published in Cracow, 1590, referred to 'sztorty', meaning dulcians. An inventory at the death of the instrument maker Bartolomiej Kiejcher in Cracow, 1599, included 'eight finished sztort … two consorts of sztort, each comprising seven items … sixteen white sztort with the double bore and finger holes, thirty white sztort, roughly bored … one white consort of sztort, unfinished, comprising seven instruments', plus boring tools, reamers, four crook mandrels, and sztort reeds.[130] Tommaso Chiari, a maker at the Polish court in Cracow in 1606, was reported to have made dulcians. Piwkowski cited sixteen sztort players active in Poland during the years 1600–41.[131] Jarzebski (d. 1648/9), Mielczewski (d. 1651), and Pekiel (d. 1670), composers at courts in Warsaw and Cracow, wrote ensemble or solo sonatas for dulcian.[132]

The makers Bartholomäus Hess and Paul Hess worked in Breslau c.1553–85, producing dulcians for distant customers and doubtless local ones as well. Among composers with links to Breslau and specifying dulcian in their scores were Schütz (*Syncharma musicum*, 1621), Bertoli, and Selma y Salaverde.[133] Numerous scores calling for dulcian are preserved in the Bohn Collection (formerly Staatsbibliothek Breslau, now Staatsbibliothek, Berlin).[134]

The Lutheran Hofkapelle of Dresden in 1593 owned eight 'Dolzom'. Praetorius, who worked with Schütz at the Hofkapelle from 1613 until 1616, probably knew some of these instruments.[135] Several of Schütz's compositions demand dulcians of a size larger than Choristfagott. In his compositions for Dresden, Schütz used dulcians freely, as did (later) his choirboy pupils Pohle, Thieme, Vierdanck, and Weckmann, and his cousin Albert. Schütz's successors at Dresden, Vincenzo Albrici and Giuseppe Peranda, continued the rich tradition of dulcian usage.[136] The Dresden Stadtpfeifer in 1606 played 'crumhorns, recorders, flutes, dulcians, trumpets and cornetts. They were required to perform four-part music from the tower, to "strengthen and enhance" the choir of the Kreuzkirche on feast days, Sundays, and at weddings.' Dulcians were still in the inventories of the Tragoner-Schallmeipfeifer and the royal instrument chamber in 1680–1.[137]

Christoph Straus, a Viennese church musician, scored for 'fagot grande' in choral works of 1613 and 1631.[138] When Ferdinand II became Habsburg emperor in 1619, he discharged most of the existing Kapelle (including Straus, who had joined in 1616). He installed many Italian musicians, beginning with members of his archducal Kapelle in Graz. Among those engaged was Giovanni Sansoni, a virtuoso on cornetto, dulcian, and sackbut, reputedly with Venetian experience.[139] In 1637 Sansoni was the highest-paid instrumentalist at court by a factor of nearly three to one. Bertoli praised Sansoni in the preface to his bassoon sonatas (1645). In 1648 Schütz sent choirboys, after their voices broke, to Sansoni, for training as instrumentalists. Sansoni possibly taught the court cornettist Schmelzer, who composed numerous ballet suites and ensemble sonatas that call for dulcian.

As an essential ingredient of the exported Venetian musical style, the dulcian found a warm and enduring reception in Vienna. Two emperors – Ferdinand III and Leopold I – scored for dulcian in their own sacred concertos. Giovanni Valentini, music teacher of Ferdinand III, composed sonatas for mixed ensemble including dulcians.[140] Ensemble sonatas for strings by the court lutenist Marc-Antonio Ferro included alternative scorings for two cornets, dulcians, trombone, and theorbo.[141]

In Cesti's opera *Il Pomo d'oro* (composed 1666 for Venice, performed 1667 in Vienna), a dulcian figures in two underworld scenes – the court of Pluto and Proserpine in Act I and Charon's post at the river Styx in Act II – along with cornetti, trombones, and regal, an ensemble evoking the underworld in the growling Venetian tradition.[142] The dulcian player may have been Pietro Aut[en]garden, who left the Kapelle for San Marco in 1674, or Giro (Siro) Mangiarotti, who served from 1662 to 1684.[143]

Portugal

The one surviving instrument of Portuguese provenance, now in Lisbon, is idiosyncratic, lacking one of the two lower thumb holes.[144] Pedro de Cristo in 1571 became a professed monk, organist, bajonista, and chapelmaster at the monastery of Santa Cruz, Coimbra, dying in 1618. Cristo's successor in 1627 was Pedro de Esperança, who had composed four Christmas responsories c.1615, calling for fagotilho, violin, baixão, and gamba. The fagotilho part, lying in the range C4 to F5, 'could be played only on a descant bajoncillo in C3' (range G2 to G4).[145] A distinguished player of the fagote, Antonio Marques Fagote was chapelmaster to D. João IV (reigned 1640–56).[146] Dulcians (baixàos) took a role in secular music parties, as captured in two sets of decorative tiles of the eighteenth century, from the Marqueses de Frontiera Palace, Lisbon, and Convent of Nostra Senora de Graça, Tores Vedras.[147]

England

An inventory made at the death of Henry VIII in 1547 included, among many other instruments, thirteen *dulceuses*; these were 'short instruments ... covered in leather'. These dulceuses were probably dulcians, and possibly produced by the Bassanos in England or Italy.[148] A Suffolk account book of 1574 recorded payment 'for an instrument called a curtall'.[149] Bassano exports may lie behind a mention in Danzig, 1594, of 'four little English dulcians'.[150]

Kilbey cited archival evidence of curtals (dulcians) in use in Exeter (1575), Kings Lynn (1593), Chester (1614), and Coventry (1627). But neither curtals nor music specifically demanding them survives in England, possibly due to the Puritans' prohibition of instrumental church music during the Commonwealth (1642–60). If many instruments perished during this era, however, the demand later surged:

> [C]urtals would have been especially valued after the Restoration in 1660. This was because an entire generation of choirboys had been skipped during the hostilities, making it even more necessary for the singers to be provided with a solid lead from the bass part. . . .[151]

On 17 April 1661, just after the restoration of the monarchy, the installation of the Knights of the Garter at Windsor included two instrumental pairs, each consisting of a double sackbut and a double curtal. During 'the grand procession', a wind pair joined each of the two choirs, helping them 'keep together in both time and tune'. In 1662 Robert Strong and Edward Strong were required 'to attend with their double *curtolls* in his Majesty's Chappell Royall at Whitehall . . . every Sunday and Holy day'.[152] Roger North, writing in 1676 of York and Durham, described the 'double curtaile' as one of the 'ordinary wind instruments in the Quires . . . which supply the want of voices, very notorious here'.[153]

Misleading labels for ensembles sometimes obscure the uses to which curtals were put. A curtal could take the bass part, for example, in a recorder consort. After the musician Aurthur Ondum died at Boston in 1607, his estate included 'one double curtal instrument, the fourth part of a noyse of recorders'.[154] In fact, the term curtal was neither necessary nor sufficient to denote an English dulcian. Around 1690–1700, James Talbot in Cambridge described the *Fagot* (one piece) as 'disused', replaced now by the *basson* (four joints).[155] Conversely, some later references to the 'double curtal' in England are to the four-joint bassoon.

Spanish and Portuguese colonies

The Spanish colonization of the new world spread from the Caribbean (1490s), to Mexico (1520s), to Peru (1530s), to the Philippines (1570s). (The Portuguese pursued a similar policy in Brazil beginning in 1549; see below.) Under Spanish legislation, the Ordenanzas of 1573,

> . . . in order to persuade the native Americans who resisted the Catholic faith, the Spanish authorities allowed the use of 'singers and high and low minstrels' to induce them to congregate in towns. In 1618 additional legislation ordered that in the new native towns with populations of a hundred or more, there were to be two or three [native] musicians exempted from paying their tribute.[156]

> The choirmasters in the newly established churches usually came from Spain, but most of the musicians were born in Latin America, and included native Americans as well as black slaves and freemen. . . . Some of the black musicians were part of

the triangular slave trade established at this date. . . . Other slaves were shipped to Spain for instrumental lessons before being sent to Latin America.[157]

The native musicians were called *yanaconas*, meaning 'service natives' or 'service Indians'.[158] Like many civic or military musicians in Europe, they often wore colorful uniforms and hats.[159] Their activity was strictly regulated by the church, which sought to preserve the exclusivity of such music. During the years 1580–82, Pedro Serrano, an instrumentalist forbidden by contract to perform outside the church without permission, was accused of playing with his native musicians on the streets of Cuzco at night, 'offering his services to anyone'.[160] Individual players were sometimes named after their instruments, including one 'Bajonero' (Santafé, 1595–1630) and 'El Bajón' (New Mexico, 1698).[161] Among the service natives who played bajón were Juan Bermudo de Castro, a black slave (also a carpenter) owned by the Jesuits in Santafé (present-day Bogota, Colombia), in 1651; and the Native American José Soraca, who was an organist, bajonista, and cornett player in Santafé in 1709.

The broad term *chirimía* (literally, shawm or shawm player) sometimes referred to players of other wind instruments, including bajones or dulcians.[162] In 1568, Lieciando Juan de Ovando, an inspector from the Franciscan Council of Indies, reported that

> Polyphonic music is everywhere, and accompaniment of flutes and chirimías is common. In a number of places dulcians and reeds along with viols and other types of instruments are used.[163]

In 1588, a bajón was used for the first time in the cathedral in Mexico City. A painting in the Convento de la Merced, Cuzco, Peru (c.1595), shows a bajonista playing what appears to be an innovative three-piece instrument. A bajón was purchased in Cuzco in 1606. Between 1632 and c.1650, the bajonista Simón Martínez collaborated with the turner Baltasar Rodríguez to produce double-reed instruments in Puebla, Mexico. They were encouraged in this work by Juan Gutiérrez de Padilla, the maestro de capilla at Puebla Cathedral (then the largest in Latin America). In 1641 they produced a batch including thirty bajones grandes, twenty bajones tenores, and twenty bajicos tiples (trebles), among other instruments, for sale in Nexapa and other villages.[164] Two more makers were documented in Puebla by 1719, when they exported bajones to markets in Caracas and Veracruz.[165]

In Argentina, the Tyrolean Father Antonio Sepp arrived at Buenos Aires in April 1691, soon departing for the Church of the Reduction of Yapeyú.[166] After a year of labor, he had trained ten fagotistas, among dozens of other players, and installed a factory to make musical instruments. He wrote:

> The Indians make very good musical instruments, among them trumpets, clarinets, harps, clavichords, psalteries, fagotes, chirimías, theorbos, violins, flautas, guitars, etc. . . . We recently made some drills (or reamers) of iron for the making of fagots and chirimías, enabling us to make instruments as perfect as those made in Europe.[167]

Gutierre Fernandéz Hidalgo (c.1545–1622) may have been a force in the spread of the bajón. The instrument's use is recorded in cathedrals or convents at Lima, Peru, c.1590; Cuzco, Peru, c.1595; and La Plata, Bolivia, c.1607, in each instance during Hidalgo's service as maestro de capilla. Bajonistas played early in the morning on major feast days and during vespers on the preceding day (as documented in Santafé, 1651). They played in processions for funerals; an anonymous painting in Michoacán, Mexico, shows 'three bajonistas, each in his own procession of mourners and each accompanied by one or more singers'.[168] Processions were regularly staged for Corpus Christi,[169] but they might also be staged for extraordinary reasons, such as the transportation of the image of Our Lady of Chiquinquirá, brought to Santafé in 1633, after the city suffered from a deadly plague. 'The image was escorted by four bands of chirimías' in a one-hundred-mile journey.[170] The inventory of a newly established church at Fontibón (near Santafé) in 1639 included three cornetts, two bajones, and three sets of shawms; five Indian players were exempted from paying tribute.[171]

At La Plata cathedral in 1607 the bajón was played by the Creole or African slave Alejandro de la Cruz; both instrument and player were property of the church. Of six wind players in the cathedral at La Plata during 1610–11, three were natives and two were mulattos or blacks. Among these was Antón de Toledo, called 'Mulato Bajón', who also played the trombone.[172] Repairs to the cathedral bajones were carried out between 1610 and 1613 by Alejandro Alemán, apparently a German metalworker drawn by the nearby silver deposits.[173]

Fray Alonso de Benavides (c.1579–c.1635) was the supervisor of Franciscan missionaries in the New Mexico area. Arriving in Santa Fe in 1626 with religious books and musical instruments, including a bajón, he and his missionaries established music schools and choirs in more than ten mission towns, including Santa Clara and El Paso. His reports mentioned use of the shawms and bajón to accompany polyphonic music in the services:

> A contract dated 1631 specifies that shawms, bajones, and trumpets, and other musical supplies as well, were to be sent to missions for every five friars in the field.[174] Between 1620 and 1630, there were as many as sixty-six Franciscans working in New Mexico at any given time. This figure suggests that at least thirteen bajones and as many as forty chirimías in consort were in used in New Mexico. . . .[175]

Franciscan bajonistas included Fray Roque de Figueredo, recorded at Hawikuh, New Mexico, in 1628.[176]

In a ceiling painting in the Michoacán village of Nurio, a bajón-playing angel reads from an angel singer's part book in baritone clef. Starner conjectured that the anonymous artist (1600–50) had seen bajónes first hand, possibly instruments made in nearby Paracho.[177]

Other local evidence of early bajón usage dates as follows: Cajamarca, Peru, c.1610; Guatemala, c.1610; Paraguay, 1647; Topaga, Colombia, 1669; Acoma Pueblo (present-day Arizona), 1672; Fómeque, Colombia, 1676; San Ignacio de Chicamocha, Colombia, 1719; Betoye, Chile, 1722; Santo Regis de Guanapalo, Colombia, 1728;

New Granada (a territory comprising parts of Panama and northern South America), 1741; and Santiago, Cuba, 1764.[178]

The Jesuit order was expelled from the Spanish and Portuguese dominions in 1767–8, prompting a number of inventories. In Trinidad, Bolivia, a 1767 inventory of an organ and spinet maker's shop included 'five planes of which three are long for making bajones and shawms'.[179] Two dulcians survive from the Church of San Rafael, Concepción, Bolivia, where they were listed in a 1767 inventory. They are made of indigenous materials: wood of cedar and a reed of thin horn.[180] Inventories of the instruments left behind by the Jesuits included two to five bajones and bajoncillos in each of ten different Argentine cities, as well two bajones and a fagot in Santiago, Chile. The bajones were not abandoned by native players, however: when Carlos IV was crowned king of Spain in 1789, bajones were played during the coronation festivities in Córdoba, Argentina.[181]

Spanish missionaries used the bajón (and music generally) as a tool, powerful and seemingly simple, to evangelize the native peoples of the New World. What the native musicians took away from this cross-cultural transaction was more complex. Starner reported that:

> ... musicians were held in high esteem by Aztec society, where there was little separation between the secular and the sacred. Often, the role of church musician was used as a stepping stone to higher political office. Musicians not only contributed large sums of money for the maintenance of the church and the purchase of musical instruments and music manuscripts, they also acted as witnesses for various community transactions.[182]

Bermúdez viewed the colonial musical experience in a favorable light: a new element assimilated into native traditions and 'an important factor in the development of modern Indian musical identity'.[183] Baker saw in the native reaction 'subtle attempts by the indigenous elite to resist the orchestration of the Spanish authorities', 'a certain desire for equality through cultural assimilation, and a rejection of the subordinate status associated with cultural difference ...'.[184]

Portuguese missionaries used musical instruments in a similar way. 'From the time of their arrival in Brazil in 1549 until their expulsion in 1759, the Jesuits made extensive use of music in their attempt to bring about the conversion of the Indians to the Catholic faith.'[185] The use of a *doçaina* (dulcian) by Jesuit missionaries in Brazil was recorded in 1602.[186] Father Simaõ de Vasconcellos in 1663 cited the use of both baixões and fagotes by native players; the difference, if any, between the various terms is not clear.[187] The Portuguese Frei Manoel da Luz (1655–1743), a teacher in Bahia, played *baixõ*.[188] A school of music was reported at the cathedral of Olinda, where baixão and fagote were taught in 1697.[189]

Wherever European Catholic missionaries traveled during the age of colonization, the dulcian (under whatever name) was likely to accompany them. Irving reported that the bajón was introduced to the Philippines by the Jesuit Luis Serrano (d. 1603), 'who played in the choir, and taught the Filipinos to make and play it'.[190] Under the Portuguese Jesuit Tomás Pereira, palace musician to Kangxi, several priests joined in a quintet, including a 'bassoon', before the emperor of China, in Peking, 1699.[191]

France

A kingdom nearly encircled by Habsburg powers, France was politically isolated during the era of the dulcian. Possibly for this reason, there is no evidence of dulcian use at the French court. Nor were dulcians used in Parisian churches, which followed an austere liturgy permitting no instruments. 'Fagots' were used, however, in provincial choir schools. Michael Tornatoris was appointed player of the fagot (dulcian) at the church of Notre Dame des Doms in Avignon in 1602.[192] Thomas de Villers (1625–1713) in 1667 supplied a basson to the parish of Notre-Dame de la Couture de Bernay and repaired another one. Described as an organ builder, he may also have made the basson he supplied.[193] Use is also documented in Chartres (1655) and Rouen (after 1626).[194] Mersenne acknowledged this churchly use:

> Musicians have invented several instruments to be blended with voices in order to remedy the shortcomings of bass and dessus singers. Deep bass voices are very scarce, so the basson, the sackbut, and the serpent are used. . . .[195]

The four instruments shown in propositions 24–5 of Mersenne's *Harmonie universelle* stand outside the dulcian and ecclesiastical traditions; they are discussed in chapter 3. Pierre Trichet, a collector in Bordeaux, published an inventory of his instruments in 1631 that included a set of four bassons. According to his later description (c.1641), the smallest of these was a *dessus de basson* with ten holes – most likely a descant or alto dulcian.[196] In 1685, the evangelical Neue Kirche of Strasbourg owned *a fagott*, which may have been a dulcian or a baroque bassoon.[197]

Scandinavia

The dulcian may have come to Denmark along with the composer Heinrich Schütz, who was called to Copenhagen to provide music for royal weddings in 1633–4 and 1642–4.[198] Or it may have come at the behest of Matthias Weckmann, a dulcian player who accompanied Schütz in 1642 and remained as a court composer until 1647.[199] In 1650, 'dulcian' was defined in a dictionary published at Vodingbord. By 1670, one of the five shawm players in the military music of Christian V played dulcian.[200] By 1676, a dulcian was mentioned at court. The vagaries of Danish usage make many later references ambiguous.[201] In 1701, an orchestra at Nykobing included transverse flutes and violins; in this fashionable French company, perhaps the 'shawms' and 'dulcianer' mentioned were oboes and baroque bassoons. In 1704, the death inventory of Peder Hoyelses at Nykobing Folster included two 'franske Dulcianer', one new and one old; and two 'Chormesse Dulcianer'. The first two were likely baroque bassoons, while the latter two, at choir pitch, were either dulcians or bassoons.

Gustav Düben the Elder, Kapellmeister at the Royal Swedish Court 1660–90, assembled manuscripts of ensemble sonatas including dulcian by Albrici, Bertali,

Forcheim, Förster, Nicolai, Pohle, J. H. Schmelzer, Thieme, and Weckmann.[202] Around 1682, 'every regiment in the Swedish army had three shawms and one dulcian'.[203] An invoice from the Dutch maker Richard Haka to an official of the Swedish navy, dated 1685, records the sale of both dulcians and baroque bassoons, and also underscores the broad ambiguity of much terminology. Among the 'German shawms' listed were 'six maple bass dulcians at choir pitch'.[204] In 1691 Johan Kiörning obtained a license to supply instruments to the Swedish army, including dulcianer.[205] Dulcians (dulcian, dulsian) were used at the cathedral of Turku (now Abo), Finland, in 1660, and by a Turku Stadtpfeifer in 1663.[206]

The twilight of the dulcian

An emerging vogue for the multipartite French basson, often at a lower and incompatible pitch, led to the gradual extinction of the dulcian. Occasionally we can glimpse the old instruments in their demise. In Nuremberg in 1712, various instruments removed from the music gallery of the Frauenkirche were to be brought 'to the middle turret of the town hall for safe keeping', including three dulcians. A quartbass dulcian, however, remained in use, possibly because the Kapellmeister had no replacement available.[207] A 1718 inventory of instruments owned by the Württemberg court shows a similar disuse of dulcians after French bassons were adopted. J. S. Bach scored for fagotto at chorton (probably a dulcian) in some of his early cantatas (see chapter 4). By 1738, Eisel wrote in Erfurt that

> The Teutschen bassoons, Fagotte or bombardi, as used by our German ancestors (before music had become clothed in Italian and French fashion) are no longer in use and accordingly it is unnecessary to waste paper with a description of them. He who is a connoisseur of antiques can inform himself about them from the accompanying chart.[208]

Yet the instrument faded from use only gradually, driven mostly by local pitch standards. A procession of the Jewish Musicians' Guild in Prague, 1741, to celebrate the birthday of crown prince Joseph, included one dulcian player.[209]

In Spain, the bassoon was at first used mostly in secular music, including opera, while the bajón continued in sacred use. The old and the new coexisted in Madrid in 1739, when the fagot was used 'to supplement the bajón in facistol music since it was of the same tone, although not as resonant as the bajón, and because the two bajonistas were very elderly, infirm and unable to play'.[210] Meanwhile, the bajón itself evolved into a three- or four-joint instrument with several keys. Surviving examples preserve the range and Dorian scale of the old bajón. Fernando Llop advertised in Madrid, 1785, that he made *fagots* as well as three- and one-piece bajones.[211] Two surviving three-piece bajones are anonymous, while one four-part instrument is by Claret and three are by Segarra of Valencia.[212]

Selected church records show the bajón's role ebbing away. In Palencia, in 1828, 'the chapter decided that bajones would only be used in the invitorios, anthems and responses, but no longer during the psalms'. 'In June 1834 it was proposed that the bajonistas in the Capilla Real [Madrid] should be replaced by bassoonists'.[213] In some cathedrals, the ophicleide supplanted the bajón: Valladolid (1843), Tuy (1846), Segovia (1850), and Palencia (1860).[214] Toledo's bajón era came to a documented end in 1871, when the cathedral sold four bajoncillos made by Melchor Rodríguez 'which had until recently been kept . . . for use at Christmas'. Church use of bajones persisted at Ciudad Rodrigo (1901), Santo Domingo de la Calzada (1902), and Jaca (1920).[215]

The rebirth of the dulcian

The twentieth-century rediscovery of early repertory and instruments created a market for reproduction dulcians. Among the first revivalists was Otto Steinkopf, who produced dulcians in various sizes under his own mark from c.1955 until 1964, when he began to collaborate with Moeck Verlag of Celle. Gunter Körber, an early associate of Steinkopf, later produced dulcians under his own mark, as did Rainer Weber of Bayerbach, Bavaria (price list by 1958). Later German makers included Adler of Markneukirchen, Bernhard Junghänel, Martin Praetorius, and Guntram Wolf. English makers included John Cousen, Barbara Stanley, Graham Lyndon-Jones, Maggie Lyndon-Jones (later Kilbey), A. Eric Moulder, and The Early Music Shop of Bradford (under the brand name of Wood). Laurent Verjat and Olivier Cottet produced dulcians in France. American makers included Robert Cronin, Philip Levin, and Leslie Ross. Many surviving original dulcians appear to sound at a higher pitch than the modern standard of A-440; reproductions have been made variously in modern, lower and higher pitches. Some makers of reproduction instruments added tone holes to obtain certain chromatic pitches, and many drill a vent hole in the crook to ease production of the overblown upper registers. Most reproductions to date have followed the Speer fingerings (or some modernized version of Speer), although Leslie Ross has occasionally made one-piece bajones with Spanish tuning, as well as a three-piece bajón.

Chapter 3

The bassoon idea: early relatives

The instruments discussed in this chapter partake of the bassoon idea, but only as cousins, rather than ancestors. Each lacked at least one of the bassoon's essential characteristics – a direct-blown double reed; a folded, conical bore capable of over-blowing; a controllable extension bore; and chimney-shaped finger holes. Many of them have nevertheless been called a 'bassoon' by early or later writers. The following discussion briefly compares each instrument with the bassoon concept.

The length of a bass woodwind instrument – whether folded or not – will often require it to be held more or less parallel to the player's torso, so that the player's two arms can occupy a comfortable position. A metal crook will usually connect the reed to the body of the instrument. (The ingenious racket is an exception, as are the racket drone and the phagotum.) Once a maker has decided to fold the bore of a woodwind instrument, several options are open. A simple folding in half (180 degrees) – as seen in the bassoon, sordun, kortholt, and courtaut – is a common choice. Alternatively, the bore can be folded more than once. In the racket of the sixteenth century, most of the parallel bores were arranged along the circumference of a cylindrical billet and connected in series; the reed was inserted into an unfingered central bore. The racket bassoon of the eighteenth century had a similar pattern of boring, except that the central bore usually acted as the 'bell'. When multiple parallel bores are drilled in a billet of wood, some or all can be left unconnected and played in parallel, as in the multi-reeded racket drone. They can even be connected in series but blown from either end, as in the doppioni. (Once elaborate key systems were developed, the folds could be nested, as in a modern contrabassoon.) If the sounding tube is made of metal rather than wood, the bores can have a helical bend, as in the Tartölt, rather than a 180-degree bend (Ill. 12).

Masel noted in Praetorius a lingering preference for low-register instruments, which had resulted in a profusion of new designs for bass woodwinds, many of them cylindrical in bore. Most of these designs did not survive long into the baroque era, as he noted:

> In the continuo period, different musical elements were favored: a better-carrying tone, stepped dynamics, varied articulations, expressive manners, and a greater range of pitch contributed to expressivity and soloistic presence.[1]

The quest for a broader compass tended to favor conical instruments, which could overblow at the octave without the addition of upper or lower extension keys.[2] The

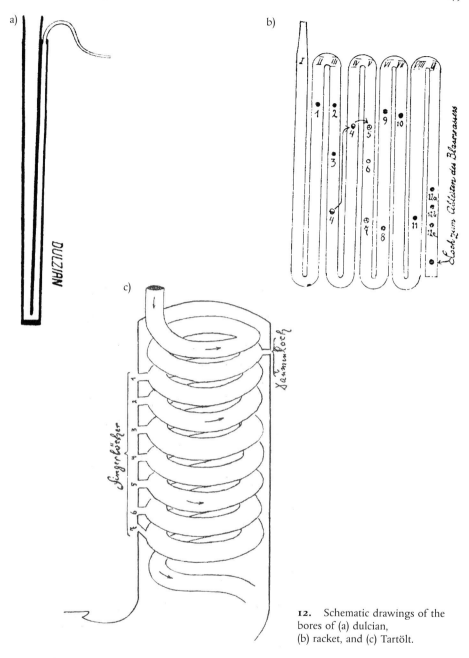

12. Schematic drawings of the
bores of (a) dulcian,
(b) racket, and (c) Tartölt.

pirouette – the disc at the base of an exposed reed – encouraged a loose embouchure
and a forceful but unmodulated sound. The racket was first seen with a pirouette, later
with the pirouette removed; this would have allowed overblowing, a practice not
envisioned in the original design. The pirouette was eventually omitted from shawms
as well. Wind caps, which carried the pirouette idea to an even more inflexible
extreme, also fell from fashion.

The devising of clever fingering systems that spanned more than an octave with few if any keys showed ingenuity by makers. But these idiosyncratic systems would have made life hard for consort musicians, who often doubled on several different wind instruments. A player who makes such rapid transitions between instruments will benefit from having as much commonality as possible in the fingering patterns. The early racket, the sordun (and the similar kortholt and courtaut), and the basse de musette de Poitou departed in important ways from the archetypal European fingering patterns; none survived as such.

The low-register shawm

The soprano or descant medieval shawm was long played in monophonic music. The 'bombard', a larger, tenor version, emerged by the late fourteenth century to play the tenor line in improvised two- and three-voice consort music.[3] The earliest surviving European shawms have a long bore extension below the lowest fingered hole; the extension is drilled with up to five resonance vents, which help to strengthen and stabilize various higher pitches (Ill. 13).

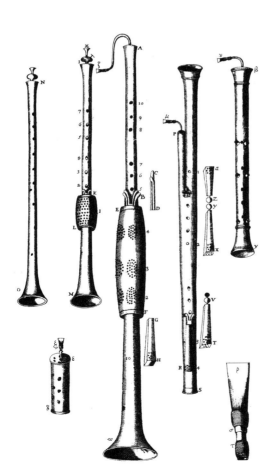

13. From top left: French *dessus de hautbois* or treble shawm; *taille de hautbois* or alto shawm; *basse de hautbois* or bass shawm; *basson* or *fagot*; *courtaut*. At bottom left, *cervelat* or racket; at bottom right, double reed for unspecified instrument. Mersenne, *Harmonie universelle* (Paris, 1636).

On larger sizes of shawm, three such vent holes were eventually provided with open-standing keys, bringing them under control of the player's fingers and adding a useful lower extension to the instrument's range. A curved crook brought the reed within convenient range of the player's mouth. The extension bore of these large shawms – often called 'Pommer', 'bombarde', or 'bombardono' – was often relatively narrow.[4] Between 1535 and 1551, tenor and bass Pommers were documented at Nuremberg, Augsburg, York, and Ghent.[5] A 1555 Spanish inventory of Mary of Austria, Queen of Hungary, included two 'contrebass of the shawms (chirimias)', which were in two pieces, each instrument being in a great case.[6] The exact pitch of these shawms is not known, but very large shawms were known by 1596, when an inventory at Schloß Ambras included three 'grosse päsz Schallmeien', in addition to two 'päs'.[7]

Makers of bass or larger Pommers included Hans Drebs (fl. Leipzig, 1589–1640), Hans Fischer (fl. late sixteenth century), and G. Strehli (fl. early eighteenth century); other marks on surviving basses include 'GK', 'MH', and the 'double silk-moth' that has been associated with the Bassano family. Siegmund Schnitzer (fl. Nuremberg, 1547–57) was recorded as the first to make a contrabass woodwind instrument, the Grossdoppelbasspommer; surviving Pommers in this size bear the marks 'HD' (Hinrich Ditmer, fl. 1685) and 'W'.

Among the fewer than fifty original European shawms, fewer than a dozen Pommers survive from before 1700. Most are not closely datable.[8] Two basset (or tenor) Pommers (lowest note G_2) survive in Berlin, and one in Prague. Two basses (lowest note C_2) survive, in Sopron, Hungary, and Nuremberg, together with fragments in Salamanca and Braunschweig. Four Gross-quint Pommers (lowest note F_1) survive, in Lübeck, Berlin, Salzburg, and Prague. John Hanchet, a maker of reproduction shawms who has examined virtually all of the existing originals, noted the expense of seasoning a large billet of wood for the shawm's broad bell. Partly for the last reason, the larger Pommers were often made in two pieces.

Players of the *basse taille de haultbois* were documented at the French court by 1571.[9] A bass shawm with an upward-bent bell is shown in an illustration of the obsequies of Charles II of Lorraine at Nancy, 1608.[10] In 1636 Mersenne illustrated the bass shawm and showed a six-voice score of a pavane by Henri le Jeune, as played by the *Douze grands hautbois du roi*. The sixth and lowest voice was marked 'basse de hautbois'; Mersenne said that it could play two octaves in range, beginning at C_2. During the period 1611–27, three players in Paris are known to have played both large shawms and bass violin in dance ensembles. The estate of one of these, Ancelot Duingue, in 1628 included a bass shawm, a bass violin, and a 'basson'.[11]

A bombard is called for in scorings by Buxtehude, Cazzati, Freisslich, Hammerschmidt, Knüpfer, Merula, Mielczewski, Pekiel, Rózicki, Schein, and Weckmannn, and a 'bombardo grosso' in works by Bütner and Croatti. An early Franco-Flemish taste for such instruments may be evident in the use of one or more 'Pumart' in instrumental works by Gasswin, Lasso, Monte, Utendal, and Wert, although Clavius, Andrea Gabrieli, Lange, and Striggio also made similar demands.[12]

In the narrowest usage, a bombardo was a bass Pommer or shawm. Yet dulcians may sometimes lie beneath these misleading labels. 'Bombard' and 'bombardone' were used – at times between 1671 and 1789, at least – to refer to bass or contrabass dulcians. Brossard's equation of bombardo and basson was noted above, and Eppelsheim suggested that Martin Fuhrmann (1706) and his contemporaries might have referred to contrabass dulcians as octav Bombart, großer Baß-bommert, etc.[13]

The racket

The racket was a squat cylindrical billet drilled with nine parallel, cylindrical bores. The double reed was mounted in the central bore, which was connected in series to eight more bores arranged concentrically around it. Vent holes drilled in an ingenious pattern allowed the player to control the effective length of the bore with his ten fingers, obtaining a range of an eleventh or twelfth without overblowing. The tiny descant racket reached as low as G2 with a height of only 12 cm (Ill. 14; see also Ill. 6). Multiplied by the nine bores, however, the sounding length was more than a meter. (In surviving diskants, the bores have a diameter of 5 mm.) Three larger sizes reached still lower depths of pitch: Tenor-Alt (18 cm to C2), Bass (25 cm to F1), and Gross Bass (35 cm to D1 or C1).[14] Martin Reiff is the one known maker.

    With no visible bell and a startling depth of pitch, the racket was possibly designed to mystify the onlooker. Seventeen vents were arranged to produce eleven pitches. The configuration of a surviving racket, illustrated by Masel, is o + 1 + 3 + 3 + 4 + 2 + 1 + 1 + 2. This tally reflects occasional grouping of several multiple vents under a single fingertip, which demanded great subtlety from the maker.

    The esoteric fingering of the renaissance racket departed significantly from the archetypical woodwind fingering. The left index finger – using both the middle phalange and the fingertip – controlled two diatonic steps below the 'open' pitch; the fingering descends as follows from the open pitch: L1 phalange, L1 tip, L2, L3, R1 tip, R2, R3, R4, R1 phalange, LT, RT, L4.

    Waterhouse noted:

> the player's lips control the reed blades but are supported and helped very effectively by the pirouette to produce and maintain the loose embouchure demanded by the low tessitura; this device also adds, surprisingly, a considerable degree of resonance to the tone. Praetorius . . . indicated that . . . an expert could produce more notes with a good reed, but that 'falsetto' playing was seldom used.[15]

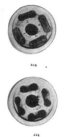

14. Descant rackets with details showing view from the top and bottom of the cylinder (covers and corks removed). Sammlung alter Musikinstrumente, Vienna.

Mersenne's racket had no pirouette in either picture, but a total of nineteen holes, more than any surviving racket.[16]

The so-called racket drone of the musette bagpipe predated evidence of the racket itself[17] (Ill. 15). An illumination (datable to 1565–70) by Hans Mielich in Munich is early evidence of the racket in use. The Ambras inventory (1596) implies that rackets participated in a mixed ensemble: two large flutes, two *cordali* (rackets), and two fifes.[18] Both Praetorius and an inventory from Kassel, 1613, described 'consorts' (tuned sets, not necessarily all used at once) of seven rackets.[19]

The sordun, Kortholt, courtaut and Sorduen-bas

Each of these double-reed instruments involves a cylindrical bore folded into a U-shaped, front-and-rear configuration within a single wooden billet. The player's upper thumb and finger tips covered seven or eight holes on the descending bore, following a traditional woodwind schema. The ascending bores of the courtaut and Kortholt were controlled, however, by the lower thumb and the second phalanges of the two index fingers. The tone hole controlled by the lower little finger led on the courtaut and Kortholt to a tone hole on the up bore; on the sordun, this tone hole led to the instrument's down bore. As multi-bored cylindrical woodwinds, these

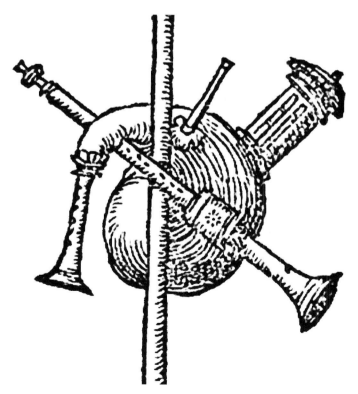

15. Alto shawm and mouth-blown musette with shuttle drone. Paradin, *Devises heroïques* (Lyon, 1551).

instruments have some schematic resemblance to the individual chanters of the phagotum. In fact, the surviving bass sorduns also have a short third bore into which the crook inserts (Ill. 16).

The three instruments differed from one another in various other details, including the presence or absence of upper extension keys, tétines, and a wind cap. The surviving sorduns in Vienna have a layout of 8 down + 4 up; they were played with a bare reed; on the larger sizes a crook was present. The key work of the Kortholt shown by Praetorius had one or more upper extension keys and a windcap.[20] The courtaut shown by Mersenne has a layout of 7 down + 3 up; short tubes called tétines projected from its body, enabling the phalanges of the performer's two index fingers and lower little finger to close the vents more easily. Trichet, unlike Mersenne, described the courtaut as having a windcap; Masel disagreed, believing that Trichet had simply misunderstood Mersenne, upon whose text he was relying.[21]

Zacconi in 1592 referred to 'sordoni' and Praetorius in 1618–20 to Sordunen.[22] The Kortholt is known mostly from Praetorius.[23] A Parisian inventory of 1632 contained one courtaut; the instrument was later described by Mersenne (1635–6) and Trichet (c.1640).[24] The use of the courtaut with musettes, reported by both Mersenne and Trichet, points up the similarity of sound between a musette chanter and this low-register instrument.

All these names were used freely during the period. Manfredo Settala in 1664 used the term 'courtaut' in reference to a racket, while the Ambras inventory of 1596, mentioned above, refers to 'cordali'. Mersenne termed the courtaut 'a fagot, or short-ened basson'; he called the racket 'nothing other than a courtaut, or a fagot so contracted and small that it can be concealed in one's hand'.[25]

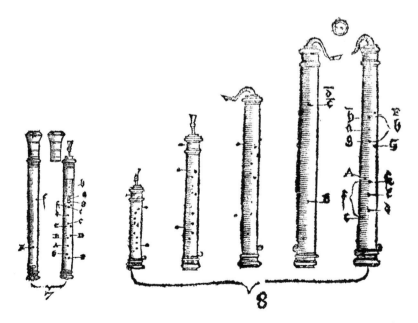

16. Kortholts (no. 7) and sorduns (no. 8). Praetorius, *Syntagma Musicum II: De Organographia* (Wolfenbüttel, 1618–20).

The 'Sorduen-bas' illustrated by Praetorius was something different, however, in both name and form. As shown, its tone hole layout (6 down + 4 up, or possibly 7 down + 3 up) resembles the dulcian rather than the sordun, although it still appears, like Praetorius's sordanen, to have front-and-rear bores in an outwardly cylindrical body (Ill. 6).[26]

The racket-bassoon

By 1707 Johann Christoph Denner had built a racket with a bore and fingering more like the dulcian or baroque bassoon.[27] Several other makers made similar instruments, although details sometimes differed. On some exemplars, a leather binding helped to seal the body or to conceal corrections. The bell was occasionally invisible, a mere hole at the end of the central bore. When present, the bell is sometimes hollowed out, pear-like, and decorated with a crown of brass, as on some baroque bassoons. Projecting bushes (outwardly similar to the tétines of the courtaut) were occasionally added to those holes stopped with the phalanges of the fingers (Wyne). These baroque-era instruments, called racket-bassoons, had a crook (sometimes coiled to trap condensation before it entered the body), but no pirouette (Ill. 17).

Waterhouse noted that the wooden body of the Denner racket-bassoon has ten cylindrical bores increasing in size from 10 mm to 23 mm. In a surviving racket by Bizet, each of the individual bores has a slight degree of conicity, as Weber pointed out.[28] The ten surviving instruments were built in at least three sizes: tenor (Denner);

a)   b)

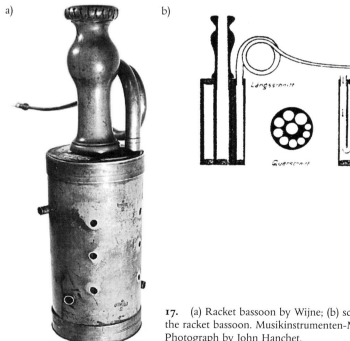

17. (a) Racket bassoon by Wijne; (b) schematic drawing of the racket bassoon. Musikinstrumenten-Museum, Berlin. Photograph by John Hanchet.

bass (Bizey), and great bass (Wyne).[29] One exemplar in Paris has two stamps: 'Bizey' over 'Rozet'.

The evolution toward this new type may have begun earlier than Denner. Possibly drawing a distinction, an inventory from Innsbruck, 1664/5, contained both 'eight rackets covered with black leather' and 'six ivory rackets as well as other old things'.[30] The latest surviving exemplars, by Heinrich Carl Tölcke (1720–98) of Brunswick and Wilhelmus Wyne (1730–1816) of Nijmegen, are datable to the end of the eighteenth century.[31]

The stepped-cylindrical bore (roughly speaking) produced a larger tone than that of the renaissance racket. Played without a pirouette, the racket-bassoon used mostly bassoon-like fingerings and produced a second-mode response by over-blowing. In a schematic drawing by Weber, the layout is 3 + 0 + 3 + 0 + 1 + 1 + 1 + 1.[32]

Most chromatic tones were obtainable by fork fingerings, but two or three chromatic keys were sometimes added. Usually the player used ten fingers to cover eleven tone holes. The downward extension (below the seven-finger note) was normally four diatonic pitches (bassoon-like), but sometimes only three (Stingelwagner).

Despite its unconventionality, the racket idea seized the imagination of leading woodwind makers of the late seventeenth/eighteenth century in Germany, France, Holland, and England. They brought the acoustical design and fingering closer to that of the conventional baroque bassoon, while retaining most of the artifice of the original renaissance design. Stanesby Jr., however, retreated to an older design – much harder to make and to play – in attempting to copy Mersenne's 1635 design for Lord Paisley.

The Bizey racket-bassoon helped in the performance of chant in the choir school of Dijon, Chouquet conjectured.[33] An observer of the later eighteenth century remarked that 'they are very agreeable to play, and have very majestic basses for such a small volume. . . . One can carry these types of bassoons in the pocket, and for accompaniment they make the same effect as a large bassoon.'[34] In both renaissance- and baroque-era versions, the racket appealed to wealthy collectors and connoisseurs as a functional puzzle. Among the owners were court officials, aristocrats, and connoisseurs, including Carl Schurf (marshal of the Tyrolean army), Manfredo Settala (Jesuit priest and librarian of the Ambrosian library), and Lord Paisley of Scotland (probably James Hamilton, the seventh earl of Abercorn and also a scientist).

The doppioni

The name 'doppioni' is known from theoretical mentions (Zacconi 1592 and Cerone 1613), which were not illustrated. The following statements are based on a tentative identification of two surviving instruments (Verona, Accademia Filarmonica) as doppioni. Each of the Verona instruments is a conceptual puzzle, playable via a double reed in either of two ways. Two conical bores are drilled side by side in one billet of wood, connecting at the distal end. One bore of each instrument is of larger diameter, with finger holes drilled lower. The player could insert a crook into either bore, thereby choosing a different range of pitches (tuned about a fourth apart).[35] In either choice, he was playing a double-reed instrument having a complex bore of two cones, opposed end to end – an ingenious twist on the bassoon concept. Weber and Van der Meer hypothesized that the instrument originally had a windcap and did not overblow, but later was blown without the windcap.[36] The doppioni may have been short-lived or rare. Praetorius, though he read of it in Zacconi, had not seen an example. The larger of the instruments surviving at Verona shows signs of trial-and-error experimentation; several finger holes have been moved once or twice, presumably in an effort to discover a proper tuning.

The Tartölt

The one existing consort of these instruments – two trebles, two tenors, and a bass – was recorded in a 1596 inventory at Ambras Castle. Painted green, red, and gold, the Tartölt resembles a dragon. The player blows into a double reed mounted on the tail end; on the bell end, a trembling iron tongue protrudes from the dragon's mouth (Ill. 18). The vividly modelled metal skin conceals an internal tube of yellow bronze coiled into a helix of nine or ten turns. Although the tube is cylindrical, the conical crook (forming the dragon's tail) reportedly causes the instrument to overblow at the octave, like a thoroughly conical instrument. The instruments of the surviving consort are not currently playable; Brown described their lowest pitches as A2, D3, and A3; Masel described them as F2, C3, and G3. Reichmann & Körber showed reproduction Tartölts at the Frankfurt Musikmesse in 1982; some players were able to sound a range of two and a half octaves.[37]

Brown described the Tartölt as a racket; the bore diameter is comparable (6 mm for the diskant, versus 5 mm for the Vienna diskant rackets). But no pirouette is present and the fingering system is a conventional seven fingers plus thumb, far simpler than that of the early racket. Dragon-like instruments of unspecified sorts, inspired by the encounters of Hercules and Apollo with water snakes, were reported in the intermedii of sixteenth-century Italy.[38]

18. Set of five Tartölten and original case. Sammlung alter Musikinstrumente, Vienna.

The basse de musette de Poitou

By 1625, some enterprising maker had adapted the design of a French descant bagpipe chanter into a family including alto and bass sizes. The 'basse de musette de Poitou' (it is labelled 'basse de hautbois' by Mersenne in the only surviving picture) was the boldest of these adaptations.[39] As on the courtaut, two bores arranged front and rear accommodate a low-register extension.[40] Here, however, the two bores were contained in separate billets and fingered by a unique system. The player's fingers covered six holes on the down bore, while two more holes on the up bore were apparently covered by the palms of the player's hands. The lower thumb covered one more hole, while the upper thumb covered one open hole and operated an open-standing key; the layout was thus 6 down + 5 up (Ill. 19).

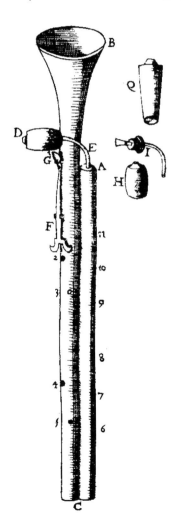

In the inconstant scale of Mersenne's illustration, the bell of the basse appears almost as small as that of the dessus; the depiction of the basse may instead be in scale with the illustrated cornemuse. It appears to have been a fragile instrument; possibly a leather wrapping, not shown in Mersenne's illustration, served to bind the two billets securely together, making the connection between the two billets airtight. The innovative design of the basse de musette de Poitou may have served as a model for the proto-bassoons that Mersenne showed elsewhere in his treatises. The bore was probably conical, as Mersenne wrote that the range of the hautbois de Poitou family was similar to that of the conventional hautbois or shawms.[41]

Archival records indicate that the basse de hautbois de Poitou or 'basse-contre de musette' de Poitou was in regular use at the French court by 1625, probably continuing until 1667 or later. Mersenne shows a four-part setting for the group.[42] Lully's music for *Le Bourgeois gentilhomme* (1670) included a 'Menuet pour les hautbois en poitevin' (treble/treble/bass clefs); the label, however, may refer to the onstage costumes of the players, rather than to the design of their instruments.

19.   *Basse de musette de Poitou.*
Mersenne, *Harmonie universelle*
(Paris, 1636).

The proto-bassoons of Mersenne and Trichet

The four proto-bassoons shown in Marin Mersenne's *Harmonicorum libri XII* (Paris, 1635) and *Harmonie universelle* (Paris, 1636) are the last detailed evidence of bass double-reed instruments in France before Hotteterre's unexplained 'basson' of 1668.[43] The Mersenne instruments have often been described as curtals or dulcians, but this view is short-sighted; the four instruments in fact reject, in varying degrees, the neat, logical design of the dulcian (known in provincial France, and evidently to Mersenne in Paris). Three at least, and probably all four of Mersenne's proto-bassoons, had seven tone holes in the down bore, unlike most surviving dulcians. Three of them, moreover, had a front-and-back configuration of the two bores (the up bore was held closest to the player, the reverse of a saxophone's layout). The short crooks suggest that they would have been held close to the player's torso (Ills. 20, 21).

No two of the four illustrated proto-bassoons are exactly alike. Mersenne in *Harmonicorum libri XII* defined 'basson' as 'barytonum', or a low-pitched instrument; he defined 'fagot' as 'tibia contracta', or a folded instrument. His usage in one instance equates the terms 'fagot' and 'basson', and in another instance the terms 'basson' and 'tarot'.[44] The first two of the proto-bassoons illustrated by Mersenne are essentially anti-dulcians, extreme in their avoidance of dulcian design features. Mersenne's Latin text (and the negative coloration scheme of Ill. 21) indicates two wooden tubes, arranged front and back. They were possibly covered with leather for stability and air-tightness. His measurements indicate that the instrument on the left had approximately the sounding length of a basset shawm.[45] The layout is 7 down + 4 up. Unlike

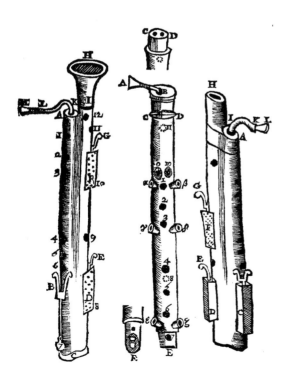

20. Two proto-bassoons (left and right) and a *courtaut*. Mersenne, *Harmonie universelle* (Paris, 1636).

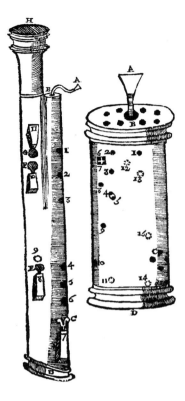

21. Proto-bassoon (left) and *cervelat* or racket (shown in much larger scale). Mersenne, *Harmonie universelle* (Paris, 1636).

shawms or dulcians, however, it has a twelfth tone hole. On an instrument in F2, this would presumably add a low E2 or Eb2 at the bottom of the range (Mersenne does not comment on the ranges of any of these instruments). The instrument on the right has neither a twelfth tone hole nor a detachable bell, and may be of a smaller size. Its layout is 7 down + 3 up.

The other two proto-bassoons show a gradual accommodation to the design of the conventional dulcian. Ill. 21 shows a bass instrument (apparently to B1 or Bb1) made of one piece of wood ('ex uno frustrum ligni'), although it still has a front-and-back configuration and a 7 down + 4 up layout of tone holes.[46] The unnamed maker went to the trouble of modelling a cleft or recess in the instrument's torso (between the top portion of the two bores). Except for a trivial reduction in weight, this has only a decorative effect, possibly a reference to the genuine two-piece construction of the anti-dulcians shown earlier. The fourth proto-bassoon (Ill. 13) has a similar cleft, as well as a dulcian-like left-and-right layout. It appears to have a 7 down + 4 up layout of tone holes and a one-piece body, although Mersenne did not comment on these issues[47]. Illustrated in a plate with shawms used by the Douze Grands Hautbois, it may have been produced for royal use, as the fleur-de-lis would suggest.

No instruments of this description survive. The basson listed in the estate of Ancelot Duingue in 1628 may have resembled one of these instruments.[48] A brief verbal description by Pierre Trichet of Bordeaux suggests that he owned three bassons of this approximate type.[49]

Why were French makers so much at pains to avoid the widely accepted design of the dulcian? Mersenne offered no comment on this evident antipathy, but its roots may have been political. France had supported Sweden in an invasion of the Habsburg Empire in 1630 and would declare war on Spain in 1635. It may be that a long-standing association of the dulcian with Habsburg courts and armies was strong enough to provoke makers at the French court into producing an anti-dulcian.

The basse de cromorne and contrebasse de hautbois

The term 'basse de cromorne' referred to a contrabass oboe in use at the French court during the later seventeenth century. It was related to the bassoon only in the sense that it played the bass line. Nevertheless, an early dictionary wrongly defined the basse de cromorne in 1703 as 'a sort of bassoon'; the long-echoing consequences of this error are reviewed in chapter 1. The basse de cromorne also has been confused with the bass crumhorn, because of the similarity of its name. The name appears to have been borrowed from a stop on French organs, not from the crumhorn itself[50] (Ill. 22).

The instrument outlived the cromorne name, later coming to be called simply 'basse de hautbois' or 'contrebasse de hautbois'. In the Museé de la musique, Paris, is a contrebasse de hautbois by Christophe Delusse, apparently made shortly before 1781. It was used at the Opéra in Paris c.1781, played by the bassoonist Marchand.[51] An instrument that corresponds closely in size and features survives in the collection at Trossingen, in Baden-Württemberg. It bears the stamp of Johann Christoph Heise, who lived at Kassel 1703–83.[52]

The seven-finger note of the basse de cromorne was C2, and one extension key was sometimes present, giving a lowest pitch of B♭1 or B1; the upper range extended to C4 or above. A straightforward illustration of a basse de cromorne has been available since 1761 in a published source: the *Notionaire* of François-Alexandre-Pierre de Garsault, published in Paris.[53] Garsault shows an oboe-like woodwind large enough to require an acutely angled crook and open-standing keys to cover finger-holes 1, 3, 4, and 6, plus the traditional key for tone hole 7. These five keys are also illustrated in an earlier, unlabelled picture of a smaller cromorne,[54] but Garsault's instrument has three more keys: one for an extension of the bass register (presumably to B♭1 or B1), one for a chromatic half step, and one register key. The Delusse instrument strongly resembles Garsault's cromorne, with a lower extension to B♭1 and with a few chromatic keys added.

The basse de cromorne was the longest surviving member of a family of several sizes. The smaller sizes (sometimes lacking the keys for holes 1, 3, 4, and 6) had apparently fallen out of use by the early eighteenth century, and none are known to survive. By Garsault's time, the name cromorne was largely forgotten.

The cromorne was described in 1651 as 'newly invented', when Michel Danican Philidor served as 'quinte de cromorne' in a royal ensemble of cromornes et trompettes marines.[55] The Philidor collection includes a suite for four cromornes, the bass part descending to B1, composed c.1660.[56] Around this time, the basse de cromorne was

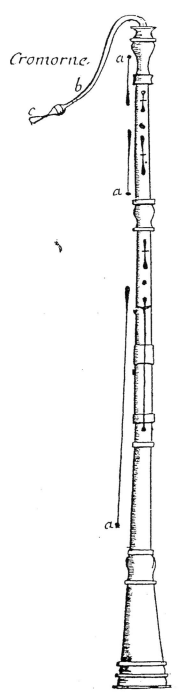

22. *Basse de cromorne.* Garsault, *Notionaire ou mémorial raisonné* (Paris, 1761).

possibly also used as a bass to the newly invented baroque oboe.[57]

Beginning in the 1670s, the bass cromorne was used in the royal chapel of France. In 1674, Charpentier gave it an obbligato part in his *Messe pour plusieurs instruments*, H. 513. André Danican Philidor was named 'basse de cromorne' in the chapel in 1682. The frequent use of the cromorne in both the royal chapel and the royal chamber music seems linked to the Philidor family and to M. R. de Lalande, a composer and master of the royal chamber music.

The basse de cromorne would have had a noticeably more powerful tone than the bassoon. The choke, or smallest bore diameter, of the Heise instrument measures 20.5 mm. Meanwhile, the choke of surviving baroque bassoons is usually in the region of 9–10 mm (both measurements exclude the crooks). Moreover, the key-covered holes of the basse de cromorne could be large and relatively low on the bore, leading to a greater possible loudness. An instrument with as little resistance as this would quickly drain the player's lungs of air. Garnier commented in 1761 that players of the bass cromorne complained of fatigue in the chest. Modern players of reproduction cromornes echo this complaint.[58]

The basson d'amour

A family of highly decorative, shawm-like woodwinds was used to accompany psalms in Swiss church music between c.1750 and 1810 (Finkelman) or 1850 (Girard).[59] Of the three sizes, the middle size (analogous to the modern heckelphone) is called 'basse de musette', while the largest is called 'basson d'amour', after its folded bore and its hollow, spherical brass bell (Ill. 23). These latter-day names are deceptive as to nationality; the instruments were used to accompany the singing of psalms in German-speaking churches in Protestant Switzerland. Despite its bassoon-like size and appearance, the basson d'amour was played with a pirouette, and

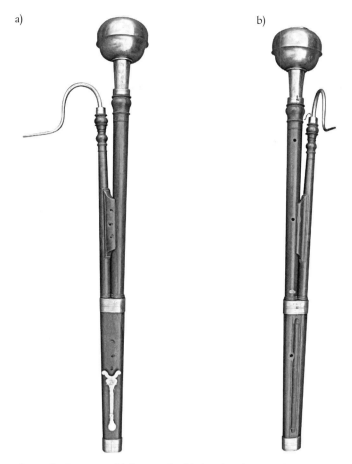

23. *Basson d'amour* by Jeanneret: (a) finger side; (b) thumb side. Waterhouse Collection.

the lowest note obtainable was often E2, as there are sometimes no thumb keys covering the vent holes; the layout of such an instrument is thus 6 down + 2 up. Some of the sixteen existing basses, however, are provided with two bassoon-like thumb keys, and a part-book dating from Gurzelen, 1781, refers to the instrument as a 'Facot'. Most of the surviving bassons d'amour bear the mark 'I.IR.', indicating Jean (or Jacques) Jeanneret (fl. 1764–86) of La Chaux du Milieu, near Neuchâtel. One other is signed I.F.R.[60]

Chapter 4

The baroque bassoon

Evidence suggests that the four-piece baroque bassoon arose in France by 1668, when Nicolas II Hotteterre played 'basson' in the royal chapel of Louis XIV.[1] This seemingly innocuous information is significant because: (1) no bass woodwind is known to have played earlier in the royal chapel, (2) the royal chapel and opera underwent an abrupt shift in performing pitch during the years 1664–70, and (3) the Hotteterres were credited (by a writer of the eighteenth century) with a role in producing the baroque hautbois.[2]

The precise form of Nicolas Hotteterre's basson of 1668 can only be conjectured. By 1685, however, the four-piece, three-key instrument is documented – dozens of such instruments survive today. The upper part of the down bore came now to be called the tenor joint or wing joint. The 'wing' or 'épaule' (French for 'shoulder') was an ingenious abstraction, allowing the chimneys of holes 1 through 3 to be accommodated in a relatively short and slender joint. To provide chimneys for holes 4 through 8, the maker drew on the dulcian's double-bored body design. Two sockets were drilled into the top of this boot or butt joint; into these sockets were inserted the wing joint and the long or bass joint, which contained tone holes 9 through 11. Atop the long or bass joint sat a detachable bell.

Important differences between the baroque bassoon and the dulcian lay, from the player's perspective, in (1) a further extension of the up bore (producing an additional lower tone, B♭1) and (2) a redistribution of the up bore tone holes (control of hole 9 was transferred from the lower thumb to the upper thumb). In consequence, (3) the upper thumb now controlled one open hole and two open-standing keys, while the lower controlled only one open hole, all of these being more proportionately distributed on the up bore. (4) The vents for E2 and below were no longer chimneys. The maker had a somewhat safer task, because (5) each of the four joints could be bored and turned separately, reducing risk and allowing easier access by reaming tools. The separate joints allowed for a complex bore profile, including a reverse taper frequently seen in the bell and cylindrical 'chambers', which some makers employed to manipulate the scale, voicing, and tone hole placement.[3] In addition, (6) the crook was lengthened (and the wooden down bore reciprocally shortened), which had significant acoustical consequences. The new layout was 6 down + 5 up, in contrast to the 7 down + 4 up of Mersenne's proto-bassoons,[4] or the 6 down + 4 up of the dulcian. The inventor of the four-piece baroque bassoon – possibly Nicolas Hotteterre – set the iconic pattern for bassoons to the present day.

The new French performing pitch, called 'ton de l'opéra' but also used in the royal chapel, was a minor third lower (A4 = c.390 Hz) than the old 'ton de l'écurie'. The bassoons used in other countries, however, were seldom as low as this. When bassoons for English use were ordered from the Parisian maker Jacques Rippert in 1711, the customer specified that they were to be tuned 'a quarter-tone higher than the pitch of the Opéra in Paris'.[5] The pitch in Venice was in the 430–440 range by around 1740, followed soon by Prague and Vienna.[6] Some surviving bassoons by J. W. Kenigsperger clothe an old-fashioned Chorton pitch in a showy and fashionable exterior.[7] Even in Paris, the Concert Spirituel attracted visiting performers who probably played at a pitch closer to A-435.[8]

During the seventeenth century, the texture of ensemble music shifted from the consort toward a polarized texture of bass versus one or two higher voices. Larger ensemble sonatas and concertos were still seen, but the trio sonata (already well known in Venice – see chapter 2) became the stereotype. This texture often characterized the orchestral suite (ouverture), especially in movements where two oboes and a bassoon played soli. To accommodate this thinner texture, the range of individual instrumental voices increased. For the bassoon family, the result of these trends was one favored size – the bass, analogous to the old Choristfagott, but with the range extended down to Bb1 and up to G4 or even higher. In addition, the new baroque bassoon, with more tonal and dynamic range, could mirror the expressiveness of the new transverse flute and baroque oboe. Mattheson in 1713 defined 'the proud bassoon' as the 'fundamental' or accompaniment of the oboe:

> It is, however, easier to play than the oboe, because it does not require the same finesse or manners (but yet others, however); all who want to play it should, particularly in the high register, find full work in [cultivating] daintiness and speed. One has to depend especially with bassoons and oboes on good reeds, and the best *maîtres* labor to make them after their own embouchures, for a good reed is half the playing. . . .[9]

Mattheson's comment, that 'the bombardi, which were formerly found in place of the bassoon, are no longer fashionable', needs to be taken with a grain of salt. At courts where bombardi (here meaning dulcians) were in use, the abandonment of the dulcian often came only when the old Chorton pitch was abandoned. The French term basson in this era almost invariably denoted the new four-piece baroque bassoon, while the terms Fagott, fagotto, and curtal could indicate the new bassoon or the old dulcian.

The bassoon often served as a continuo instrument in the absence of oboes and even, at times, in secco recitative. Christian Heinrich Stölzel, from c.1719 a Fagottist and violinist in the Gotha court Kapelle, held the additional title of accompanist, suggesting that he also played exposed continuo parts, unlike the other bassoonists in the same Kapelle.[10] The bassoon was not confined to the bass line, however. From the 1690s, composers in North Germany had included obbligatos for one or more bassoons in their operas (as described below), while Delalande sometimes gave the bassoon a tenor line. André Danican Philidor in 1700 published a book of pieces (dances, airs, etc.) for two viols, bass violins [*sic*] or bassoons. In 1728 Telemann published the first known sonata for the four-piece instrument. In 1733 Galliard published a set of six sonatas, the first known set for the baroque bassoon.

The French basson *is exported to other lands*

In 1685, the Amsterdam maker Richard Haka sold to a representative of the Swedish navy a 'French dulcian basson in four pieces' (Ill. 24). Prior to this, however, a half-century or so of the bassoon's history is known mostly by inference.

A powerful vogue for French music, inspired by the court music of Louis XIV, gripped potentates throughout Europe. In 1670, the duke of Württemberg complained that 'the current instrumentalists can't even play a courant in a perfect French manner'. He financed travel to the French court by Johann Fischer, who served under Lully as a copyist during the years 1665–71, and Johann Sigismund Kusser, who studied under Lully. Returning in 1671 and 1682, respectively, they helped transplant the French orchestral style to Württemberg, the second most prestigious Kapelle in Europe after Dresden. German courts were also visited by French-born oboists and bassoonists, many of whom received permanent employment.[11] A troupe of French 'Hauboisten',

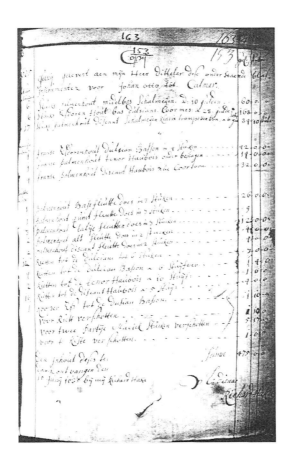

24. Detail of an invoice by Richard Haka documenting the sale of a four-piece French bassoon to the Swedish navy, 1685. Swedish National Archives.

probably including one or more bassons, was active in Hamburg in 1681. Throughout the seventeenth century, and most of the eighteenth century, it was common for other woodwind players to double on the bassoon, which was considered one of the haut-bois. In the Bavarian Hofkapelle, for example, Toussaint Poullain was recorded as both hauboiste and bassoniste during the period 1695–1705.[12]

The baroque bassoon was used earlier and more often than surviving scores or parts show:

> Unspecified wind instruments were sometimes used in ripieno sections, as we know from the 'strings only' before a slow middle movement; and in some German orchestras all available wind instruments may have joined in concertos which were performed only by strings and continuo in Italy. This ad libitum practice required no parts which differed from those supplied to string and continuo players.[13]

France

Three members of the Hotteterre family owned bassoon parts or tools for making bassoons: Nicolas II (bassoon making documented by 1694), Colin or Nicolas III (by 1708), and Martin (by 1711). The earliest baroque bassoons of French manufacture known to survive are those of Charles Bizey (fl. Paris, 1716–p1752), whose customers included the Opéra, the Théatre Italien, and the military.[14] The French-sounding name 'Dondeine' appears on a surviving four-key baroque bassoon (Bate Collection). Other known French bassoon makers of the period included Le Breton, Jacques Delusse, J. B. Fortier, Gilles Lot, Martin Lot, Thomas Lot, Naust, Rippert, and Paul Villars.[15] Iconographic evidence suggests that early French bassoons had a plain-turned body, a cylindrical bore in the bell joint, and three keys[16] (Ill. 25).

25. The bell of a four-piece baroque bassoon is visible in the frontispiece of Marais, *Pièces en trio* (Paris, 1692). Waterhouse Collection.

Use of the baroque bassoon in France during the era of Louis XIV occurred in four different contexts — the royal chapel, the opera, the royal chamber music, and the Grande Écurie. The use of symphonists or instrumentalists in the royal chapel dated from shortly after Lully's arrival at court. A post was created for basson in the royal chapel in 1668, occupied by Nicolas II Hotteterre until his death in 1694.[17] Charpentier scored for bassoon in a dozen of his works for the royal chapel between 1670/1 and 1702[18] (Ex. 4.1).

Prior to Lully, wind instruments were heard in opera as self-contained consorts that were combined rarely, if at all, with strings. Lully added wind and percussion instruments to the royal violin ensembles for his stage works, seeking to evoke the associations of classical antiquity.[19] The oboe was associated with the Greek aulos, shepherds, Bacchus, and jollity. The bassoon, grouped with the oboe (or a pair of oboes) as a suitable bass, took on some of its associations.

Lully's music for *Le Bourgeois gentilhomme* (1670) included a 'Menuet pour les hautbois en poitevin', written in treble/treble/bass clefs.[20] The oboe was called for in two works by Cambert dating from 1671, while movements from five stage works by Lully, 1672–7, called for 'hautbois'. In any of these works, the bass may have been taken by the basse de cromorne or by the new baroque bassoon.[21] Two instrumental works for the stage by Charpentier dating from 1679 called for bassons.[22] Two Lully works from 1680–1 – *Triomphe de l'Amour* and *Proserpine* – included passages explicitly labeled for two oboes and bassoon.

Lully had used the bassoon as a bass in phalanx with the oboes, a traditional role that would still be heard in symphonies of Haydn. But Lully's successor in French opera, Jean-Philippe Rameau, began to work with a rich palette of individual orchestral colors. He chose the bassoon for important new tasks:

Ex. 4.1. Charpentier, 'Offerte pour l'orgue et pour les violons, flûtes, et hautbois', H. 514 (1670/1). The note indicates that the bass line is for 'serpent, cromorne, bassoon, and organ'.

The bassoon is the instrument whose role Rameau does more to transform than any other. . . . [B]y the end of his life it is perhaps the most independent and versatile of the wind instruments. [In the 1730s] the bassoon's main function when it is not doubling is to provide the bass of the trio des hautbois, and occasionally to supply brief passages in the tenor register [at times doubling the viola line]. There are also important bassoon obbligatos. . . . The huge and rapid expansion in the bassoon's role comes in the later 1740s. There are hints of it in the powerful new bassoon obbligatos in the 1742 version of *Hippolyte* and the 1744 *Dardanus* and in the parts for divided bassoons that first appear in *La princesse de Navarre*.[23]

Les fêtes de l'Hymen (1747) has twenty-two movements with independent bassoon parts, while *Naïs* (1749) has thirty-seven, including 'Non, je ne puis assez punir', an air with two obbligato bassoons. Rameau's revisions of the 1750s often enlarged the role of the two bassoons. The 1756 rewrite of *Zoroastre* includes 'Osons achever' (iii), an aria accompanied by 'bassoons darkly sustaining against urgently syncopated strings', as well as recitative accompanied by two bassoons alone.[24]

In Rameau's writing, the first and often the second bassoon took on tenor roles, with ascents to A4 not uncommon.[25] In the bassoon obbligato to 'Lieux funestes', the F minor prison monologue from *Dardanus* [1744, 4.i], Sadler found 'an almost Beethovenian intensity'.[26] The bassoon begins the aria with unaccompanied leaps, continues through a suspension-laden, twenty-measure ritournelle with strings, then accompanies the tenor singer throughout the first section, often weaving a duet in their shared range (Ex. 4.2).

Ex. 4.2. Rameau, *Dardanus*, Act 4, scene 1, 'Lieux funestes' (1744).

In *Les Paladins* (1760) Rameau took the bassoon up to Bb4, and then in *Les Boréades* (rehearsed in 1763 but not performed) to B4. While Bb4 is possible on a four-key bassoon, the demand for B4 suggests that Rameau's player may have had help from a wing key, which is seen on several surviving bassoons by Prudent Thierrot.[27]

Sadler wrote that Rameau 'captured the dignity of Telaira's sorrow' through his harmony and somber bassoon obbligato in 'Tristes apprêts' (*Castor et Pollux*, 1736).[28] The two bassoons in unison supply the steady rhythm and often ascend above the strings and the tenor voice. In 'Pour prix d'un projet' (*Hippolyte et Aricie*, 1742 version), the two bassoons enter into three-voice imitative counterpoint with the bass singer, establishing a subdued, march-like tread. In doing so, they are sometimes above, sometimes below the singer; sometimes proceeding in thirds, sometimes separated by an interval of two octaves. The second bassoon descends briefly to B1, undoubled by the continuo.[29]

Borjon in 1672 wrote of combining bassoons with musettes, flutes or recorders, and cromornes in chamber music.[30] Music for the royal chamber, however, included not only music for small ensembles, but even suites for orchestra.[31] Lully created two posts for bassoons in his *Petits violons du chambre du roi* in 1690, which lasted until the ensemble was dissolved in 1716. The posts were occupied by Jacques Danican Philidor (followed in 1708 by his son Pierre) and by Pierre Ferrier. Their repertory presumably included Marais's estimable *Pièces en trio* (1692); an engraving on the title page showed a bassoon, along with other woodwinds and strings. André Philidor published an album of single-movement duos for bass instruments, notable for its early date (1700)

26.   Dedication to Louis XIV by the bassoonist and composer André Danican-Philidor. *Pièces à deux basse de viole, basse de violon et basson* (Versailles and Paris, 1700).

as well as Philidor's dedication to Louis XIV: 'Your Majesty, having done me the honor several times of wanting to hear me play the bassoon, and having claimed to be satisfied by this, I take the liberty, Sire, of presenting you with my pieces for two basses . . .'[32] (Ill. 26).

François Couperin published his *Concerts royaux* in 1722 and his *Les Gouts Réünis* in 1724, the two suites comprising his 'apotheosis of the contemporary dance'. The instrumentation is ad libitum, although the composer wrote that they were played, at the king's Sunday afternoon concerts, by harpsichord (Couperin), violin, viola da gamba, oboe, and bassoon (François Dubois).[33] Rameau's *Pièces de clavecin en concert* (1741) are likewise ensemble suites of distinction. The ad libitum scoring was by no means limited to oboe/oboe/bassoon. A listener wrote:

> There is no accompaniment more beautiful than those where a composer knows how to mingle tastefully the sounds of one or more bassoons with those of violins and flutes. The sustained notes of the bassoon near the top of its range make an admirable effect. M. Rameau and M. Mondonville have given perfect models of these accompaniments; to them, an instrument [sometimes] valued only for the force of its sounds has seemed a pleasant and touching instrument, equally capable of pleasing the ear and interesting the heart.[34]

The caprices, suites, or simphonies of Delalande (c.1690–1726), Mouret (1729), Aubert (1730–7), and Jean-Fery Rebel (1734–8) call for bassoon in a quasi-orchestral setting, sometimes as an obbligato and/or tenor voice.

Some of the musicians of the French court were an administrative unit of the royal stables or Écurie, through their association with military campaigns, equestrian ballets, and other emblematic activities. French bassoons (multi-piece instruments) probably were introduced into the Écurie along with the new transverse flutes c.1667–9, or shortly afterwards.[35] The Douze Grands Hautbois were heard 'in outdoor ceremonies, on military campaigns, as background music for social occasions, as dance-bands, and in dramatic works (sometimes even as quasi-actors on the stage)'.[36]

Two military regiments called *mousquetaires* or *plaisirs du roi* had shawm bands attached, playing works like Lully's 'Première marche des mousquetaires', LWV 10 (1658). After adopting baroque oboes and bassoons, these mousquetaire bands played not only military music but also for ballets, plays and balls.[37] Some of their repertoire can be seen in a manuscript volume in the Bibliothèque nationale, its early eighteenth-century binding labeled 'Pour les comédies/Basson des mousquetaires'.[38] This bulging retrospective of Lully's oeuvre, likely copied in 1686 or shortly thereafter, is an early example of French *musique de harmonie*. As in other lands of Europe, a 'harmonie' was understood to be a wind ensemble. Descended from ancient shawm bands, harmonie ensembles were by the mid-eigthteenth century organized in pairs of treble wood-winds, with one or two bassoon parts. Even within an operatic or symphonic orchestra, the winds were referred to as 'the harmonie', and sometimes scored in opposition to the string body.

The reign of Louis XIV saw the full flowering of the French 'classic' or high baroque style, 'music of depth and sincerity' performed under royal sponsorship. From c.1726, a new style, called galant, or rococo, or Louis XV style, began to offer a graceful mix of 'lightness, nonchalance, and frivolity' in works performed at public concerts or sold through published editions.[39] Both styles were heard at the Concert Spirituel des Tuileries, a series founded by Anne Danican Philidor in 1725 and open to the paying public. Cantatas by Campra, Clérambault, Dupuits, Gilles, Michel, and Mondonville sometimes called for the bassoon.[40] Invariably in the Italianate galant vein were concertos for wind instruments.[41] Italian bassoonists appearing at the Concert Spirituel included Paolo Besozzi (1735) and Federico della Valle (1752). The resident orchestra of the Concert Spirituel included three bassoonists (Garnier, Brunel, and Capel, also members of the Opéra orchestra) in 1751.[42]

Joseph Bodin de Boismortier embodied the new breed of galant composer. Settling in Paris in 1723, he held no royal post, but composed ballets, pastorales, and sacred works, some which were performed at the Concert Spirituel. He received a royal privilege to engrave and publish his instrumental compositions, which ran to around one hundred opus numbers. Among these were eight sets of works for one or more bassoons, including the Concerto, op. 26, no. 6 (1729), which was scored for solo cello, viol, or bassoon, along with two violins and continuo. Considered as a bassoon concerto, it is the earliest known French concerto for a wind instrument, Bukoff noted. In the interest of selling more copies, Boismortier and other composers often specified a variety of performance options: bassoon or cello, or viol, or even treble-clef instruments. An exception is Boismortier's op. 37 (1732): the Concerto à 4 in E minor is scored for bassoon, with no options listed.[43] Other works specifying bassoons (among other possibilities) included duos by Santo Lapis, Braun, Masse, Guillemant, and Dupuits.[44]

Other public concert series arose. Michel Corrette's *Concertos comiques*, for four-part winds and/or violin, were heard at the Opéra-Comique and Comédie-Italienne between 1732 and 1742.[45] Corrette's works include *Le phénix*, a concerto for four cellos, viols or bassoons (c.1734), and *Les Délices de la solitude*, six sonatas for cello, viol, or

Ex. 4.3. Dard, Sonata, op. 2, no. 5, Adagio (1759).

bassoon and continuo, op. 20 (1739). The six sonatas for bassoon or violoncello and continuo, op. 2, of Antoine Dard (1759) are virtuosic works notable for their 'hyper-ornamentation', fastidious marking of articulations, and the through-composition of slow movements in an arioso style[46] (Ex. 4.3).

The flutist Jacques-Christophe Naudot published six concertos for flute, bassoon, and strings, op. 11 (1735–7). As music director for a Masonic lodge, he composed marches for winds. Michel Blavet, likewise a virtuoso flutist and also a bassoonist, composed Masonic marches for winds.[47] The Masonic marches flourished, spreading from France to Germany and the Netherlands.

England, Scotland, Ireland, and English colonies

The bassoon was known in England before 1685, when the monarch Charles II died; James Talbot wrote that the sackbut's use in combination with shawms 'was left off towards the latter end of K[ing] Ch[arles] 2nd & gave place to the Fr[ench] basson'.[48] In 1677 four French woodwind players were engaged at the English court, and by 1678 three more at the Chapel Royal. Their instruments likely included a bassoon, on which oboists commonly doubled; the bassoon was often termed the basse de hautbois in England.[49] An early drawing and brief description by Randle Holme, dating from c.1688 or before, showed an instrument without parallel among surviving English bassoons.[50] The provenance of Holme's 'double curtaille' is unknown, but it shares many similarities of form with Dutch instruments of the following decade.[51] Talbot in 1690–1700 described the 'fagot' ('entyre' or one piece) as 'disused', in contrast to the 'basson' in 'four joynts', which he also called the 'bass hautbois'.

The English maker J. Ashbury of London advertised bassoons by 1698.[52] But France continued to be a source for imported bassoons: a 1711 letter from England (quoted above) documented an order to the maker Rippert in Paris for two bassoons. Pierre Jaillard Bressan (1663–1731) emigrated from France to London in 1688. A famous maker of recorders, flutes, and oboes, he left three bassoons at his death, now lost. A bassoon by his presumed apprentice, John Just Schuchart, survives in a Japanese collection. One bassoon by Thomas Stanesby Senior (fl. 1691–1734) and one by his son Thomas Stanesby Junior (1692–1754) are in the Waterhouse collection (Ills. 27, 28). The language of the son's trade card implies a typical division of labor: assistants did the preliminary work, while Stanesby himself did the finishing, including fine tuning and voicing.[53] The maker George Brown (fl. Dublin, 1748–53; London, 1753–61) traveled to Oxford in 1757, offering his bassoons and other woodwinds for sale. In 1766 he advertised a 'peculiar method ... of his own invention, of making reeds for hautboys and bassoons, which are esteemed preferable to other reeds'.[54] Surviving English bassoons of the era have a reverse-tapered bore in the bell, which mirrors the taper of the upper long joint. Dart argued that Thomas Stanesby Senior used bore perturbations in the long joint to offset the effect of smaller tone holes, which in turn moderated the volume of the low pitches venting there.[55]

In the company of French-style oboes, the bassoon took root in the English musical establishment. John Blow and Henry Purcell scored for bassoon in their odes during the 1680s. After the death of Queen Mary in 1695, Paisible's 'Queen's Farewell' for

27. Bells of bassoons by Thomas Stanesby senior (left), Gottlieb Wietfelt (center), and, HKI. C.W. Waterhouse Collection.

28. Boots of bassoons by Thomas Stanesby senior (left), HKI. C.W. (center), and Gottlieb Wietfelt. Waterhouse Collection.

two oboes, tenor, and bassoon was played at her funeral.[56] After the death of Charles II, many royal musicians also performed in public concerts.

The orchestral bassoons frequently doubled the continuo line, so that separate scoring was not always indicated:

> 'Grand chorus' or 'play all' is contrasted with the term 'vers' for solo voice with small ensemble accompaniment in works by [Henry Purcell,] Eccles, Jeremiah Clarke, Daniel Purcell and Finger; and trio sections are scored for two oboes and bassoon, in the French style.[57]

Just prior to Handel's arrival in 1710, the Haymarket royal theater employed four bassoons. The recorded number of bassoons there later varied between two (1720), three (1728), and four (1733).[58] In 1709–11, the principal bassoon and oboe were paid as much as the leading violinists.[59]

Handel used the bassoon's timbre as an important color in his orchestral palette. He created a somber backing for the soprano singer in 'Scherza infida' (*Ariodante* 2, iii): over a pizzicato bass, the violins and viola are muted, while the two bassoons (in unison) supply a cantus firmus of slowly descending scales. He chose the bassoon as obbligatist in arias from *Rinaldo, Rodelinda, Amadigi, Apollo,* and *l'Allegro, il penseroso ed il moderato*.[60] One of the Concerti grossi, op. 3, no. 1, calls for two bassoons, as does the fourth of the Coronation Anthems, 'Zadok the Priest'.

The bassoons in Handel's oratorios often departed from the continuo to play *colla voce*; the upper of two sometimes played with the tenor or even alto voices. The oratorios were frequently presented along with concertos, including Handel's *Concerti a due cori*, which expand on the Lullian model by grouping bassoons with pairs of oboes into two wind trios, which are contrasted with the strings and with one another.[61]

'Oboes' reported in the royal Horse Grenadier Guards (1678) and the Foot Guards (1684–5) probably included bassoons as well.[62] The royal model was eventually imitated by persons of lesser social rank. In 1702 the following advertisement appeared in The *Daily Courant of London*: 'A person of quality that is going beyond sea to reside wants a set of hautboys to come along with him, to accompany him; the number must be six, whereof two must be curtals [bassoons]'.[63] Handel wrote marches, minuets, and other works for a harmonie ensemble of oboes, horns, and one or two bassoons (some published in 1729; others dating from the 1740s).[64] A wind octet (pairs of oboes, clarinets, horns, and bassoons) is pictured at the head of a company of grenadiers in an engraving of 1753.[65]

Musica Bellicosa, or Warlike Music, a collection of sixty-eight 'marches and trumpet-tunes' published in London, 1730, included a fingering chart for bassoon. Aside from the low-register fingerings found in Talbot, this is the earliest known English fingering chart for the bassoon. Here and in *Apollo's Cabinet, or The Muse's Delight* (Liverpool, 1756), the lowest key is described as the 'double B-mi key', and no Bb1 is mentioned. Pitches from F#3 to G4 carry the label 'pincht notes', meaning overblown. Handel's *Music for the Royal Fireworks* was likewise billed as 'warlike music'. His score specified twenty-four oboes, twelve bassoons, one double bassoon, nine each of horns

and trumpets, and timpani. Experts disagree on whether it was first performed in 1749
by these forces, or with reduced winds and added strings.[66]

A bassoon concerto by William Boyce, performed at a London tavern in 1742, is
lost. But Stockigt cited two arias with bassoon obbligato by Boyce.[67] Thomas Arne
wrote with imagination for bassoons in his overtures to *Alfred* (1740) and *Artaxerxes*
(1762).[68]

Handel was only the most prominent of German composers residing in London.
Johann Friedrich Lampe came from Saxony to London in 1725, joining the orchestra
of the King's Theater as a bassonist. He played for both Handel and Arne, and
composed many works for the stage. Johann Ernst Galliard, a German oboist taught
by an expatriate Frenchman at Celle during the 1690s, emigrated to London, where
in 1733 he published six sonatas for bassoon and continuo, at the request of one
Kennedy (probably identifiable with Kenny, a bassoonist in Handel's orchestra).[69]
Galliard in 1744 composed 'a new concerto grosso for twenty-four bassoons', accompanied by the cellist Caporale.[70]

John Miller, a bassoon soloist from 1750, was principal (among four bassoons) at the
Foundling Hospital performances of Handel's *Messiah* (1754, 1758). At his death in 1770
he was a member of the Covent Garden orchestra. He assisted the maker Caleb Gedney
in the finishing of bassoons (see chapter 5). The Italian Luigi Merci (Louis Mercy)
published six sonatas for bassoon (or cello) and continuo (op. 3, c.1735), as well as other
sets for recorder (or bassoon) and continuo, and later for flute (or bassoon) and continuo.

The baroque bassoon was introduced to Edinburgh by 1696, when John Munro
and Malcolm McGibbon, professional oboists in Edinburgh, 'successfully petitioned
the town council to be allowed to teach the waits to play the modern French oboe
and "double curtle" '. A bassoon was among the band of the Edinburgh Assembly, an
aristocratic dancing-club.[71]

A bassoon figured in the estate of a resident of the Cape of Good Hope in 1747.
Bassoonists were presumably among the military Hauboisten mentioned there in
1741.[72] In a 1753 New York advertisement, Charles Love, a 'musician from London',
offered to teach bassoon and many other instruments. In Virginia, in 1757, a planta-
tion owner alleged of his servant: 'Charles Love, a tall thin man, about sixty years of
age; he professes music, dancing, fencing, and plays extremely well on the violin, and
all wind instruments; he stole when he went away a very good bassoon, made by
Schuchart', along with other instruments.[73]

German states

Bassoon makers in this era who lived within the boundaries of today's Germany
belonged to various traditions, old and new. Nuremberg was home to a powerful guild
of wood turners, whose influence was only beginning to wane (Ill. 29). The highly
regarded Kapelle of Dresden was probably a factor in attracting Augustin Grenser to
settle there. The free city of Leipzig, home to the bassoon makers Eichentopf,[74] Sattler,
and Poerschmann, was an emerging trade center. Mathäus Hirschstein, a dealer in
woodwind instruments, bought products from such makers and distributed them
throughout Europe by land and sea.[75]

29. *Der Pfeiffenmacher*, by Christoph Weigel (Nuremberg, 1698). Both the dulcian and the bassoon match the style of surviving instruments by J. C. Denner.

In Nuremberg, the dulcian maker J. C. Denner in 1696 had to seek permission from his restrictive guild before manufacturing 'French musical instruments, mostly oboe and recorder'; such instruments had been invented in France about a dozen years earlier, he claimed. This category evidently included bassoons; several three-key instruments survive bearing Denner's stamp, made before his death in 1707. His son Jacob Denner made bassoons, of which three survive. The upper joints of some of these bassoons have a flamboyant outer style: raised rings serving as key mounts on the long joint, with the E and C vents sited near its extreme ends; a narrowly columnar wing joint broken by a stepped épaule and sometimes a flared finial reminiscent of a pirouette; and a bulbous and decoratively turned bell with a reverse-tapered bore.[76]

Haynes listed nineteen German cities or courts, from Celle in 1680 to Weimar in 1701, where French oboes or oboists (and probably bassoons or bassoonists) were imported.[77] Hutchings listed 115 works composed in the French style 1678–1704 by the German composers Mayer, Kusser, Erlebach, Muffat, J. K. F. Fischer, Pez, Chmierer, Johann Fischer, and J. P. Krieger. [78] In Württemberg, a lengthy ducal decree of 1686 showed efforts to re-train and integrate existing wind players into the court's French-style violin band, including special twice-weekly wind rehearsals.[79] For several years prior to 1706, vice-Kapellmeister Theodor Schwartzkopff, who had studied in Paris in the mid-1680s, taught oboe, recorders and other instruments to court musicians.

During the late seventeenth century the Saxon court at Dresden had maintained a generous variety of separate ensembles – violins, shawms, bagpipes, hammered dulcimers, trumpets, and drums, in addition to two chapel choirs that each had six or seven instrumentalists attached, including one dulcian. During these years, the young heir to the electoral throne of Saxony visited the French court at Versailles, 'where he was received twice by Louis XIV and where he attended both opera and spoken theater'.[80] After he succeeded his brother as elector in 1694, August I began to transform the Dresden court Kapelle into the foremost baroque orchestra in Germany, with a rich complement of French-style woodwinds. Records show three bassoons in the Kapelle in 1697, the number gradually increasing to six in 1756.[81]

The Dresden Kapelle attracted works from a number of important composers during the early eighteenth century. A trio sonata and two sonatas à 4, scored by Lotti for oboes and bassoons, probably date from his visit to Dresden in 1717–19. Both Fasch and Zelenka also wrote sonatas for two oboes and one or two bassoons, works of great character and virtuosity. Zelenka wrote for 'fagotti con sordini' in the oratorio *Gesù al Calvario*.[82] Stockigt 2008 listed four arias with bassoon obbligato by Zelenka, plus two each by Fasch and Heinichen, who also composed works for the Dresden orchestra. Fasch eventually wrote more than sixty overture-suites for the Dresden court orchestra, a number of such works surpassed only by Graupner's eighty for Darmstadt, and Telemann's 125 for various courts (see below).[83]

Pisendel, the concertmaster at Dresden, by 1727 'routinely added oboes and bassoons' to sacred works of Zelenka, Heinichen, and Ristori to supplement the original string scoring. Oboes and bassoon were also given concertante passages in Pisendel's arrangements of three Vivaldi concertos for violin.[84] Two of Vivaldi's own concertos for multiple instruments, RV 576 and RV 577 ('per l'orchestra di Dresda'), each containing obbligato bassoon parts, were supplied to the Dresden orchestra.[85]

Carl Augstin Grenser (1720–1807) came to Dresden in 1739, establishing his own business in 1744, selling woodwinds to the court and in 1753 receiving a court appointment as maker.[86] Grenser's work spanned the years of transition between the baroque bassoon and the newer classical bassoon. In bassoons from Leipzig and Dresden, the wing joints often have a smooth exterior profile concealing a complex interior bore; all keys are mounted in wooden blocks; the bell joints usually have a hollow chamber near the terminal opening, which is ornamented with a distinctive crown of metal. These characteristics are generally true of bassoons by Scherer (Butzbach) and the Wietfelt family of Burgdorf.[87]

J. S. Bach and the bassoon

When J. A. Hasse won the position of Kapellmeister in Dresden in 1731, one of the disappointed contenders was J. S. Bach.[88] Working in nearby Leipzig since 1723, Bach looked to Dresden as a model of orchestral practice: the salaried musicians 'have no worries about feeding themselves . . . so they can excel on a single instrument'.[89] In 1733, Bach composed his Missa BWV 232-I for the Dresden Kapelle, dedicating it to the new Elector of Saxony, Friedrich August II. The 1733 Gloria includes a movement

('Quoniam') with a remarkable obbligato for two bassoons, later reused in Bachs's Mass in B minor, assembled c.1747–9.

Bach had begun his career in Thuringia, progressing via Anhalt to Leipzig. He used the bassoon in dozens of compositions for orchestra, both with and without vocalists. Old misconceptions and lingering uncertainty surround some of his bassoon usage, however. Original bassoon parts exist for about thirty vocal works, and the bassoonist may have played either continuo or *colla parte* with the choral basses in other works. Bach scholars have disagreed on the dating of various works, bringing into question which performing forces Bach had at hand for a given work. Surviving bassoon parts are sometimes written at transposing pitches, the source of further confusion.

Bach's earliest known use of the bassoon was in Mühlhausen, where his autograph score for Cantata 71 (1708) called for 'bassono', descending to B♭1. In this work and Cantata 131, the bassoon is scored a major second above the strings, implying that the bassoon was at Cammerton, while the strings were tuned to Chorton (traditional high pitch), along with the organ. In Cantata 150, a funeral composition performed without the church organ, the bassoon is written a minor third higher than the two violins and continuo, indicating that they played at a still higher pitch. Such low-pitch bassoons were evidently new instruments in the French style, not dulcians.

Bach took up a new post at Weimar in 1708. Writing out his own instrumental parts during this period, he frequently edited the bassoon line, marking it in or out in contrast to the string continuo, and sometimes thinning the part or displacing the bassoon line by an octave. 'The only standard rule is that the bassoon participates in the framing outer movements of the cantata'.[90]

Bach's bassoon parts from the Weimar years fall into two groups. Some are written at the ensemble pitch, others a minor third higher, implying that two different instruments were available to the court orchestra (possibly an old dulcian at high pitch and a new baroque bassoon at Kammerton).[91] The majority, marked fagotto, are written at Chorton, the ensemble pitch. Of parts from Weimar marked 'bassono', most are written a minor third higher.[92] Bach 'took special advantage of the versatility of the modern bassoon at Tief-Cammerton by writing in its lowest register', at times displacing the bassoon line an octave lower than the continuo.[93] To the string and organ players present, the B♭1 written in the bassoon part in Cantata 31 sounded as G1 and was notated as such in the full score. This notational solution to a clash of pitch standards has given rise to the misconception that Bach wrote in this cantata for a contrabassoon.

Bach virtually always prepared a part for his Weimar bassoonist, who in 1708 protested 'that he had never been asked to play a demisemiquaver!'[94] Terry was struck by 'Du musst glauben' (the alto/tenor duet, cantata 155); he observed that

> ... the bassoon wreathes an embroidery of almost delirious ecstasy and confident faith, expressed in a formula of both emotions. The instrument skips with agile fluency, in a manner to astonish the bassoon player. .... Indeed in the literature of the instrument this obbligato is a landmark, alike in Bach's adventurous experimentalism and in the general recognition of its qualities as an orchestral voice.[95]

The bassoon line descends to G1 in the score; in the original bassoon part, the scoring would have lain a minor third higher.

In Cöthen from 1717, Bach served as Kapellmeister. The Brandenburg Concerto no. 1 and the orchestral suites nos. 1 and 4 are usually dated to this period, although experts have disagreed. All have obbligato parts for bassoon, sometimes joining the oboes in a Lullian trio texture. In the second bourée of Suite no. 4, Bach opposes the four-voice oboe band to the tutti of the first bourée. He chose to give the melody to the bassoonist, whose fingers and lung power are challenged by a whirlwind of passage work in B minor (Ex. 4.4).

Bach moved to Leipzig in 1723. There, in the year 1730, the bassoon part was played by an apprentice Stadtpfeifer.[96] But other bassoonists were available in two (later three) collegia, low-paid orchestras staffed by law students and aspiring musicians. Bach himself directed one of these (founded by Telemann in 1704) for much of the period 1727 to c.1744.[97] The woodwind maker Johann Poerschmann was a bassoonist in a successor orchestra, the 'Große Concert', in 1746–8.[98]

In many bassoon parts from the Leipzig cantatas, Bach himself scored an obbligato bassoon line in the opening movement. Subsequent movements seldom deviate from the continuo line, however, because Bach in these years usually left them to a copyist, who merely replicated the string and keyboard continuo line. This implies 'that the bassoonist regularly played in all notated movements, which marks a striking change from Bach's [more "orchestrated"] practice at Weimar'. However, a few autograph bassoon parts survive from Bach's years in Leipzig. His parts for the B minor Mass and St. John Passion 'reduce the bassoon's involvement much like the Weimar cases'.[99] Dreyfus noted that Bach opted to use the bassoon in the most varied instrumentations:

> Bach calls for the bassoon in large-scale works with brass and drums, but he also includes it in works with intimate ensembles, such as in Cantatas 42, 44, 66, 70, 97, 173, 177, 186, and 194. . . . There are works with bassoon but without oboes, and

Ex. 4.4. J. S. Bach, Orchestral Suite no. 4, Bourrée II (c.1720).

there are a number of cantatas using oboes in which the bassoon, but not the oboes, is specified in certain movements.[100]

In the sinfonia of Easter Oratorio the bassoon diverges at times from the simple continuo line to play a florid line in trio with the violins. Experts have disagreed about whether the bassoon normally joined the continuo line.[101] Dreyfus noted that Bach occasionally had two bassoons at his disposal:

> [T]he plural appears in the scores for Cantatas 75, 119, 194, and 208, as well as the scores for the Magnificat (BWV 243), the St. John Passion, and the Christmas Oratorio (BWV 248). Indeed it seems credible that Bach's orchestral ideal included two bassoons.[102]

Dreyfus rated the first movement of Cantata 42 as 'a full-fledged concerto movement hiding behind the name of a sinfonia'.[103] Other movements with bassoon obbligato occur in cantatas 42, 143, 149, 155, 173a, 177, 197, 202, and 1088.[104]

In an anecdote dating from 4 August 1705 in Arnstadt, Bach and his cousin Barbara

> ... fell in with six students who had been to a christening feast; one of these was [J. H.] Geyersbach [b. 1682], who asked why Bach had insulted him (or his bassoon), and struck him in the face with a stick. Bach drew his sword, but another student separated them. Bach complained to the consistory ... and an inquiry was held.[105]

In 1945, David and Mendel translated 'Zippelfagottist', Bach's epithet for Geyersbach, as 'nanny-goat bassoonist'.[106] This pungent mistranslation caused some collateral damage to the image of the baroque bassoon itself, whose voice had not been heard within living memory. Later writers have pointed out that the David and Mendel confused 'Zippel' with 'Zickel', meaning a little goat. According to Botwinick's recent survey of the discussion, a better translation of Zippel would be 'dumbbell', 'lout', or 'dunce'.[107] Whether Geyersbach deserved this insult cannot be answered here.

North Germany

By 1681, a team of French 'Hauboisten' was active at Hamburg. In operas for Hamburg or Hanover by Kusser, Steffani, Keiser, and Telemann in the years 1694–1730, obbligatos for bassoon often conveyed darker emotions:

> The musty, insidious sound character gave the composer's palette the right colors to represent misfortune, doom, blame or atonement; it was preferred in scenes involving unhappy or forbidden love, or adultery.[108]

Kusser's *Erindo* (Hamburg, 1694) contained an aria for two obbligato bassoons. In *Octavia* (Hamburg, 1705), Act 1, scene.8, when Octavia finds herself deceived, 'Keiser required darkly coloured consorts of five bassoons which were reinforced by

Ex. 4.5. Keiser, *Octavia*, 'Geloso sospetto' (1705).

continuo'[109] (Ex. 4.5). (In the occasional numbers demanding three or more bassoon parts, the additional lines were played by oboists or even by violin or viola players.)

Inspired by the ballets and operas of Lully and Campra, the Germans Graun and Fasch wrote dozens of overtures or suites with obbligato bassoon parts. Telemann wrote more than 125 of these free-standing works for concert use by collegia musica and court orchestras in Hamburg, Dresden, and elsewhere.[110] Among his later overture-suites are seventeen with obbligato bassoon parts.[111] He also wrote arias with obbligato bassoon, concertos for solo bassoon with recorder (TWV 52: F1) and with two violins (TWV 53: D4), and a quartet for bassoon, two flutes, and continuo (TWV 43).[112]

The electoral court in Berlin and Potsdam was a base for C. P. E. Bach, a son of Sebastian, who wrote numerous pieces of harmonie music and trio sonatas specifying bassoon (H. 588–9; Wq. 92). Quantz and the Graun brothers, who served the electoral courts in both Berlin and Dresden, wrote solos, sonatas, trio sonatas, and harmonie works requiring bassoon.

Looking back in 1726, Hans Friedrich von Fleming described the recent transformation of Leipzig military bands from a quartet of renaissance instruments into a sextet of French-style baroque instruments: 'when Schalmeyen were still in fashion, the military ensemble was only four men – two discants, one alto, and one dulcian. After the hautbois replaced these, there were six men ... two discant oboes, two tailles, and two bassons'.[113] The ensemble was sometimes larger: a set of parts for Krieger's *Lustige Feld-Musik* (1704) provided 'three copies of the first treble part, two of the second treble, one for the tenor, and three for the bassoon'.[114] The tailles were increasingly replaced by horns, a trend evident as early as 1711, when J. G. C. Störl wrote a 'march for pairs of oboes, horns and bassoons'.[115] Telemann's 'Frankfurter' march for three oboes, two horns, and bassoon dates from 1716.

In 1724 King Friedrich Wilhelm of Prussia founded a Hoboistenschule in Potsdam, 'the first educational institution for military musicians'.[116] Under his son and successor, Friedrich II (from 1740), the school provided instruments for the students. 'Friedrich inherited an army that supported nearly 2,000 regimental musicians, many of them hautboists, and the number increased during his reign'.[117] This number would have included hundreds of bassoonists. Aside from marches, the wind bands performed entertainment music as requested by the officers who individually employed them:

> Every morning the Hautboisten perform a little morning piece in front of the officers' quarters, a march which is pleasing to them, a little Entrée and a few minuets, for which the commander has a special liking. This is also repeated in the evenings or whenever the commander has guests or parties.[118]

At times they provided music for processions and other non-military ceremonies.[119]

> The employers of Hautboisten were regimental officers, city governments, and almost any aristocrat who maintained a court.... Owens reports that the Württemberg court Hauboisten Bande was regularly used for church music in the early eighteenth century. Four- and five-part bands were included in cantatas by Liebe (Zschopau), Kegel (Gera), Schulze (Meissen), Zachow (Halle) and Boxberg (Görlitz).[120]

Among more than 500 surviving pieces for hautboy band (mostly from 1670 to 1740), Haynes singled out works of particular merit by Desmazures, Erlebach, Fischer, Müller, Paisible, Pez, Prin, and Wieland.[121] Also worthy of note was Fasch's concerto for 24 instruments (FWV L:D13).[122]

Austria, Central Europe, and Switzerland

In 1696 the abbot of Kremsmünster Abbey sent two musicians to Passau to learn 'Hubua und Fagot'.[123] The following year, a 'Fagot französich Ton' and twelve reeds were ordered for use at the abbey. According to Hubmann, surviving very early instruments – for example, those from the Cistercian cloister Wilhering in Upper Austria or from Neuberg in Styria – suggest that the baroque bassoon had a very sudden spread.[124] Two surviving bassoons – one from Kremsmünster Abbey and another signed by M. Deper of Vienna – are turned in a florid style that recalls the Denners.[125] Young tentatively attributed a bassoon from Wilhering, of somewhat similar outer appearance, to Christoph Sturmb.[126] Around 1750 Christoph Weigel illustrated a bassoon of similar appearance in the hands of an Austrian military musician.[127] This scattered evidence suggests that an indigenous Austrian style may have existed, outwardly resembling the Nuremberg style of Denner more than the Saxon style.

A work by F. T. Richter, the imperial court organist, in 1697 called for flutes, oboes, and bassoons, probably of the new French type.[128] J. J. Fux, joining the court as composer in 1698, immediately began to score for bassoon in orchestral works, where it generally strengthened the continuo line. In Masses and oratorios by Fux, the bassoon part tended to play colla voce.[129] Obbligato parts for bassoon in three of Fux's Viennese operas and one oratorio date from the years 1708–28.[130] The operas of Ziani (to 1714) also call for bassoon. A suviving manuscript volume in a Viennese library contains twelve arias, each with bassoon obbligato, by the composers Caldara, Conti, Fux, Porsile, and Reutter.[131] Fux scored for fagotto in thirty-three ensemble sonatas.[132]

The early flowering of a Bohemian wind-instrument culture included bassoon concertos, trio sonatas, and orchestral overtures by Anton Reichenauer. His Vivaldian style, seen in surviving works of the 1720s, probably stems from his service to Count Wenzel von Morzin, the dedicatee of Vivaldi's *Four Seasons* (1725) and Bassoon Concerto RV 496.[133] Other Bohemian composers, including Wendler, Neruda, and Laube, also produced bassoon concertos in a Vivaldian style.[134] Wendler, a Cistercian monk who played bassoon before Empress Maria Theresia in Prague in 1743, was invited to join the imperial Kapelle as a virtuoso, but declined.[135] Troupes of Bohemian instrumentalists visited Leipzig, where they played in taverns and coffeehouses during the city's annual fairs. In doing so, they encroached on the privileged turf of the city's Stadtpfeifer, who complained to city officials during the 1730s.

Jeremias Schlegel (d.1792) was a bassoon maker in Basel by 1752. Surviving five- and six-key bassoons by him probably date from later, however. Bassoonists active in Switzerland included Grobet (Vallorbe, 1756), Guignard (Le Lieu, 1757), and Jaccard (Lausanne, 1752).[136]

Italy

The new French oboes – and usually baroque bassoons along with them – had arrived in Venice by the 1690s, and in Parma, Naples, Milan, Rome, and Florence by 1709.[137] According to Padre Martini, Pietro Betinozzi, who had learned the hautboy, flute, and bassoon in Ansbach, introduced them to Bologna in 1702.[138]

In Parma, Duke Antonio Farnese founded the Guardia Irlandese, an oboe band, in 1702. Among the members was Cristoforo Besozzi (1661–1725), an oboist, bassoonist, and father of three famous double-reed players. One son, Paolo Girolamo Besozzi

(1704–78), also a bassoonist and oboist, joined the band as a youth. In 1731, Paolo settled in Turin with his brother Alessandro, an oboist.[139] Charles Burney heard the two play oboe/bassoon duets together in 1770 and recorded his impression:

> So much expression! Such delicacy! Such a perfect acquiescence and agreement together, that many of the passages seem heart-felt sighs, breathed through the same reed. No brilliancy of execution is aimed at, all are notes of meaning. The imitations are exact; the melody is pretty equally distributed between the two instruments; each *forte, piano, crescendo, diminuendo*, and *appoggiatura*, is observed with a minute exactness, which could be attained only by such a long residence and study together.[140]

Koenigsbeck attributed a surviving sonata in Bb for bassoon and continuo to Paolo Girolamo.[141] According to Salvetti and Keahey, Alessandro left 'hundreds of works for chamber ensemble', often jointly attributed to Paolo Girolamo.[142] Their great-nephew Carlo Besozzi (1738–p1798) wrote seventeen sonatas in the galant style for bassoon, two oboes, and two horns, and seven more adding a pair of English horns.[143]

In a painting showing the opening of Teatro Regio, 1740, two bassoonists stand at either extreme side of the orchestra pit, next to the ripieno basses, a common practice.[144] Haynes suggested that these bassoonists were probably Paolo Besozzi and Carlo Palanca, who were employed there. He further suggested that the Besozzi brothers probably used an oboe and bassoon by Palanca in the duets they performed in Paris in 1735.[145] Bassoons by Palanca and by I. Biglioni of Rome survive.

Venice was home to conservatories where orphan girls performed Saturdays and Sundays in vespers services, attracting tourists and charitable donations.[146] The services included both sacred vocal works and concertos featuring instrumental soloists. In the orchestral practice at the Ospedale della Pietà, 'the exclusively female performers were screened off from the congregation-cum-audience by grilles and black gauze'. Because there were no visual cues, 'the introduction of a new timbre . . . created a surprising effect.' This was a possible reason for Vivaldi's often innovative scoring, and it protected the modesty of the girls in an age when inflated cheeks were considered objectionable.[147]

In 1795, according to a visitor, the girls had 'protectors' or patrons, outsiders who provided for their material comforts. The protectors were entertained at musical soirées. Such soirées may have been the venue, decades earlier, for chamber works such as Vivaldi's trio sonata for recorder, bassoon, and continuo, RV 86, and the sonata à 4, Anh. 66.[148] The often virtuosic works for solo bassoon demonstrate the accomplishment of the resident bassoonists. None are known by name, and some may have remained in the ospedale into their middle age.[149]

Inventories show a fagotto (dulcian) present at the Pietà as early as 1662.[150] Vivaldi was associated with the Pietà from 1703 to 1740. Ludovico Ertman (Ludwig Erdmann, 1683–1759) taught oboe and other wind instruments during 1707–9, but other bassoon teachers there are not known.[151] Most of Vivaldi's thirty-eight concertos for bassoon solo (two of these are incomplete; a thirty-ninth is for oboe and bassoon) date from 1720–41.[152] Selfridge-Feld wrote:

Vivaldi treats the bassoon with remarkable ease and familiarity, writing in what seems a far freer vein than for other wind instruments. The instrument's idiom is closely modeled on that for the violin. Arpeggios, rapid scales, Alberti figurations and so forth are standard elements of its language. Leaps spanning almost the entire range of the instrument (C2–G4) are seen.[153]

Fertonani found Vivaldi's bassoon to be a 'fascinating and mysterious soloist' with a dual personality. 'It rumbles and gurgles in the depths of its low register, but is capable of cantabile rushes of intensity, perhaps unexpected, in its tenor range (an effect also seen in his cello concertos)'.[154] The mercurial concerto RV 501, 'La Notte', for example, 'evokes a mysterious and disquieting air'.[155] Fertonani credited Vivaldi with a sensibility for 'the chiaroscuro of major and minor'. Though most of the bassoon concertos remain between C2 and G4, one ascends twice to A4,[156] while one descends to B1, and another to B♭1.[157]

Of Vivaldi's twenty-two chamber concertos, seventeen call for bassoon. (An eighteenth, RV 751, now lost, called for two bassoons.) The concerto RV 573, also lost, was written for the harmonie scoring of two oboes, two horns, and two bassoons, while a surviving chamber concerto, RV 97, is scored for viola d'amore, two oboes, bassoon, and two horns.[158] In ten of Vivaldi's concertos for multiple instruments, the bassoon line is frequently combined with a pair of treble instruments, giving the iconic trio-sonata texture of the baroque.[159] Stockigt 2008 listed three Vivaldi opera arias with bassoon obbligato.

The Netherlands

In 1685, the Amsterdam maker Richard Haka sold to a representative of the Swedish navy a 'French dulcian bassoon in four pieces' as well as four dulcian bassoons at chorton, and various other shawms and oboes.[160] An instrument by Haka, now at Sondershausen, probably the earliest datable baroque bassoon, has an ornately turned body, four keys, and a cylindrical bell joint. Similar bassoons (albeit left-handed) are shown on the title page of Sebastian Konink's *Trios pour la flûte, le violon, le hautbois et toutes sortes d'instruments* (Amsterdam, [1696]) and on the undated trade card of Haka's nephew and apprentice Coenraad Rykel. At some point during his years of apprenticeship (c.1679–86), Rykel played 'basson' in theater performances. A four-key bassoon by Rykel, missing its original bell, was recently discovered. Its key for A♭ is operated by RT, rather than the usual R4.

Other Dutch makers producing bassoons prior to 1692 were van Heerde, de Jager, and Parent. Another Haka apprentice, Abraham van Aardenberg, made bassoons by 1698. Other Dutch makers or sellers of bassoons included Thomas Boekhout, Jan Boekhout, van Driel, van Nieuwenhoven, H. Richters, Terton, and Robert Wyne.[161]

Two four-key bassoons bearing the stamp of Joannes Hyacinthus Rottenburgh (fl. Brussels, c.1700–75) are known. A son, Godfridus Adrianus, also made bassoons; an octave bassoon by him survives.[162] One 'Rottenburgh' sold a bassoon to the church of St. Eloi in Dunquerque in 1765.[163] A bassoon by J. B. Willems of Brussels was sold in a 1754 auction.[164]

Scandinavia

'Dulcianer' were reported in use by the military and civic musicians in Trondheim, Norway, by 1702.[165] A fingering chart from Trondheim, 1744, shows a four-key bassoon, elaborately turned in the style of Haka or Denner. The author, Johann Daniel Berlin, called the instrument 'Dulcian or Fagott, or Bass-Fagott'.

In 1702, Andreas Weiss, Kunstdrejer, delivered six 'fagotter' to the Hofviolonerne of Denmark: two for the royal chapel (of nine players), two for the Fodgarden (six Hoboister), two for the Grenaderkorpset (six Hoboister).[166] Two 'franske dulcianer', one new and one old, and two 'chormesse dulcianer' were documented in a death inventory made in Nykobing Falster, Denmark, in 1704.[167] *Hofvioloner*, a 1704 painting by Benoît Le Coffre, shows two bassoonists, amid oboe, three violins or violas, one string bass, and one cembalist. The one clearly visible bassoon is baroque in style.[168] Gottfried Klauen, Blokkedrejer, made a basson in Copenhagen by 1751.[169] A city musician, Andreas Berg, left a 'dulcian', probably a baroque bassoon, at his death in 1764.[170]

Use of the 'dulcian' was recorded in the Turku Regimental band in 1693, and in the cathedral of Aabo (Turku) Finland in 1693–6.[171]

Poland and Russia

Baroque bassoons (Fagotte) were at first used only in 'the best Kapellen', according to Bula, while dulcians (sztorten) remained generally in use. Fagottists active in Poland included Krause (Breslau, 1754), Fritsch, and Jarkowski (both at the court of Count von Branicki, 1754–7).[172] Piwkowski listed ten Fagottists active in Poland between 1713 and 1761.[173] Two works by Jacek Różycki (d. 1707) called for Fagott, as did works of Gorzycki and Żebrowski.[174]

Some of the earliest known bassoonists in Russia were recruited for an opera orchestra at the imperial court of St. Petersburg in 1731. A bassoonist named Plesch (possibly from a musical family of Berliners named Glösch) was engaged.[175] A Viennese bassoonist named Friedrich served from 1731, apparently until his death in 1752 or 1757. 'He played the "fagot" or basson, which is ordinarily very unpleasant and raucous, with extraordinary pleasance and with a double reed. He won admiration by playing concertos and solos.'[176]

Spain, Portugal, and their colonies

Even while the bajón persisted in Spain and its colonies, the newer fagote was occasionally heard. The eight 'Canciones' of the Spaniard Rodriguez de Hita, drawn from a larger work (Palencia, Ms dated 1751), are trio sonatas for oboes and bassoon. The Mexico City Cathedral Chapter ordered 'fagotes in B♭' (bassoons) from Spain in 1759.[177]

Chapter 5

The classical bassoon, c.1760–1830

The development of the bassoon during this period was incremental rather than revolutionary, driven by four trends: a need to perform fluently in increasingly remote keys, a need for a more powerful sound, composers' increasing use of the instrument's tenor register, and changes in standard pitch (usually rising).

Nearly all the chromatic degrees of the bassoon's scale were obtainable on the baroque instrument through cross-fingering or half-holing. But the pitches produced by these techniques were sometimes unmatched in tone quality, limited in dynamic range, or difficult to finger at speed. An original key for E♭2 was included in a French fingering chart published c.1775.[1] A key for RT – co-opted after Ozi's time for producing F#2 – was added late in the century, and keys for C#3/C#4 and B♭2/B♭3 early in the nineteenth century.

By 1772, in his Farewell Symphony no. 45, Haydn expected a bassoonist to handle an obbligato part in the key of F# minor (sometimes venturing into the parallel major). Late in the century, even works set in less extreme keys might veer into highly chromatic territory. Tromlitz, the flutist, noted such abrupt harmonic turns in compositions by 1800; unless a flutist could match a violinist in these, Tromlitz wrote, 'he remains always only an organ grinder'.[2] Bassoonists were under the same demands, and their efforts sometimes fell short. Composers writing solos for bassoon in five or six sharps or flats were met with 'a failure in the attempt to execute them by the most experienced artists', an English writer noted in 1830.[3]

Bassoons of this period often have a narrower bore, thinner walls, and a higher pitch level than earlier bassoons. The narrower bore facilitated overblowing, so that notes up to A4 or higher could be produced by skillful players. The Berlin makers Griesling & Schlott (fl. 1801–35) wrote that the wing key for A4 was unneeded, 'because this tone speaks very easily on our instrument'.[4] Yet one or more new register keys were sometimes installed on the wing joint – what today's players call the A4 and C5 keys.

The new classical bassoon produced a more penetrating sound, especially in the upper register. The demand for this can be seen in Haydn's symphony no. 8 (c.1761). In the Andante second movement, the solo bassoon has frequent tenor duets with a solo cello. In tutti passages of the fourth movement, the bassoon has numerous passages rising to A4. This brighter, more powerful sound resulted partly from the thinner walls, which reduced the chimney depth. Another factor was a new attitude by classical makers to the bore of the bell. Inverted tapers, chokes, and chambers were

common at the start of this period; by 1830, bells were more often genuinely cylindrical, slightly choked, or flaring. Among the rich variety of bell bores seen during
the period, the trend was toward more openness.[5] In an acoustical analysis, Krüger
found that a bassoon by Tauber of Vienna (fl. 1798–1829) had significantly higher
formants than two baroque bassoons, accounting for a generally brighter sound as
perceived by listeners. The formants (regions of high resonance within the frequency
spectrum) occurred at nearly harmonic intervals, which magnified their resonant
effect.[6]

Composers liked what they heard of the tenor register of the bassoon – it became
the favored instrument for doubling singers, violins, or the treble woodwinds at the
lower octave (or sometimes the double octave). This sort of scoring – typical of
Viennese classical composers but also seen elsewhere – gave the featured melody a
vivid, 'shadowed', almost palpable presence and the orchestral texture a new illusion
of depth or three-dimensional space. The sound of this subtle but irresistible scoring
technique is engraved on the aural memories of countless listeners today. When Koch
described the bassoon in 1802 as 'the instrument of love', he was thinking of its
beguiling tenor register.[7]

A new consciousness arose of the bassoon's colorful bass register, as well. In 1768
Haydn noted the advantage of including a bassoon among the strings in order to give
more definition to the bass line.[8] These lessons were not lost on Mozart, who opened
his *Marriage of Figaro* overture with cellos and bassoons at the unison. A few seconds
later, he entrusted the new theme in A major to the first violins, doubled at the lower
octave by the first bassoon (mm 110ff.). Forkel wrote in 1782 that the bassoon,
supplying husky bass and transparent tenor, is 'what turns etchings into paintings'.[9]
Fröhlich's comments in 1829 on the bright/dark of the bassoon's tones likewise
suggested that composers had employed the bassoon to introduce chiaroscuro into
their *Tonkunstwerke*.[10]

The increasing popularity of public concerts entailed a trend toward larger
performing spaces, and a resultant demand for bassoonists (like other instrumentalists)
to create a strong sound. In Paris, 'operas were performed in the Grande Salle of the
Palais Royal until 1763; subsequent performances were in the Salle des Machines,
which could seat nearly 8,000'.[11] Spitzer reported eight bassoons in the Opéra
orchestra in 1773, although a more typical number in European classical orchestras
was two to four.[12]

Pierre Cugnier (b.1740) observed in 1780 that pitch at the Concert Spirituel had
risen during his career, so that newer bassoons tended to be higher and thus
smaller. Older, lower-pitched bassoons were still in use in the Sainte-Chapelle, Paris,
and the royal chapel, Versailles, where organs were still at low pitch, and at the Paris
Opera, 'where one changes pitch according to whether the roles are lower or less
high; thus the pitch is sometimes so low that all the wind instruments are necessarily
out of tune. . . .'[13] In the 1790s the 'ton d'orchestre' (A = c.435) was officially adopted
by the conservatoire, although slightly lower pitches were still reported in various
Parisian theaters in 1823.[14] Ellis traced the European rise in tuning pitch during much
of the nineteenth century to the gift of sharp-pitch woodwinds to an Austrian regiment in 1814. Another regiment received even sharper wind instruments in 1820.

These regimental pitches affected theaters, which were dependent on military musicians.[15]

'Manufactory' production, involving division of labor and larger-scale production, was evident in parts of England, France, and Germany. Dealers became more common, commissioning or purchasing instruments from makers. The dealer, sometimes adding his own stamp, then distributed the instruments via traders or direct foreign export along established trade routes – an early example of trade liberalism or free trade. Following close behind was patent protection for woodwind makers and traders, seen in Britain around the end of the eighteenth century. A patent law of 1830 (the Gewerbeordnung) brought forth 'a veritable flood of patent applications' in German states.[16]

France

An inventory at the death of the wife of the maker Thomas Lot III in 1765 showed a manufactory scale of production: 72 bassoons among 400 instruments.[17] The after-death inventory of the property of Prudent Thierriot (1730–86) also indicated a manufactory; it included 58 bassoons, 125 bassoons in progress, and 21 bassoons 'de hazard' (among 143 clarinets, 22 oboes, 177 flutes, etc.). Some bassoons were 'en blanc', or unstained; others with ferrules, others with keys. Seven boxes of bassoon and oboe reeds were counted; quantities of cane in the inventory implied production within the Prudent shop. Prudent was related by birth or marriage to other prominent bassoon makers: Charles Bizey, Dominique Porthaux, and Nicolas Winnen. Both Prudent and Bizey supplied musicians of the Opéra, Théâtre Italien, and military.[18]

In 1760 Garsault illustrated a bassoon with a two-ring wooden finial on the bell and a narrow, metal-bound receiver – characteristics that would persist through the century on most French instruments. The bassoon was held high, with the right thumb 'at the level of the navel'.[19] Laborde's engraving of a bassoonist bears this out, as does the acute bending of some surviving crooks. A vent hole drilled in the crook was familiar to Cugnier in 1780, as was the possibility of a key for the left thumb to close the hole. Cugnier noted:

> The intonation of the bassoon, like all wind instruments, depends on the interior bore of its joints, and that of the holes that communicate with the bore or interior channel of the instrument. The luthiers who make these instruments generally make them in small quantities [relative to clarinets and flutes], and don't have equal success in the making; the one who is most experienced in this type must therefore be preferred.[20]

Cugnier was possibly speaking of Prudent Thierriot. Ozi in 1787 complained of two problems facing bassoonists: an imperfect scale and a lack of volume. The maker of his bassoon at the time, Keller of Strasbourg, moved the G# key lower on the bore and added a key for right thumb; the larger bore and crook delivered a larger sound.[21]

Fétis reported dissatisfaction with the bassoon's capabilities by 1780, when

Delusse, the Parisian maker, tried to make it produce sounds of a better quality, without being able, however, to correct its defects of intonation. Asked by the distinguished bassoonists Delcambre, and especially Fougas, at the beginning of the nineteenth century, the Parisian maker Adler made numerous experiments around 1809, seeking to correct some bad notes by the addition of several keys.[22]

Simiot of Lyon added a tuning slide and keys for B1 and C#2 by 1808; a metal U-tube in 1817; and a water key and a rack-and-pinion tuning slide by 1823.[23] An informal survey of bell types shows examples of the inverted taper (Porthaux); the choke (Winnen, Savary père, Savary jeune, Simiot & Brelet); and the orthogonal taper (Bühner & Keller, Auguste Buffet).[24] Other variations were seen in the period, including a dramatically flared wooden bell for military use (Rust) and a metal bell terminated by a dragon's head (Sautermeister).[25]

The fluctuation of pitch standards caused particular problems for players of the bassoon, which was more expensive to replace than the smaller woodwinds. Small adjustments to the sharp side could be made by using a shorter reed or crook. Cugnier noted that reeds in current use varied in length from 28 to 32 lignes, or 66 to 71.5 mm.[26] In later decades bassoon makers devised two partial solutions to the problem: multiple wing joints (*corps de rechange*), and a single or double tuning slide (*pompe d'accorde*) in the wing joint. Makers in Lyon included Jeantet, Rust, and Sautermeister & Muller.[27] Other makers included Cuvillier (St. Omer), Jung (Marseilles), and Roustaneq (Toulon).[28]

International trade advanced. By 1829, the publisher/maker Schott offered German-made bassoons and contras in their Paris and Antwerp shops. Küffner's method, published by Schott in 1829 with parallel French and German texts, was for a ten-key bassoon with keys for Eb2 (for L4, in the German style), F#2, Bb2/Bb3, C#3/C#4, and two wing keys, in addition to the basic four. Fétis noted in 1828 that 'Adler of Paris has noted Almenräder's improvements, and Gebauer teaches it to his students'.[29]

France: Players and pedagogy

Cugnier identified five roles for the bassoon: playing the bass part; accompanying the voice, especially the bass voice; playing in pairs with clarinets and horns in musique d'harmonie; accompanying pieces arranged for harp[30]; and 'in nearly all types of music', including concertos.[31] Cugnier stressed that the bassoonist must imitate the singing voice:

> ... taking care to make short and long syllables, the same as the voice ... the sound of the instrument must be managed in a manner that mixes with that of the voice, and the tongue stroke must be softened in proportion to the syllables that the voice pronounces.[32]

The lips should be placed halfway between tip and first wire, but

... the reed could be advanced into the mouth a little further than this halfway mark in order to sustain the tones in pieces of music such as Rameau's operas, where a louder tone is desired for continuo playing. This type of sound, [Cugnier] maintains, is quite unlike the sound used in concerto playing.[33]

This comment, surprising to the present-day reader, implies that concertos were played with a modest, intimate sound, at least at times.

Cugnier advised the bassoonist to avoid buzzing (*sifflement*), but the bassoon's tone must not 'be entirely without the kind of piercing quality proper to it ... which gives it the necessary timbre; for then it would resemble that of the serpent, which would be equally disagreeable'. He advised the player to rotate the reed on the crook slightly to the right or left, so that the reed was held obliquely between the lips. This was 'in order to keep the reed from closing on high notes due to increased lip pressure'.[34] Cugnier noted that the bassoon's scale was usually uneven, necessitating the use of compensatory fingerings not shown in his chart:

> ... there are always some tones a little stronger or weaker; the ear must guide the embouchure, giving a little more force to the weak tones, and diminishing those that are a little strong. For example, it is rare that the two A's, lying an octave apart and fingered 123 45, are exactly in tune, like the other tones notated here [A♭2/A♭3, B♭2/B♭3, B2/B3], when one uses the simple fingering shown in the table. There are special fingerings to rectify this fault; for some tones, there are several fingerings, according to the passages where they are used. ... One should ... choose an able master who knows the fingerings and who can teach them, and practice them so that they become habitual.[35]

Cugnier gave examples of middle-register passages in E major and E♭ minor that should be avoided by composers 'in accompaniments and solos':

> The above passages are too difficult and even almost impossible at speed, because of the two keys 7 and 8 [A♭ and F], which must be touched alternately with the little finger of the right hand ... this makes for embarrassment in the movements, and a disagreeable clicking.

However, the bassoon 'can play the same part as the violoncello in all symphonies and other pieces of great effect, in all keys'.[36]

The Institut nationale de musique was founded in Paris in 1793, in the wake of the revolution. All the founding professors were members of the Garde Nationale, including the bassoonist Thomas Delcambre, who held the high rank of sergeant. In a planning document, the numbers of intended professors were heavily weighted toward clarinet, bassoon, and horn, which together comprised harmonie ensembles, the musical mainstays of patriotic 'fêtes publiques'.[37] Renamed in 1795, the Conservatoire nationale supérieure de musique dominated musical pedagogy in France for more than two centuries. Its professors of bassoon, who also performed in orchestras at the Opéra and elsewhere, wielded a great influence on both performing style and the bassoons made in France. Wind music was held in such high regard in 1799 that professors, including Delcambre and Ozi, performed extraneous musical selections between acts at the Opéra. From 1795 to 1802, there were five bassoon professors. After 1802 there were two, including Ozi until his death (1813). After 1813 the sole bassoon professor was Delcambre, who served from 1795 until 1824.[38] In the years An V (1797) and An VIII (1800), at least, bassoonists winning the premier prix at the conservatoire were awarded bassoons.[39] Beginning in 1802, students performed musical works in public exercises. During the Napoleonic campaigns, the number of bassoon pupils waned: three in 1808, none in 1809–11, no records for 1812–17, two in 1818, etc.

Like Cugnier, Ozi held up the vocal art as a model for bassoonists. His bassoon method of 1787 advised the bassoonist 'to imitate a beautiful human voice, and I dare say that of all instruments [the bassoon] is the most likely to approach it. . . .'[40] Part of the imitation was 'nuances', or subtle fluctuations of volume; 'a succession of sounds without nuances would produce monotony and destroy the charm of the music'.[41] In his second method for bassoon (1803; commissioned by the conservatoire) Ozi quoted the *Méthode de chant du conservatoire* as to principles of phrasing.[42] He distinguished between strongly taken breaths (fast tempos), and a more regular type of breathing, to match up with musical phrases. In the latter, the player could shorten a long note to take a breath, or leave out a repeated note in order to breathe. Ozi recognized three types of articulation: slurred, short tongued, and 'marked' (longer tongued). In order to achieve the song-like style on the classical bassoon, Ozi 1803 offered six other 'modifications' (compensatory fingerings comparable to those of Cugnier).[43]

Ozi in 1787 maintained that the oblique embouchure, described earlier by Cugnier, 'eliminated the undesirable practice of turning [tilting] the head to the right or left while playing the bassoon'. He included a brief chapter on choosing and adjusting reeds. Among his counsels was: if the reed is dull, or if doesn't vibrate enough, one must remove a little rind from the cane, and scrape lightly all over, down to the bottom of the blade.[44] The corresponding section of Ozi 1803 was longer and completely rewritten, now giving dimensions and detailed directions for making reeds. His most eyebrow-raising specification was an internal gouge reduced to an overall thickness of one-quarter line (0.55 mm), and thinned further in the region of the blades.[45] Such an extremely thin gouge produces a reed with very little pith and water absorption. This gouge measurement was retained through several editions of his method (Ill. 30).

For initial scraping of the reed, Ozi called for the unopened reed to be held tip down, steadied against the maker's palm. (Plaques were not yet documented, and the mandrel was apparently used only in the forming process.) Ozi recommended beginning the scrape 5 lines (5/12 inch) above the top wire, but his illustration showed a much shorter scrape, possibly 5/12 inch total. He mentioned that the aperture of the reed could be adjusted by compressing the first or second wires from the sides.[46]

Aside from teaching bassoon, Ozi held another office that reflected the revolutionary roots of the conservatoire. The Garde Nationale of France, to which Ozi belonged, established the Magasin de musique à l'usage des fêtes nationales, to publish

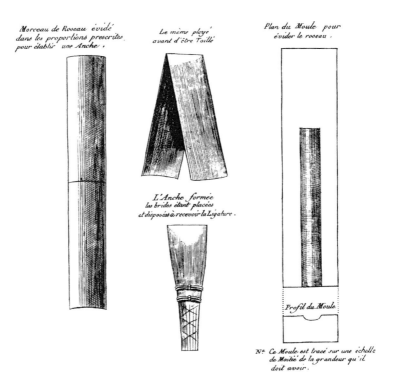

Morceau de Roseau évidé dans les proportions prescrites pour établir une Anche.

Le même ployé avant d'être Taillé

Plan du Moule pour évider le roseau.

L'Anche formée les brides étant placées et disposées à recevoir la Ligature.

Profil du Moule

N.ª Ce Moule est tracé sur une échelle de Moitié de la grandeur qu'il doit avoir.

30.   A drawing of cane, a gouging mould, and a finished reed. The treatise explains that the cane is gouged thinner towards the reed's tip. Ozi, *Nouvelle méthode de basson* (Paris, 1803).

patriotic music during the years of the first republic. 'The profits were to be used to support widows and children of the National Guard's musicians.' From 1797 until his death, Ozi was manager of the firm, which was renamed the Imprimerie du Conservatoire and increasingly devoted to pedagogical works.[47]

Castil-Blaze wrote in 1821 that the tones of the bassoon were 'tender and melancholy, full of vigor and feeling … inviting contemplation, inspiring gentle piety if they accompany religious songs'. He called the bassoon

a universal instrument [which] inflects a solo with as much grace as suavity. . . . Possessing the timbre that agrees best with all instruments, it doubles the bass, the *viole*, the clarinet, and the flute in turn. . . . Its rumbling pedal notes and its middle notes provide accompaniment, and its last octave gives a pure and sonorous melody.[48]

France: Repertory

Gossec's *Messe des morts* (1760) included orchestral effects worthy of Berlioz: 'The audience was alarmed by the dreadful and sinister effect of the three trombones together with four clarinets, four trumpets, four horns and eight bassoons, hidden in the distance and in a lofty part of the church, to announce the last judgment, while the orchestra expressed terror with a muted tremolo in all the strings.'[49]

Operatic composers in Paris, the artistic heirs of Rameau, drew on the bassoon as a color of the orchestral palette even in opéra-comique, including a solo in Monsigny's *Aline, reine de Golconde* (1766). The bassoon expresses the sorrow of the father in Gluck's tragedy *Iphigénie en Aulide* (1774; Act 1, scenes 1 and 3).[50] Gluck also scored an aria and chorus in *Armide* (1777), Act 5, for solo bassoon and strings. In the opéra-comique *Richard Cœur-de-Lion* (1784; Act 2, scene 1) Grétry used muted violins, violas, flutes, bassoon (all pianissimo), tripled in octaves to conjure a magical effect during a nocturnal march. An aria from Cherubini's *Médée* (Paris, 1797) includes a dramatic obbligato for bassoon, leaping from C5 to C2. Méhul's overture to *Adrien* (1799) included writing for bassoons in four parts. The overture to Reicha's *Sapho* (1822) included an introduction scored for bassoon, horn, two harps, and glass harmonica.[51]

Public concert series flourished, including the long-lived Concert Spirituel, where Mozart's 'Paris' symphony (K. 297) received its premiere in 1778. Haydn's Six 'Paris' symphonies (nos. 82–87; 1787) were written for the concerts of the Loge Olympique, said to have the best orchestra (65 members) in Paris 'and perhaps in all of Europe'.[52]

At the Concert Spirituel, sixteen bassoon soloists had appeared by 1786.[53] Among these was Ozi, who debuted in 1779. During the next two decades he performed his own bassoon concertos and concertantes there, as well as works by Deshayes and Devienne, in a total of thirty-seven solo appearances.[54] His obituary in 1813 noted the 'melancholic and touching accent' that characterizes the bassoon. 'After 1780 bassoon soloists appear on the series more often than flutists, oboists, or cellists', Griswold noted.[55]

A favorite Parisian genre from 1773, the symphonie concertante was a concerto for multiple soloists. This 'many-sided conversation' among instrumental voices was marked by surface appeal and repetition.[56] One of the leading composers of such works was Giuseppe Cambini (1746–1825), 'the galant Parisian composer par excellence – facile, charming, brilliant, very occasionally novel, and limited in both imagination and purpose'.[57] Ozi himself wrote concertantes for two bassoons and for clarinet and bassoon.[58] François Devienne, known first as a flutist, was also a professional bassoonist and composer. He appeared at the Concert Spirituel as a bassoon soloist in 1784 playing his own bassoon concerto, and in 1787 playing the solo bassoon part in his own concertante for flute, clarinet, and bassoon.[59] During the years 1803–24, bassoon students at the Paris Conservatoire performed in concertantes by Reicha, Widerkehr, Catel, Lefevre, Devienne, Jadin, and Brod.[60]

During the coming decades, ensembles for galant chamber music in Paris would often include the bassoon. Both Ozi and Devienne wrote numerous chamber works for bassoon with strings or other winds.[61] Works by the Bohemian oboist Charles Bochsa père (1755–1821) included a trio with oboe and harp, and quartets for mixed winds (as well as traditional harmonie works).

The Bohemian Antoine Reicha was a professor of fugue and counterpoint at the Conservatoire in Paris from 1818 until his death in 1836.[62] Also an experienced flutist, he composed a quintet for the combination of flute, oboe, clarinet, horn, and bassoon around 1810.[63] Reicha characterized it as a failure, but a performance of later quintets in 1814 was acclaimed in the Parisian press. Among the performers was the bassoonist Antoine Nicolas Henry, an Ozi pupil who had won a first prize in 1803. A quintet including Henry performed a cycle of Reicha's quintets in Paris during 1818–19, again winning praise.[64] The composer's four collections of six wind quintets, published c.1817–20, were each reprinted multiple times within a few years by French and German publishers. The preface to the Simrock edition cited the precedent of the Haydn and Mozart masterpieces for string quartet.[65] Reicha composed a set of variations for bassoon and string quartet, as well as other works for bassoon with other winds and strings.

Cambini's three *Quintetti concertants*, op. 4, were published between 1812 and 1822, judging by the address of Sieber, the publisher.[66] The first opus of Franz Danzi's quintets, op. 56, was also published in Paris, c.1819–21. Three virtuosic quintets by the bassoonist F. R. Gebauer were published c.1820–30. Works were composed for many other sub-groupings of the five instruments, by these composers and many others.

In 1762 Louis XV established a musical force of four bassoons, four horns, four oboes, and four clarinets in his Swiss Guards.[67] Instructions for composing or arranging suitable music soon followed. In 1764 Valentin Roeser, a clarinetist in the service of the prince of Monaco, published a method for composers 'with remarks on the harmonie of two clarinets, two horns, and two bassoons'.[68] This new standard ensemble of paired winds was popular in both military and civilian contexts; both the repertory and the players frequently overlapped.[69] By 1767 the duke of Orleans also sponsored a harmonie ensemble.[70] Louis-Joseph Francoeur in 1772 published another treatise on scoring for wind sextet; one part was to be played by the two bassoons.[71] French Masonic lodges maintained *colonnes d'harmonie* until about 1830.[72]

Between 1783 and 1786 Ozi was employed by the duke of Orléans; he prepared seventeen of his thirty-two *Nouvelles suites* for harmonie for the duke's salon, a hub of aristocratic night life. The duke was 'the head of Freemasonry of all of France',[73] while Ozi was a member of three Masonic lodges and one Masonic musical society.[74] Ozi's suites – arrangements of overtures, ballets, and arias from popular operas – coincided with his membership in the three lodges.[75] Other prolific composers or arrangers included Bochsa, Cambini, Catel, Devienne, Deshayes, Roeser and Soler; the 1799 Sieber catalogue listed more than one hundred works of harmonie music.[76] Among works excerpted were operas by Gluck, Gossec, Méhul, and Spontini. Cherubini during 1800–14 wrote fourteen marches for winds; his *Morceau pour basson* has been dated to 1823.[77]

In 1809–20, a typical French infantry band still included two bassoons, although it had expanded to include eight to ten other woodwinds, six to eight brass, and four percussionists. A French infantry band of 1829 included six bassoons and twenty other woodwinds.[78] Military bandsmen were sometimes bassoonists of distinction. C. D. J. Barizel was chief of military music in Napoleon's Spanish campaign (1808); then played at the Opéra; served 1815 in Napoleon's Russian campaign, receiving the Legion of Honor; and in 1839 became bassoon professor at the conservatoire. Adolphe Reickmans served in the army 1820–33; he then played bassoon at the Opéra, later becoming director of a Dutch regimental band.

Germany

In 1772 F. G. A. Kirst of Potsdam received a privileged appointment to supply wood-wind instruments to the Prussian army.[79] By 1800, Kirst was leveraging his expertise and dividing the labor within his shop of six to seven workers. 'None of his workers completes an instrument', an observer noted.

> One drills, the other polishes, the third makes the keys, a fourth stains, etc.; he does the voicing himself. None of his workers has become independent, nor can most of them leave because they are soldiers. By such an arrangement . . . he has driven his prices to the highest level.[80]

The leverage was even greater in Leipzig, which was a free city, allowing open trade. During the 1780s, Johann August Crone of Leipzig, working together with the brass maker Johann Friedrich Schwabe, employed 'thirty makers and ten to twelve apprentices'. One of these suppliers was Carl Wilhelm Sattler, an independent maker, who during times of slow business made piecework for other workshops.[81] Sattler in 1788 sent Crone thirty-eight bassoons of the specified 'Wietfelt model' with E♭2 key, then another thirty-two ordinary bassoons. 'Crone commissioned Sattler to do the work, then stamped the instrument with his own name and sold it for a profit'. Meanwhile, Sattler himself subcontracted work to Gregorius Ludewig, who manufactured the metal parts for the bassoons. Ludewig, an established brass instrument maker, shared a stand with Sattler at the three annual trade fairs in Leipzig. The trade of Crone and Schwabe suffered when Napoleon sent troops into Leipzig in 1806, but the Crone firm survived both the occupation and its founder, still existing in 1829.[82]

Dresden became famous in this era for the quality of woodwinds, including bassoons, by Augustin Grenser, Heinrich Grenser, and Jakob Grundmann. Augustin Grenser made the typical four-key bassoon, but sometimes added the new E♭ key, which he usually located for LT in the French style.[83] He supplied bassoons to Leopold Mozart for the Salzburg Hofkapelle in 1772 and to the Mecklenburg regiment at Ludwigslust in 1788. During 1796/7 the two Grensers had four journeymen active in a manufactory, comparable to that of Kirst in Potsdam. Taking over direction of the firm in 1796, Heinrich Grenser probably doubled the number of employees and outsourced some of the work.[84] An after-death inventory included thirty-five bassoon reamers, seven lathes, and a polishing machine (a type of lathe). Also present were cane for making reeds, and *Schachtelhalm* or Dutch rush, an abrasive used in making both instruments and reeds.[85] Heinrich Grenser delivered instruments to Kassel, Gotha, Chemnitz, Frankfurt, Aschersleben, Darmstadt, Lübeck, Riga, Salzburg, and Stockholm.[86] According to Haynes, Grenser instruments are normally pitched around A = 433, although many Dresden makers also made instruments at both A = c.415 (for north German use) and A = c.440 (for export).[87]

On almost all the surviving bassoons by Heinrich Grenser, the keys are mounted in saddles; this marked a break with the work of his uncle, who favored block mounting for most keys (Ill. 31). On the wing, the younger Grenser 'altered the C5 key, moving it higher up'. Unlike his uncle, Heinrich Grenser placed the E♭ key for L4 (Ill. 32).

31.   Right-hand keys mounted in blocks on a bassoon by J. F. Grundmann (above); the same keys mounted in saddles on a bassoon by F. G. A. Kirst (top). Waterhouse Collection.

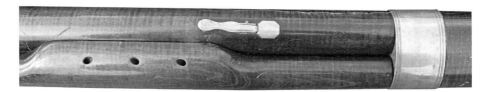

32.   E♭ key for L4 on a bassoon by J. F. Grundmann of Dresden (above); E♭ key for LT on a bassoon by N. Winnen of Paris (top). Waterhouse Collection.

According to Fröhlich, Heinrich Grenser added a C#3/C#4 key for L4;[88] later moved to the LT side of the wing joint, this was the direct ancestor of the Heckel-system C#3/C#4 key. Seventeen of the fifty-one surviving bassoon bells by Heinrich Grenser (as surveyed by Young) have a small vent drilled at the mid-length.[89] Almenräder later explained that the vent was to improve the quality of C2; it could also benefit D2, he noted.[90]

 After Grenser's death in 1813, his successor was the journeyman Samuel Wiesner. When Wiesner married Grenser's widow in 1817, the firm became known as H. Grenser & Wiesner.[91] The firm, later known as Wiesner, continued to offer the 'Dresden bassoon' until 1867, while offering added keys to meet the newer demands.[92]

Other Saxon makers included Floth (Grundmann's successor; Dresden), Huittl (Graslitz), and J. G. Jaeger (Neukirchen). Most of the Saxon makers offered *corps de rechange* wing joints, and some later German makers offered tuning slides, including Rank and Stengel.[93]

Germany: Players and pedagogy

Two early translations into German of Ozi's second treatise (1803) highlighted differences of practice between Germany and France. Established national preferences of reed, embouchure, and instrument prompted one anonymous German translator to revise Ozi's fingerings for Eb2 (L4 instead of LT), and F#2 (RT key instead of RT fork).[94] These translations marked the divergence of French and German finger technique.

Joseph Fröhlich, appointed to the music faculty of the university of Würzburg in 1812, wrote tutors for most instruments. His *Fagott Schule* (1810/11) borrowed from Ozi, but included much original material.[95] The author advised the beginner to start with a used, even a 'worn-out' instrument rather than a new one: 'the first speaks more easily, being well blown-in, and one is thus not in danger of finding tones fading [breaking] so easily, as with a new one. Furthermore, the wood cracks or shrinks more easily with a new instrument, especially if it is made of boxwood.' If the bassoonist needs to tune his bassoon to a lower pitch, he can avail himself of a longer crook, or better, a longer wing joint. Some bassoons, Fröhlich noted, had three wing joints and three crooks. Many bassoons then had four keys, while some also had Eb2 and F#2. Only 'the newest, most complete bassoons have high A4 and C5 keys'.[96]

Fröhlich compared the bassoon's utterance to both 'a beautifully full tenor voice' and, in its low register, to a majestic bass voice, 'able to express the most elevated feelings'. He advised the advanced student to practice scales in thirds, fourths, and fifths, as outlined in vocal methods.[97] Fröhlich recognized two styles of articulation: slurred and staccato.[98] He took equal temperament as a given, counseling the bassoonist to practice 'singing' opera arias and other vocal music in all keys, especially difficult ones.[99]

Fröhlich showed multiple fingering possibilities (*Kunstgriffen*) for the average bassoon, which could improve dull or bad tones. 'The table is intended for the Dresden bassoon so common among us, yet other fingerings, including those in the Parisian bassoon method [Ozi], are also given'. His prose specified further alternate or basic fingerings up to D#5.[100]

Fröhlich again called for an oblique embouchure. In ascending, the players should draw the lips in a bit, giving them more force to produce the tones; in descending, conversely, a certain slackness of the lips is called for.[101] His 1810 instructions for reed making showed two different finished reeds, one 'after the model of the Parisian bassoon method [Ozi]', the other shorter of both tube and blade, and of about the same breadth as the 'Parisian' model. He recommended a form (template or shaper) of parchment, brass, or cardboard.[102] In Fröhlich's second treatise of 1829, the finished reeds appear strikingly narrower at the throat. They also have a third wire at the butt, rather than the thread binding shown in 1810.

The newly formed reed, after removal from the mandrel, was held inverted with the tip against the maker's palm for scraping. The adequacy of the scraping was first judged by the crowing (*Erzitterung*); only later was the reed tried on the bassoon. It was smoothed, if necessary, with the penknife blade and/or sandpaper.[103] In both works, Fröhlich, like Ozi, advised that the tip aperture could be adjusted by compressing the wires; he recommended that the wires be oval, not flat. In 1810, the blade portions of the work piece (reed-to-be) were gouged thinner than the tube portions, but in 1829 they were uniform, a surprisingly thick 3 lignes (3.3 mm, or about one-quarter inch). If a reed has become old and weak, Fröhlich recommended that a line (1/12 inch) be cut from the tip, to strengthen and improve it.

Fröhlich's already high opinion of the bassoon's powers had only increased by the writing of his second treatise in 1829. The bassoon was able, he wrote, to project 'the worthy, the virile, the solemn, the great, the sublime, composure, mildness, intimacy, emotion, longing, heartfulness, reverence, and soulful ardour'. He also noted the bright/dark (chiaroscuro) of its tones and its ability to create dark, gloomy musical pictures.[104] It has 'a soulful song, developed on a golden ladder of beautifully cultivated tones'.[105]

Two German bassoon soloists, famed in their time, predated the methods of Ozi and Fröhlich. Georg Wenzel Ritter (1748–1808) was playing at Mannheim in 1777, where he met Mozart. In 1778, Ritter moved to Paris, where Mozart wrote his *Sinfonie concertante*, K. 297b, for Ritter and three other Mannheim wind players.[106] Later serving in Munich, Ritter played the notable obbligato parts in Mozart's *Idomeneo*. He joined the Royal Prussian Kapelle in Berlin, 1788, receiving an exceptional salary and praise from Dittersdorf, Michael Kelly, and the *AmZ* for his elegance and tenderness of tone. While in Berlin, he taught Friedrich Brandt and Carl Bärmann.

Franz Anton Pfeiffer (1752–87) studied with Felix Rheiner in Munich c.1772. He was a principal or soloist at the courts of Mainz (1778–83) and Mecklenburg-Schwerin (1783–7). 'By the time of his death he was playing a bassoon that included an octave key and also a hand-rest.' Pfeiffer was apparently able to play multiphonics in 1776.[107] Two 'anonymous' works from the Schwerin court are pastiches of compositions by Pfeiffer and the composer Carl Stamitz (whom Pfeiffer had known since the 1760s). The works – a sonata in F (Mus 517) for bassoon and cello and a quartet for bassoon and strings – draw on bassoon concertos by Stamitz (who wrote at least seven) and Pfeiffer, and on chamber works with strings by both composers.[108] Forkel, writing in the *Musikalischer Almanach* 1782–4, employed his favored simile of light and shade to praise Pfeiffer.[109] According to Rhodes:

> . . . two types of tone seem to have existed side by side during the late eighteenth century, with public opinion divided as to which represented the 'true' bassoon sound. Ironically, both Rheiner and Pfeiffer were criticised for playing with the one sound or the other – Rheiner the more harsh, blustering tone, Pfeiffer the sweet, round, full tone that some found dull.[110]

Carl Bärmann, first bassoonist of the Royal Prussian Orchestra (Berlin), wrote an article in the *AmZ* in 1820. He again held up the singer's art as a model:

[T]his very instrument of ours comes the nearest to the human voice … during my six months stay at Naples in 1807, I chose the excellent composer and singing master Mosca as a teacher, who gave me the most excellent suitable instruction possible for it, as he rehearsed with me the most difficult recitative and aria on the bassoon and he accompanied me on the clavier. …

Bärmann also remarked that the bassoon's reed requires soft cane, while the oboe and clarinet required hard cane. The reed 'can be made a little rough at the opening with a small English file, whereby the tone becomes velvety'.[111] Reeds of Bärmann, narrow at the throat and with the tip roughened, possibly reflected the style of Ritter, his teacher. Griswold suggested that Bärmann was the source of the reeds pictured by Fröhlich in 1829.[112]

Christoph Gottlieb Schwarz (1768–1829), the son of a famous bassoonist (Andreas Gottlieb Schwarz), was a pupil of Ritter, and Barmann's colleague in the Berlin Kapelle. In 1823, he wrote a long letter to an amateur player who had studied with him. Schwarz had chosen a bassoon for the student – from 'among hundreds', an older one by Kirst, who had died in 1806 – and two sample reeds. He included specific advice on adjusting reeds, posture, fingering and tone production.[113] Schwarz and three colleagues in 1824 performed a bassoon quartet – among the earliest known for equal voices – composed by Georg Abraham Schneider.[114]

In contrast to the highly refined technique evident in writings by Fröhlich, Bärmann, and Schwarz, the workaday bassoonist of the time probably expected much less from his instrument. 'Already from the beginning of the 1820s, a weakness of orchestral bassoonists is tolerated; a good and strong tone is rare.' In 1822, a correspondent recommended strengthening the bassoons with a serpent in large orchestras.[115] Sundelin's orchestration manual for military musicians (1828) gave the bassoon's range as only D2 to G4.[116]

Updating the baroque-era oboe band in the Prussian military, Frederick the Great in 1763 specified an octet of two each of clarinets, oboes, horns, and bassoons. The director (by 1786) was the bassoonist Friedrich Antoni (c.1755–1830) who taught Bärmann and Georg Friedrich Brandt (1773-1836), both later famed soloists.[117] After studies with Ritter in Berlin, Brandt served at Schwerin, where the reigning duke's favorite instrument was the bassoon.[118] Following in the steps of both Rheiner and Ritter, he later entered the Bavarian Hofkapelle.[119]

In an era when both courts and regiments were often sponsored by nobles, harmonie musicians sometimes mixed military and civilian service.[120]

[I]n many areas military bandsmen were not actually soldiers, but were civilian musicians contractually attached to a regiment. … Furthermore, many harmonie musicians had previously served in military bands where they learned the professional skills which earned them places in Harmonien. …[121]

The harmonie at the Mecklenburg-Schwerin court, Ludwigslust, existed from 1798 until it was dissolved in 1839, by that time an anachronism. 'The musicians wore a green hunting livery, and they were especially active during the summer months when the duke and his entourage went to the coastal resort of Deberan for the annual "Badezeit".'[122]

Germany: Repertory

G. F. Brandt gave the first known performance of Carl Maria von Weber's concerto for bassoon (1811; op. 75; J. 127) in Prague, 1813. Once again, a critic compared the bassoon to a human voice:

> ... there is a sense here of the bassoon presented as a dramatic character – indeed, one seemingly on the brink of words at the start of the Adagio. ... As well as the cavernous mystery in the instrument's tone, Weber also discovers tenderness and dignity shot with a curious pathos. ... Although he uses the potentially comic contrast between high and very low registers, he does so sparingly, and always to make a musical point. ...

Weber revised the concerto, mostly the first movement, in Dresden in 1822.[123] Weber had written his Andante and Hungarian Rondo for his brother Fritz, a violist, in 1809; in 1813 he arranged it at Brandt's request, adding three measures to the opening Andante. Brandt played the revised work in Prague 1814; the bassoon version was published 1816.[124]

Weber turned to the bassoon at a crucial moment in the finale of *Der Freischütz* (1821), where at m 169, a brief exposed solo in the bassoon's tenor register announces the character's (Max) feelings of contrition even before he sings.[125] J. J. Reichardt, who served as Kapellmeister to the Prussian court at Berlin, scored for bassoon obbligato in several of his operas, 1789–1808. Stockigt cited other obbligato arias from Weber's *Euryanthe, Peter Schmoll*, and *Silvana*, and others from sacred works by Dittersdorf, Mysliveček, and Winter.[126]

The Bohemian Josef Mysliveček wrote wind octets, probably in Munich, 1777–8, as well as smaller chamber works including bassoon. Chamber works for bassoon with strings include three quartets for bassoon and strings by Danzi, a trio with violin and piano (among other works) by Peter von Winter, and quintets by J. E. Brandl, some of these also with piano. Danzi and Winter each wrote several bassoon concertos, as did Antonio Rosetti.

All of these three composers, like C. P. E. Bach, wrote much music for harmonie ensemble. Later works for harmonie in Germany include Spohr's Notturno and Janissary Music, op. 34; Weber's five pieces and 'Heil dir, Sappho', with chorus; and Mendelssohn's Overture and Trauermarsch.

Austria and Central Europe

In Vienna, craft guilds still held power. Some bassoon makers were guild members or *Bürger*, including Martin Lempp, Tauber, Scholl, Ehrlich, and Merklein. Non-members, called *Störer*, included the bassoon makers Rocko Baur, Friedrich Lempp, Jakob Baur, Theodor Lotz, and Raymund Grießbacher I. Members or not, makers were sometimes granted a special imperial license as 'hofbefreite' or 'k.k. Hofinstrumentmacher', including Baur (from 1780), Lotz (1788), Martin Lempp, and Griesbacher (both 1800).[127] (The prefix 'k.k.' signified imperial-royal status.)

Friedrich Lempp made woodwind instruments for various imperial-royal army regiments beginning in 1755. But he claimed in 1768 that 'since there was virtually no one else in [Lower Austria] who made bassoons and other woodwinds for the use of the common people, these instruments had to be imported from Saxony and other foreign lands'. Registered only as a musical performer in the suburbs, Lempp faced opposition from the joiners' guild. He was granted a protective license, however, partly because he belonged to the Nicolai Brotherhood, a sort of musicians' union.[128] In 1776 Lempp invited customers to specify Viennese pitch, Kammerton, or French pitch, or to send him a tuning fork.[129] His bassoons cost from 18 to 54 florins, depending on the quality of the wood, up to 27 florins for figured maple, but twice as much for boxwood. A replacement bassoon wing joint cost 6 florins in 1781.[130] Finished bassoon reeds cost 10 kreutzer apiece.

Haydn, as Vice-Kapellmeister for the Esterházy court, was responsible for purchasing instruments, including bassoons and reeds. A receipt is preserved, countersigned by Haydn and the maker Mathias Rocko Baur, who supplied bassoons to the Esterházy court in 1771.[131] A surviving bassoon by Rocko Baur has turned beads at either end of the wing épaule, a vestige of the older style practiced by Deper and others.[132] He also supplied reeds to the court, usually a few dozen per year. But during one two-month period (May and June 1769), he supplied forty-eight reeds.[133] Rocko Baur's successor was his son-in-law Jakob Baur, who also supplied reeds to the Esterházy court.[134] In his shop, *Zum goldenen Fagott*, Baur made bassoons and offered music for nine-part harmonie ensemble.[135] A surviving 5–6 key bassoon by Baur has block-mounted keys and a bell resembling the Saxon style.[136]

Leopold Prochaska was a bassoonist at the Schwarzenberg Court in Vienna. Accounts show that reeds were ordered for Prochaska in 1781, cane for reed making in 1783, and in 1790 a bassoon from Anton Lotz, a maker in Pressburg (Bratislava).[137] Theodor Lotz, probably a relative, was active in Vienna from 1785 as a bassoon maker and contra player. Friedrich Hammig, active in Vienna from 1791, offered bassoons and their reeds, among other woodwinds.[138]

Three bassoon makers active in Vienna were born in Hungary. Caspar Tauber in 1807 provided the court bassoonist Wenzel Mattuschek with two bassoons, each with two wing joints and three crooks; both leather bags and custom hardwood cases were included.[139] Stephan Koch in 1807 was 'at the sign of the golden bassoon'. He and Johan Ziegler each offered tuning slides on the wing joints of their bassoons.[140] In 1827 Ziegler sold the imperial Hofkapelle two bassoons 'with all important keys' and cases; 'the bassoons must match the organ pitch of the Hofkapelle and must have "k.k. Hofkapelle Instrument" branded on the bell'.[141] Schöllnast, born in Hungary, was active in Pressburg (Bratislava).[142] Other makers of the early nineteenth century included Merklein (Vienna), Reiha (Prague), Ruschka (Prague), F. Pitschmann (Arnsdorf), Carl Doke (Linz), and Wussinger (Klagenfurt).[143]

On Central European bassoons of this period, the bell often had an inverted taper, and a brass ring decorating the mouth. Seven keys were typical, with the possible addition of a second wing key and middle C#3/C#4 key for RT. The larger key flaps were often spade-shaped, the smaller ones lozenge- or oval-shaped. There was often an integral or added guard for the F-key flap.[144]

Austria and Central Europe: Players and pedagogy

Carl Schiringer was a double-bass player and bassoonist under Haydn at the Esterházy court.[145] Under a renewable annual contract, he received numerous benefits but was precluded from working elsewhere. This economic model of a paternalistic Hofkapelle was declining in Vienna meanwhile, in favor of a system that included elements of free enterprise.[146]

Many bassoon players, makers (Ehrlich) and composers of this period were Bohemians or Moravians. A culture of bassoon playing was long established, and since 1723 Bohemians had been Habsburg subjects, free to move about the empire in search of musical employment. In a biographical study of approximately 800 bassoonists born before 1825, Hodges documented that 83 or more were Bohemians. Beginning in 1772, the imperial Kapellmeister Leopold Gassman (himself a Bohemian) hired numerous other Bohemians, including the bassoonists Drobnal, Czerwenka, Kauzner, and Sedlaczek. Before joining the Kapelle in 1807, Mattuschek had played in the premieres of Beethoven's quintet, op. 16 (1797, with the composer at the piano) and septet, op. 20 (1800).[147]

Hundreds of surviving works featuring bassoon – harmonie music, concertantes, sonatas, etc. – show the enthusiasm of Bohemian and Moravian composers for the instrument and its woodwind brethren. Among these were Druschetzky (more than 200 works for harmonie ensemble, according to Hellyer), F. X. Dušek, Rosetti, Carl Stamitz, Mysliveček, Giovanni Punto (Stich), J. B. Vanhal, Gassmann, Leopold Kozeluch, Franz Krommer, and Antoine Reicha.[148]

August Mittag, after bassoon study with the Dresden Hofkapelle players Kummer and Schmidt, became a regimental Kapellmeister in Dresden. He moved in 1820 to Vienna, teaching at the conservatorium from 1821, and played first bassoon in the Hofkapelle from 1824. Mittag was the bassoonist of the Harmonie-Quintett, founded in Vienna in 1821. Modeled on the Reicha Quintet of Paris, they performed the twenty-four quintets of Reicha in subscription concerts, receiving great applause.[149] At the Vienna conservatorium Mittag at first used German translations of Ozi 1803, as did his counterpart at the Graz Conservatorium, Michael Delange.[150] Early professors of bassoon at the Prague Conservatory included Gabriel Rausch (c.1810–2) and Josef Bettlach (1812–37).[151]

Austria and Central Europe: Repertory

The bassoon at first served Gluck, like other Neapolitan-trained composers, mostly to strengthen the bass line, although Stockigt noted arias with bassoon obbligato as early as *La Danza* (1755). In Gluck's reform operas, it received more varied assignments. In the Elysian scenes of Orfeo (1762), the bassoon plays an important, sometimes soloistic role in expressing the woeful and wistful feelings of Orpheus, employing the expressive sound of the high range (to G4); in the last scene of the work the bassoon is almost completely in unison with the violas; it echoes the oboes in *Orfeo* (iii, 1). The bassoon is coupled with the chalumeaux to evoke a sylvan gloom and ghastly voices of subterranean gods (*Alceste*, ii, 2). Gluck used its colour to express gloom and melancholy in the ballet *Don Juan* (no. 21, exit of the statue).[152]

The novel timbre of the bassoon's tenor voice seems to have led composers in stages to a new orchestral scoring technique. In an early example – Haydn's symphony no. 7 (1761), i – the bassoon doubles the second violins at the lower octave in brief passages. A generation later, in Mozart's 1786 score to *The Marriage of Figaro*, the technique is pervasive, beginning with the A-major theme of the overture, cited above. As the curtain rises, the first bassoon and first violins play at the fifteenth as they foreshadow Figaro's melody (Ex. 5.1). In the aria no. 12, Susanna and the first violins sing in unison, doubled by the first bassoon an octave lower.

In these and countless other works, the bassoon's tenor voice assumed a discreet but crucial role in creating the three-dimensional feel of Viennese classical orchestration. Doubling the violin at the lower octave was part of the essential Viennese Classic sound – a musical pattern not in only one octave, but in two or often three, called by some authors the 'Wiener unisono'.[153]

Ex. 5.1.   Mozart, *Le Nozze di Figaro*, no. 2, 'Se a caso madama', opening (1786).

The subtle effect of chiaroscuro, added to melodies played by the violin, flute, oboe, or clarinet (or sometimes doubling a singer's voice), conjured an aura of spot-lit intensity. In making this choice, composers bypassed the horn, which at the time was less agile. They apparently preferred the bassoon's creamy tenor to the viola or cello, two voices of the string choir already at work in the orchestral tutti. This octave doubling long remained a favorite tool in the orchestrator's kit, coloring the voices of Mahler, Shostakovich, and other composers in the western mainstream.

Two bassoon parts were the rule in Haydn's symphonies by 1774. His sinfonia concertante (first performed London, 1792) included the bassoon as one of four soloists. (A thematic catalogue of Haydn's works, prepared in 1803–4 by Elßler, documented a bassoon concerto, now lost.) In 1796, Haydn's sacred music ensemble for the Esterházy palace and the Bergkirche included only one wind player – a bassoonist – among thirteen singers and instrumentalists.[154] Haydn wrote to A4 in several works and to Bb4 in Symphony no. 98 (i, iii). His bassoon boosts the violas in Symphony no. 104 and impersonates the biblical Adam in *The Creation*, III. Haydn's operas include four arias with bassoon obbligato.[155] Works for harmonie ensemble range from 1760 to Haydn's last completed composition, the *Hungarischer National Marsch* (1802). Haydn prepared his own harmonie arrangement of the slow movement of his Symphony no. 100.[156]

From 1776 to 1778, Raymund Griesbacher played clarinet and basset horn under Haydn. In 1800 he was appointed a Viennese court maker of brass and woodwind instruments, succeeded by his son (active until 1846); one eight-key bassoon bearing the mark survives. The elder Griesbacher, also a bassoonist, was possibly the dedicatee of Hummel's Concerto in F for bassoon (c.1805).[157] J. N. Hummel, who served alongside Haydn as concertmaster at the Esterházy Court from 1804 to 1811, also composed an octet and three military marches for harmonie ensemble.

Like Haydn, Mozart drew upon the bassoon as an irreplaceable orchestral color and a frequent contributor of solo lines. More than 150 of his works specify bassoon, and it probably doubled the bass line in others. Mozart's last three Masses incorporate two bassoon parts, including the haunting opening of the Requiem and an important obbligato in the Mass in C minor. All his operas written in 1770 and later have two written bassoon parts. In a survey of Mozart's vocal works, Stockigt counted nineteen arias with bassoon obbligatos. Ward observed of Mozart:

> With clarinets he liked his bassoons to have warmth and steady tone, but with the flute he made it sound more hollow, restless and perhaps more agile. The instruments together rarely sound peaceful. . . . [In] the uncommon partnership between violas and bassoons . . . Mozart's bassoons are unusually dark in tone-colouring and have an air of persuasive dignity utterly unlike their timbre with oboes or clarinets.[158]

In a letter to his father, Mozart specified ten basses, eight cellos, and six bassoons for the symphony K. 338.[159] Two written bassoon parts are standard in his symphonies beginning in 1778, and in his piano concertos beginning in 1784.

Mozart's Concerto for Bassoon, K. 191 (186e), was written for the Salzburg court in the spring of 1774. It thus predates all but two of his surviving authentic concertos for any instrument. Waterhouse conjectured that Johann Hofer (c.1745–81), the youngest of three bassoonists in the Salzburg Kapelle, might have been the first performer.[160] Sadie saw in the concerto 'Mozart's brilliant assumption of a style to exploit the instrument's special qualities – its contrasts of register, its staccato, its latent eloquence'. Girdlestone found wit, *galanterie*, and virtuosity. Ward saw in the bassoon concerto 'Mozart's answer to the instrument's critics':

> We hear the bassoon in all its moods, and are moved to laughter and to tears almost imperceptibly. . . . [T]he andante is one of Mozart's most touching pieces, endowed with a quite heartrending pathos and beauty. . . . [T]he bassoon, with its quality of universal humanity, is capable of expressing in purest sound all the emotions we express but crudely in words.[161]

If Ward's words ring familiar, it is because she was echoing the views of Cugnier, Ozi, and Fröhlich, as well as Warrack (and Sadie again, below): its tessitura and flexibility allow the bassoon to approach human speech – its wordless language lends it universality. Except for references to the bassoon's male character (tenor and bass), much the same was said of the eighteenth-century oboe.

K. Anh. 230, a concerto in F for bassoon, is a doubtful work, according to Mozart scholars. Attributed to Mozart by Max Seiffert in 1934 on purely stylistic grounds, it was later reattributed to Devienne, but a Devienne scholar rejected that attribution, leaving it an orphan at present.[162] Three other bassoon concertos allegedly by Mozart have never been traced.[163] The Sinfonia concertante, K. 297b, attributed to Mozart, is a derivative work, the shadow of a vanished original. Mozart's letters reveal that in 1778, while in Paris, he composed a *sinfonie concertante* for flute, oboe, horn and bassoon (Ritter), intended for performance at the Concert Spirituel. But the outsider Mozart was the victim of a Parisian intrigue: a concertante by Cambini, the local insider, was performed instead. Mozart, bitterly disappointed, sought to conceal the bad news from his father. An anonymous composer of c.1820–30 recomposed the lost, never-performed orchestral score on the basis of four surviving solo parts. This version is usually heard, although Robert Levin has published a reconstruction of the original version.[164]

Among the several private harmonie ensembles formed in Vienna during the 1780s was the kaiserlich-königliche Harmonie, founded in 1782 by Emperor Joseph II.[165] For this ensemble, which included the bassoonists Kauzner, Drobnal, and possibly Steiner, Mozart composed his serenades K. 361, 375, and 388. In order to preserve his publication rights, Mozart prepared his own harmonie version of *Die Entführung aus dem Serail* in 1782, immediately after the operatic version was complete, adding much new music.[166]

In 1784 Mozart composed a quintet in elevated style for keyboard, oboe, clarinet, horn, and bassoon. Sadie, himself a onetime clarinetist, conceded:

> the limited capacities of the wind instruments . . . to blend or to sustain a prolonged line, and the risk of their sound beginning to cloy. Mozart designed his melodic

material accordingly, casting it in short phrases which create and resolve tensions at a rapid rate. The result is a work of exceptional mastery and inventiveness. . . .[167]

Mozart wrote to his father that the quintet 'was applauded extraordinarily; I myself consider it the best work I have composed in my life. . . . I only wish you could have heard it.'[168]

In the Vienna of Beethoven's time two bassoons were present in most opera and symphony orchestras. The Bohemian bassoonist Valentin Czejka (1769–p1834) was the original player of many of Beethoven's bassoon parts, including the violin concerto (ii), where the bassoon assumes the top voice in a choir of violas and cellos, accompanying the solo violin; and (iii), where the bassoon alternates the rondo melodies with the solo violin. Czejka also played in symphonies 4, 5, 6, and 8, the Choral Fantasy, and *Fidelio*.[169] In the last, Beethoven pressed the bassoon into service as an ad hoc hornist in Leonore's recitative and aria 'Ach, brich noch nicht . . . Komm, Hoffnung'. Drawing on the bassoon's acoustical similarity to the horn's sound, Beethoven assigned it the highest and most chromatic part in the four-part obbligato, 'to give the effect of an almost impossibly agile and chromatic horn quartet'[170] (Ex. 5.2). A similar

Ex. 5.2. Beethoven, *Fidelio*, no. 9, 'Ach, brich noch nicht . . . Komm, Hoffnung', excerpt (1806). The bassoon plays the top stave above a trio of horns.

effect is employed in the trio of Beethoven's Symphony no. 7 and in Mendelssohn's Symphony no. 4 (iii). Beethoven used the two bassoons to replace the horns in his Symphony no. 3 (i), at the second subject.

Beethoven's works for harmonie ensemble include the Octet, op. 103; the Rondino, WoO 25, originally intended as a finale to the octet; and a sextet, op. 71. Masonic works include a march in B♭ and the *Bundeslied*, op. 122, set to a Masonic text by Goethe. Beethoven's *Ruins of Athens* music, no. 6, opposes a stage harmonie to the orchestral harmonie. The composer authorized harmonie arrangements of his Symphony no. 7 and *Fidelio*. Other works include the Trio in G, WoO 37, for flute, bassoon, and piano, and the incomplete Quintet in E♭ for oboe, bassoon, and three horns, HV 19.

Beethoven took an interest in the progress of instrument making. For a conversation in September 1825, he summoned the bassoonist August Mittag, who told Beethoven that the keys of A and E were now easier to navigate on Schott bassoons, as improved by Gottfried Weber and Carl Almenräder. Beethoven, who had read Weber's article in *Cäcilia*, twice asked Schott (his own publisher) to send him one of the improved 19-key bassoons (see chapter 6).[171] There is no evidence that he received the bassoon. In 1826 Mittag returned for a second chat, but Beethoven wrote no further works involving bassoon, so the information had no practical result.

Schubert wrote works for harmonie ensemble in 1811 (Six Minuets, D. 2d; formerly D. 995) and 1813 (the Octet, D. 71, and the Wind Nonet, 'Eine kleine Trauermusik', D. 79). Mittag played in the premiere of Schubert's octet for winds and strings, D. 803, which was commissioned in 1824 as a companion piece to the Beethoven septet.

The Habsburgs had brought an end to Ottoman rule in Vienna with a victory over the Turks in 1683. As the centenary approached in 1783, a fashion for 'Turkish' or 'Janissary' music swept over Vienna. By the 1780s a 'Turkish band' in Europe was usually one of European instruments with added percussion and a piccolo; a band reported in Vienna in 1796 included oboes, bassoons, horns, and clarinets, a trumpet, a triangle, a piccolo, a very large drum, an ordinary drum, and a pair of cymbals'.[172] Beethoven in 1809–16 wrote marches and other pieces for Türkische Musik.[173]

A 'Fagott stop' was included on some fortepianos made in Vienna between about 1795 and 1830. Pieces of paper or parchment buzzing against the lower strings supposedly produced a bassoon-like timbre.[174] The bassoon was popular enough in Vienna to figure in a hit singspiel, *Die Zauberzither oder Kaspar der Fagottist*, by Wenzel Müller (1791). The work, which includes obbligato bassoon in two arias and a duet, was revived in Cologne in 2004.[175]

The British Isles

Early in this era, many English bassoons were outwardly similar to their baroque predecessors. Examples in the Waterhouse collection by Gedney, Richard Millhouse, and William Milhouse have reverse-conical bell bores, while a Kusder bassoon has a choke bore. After a narrow-waisted bell later came into fashion, the dramatic flare of the bell opening sometimes led still to an old-fashioned choke (as in a bassoon by Goulding, Wood & Co. in the Waterhouse collection). Bodies were often heavier than

on contemporary French bassoons. The A♭ tone hole was often sited high on the bore, as in the baroque era. The E♭ key, if present, was usually located to the left of the D key, rather than on the right, as French makers placed it (Ill. 33).

The bassoonist John Miller assisted the maker Caleb Gedney in testing bassoons in 1754; after Gedney's death in 1769, he became guardian for Gedney's two daughters. According to a news-paper advertisement from 1769, the daughters 'were brought up in the business, and finished most of the instruments for some years, in their father's lifetime'. As guardian, Miller supervised their work in making 'all kinds of musical wind instruments'.[176]

By mid-century provincial bassoon makers were active, including Richard Millhouse of Newark and John Blockley of Ullesthorpe.[177] Henry John Muraeus had a shop in London at 'the Bassoon, Two Flutes, and Hautboy', 1759–66. Bassoons for the military market were advertised by John Mason (1778); Longman and Broderip (1790); William Milhouse (1791); and George Astor (1795-9).[178] In the 1790s at least three London makers – John Köhler; George Astor; and Goulding, Phipps, and D'Almaine – offered 'trumpet tops' for bassoon. These were trumpet-like brass bells targeted to the military market. A commentator observed in 1821: 'When the common wooden nozle [*sic*], or top, is exchanged for a copper trumpet, or bell-mouth, the sounds are much reinforced, and partake some-thing of the intonation of the horn.' In one order, the buyer asked that wooden or 'common tops' also be supplied for occasional use, 'which will render them fit for concerts or church music when wanted'.[179]

Other London-based bassoon makers of the classical period included Bilton, Cahusac, Gerock, Parker, and Wood.[180] Many London bassoon makers bought keys and ferrules from John Hale, a specialist key maker, whose initials I. H. were often stamped on the underside. Another key maker in London is known only by the mark 'G'.

33. Bassoon by Willis & Goodlad, London, c.1825. Tony Bingham.

The British Isles: Players and pedagogy

Ernst Eichner, a second-generation bassoonist who also served as concertmaster at Zweibrücken, toured as a bassoon soloist from 1767. In London during the spring of 1773, he appeared in twelve of the Bach-Abel concerts. He spent his last years as a bassoonist in the Prussian Hofkapelle. He wrote six concertos for bassoon, published 1778–84, and several works for harmonie ensemble.[181] Other German-born bassoonists who sojourned in London or emigrated there included A. G. Schwarz, his son Christian Gottlieb Schwarz, and George Frederick Schubert.

Leopold Mozart took his children Nannerl and Wolfgang to visit Ranelagh Gardens, London, in 1764. In a letter, he described a well-lit hall where, on three nights a week, an orchestra played from 7 until 10, followed by one or two hours of music by two clarinets, horn, and bassoon.[182] He also visited Vauxhall Gardens, where the bassoon figured in similar entertainment music nearly thirty years later. During forty trio appearances at Vauxhall Gardens in May–August 1791, the English bassoonist Jeremiah Parkinson played six clarinet and bassoon duets with the Bohemian clarinetist Franz Dworschack.[183]

London, in contrast to Esterhazy and Vienna, had evolved a free-market system of employment for musicians. A bassoonist might earn a living by combining engagements at theaters, pleasure gardens, concert societies, and royal musical ensembles. Long-term contracts and benefits beyond salary were not generally provided.[184] James Holmes, engaged for the Salomon Concerts, London, in 1802, was the original soloist in Haydn's Sinfonia Concertante. His successor as preeminent freelance bassoonist in London was John Mackintosh.[185] The first bassoon professor at the Royal Academy of Music, c.1820–5, Mackintosh also performed the Reicha wind quintets in London during 1824–5.[186]

John Thomson played bassoon, along with two oboes and four fiddles, for functions of the Old Edinburgh Club, 1776. 'These musicians were constantly playing at concerts, dances, and other gatherings in Edinburgh.'[187]

The British Isles: Repertory

From 1765 to 1781, J. C. Bach and Carl Friedrich Abel presented a series of subscription concerts in London. Included were symphonies and symphonies concertantes, including four of Bach's own concertantes for bassoon and other winds.[188] Bach also wrote two concertos for solo bassoon, as well as five arias and three Vauxhall songs with bassoon obbligato.[189]

In the Royal Regiment of Artillery, in 1764, each troop had one mounted trumpet player; dismounted, the players formed 'a band of music, consisting of two French horns, two clarinets and two bassoons'.[190] J. C. Bach composed his four symphonies (1775–81), and six sinfonien for an English military band of two clarinets, two horns, and one bassoon part. Such works were possibly played at Vauxhall or other entertainment gardens.

Among Capell Bond's six concertos (London, 1766), no. 6 is scored for solo bassoon. Stockigt noted two arias by Stephen Storace with bassoon obbligato.[191]

During the 1760s Henry Hargrave published four concertos for solo bassoon and two more for solo oboe and bassoon. Duos for bassoons were published in London by Johann Schobert (d. 1767). William Paxton published 'Six Easy Solos' for bassoon or cello and keyboard in 1780.

After the Puritan revolution left most English churches without organs, a bassoon (sometimes with other instruments) was used to accompany choir (quire) or congregational singing. Church bassoonists were documented in Sussex, Northamptonshire, and Shropshire. Flourishing from about 1730 to 1880, the so-called West Gallery music reached its fullest currency between about 1780 and 1840.[192] The volunteer players catered to all musical needs of their villages.[193]

Other European countries

By around 1750, the community musicians of Antwerp were hired by competition to form a sextet of oboes, clarinets, and bassoons.[194] At Liège, when a royal school of music was founded in 1827, the professor of bassoon was Joseph Ferdinand Bacha, a native of the town. C. J. J. Tuerlinckx worked from age nine in the family's woodwind and brass workshop in Malines, Belgium, succeeding his father in 1827. Also a composer and scientist, he played bassoon and other woodwinds.[195]

A surviving bassoon by Wilhelmus Wyne of Nijmegen (d. 1816) has both a wooden bell and a trumpet bell. The maker Ludwig Embach (fl. Amsterdam, 1820–44) exhibited a fourteen-key bassoon in Haarlem in 1824.

Many bassoons and contrabassoons that survive in Italian collections are Austrian instruments, reflecting the Habsburg dominion over northern Italy until c.1860. The Bohemian bassoonist Valentin Czejka in 1822 became the bandmaster for an Austrian regiment stationed in Naples.[196]

Pressure from the guilds of turners and joiners apparently discouraged the making of woodwinds in Venice during the later eighteenth century. Andrea Fornari, officially authorized to make woodwind instruments there in 1792, listed a 'fagotto corista' among instruments 'of my own invention, all improved'.[197] Bassoons survive by Berti and Magazzari (both of Bologna), Biglioni (Rome), Piana (Milan), Guglielminetti (Novara), and Palanca (Turin).[198]

Gaetano Grossi (c.1750–1807), bassoonist in the Regia orchestra of Parma under the maestro Alessandro Rolla, was possibly the original performer of Rolla's bassoon concerto and chamber works involving bassoon.[199] Grossi himself composed a concerto and quartets for bassoon.[200] Giovanni Simon Mayr (1763–1845), a German composer of Italian operas long resident in Bergamo, included obbligato bassoon in arias of three operas and an oratorio. He also wrote a bassoon concerto and more than two dozen works for harmonie ensemble; these may have been connected with a school of music he founded in Bergamo in 1805.[201]

From 1809 to 1830, Gaudenzio Lavaria was principal bassoonist at La Scala and the Teatro della Cannobiana. When the Conservatory of Milan was founded in 1808, the teacher of flute, oboe, and bassoon was Giuseppe Buccinelli.[202] In Bologna, Luigi Tartagnini was professor of bassoon at the Liceo musicale in 1813–16.

Rossini wrote unique solos for bassoon in the overtures to *Cenerentola* and *Semiramide*. His early operas *Ciro in Babilonia* (1812) and *Il Signor Bruschino* (1813) include arias with obbligato bassoon. A duet for bassoon and piano by Rossini was performed in Bologna on 19 April 1807.[203] In 1812 Rossini wrote an Andante, Theme, and Variations for wind quartet and a terzetto for bassoon, horn, and piano, now lost. The attribution of a 'concerto da esperimento' (examination piece for the Liceo of Bologna) to Rossini is uncertain, although the attractive work has been published, performed, and recorded under his name.[204]

Stockigt noted arias with bassoon obbligato by Cimarosa, Galuppi, Paër, Paisiello, Righini, Salieri, and Sarti.[205] Best remembered among all such arias is 'Una furtive lagrima' from *l'Elisir d'amore* (1832), in the key of Bb minor, where Donizetti chose the bassoon to set the mournful tone for the tenor singer. Donizetti also wrote a trio for flute, bassoon, and piano; and harmonie music, including a Sinfonia in G Minor (1817), and Three Marches (Turkish), 1835. In 1800 Nicolo Paganini composed three duets for bassoon with violin, among his earliest known works; he later wrote a concertino for bassoon, horn, and orchestra.[206]

Swiss bassoon makers, scattered across northern Switzerland, included Ammann (Alt St. Johann), Fleischmann (Baden), Hirsbrunner (Sumiswald), Kaiser (Zug), Lutz (Wolfhalden), Jeremias Schlegel (Basel), Seelhoffer (Kehrsatz/Bern), Streuli (Horgen), and Sutter (Appenzell).[207] Bassoonists active in Basel included Matuska (1760), Meylan (1760), and Bayer (1778); players in Neuchâtel included Glase (1789), Gaveaux (1790-02), and Nussbaum (1802). Other reported players included Nübe (Lausanne, 1757–1804), Décombaz (Vaud, 1774), Brunette (Chasin, 1797), Haller (Bern, 1804), and Hirzel (Zürich, 1824–8).[208]

French-made bassoons from this period are found in many Iberian collections, but native makers were known. Salvador Xuriach was employed as 'baixo' (player of bassoon or dulcian) at the Barcelona cathedral during the 1780s. A five-key bassoon bearing the mark of the Xuriach family survives, as do two seven-key instruments (one of them incomplete) by Oms of Barcelona.[209] The Spanish or Catalan Juan Bautista Pla, active as an oboist from before 1747, served as a bassoonist at the Portuguese court in 1769–73.[210] Bassoonists active in Lisbon included Bies (c.1800), Calveti (1822), and Martius (1822).[211]

Lorents Nicolaj Berg published a fingering chart (Kristiansand, 1782) for four-key bassoon, labeled 'dulcian'. Two bassoons were reported in a Norwegian regimental band in 1798.[212] Georg Johann Abraham Berwald, uncle of the composer Franz Berwald, was a bassoonist and later a violinist in the Stockholm court orchestra during 1782 to 1800. Over the period 1795–9, he toured as a bassoon soloist in northern European cities; in Leipzig, 1798, he played a bassoon concerto by 'Grenser', probably Johann Friedrich Grenser[213]. Severin Preumayr, a German bassoonist active at Coblenz c.1782, had three bassoonist sons who often performed trios. All served in the royal kapelle of Stockholm during the period 1811–35. One of the Preumayr sons, Frans, married the daughter of the composer Bernhard Crusell, who wrote a virtuosic concerto for Frans.[214] Resident bassoon makers included Finnish-born Peter Apelberg and native-born Friderich Coppy.[215] From 1773, two of the royal chapel bassoonists also served in a military octet. Music by Ernst Hartmann for the play *Balders Dod* (royal theater, 1779–92) called for two bassoons. From 1786, many of the chapel bassoonists were German- or Bohemian-born. Several hailed from Dresden or used bassoons by Dresden makers, including the Grensers. During the years 1800–4, Carl Gottfried Donath performed bassoon concertos by Ozi and Devienne at the royal theater.[216]

In the second movement of his Piano Concerto no. 1 (first performed at the National Theater, Warsaw, 1830), Chopin chose the bassoon to present the lyrical B major theme. The premiere was presumably played by Nicolas Prudent Winnen, the long-time principal bassoonist there, professor at Warsaw conservatory, and son of the Parisian maker of bassoons. Other players active in Poland during this period included Horoszkiewicz, Krause, Mertke, Michalowski, Praetorius, Stankiewicz, and Tokarzewski.[217]

A Franconian bassoonist named Zahn joined the Imperial Chapel at St. Petersburg in 1761, spending twenty years there.[218] The Bohemian bassoonist Anton Bullandt (c.1750–1821) appeared in St. Petersburg from 1780, performing his own opéra-comiques and probably his own works for bassoon. (He composed a bassoon concerto by 1782 and harmonie works by 1785.) Bullandt joined the imperial opera orchestra in 1783. During a dispute with officials over his status in 1784, Bullandt opened a music store, selling keyboard instruments from England, stringed and wind instruments, and sheet music.[219] Meanwhile another bassoonist (probably the Bohemian Johann Anton Sattler) was engaged, but died in 1785. Re-engaged in the court orchestra, Bullandt served until 1801. In 1802, he became a founding member of the St. Petersburg Philharmonic Society, later a director, and in 1821 a pensioner of the society.[220] Other bassoonists active in Russia during the period included Bender, Mendel, Rauner, Reiniger, and Witt.[221] A Russian newspaper advertisement of 1791 offered a serf with musical talents:

> On sale is a very good musician who plays the viola in instrumental music and the bassoon in brass music; he is also a good footman, of a good height, twenty-one years old; price 1,200 roubles.[222]

A bassoon was the sole wind instrument chosen in Bortniansky's synfonie concertante – actually a septet for strings and fortepiano organisé (1790).[223] Glinka's chamber works included a septet for piano and winds (1823) and a *Trio pathétique* for piano, clarinet, and bassoon (1827). Military bands under Tsar Paul I (reigned 1796–1801) reportedly consisted of two clarinets, two horns and bassoon.[224]

The Americas

Early bassoon makers in the English colonies included Gottlieb (David) Wolhaupter (fl. New York, 1761–70) and Joshua Collins, an emigrant from Manchester, England (fl. Annapolis, MD, 1773).[225] London makers of bassoons who advertised in American periodicals included Collier, Gedney, Mason, and Schuchart.[226] In New York, 1787, John Jacob Astor advertised bassoons and other musical instruments from London.[227] Connecticut-born George Catlin advertised bassoons (with plain or trumpet bells) and tenoroons in Hartford, 1803; he exhibited a bassoon in Philadelphia, 1824. His former employee, John Meacham, also made bassoons.[228] Other reported bassoon makers included William Whiteley and Fisher & Metcalf.[229]

Accounts of bassoon playing during the American colonial and federal periods often documented harmonie or chamber ensembles. Early reports included Charleston (1765), Boston (1775), and New York (1779).[230] During the revolutionary war (1776–81), 'both British and American regiments maintained wind bands that gave frequent performances. Following the war, wind bands associated with taverns, coffeehouses, theatres and pleasure gardens played arrangements of theatrical and orchestral works, military pieces, and patriotic songs.'[231] Post-war reports included Providence, RI (1784), and Philadelphia (1786).[232] In 1801–17, five instrumental methods were published in New Hampshire, Massachusetts, New York, and Maine, containing identical fingering charts.[233]

A bassoon was heard in ensemble in New Orleans in 1811. In 1813, a bassoonist and fencing master named Passage 'performed the first bassoon concerto ever heard in New Orleans'. In 1814, 'Passage played a concerto [possibly only a solo], then fought an exhibition duel with another fencing master'.[234]

The United States Marine band in 1800 included one bassoon and one drum, in addition to pairs of oboes, clarinets, and horns.[235] Two distinct bassoon parts were present in fourteen *Parthien* (sextets) by the European-trained Moravian composer David Moritz Michael (fl. Bethlehem and Nazareth, PA, 1795–1815) and in William Webb's Grand Military Divertimentos (Philadelphia, c.1828).[236]

A bassoon was played in a small orchestra at the Teatro de la Ranchería in Buenos Aires, Argentina, 1783–92.[237] Jerónimo Clarach, a Spanish flutist employed there, taught 'fagot' to a mulatto servant in 1787.[238] A regimental band in Bogotá, Colombia, in 1784 probably included bassoons; its conductor, Pedro Carricarte, also directed an ensemble containing a bassoon.[239] In Brazil, Ignácio Parreira (Parreryras Neves) composed funeral music in memory of Don Pedro III (d. 1786) for an orchestra including two bassoons. Two bassoonists associated with the composer in 1787 were Luiz José da Costa and Joaquim Joze do Amaral.[240] Kaiser Don Pedro I (1798–1834) – emperor of Brazil, later king of Portugal, and himself a bassoonist – wrote Masonic choruses for male voices and military musique (harmonie ensemble).[241]

Chapter 6

The scientific bassoon, c.1830–1900

From the dawn of the symphonic era, difficult moments for bassoonists often came in transitional or developmental passages, when short motives were tossed from one woodwind to another, sometimes in extreme keys, or with chromatic alterations. Composers asked the bassoon to match the higher-pitched woodwinds in volume and fluency, in almost every tonality. The old cross-fingerings, which had sufficed in an older musical style, were less suited to the newer musical demands.[1] The more forward-looking romantic composers, including Berlioz and Wagner, subscribed to a new aesthetic, under which listeners were to be awed and even overwhelmed by larger and more aggressive orchestras, heard in larger and larger concert rooms. Yet solo passages within symphonic works were still scored for single woodwind players. As composers increasingly exploited the bassoon's higher register, players were increasingly reliant on the bassoon's higher modes of tone production, which had inherent weaknesses of intonation and loudness. The increasingly cumbersome fingerings necessary for pitch correction and maximal resonance in the tenor register made life difficult for the first bassoonists. Makers pursued varied stratagems in their attempts to remedy these shortcomings, often drawing on new theoretical insights into musical acoustics. The result was the broadest variety of bassoon designs ever to co-exist. National preferences of instrument and performance practice were increasingly evident, even as players continued international touring and emigration.

Beginning in Paris, 1806, woodwinds (among other musical instruments) were exhibited and sold at international and 'world' trade exhibitions, to both wholesale and retail buyers.[2] The new international marketplace enabled technologies to spread quickly, and encouraged entrepreneurs who could mass-produce instruments. Patents were obtainable in France from 1791 (reformed 1800, 1844), in England from 1824 (reformed 1852), and in federal Germany from 1877.[3] Modern-sounding trade names for instruments (Bassonore, patented 1844; Sarrusophone, patented 1856) were often by-products of the patent protection.

Sheet music was published at an increasing rate in centers like Amsterdam, Leipzig, Mainz, London, and Paris. Textbooks (including bassoon methods and charts) for the study of musical subjects proliferated, along with dictionaries and encyclopedias of music. Musical periodicals included concert reviews, instruction, advertisements, and even discussions of technical and acoustical matters. Positive reviews of bassoons and bassoonists appeared, but one could also read complaints about their shortcomings. Fétis in 1834 wrote that Grenser and Almenräder had undertaken the improvement of an instrument that was 'sourd et faux'.[4] Reviewing a performance by Wenzel Neukirchner in Paris, 1843, Hector Berlioz faulted his instrument (Neukirchner's own design), even while acknowledging the player's virtuosity.[5] The eruption of such complaints coincided with the flourishing of the musical press.

Trade associations, labor and benevolent societies, and educational institutions supported the interests of makers, dealers, musicians (both professional and amateur), and audiences. Publicly supported symphony orchestras were increasingly the model, including the Vienna and New York Philharmonic orchestras, both founded in the 1840s. Military bands grew in size and sophistication, expanding far beyond the old harmonie octets to include dozens of performers, among them up to three or more bassoons and contrabassoons. Many players were still doublers proficient on two or more instruments, not limited to woodwinds. They often pieced together a living as today's freelance bassoonist does: by a patchwork of concert, opera, theater, social, church, and band engagements, and by teaching.

Germany and Switzerland

Beginning in the year 1800, Germany's leading musical periodical, the *Allgemeine musikalische Zeitung* (*AmZ*), offered articles on acoustical topics by Ernst Florens Friedrich Chladni. An academically trained physicist who made his living by giving freelance lectures and inventing musical instruments, Chladni was the first to describe the longitudinal vibration of an air column, as found inside musical wind instruments. Chladni published books on musical acoustics in 1802, 1817, and 1821 with Breitkopf & Härtel of Leipzig. In 1827 he published another volume on acoustics with B. Schott's Söhne, Breitkopf's competitor in music publishing. Schott (based in Mainz, with branches in Antwerp, Brussels, and Paris) began to offer its own journal, *Cäcilia*, edited from 1824 by Gottfried Weber. Among the articles published in *Cäcilia* in 1826 was a summary by Chladni of the *Wellenlehre*, or wave theory, formulated by Ernst Heinrich Weber and Wilhelm Weber, two physicist brothers unrelated to Gottfried. Wilhelm Weber held an optimistic view that scientific insights would revolutionize the practice of musical instrument making, allowing production in large numbers and of great precision.[6] These new acoustical ideas, available for the reading, were not without effect. Normally untrained in physics, most bassoon makers did not change their artisanal ways, but there were notable exceptions, including – before 1830 – Charles Sax, Frédéric Guillaume Adler, Carl Almenräder, Jean François Simiot, and August Jehring.

Gottfried Weber, though trained as a lawyer, was a musical polymath: theorist, flutist, cellist, composer, and conductor. In August 1815, Weber submitted a lengthy treatise to the *AmZ* of Leipzig. Published in parts during 1816 and 1817, it developed ideas from Chladni's writings.

Weber might be called an acoustical fundamentalist or, in the terms of his own era, a 'mathematical' purist. His theoretical writings show no specific consideration of acoustical conditions created by the bassoon's unusually long extension bore, and he apparently considered the bassoon's chimneys to be a necessary evil, rather than the welcome source of the instrument's essential timbre. He likened the covered tones issuing through chimneys of the bassoon to 'stopped' notes on the horn. To remedy a perceived dullness and weakness, he called for the A vent (R3) to be moved lower on the bassoon's bore, allowing the tone hole to be made wider and less chimney-like.[7] The idea of placing tone holes at acoustically optimal locations ran counter to three centuries of bassoon design; tone holes were traditionally located within convenient reach of the average player's ten fingers, with a resulting compromise in hole diameters.

Weber was the conductor at the Mainz Theater, where Carl Almenräder served 1817–20 as first bassoonist. In a later treatise, Almenräder explained why he found the bassoon to be unsatisfactory:

> The famous instrument makers A. and H. Grenser in Dresden have contributed much to the improvement of the bassoon . . . their instruments [were] made of this type, with their beautiful, round, and sonorous tones. . . . But to be honest, there are various lacks, especially in the realm of purity [*Reinheit*]. These principal faults can be improved somewhat through the use of special fingerings [*Applikaturen*], but then difficulties arise, which work against fluent and attractive execution, often putting the best bassoonists in trouble when in remote tonalities.[8]

In 1817 Almenräder began work at the musical instrument factory of B. Schott Söhne in Mainz, where he was able to apply, test, and refine Weber's ideas.[9] At the Frankfurt Fair of 1819 Schott showed bassoons with the Almenräder keys, which were said to simplify fingering.[10] Almenräder moved to Cologne during 1820–2, where he performed and taught. He also produced at least thirteen flutes and seven clarinets for sale in his brother's music shop.

In 1822 Almenräder became first bassoon in the Hofkapelle of the archduke of Nassau in Biebrich, a wind-only group where he would remain for twenty years. He also resumed his work as an advisor at the nearby Schott factory.[11] In 1823 Schott published his *Treatise on the Improvement of the Bassoon*, in which Almenräder discussed innovations he had brought to the bassoon:

1. To avoid the entrance of condensed water, the C#3/4 tone hole was moved to the thumb side of the wing, now operated by LT. The tone hole was also lowered and enlarged. To make this lower location possible, the wing joint was lengthened, and the boot joint made a corresponding amount shorter. This C# key could also be used to produce E♭3.[12]

2. The A2 vent for R3 was sited lower, enlarged, and bored double; one hole led to the down bore; the other to the up bore.[13]

3. A tone hole and key were added for the A/B♭ trill, operated by R3.

4. A second A♭ (or G#) key was added for RT, facilitating slurs to and from F#.[14]

5. Tone holes and saddle-mounted keys were introduced for B1 and C#2.[15]

6. The D2 vent was enlarged and covered by a plateau.[16]

7. Pads were now wool balls covered with membrane, replacing the stuffed leather pads invented by Ivan Müller.[17]

8. The F2 key and G key were coupled so that closing F2 also closed G, to facilitate fingering.[18]

Writing in *Cäcilia* in 1825, Weber reiterated these and later improvements. Since 1823, the Bb2 tone hole was moved lower (northward on the up bore) and enlarged.[19] The Bb and F keys were actively coupled; opening the Bb2 key closed the F2 key to correct the sound and intonation (Ill. 34). *Cäcilia* in 1827 reported that Schott's bassoons were made after the inventor's design and under his own supervision, and that older bassoons could be converted to the Almenräder system. Adler of Paris exhibited an Almenräder-type bassoon in 1827, equipped with fifteen keys.[20] Weber in 1828 discussed further improvements by Almenräder:

I.   A second F# key was added for R4. Its spatula overlapped the F spatula for R4, so that when F# was opened, F was necessarily closed.[21]

II. The D2 and Eb2 vents were moved northward on the up bore (acoustically lower) and bored larger.[22]

III. The D2 vent moved northward on the up bore; the 'C2 key' was operated by a short spatula. (Figs. IV, V).[23]

IV. By means of these improvements, Weber wrote, Almenräder's bassoon now had a chromatic compass from Bb1 to Ab5, nearly four octaves.[24]

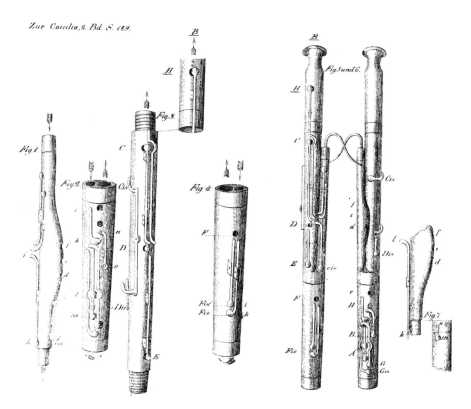

34.   Illustrations of two bassoon models made by Schott under the influence of Gottfried Weber and Carl Almenräder. *Cäcilia* 2 (1825):129.

The method writer Joseph Fröhlich noted in 1829 that bassoons with Almenräder's new system were still rare.[25] But Fétis in 1834 wrote that Almenräder had provided bassoons to artists in Germany, Holland, and Belgium.[26] In 1836 Schott received a medal from a business association for its excellent Almenräder-type bassoons and clarinets. Waterhouse reported that the Schott factory was closed around 1840.[27]

Two of Almenräder's associates in the Schott factory are known. August Jehring came from Adorf in the Vogtland, a traditional musical instrument-making region, c.1822. In 1829 Jehring sent to Adorf for his nephew Johann Adam Heckel. In 1830, apparently for reasons of health, Jehring left Schott to found his own private shop. He remained friendly with Almenräder, standing as godfather to a son born in 1832. At least three of Jehring's five surviving bassoons show evidence of the reforms known under Almenräder's name.[28]

In 1831 Almenräder contracted with Johann Adam Heckel (1812–77) in a partner-ship to be called Almenräder u. Heckel. Even during this partnership, however, Almenräder maintained business relations with Schott, serving as a proof reader, tuner, and reed maker.[29] No instruments bearing the mark 'Almenräder u. Heckel' are known.

Letters in the Schott archive document that the partnership had soured within a few years. Almenräder in May 1838 returned to Schott a defective bassoon he had repaired, complaining of Heckel's behavior and refusing to tune any further instruments from Heckel. Thereafter Heckel had the bassoons tuned by other local players and conducted business under his own name.[30] The period of collaboration between Almenräder and Heckel lasted only from 1829 to 1838, possibly weakened by the generation gap. An obituary noted that Almenräder's son Ludwig had absorbed all his father's knowledge about the bassoon; bassoons made according to this expertise were available either through Schott or from Ludwig Almenräder directly. In 1844 Ludwig Almenräder, now based in Darmstadt, exhibited instruments at Berlin.[31]

Almenräder in 1837 published an article explaining his idea of 'double venting' the pitches A♭, A, and B♭. He observed that the long extension bore of the bassoon tends to widen the octaves of A♭2, A2, and B♭2.[32] Meanwhile, 'at least on some tones, espe-cially on the lower part of the bore, the opening of one tone hole along with a higher one raises the lower tone alone, without affecting its higher octave'.[33] Thus he applied the double venting principle to the A vent (illustrated in his 1823 treatise), obtaining a pure octave between A2 and A3. Almenräder's A♭ key for RT, also illustrated in 1823, had originated as an aid to facilitate slurs from A♭3 to G♭3. Almenräder realized that a perfect A♭2/A♭3 octave could be produced by opening two RT keys at once. Because the two tone holes were too close to each other in the up bore, the octave A♭2 was initially flat; after Almenräder relocated the hole in the down bore, the flatness was cured.[34] The double venting of B♭, unmentioned in Weber's discussion of 1828, presumably dates from between then and 1835, when Almenräder wrote the article[35] (Ill. 35). This pragmatic solution to a bassoon-specific intonation problem was unfore-seen by Weber, but it survives in principle in the modern Heckel-system bassoon. Still other revisions were documented in Almenräder's method, which was under way by 1835 but published only in 1843[36] (Ill. 36).

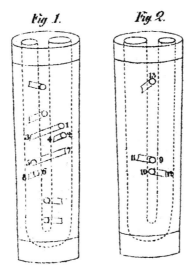

35.   Drawings used by Almenräder to explain his idea of double-venting pitches to produce in-tune octaves. *Cäcilia* 19 (1837):81.

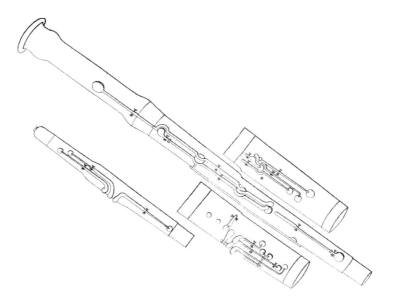

36.   The last documented innovations by Almenräder included a push-rod mechanism for B♭ and a rod-axle key for G (A vent), both operated by R3. Almenräder, *Fagottschule* (Mainz, 1843).

1. Table V showed the A♭ spatula for RT overlapping the F♯ spatula, so that the player need touch only one spatula to play A♭.
2. Table V showed the tone holes for B♭ relocated to the thumb side of the instrument, to prevent water from accumulating. The familiar spatula for R3 now operated the new key cup and lever by a push-rod passing through the septum of the boot joint.
3. Table V (unlike tables I and II) showed all keys mounted on pillars, plus a rod-axle key linkage for the double-headed A vent.[37]
4. Almenräder, possibly with Heckel, had apparently improved the B2 venting after 1823; the 1843 fingering chart no longer called for the F2 key to be closed on the lower octave.[38]

For making bassoons, Almenräder preferred American *acer saccharum* or sugar maple, writing that 'bassoons of such wood give a notably brighter and more resonant tone than those made of European maple'. Misleading readers, he wrongly equated the French term *palisander*, a type of rosewood, with sugar maple.[39]

Almenräder's former partner exhibited in Mainz in 1842, billed as 'J. A. Heckel, instrument maker in Biebrich near Wiesbaden'. A bassoon of maple wood with German silver keys, 'after the latest invention of Carl Almenräder', was priced at 90 florins. Like Ludwig Almenräder, Heckel exhibited in Berlin in 1844; the official report praised the immaculate workmanship of bassoons by both Neddermann & Meyer and J. A. Heckel, noting a newly functional layout of the keys.[40] Heckel apparently adopted the curved HECKEL/BIEBRICH stamp by 1845.[41]

Exhibiting in London in 1851, Heckel showed a 'bassoon of a new and improved construction'. Schafhäutl, Boehm's mentor and collaborator, wrote of this instrument:

> He had associated himself many years ago with an outstanding bassoonist in order to improve the lacks and shortcomings of the usual bassoon scale, and the experiment is, after much effort, quite successful. The scale is pure and the tuning uniform even if the tone, on account of the narrow tone holes, is not yet as completely free as it could be.

In voicing this criticism, Schafhäutl was likely thinking of the very large tone holes of his friend Boehm's cylindrical flute, and likewise of Sax's Boehm-inspired brass bassoon; both were displayed at the same exhibition. (In contrast, Zamminer, a physicist who published an acoustical treatise in 1855, considered the traditional bassoon exceptional to regular acoustical theory, because of its complex construction and the effect of its double reed.)[42] By 1851 Heckel was a supplier of high-pitch bassoons to the Austro-Hungarian military. Starting possibly at this time, he supplied bassoon bodies to Boosey of London until the late 1860s. Heckel also exhibited at Wiesbaden in 1846 and 1863.[43]

An undated price list by J. A. Heckel offered a bassoon 'after C. Almenroeder's [*sic*] design', with a choice of maple or palisander wood, and brass or silver keys. On a handful of his surviving bassoons, some of the keys are mounted in saddles, the others

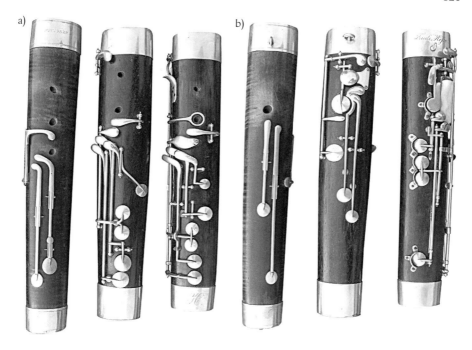

37. Boots of bassoons by Samuel Wiesner, J. A. Heckel, and H. J. Haseneier). (a) finger side; (b) thumb side. Waterhouse Collection.

on pillars. Heckel later converted all keys to pillar mounting, and many of the levers to rod-axle keys. Many of his key spatulas, except for the addition of rollers, are hardly altered today, including virtually all those for LT, the B♭ spatula for R3; and the trio of spatulas for R4 (Ill.37).

J. A. Heckel evidently decided to enlarge the E3 vent (L2). This tended to raise (and thus stabilize) E3 and E♭3, but also served to strengthen a new, post-classical fingering of E4 (1-3 456) and F4 (1-3 45-). His bassoons usually have metal bushings in the vents for B1, F#3, and A2 (double-headed), and countersunk seats for most of the other pads. The coupling of RT F# to R4 F, sometimes called the trill mechanism for F#–G#, is present on a J. A. Heckel bassoon dated 1877, where it is noted as a first-time occurrence.[44]

The bores of J. A. Heckel's bassoons, like those marked 'Schott', are longer and the tone hole lattice more open than on the Dresden bassoons of Grenser and Wiesner. J. A. Heckel made further revisions to the open-standing tone hole lattice, and his bell joints (generally conical) are slightly larger in bore diameter than in at least one of the surviving Schott bassoons (Carse Collection, Horniman Museum). Further analysis of his work awaits detailed measurements of surviving instruments.

Perhaps the most consequential innovation by J. A. Heckel was his addition of an RT touch for B♭2/B♭3. Along with the C# key for LT, this was one of the most radical alterations to nineteenth-century finger technique, giving new duties to the player's thumbs.[45] In the seven-finger archetype for conical woodwinds, the thumbs dealt only with lower and upper extensions of the compass, not with chromatic degrees of the basic seven-finger scale.[46] But the thumbs, though already busy, have a great facility for shifting along the north-south axis of the bassoon, whereas the other eight fingers cannot easily handle further duties. Almenräder's spatula for R3 B♭ was conceived as a trill key; it is usually confined to that use today, as R3 is busy operating the spatula that closes the A vent. Meanwhile, J. A. Heckel's B♭ spatula for RT is normally used for B♭2/B♭3, and also for F#4, B4, and C5.

Wilhelm Heckel (1856–1909) assumed direction of the family firm at the age of twenty-one after the death of his father Johann Adam. While he continued to offer the Almenräder design until 1885 or later, the son was also quick to develop his own new ideas. He began to number his bassoons, beginning with no. 3001. By 1879, Heckel offered a bassoon incorporating several noteworthy changes.[47] Many vents (A, G#, G, F#, F2, E2, and C#2) were moved 'lower' on the up bore; the RT G# was made independent of RT F#; and the last few inches of bell flare were moderated. An optional key covering the whisper vent was activated by the high C5 key. A spatula for LT D#3 overlapped the spatula for LT C#; pressing the D# spatula opened both vents to produce D#3 and D#4.[48] The Model 1879 represented a point of arrival for Heckel; picturing it fourteen years later, he labelled it 'the original type of Heckel-Fagott . . . the orchestral bassoon of today'. Invited by the conductor Wilhelm Jahn to Bayreuth in October 1879, Wilhelm Heckel visited Richard Wagner, who endorsed Heckel's bassoon and contrabassoon.[49] Heckel avidly reprinted this endorsement, the first of many that he would garner from noted composers, conductors, and players.

Around 1881 Heckel advertised five different models of bassoon, offered at a broad range of prices. Most expensive was the Model 1881, at 400 marks, 'with all necessary keys, of finest maple, to low A1 (our latest invention)'.[50] At 200 marks was an 18-key Almenräder model to B♭1 with brass fittings.

During a time when bassoons in use ranged from simple-system instruments to the latest innovations of W. Heckel and other makers, terms were used loosely. Wilhelm Heckel's own chart for his 1879 model named his father, himself, and Almenräder in the title.[51] Weissenborn's fingering chart (1887) had many different choices for some fingerings: for 'old-system bassoons', for 'the older Almenräder bassoons', for 'the modern bassoon', or for 'the newest Almenräder bassoons'.

In 1886 Heckel patented a moisture-resistant wooden liner for the bassoon's down bore, and in 1889 an ebonite liner.[52] The bore was lengthened and made more purely conical, while Heckel 'improved' the response of several notes: F#3, G3, C#, B2, F#4, and E♭ by 1897, presumably through adjustments to the tone holes and main bore.[53] From the vantage point of 1887, Weissenborn compared the latest Wilhelm Heckel bassoon to its precursors:

Despite the significant progress made, despite the eminence of these [Almenräder-Heckel] instruments, which everyone must acknowledge, during the reform of the bassoon, here and there, a little too much good was done. Anyone used to the mellow, heart-touching sound of the old [Grenser and Wiesner] bassoons may hear the big, strong sound imposed on the new ones, but not find it easy to sympathise with this bright, almost sharp sound. This evil can be mitigated by the used of a mellow, quiet-sounding reed. . . . [But] since December 1885 it is Wilhelm Heckel, the son of the former [J. A. Heckel], who has finally made the desired bassoons, which seem to the undersigned to combine all the excellences of the old and the new.[54]

In his ear and mind, Weissenborn guarded an ideal of the Dresden classical bassoon timbre. He regretted its dilution in the Almenräder-Heckel model. In Weissenborn's view, Wilhelm Heckel had by 1885 nudged the bassoon's timbre back toward his mental ideal, even while increasing its power. These instruments had a new timbre, richer in upper partials (above 2 kHz), on the whole, than the old Dresden bassoons, yet still mellow.[55]

Der Fagott (1899) includes a discussion of vibration and interval theory, making clear Wilhelm Heckel's grasp of the acoustical theories that inspired Weber, Almenräder, and Boehm. (Heckel even built a Boehm-inspired bassoon, which is discussed below.) 'With the old bassoons', an observer wrote, 'a non-linear, irregular bore had arisen through trial and error, constrained by the unnatural piecing of the instrument into joints.'[56] According to his own son, Wilhelm Heckel believed that:

. . . a uniform speech demanded a uniform angle of the bore. . . . With the help of micrometer screws, which were graduated in hundredths of a millimeter, he was able to control the progress of the bore to this tolerance.[57]

Yet this regularity was by no means an ironclad rule. Experimentation continued, often hidden from the naked eye. Measurements reveal, for example, that on W. Heckel's bassoon 3229 (c.1878), the bell bore is choked rather than conical, and the B_1 tone hole is moved significantly 'lower' on the bore (c.16 cm below the bell opening, vs. 23 cm on 3717). On 3717 (c.1885), the bell bore is essentially cylindrical, whereas on 4607 (c.1905) the bell bore is more conical. The Heckel-type bassoon – in 1885 and today – does not have an evenly progressive lattice of tone-hole diameters. The second finger hole is quite large, while the vents for B_1 and D_2 are quite small. Heckel was guided by his own ear, and by the evolving requirements of his customers.

Under Wilhelm Heckel the firm's bassoons spread beyond Germany. An advertisement from the *Military Musical Almanac*, 1889, listed bassoonists using the Heckel bassoon in Vienna, St. Petersburg, Warsaw, and Prague. (W. Heckel was the dedicatee of volume two of Concert Studies by Ludwig Milde, professor at Prague.) A Heckel catalogue issued in early 1898 cited players in London, Amsterdam, Moscow, Budapest, Odessa, Dundee, The Hague, Liège, Brighouse, New York, Boston, Constantinople, Jamaica, and Gateshead. The Heckel factory was equipped by 1899 with electric power and steam heat. Five harmoniums at different pitch levels were available to meet different tuning needs.[58] Heckel invited visitors to visit his factory and museum.

Even after beginning to offer his own distinctive models, Wilhelm Heckel referred for a time to all his products as the 'Almenräder-Heckelfagott'. In an advertisement of 1889, however, Almenräder's name was absent, and by 1899 Heckel began to identify his product as the 'Heckelfagott'. This was a fair distinction, so far had he departed from Almenräder's measurements and proportions. The marketplace of the twentieth century ratified Wilhelm Heckel's conception of the bassoon's sound, while allowing a few subtle refinements. Makers in an increasing number of countries (including successors in the Heckel firm) made their own additions or modifications to Wilhelm Heckel's basic designs of 1879–1909. His core ideas of bore, tone-hole lattice, and key work are recognizable in most of the hundreds of thousands of bassoons that exist in the world today. Virtually all German-system bassoons of the twentieth and twenty-first centuries (and many from the 1880s–90s) can justly be called Heckel-system bassoons.

During the reforms of the bassoon in the nineteenth century, many players and makers made do with older designs. Breitkopf & Härtel reprinted its 1806 German translation of Ozi (for seven-key bassoon), using the original plates, in 1898. André reprinted its 1805 German translation of Ozi as late as 1897. Such instruments and methods lagged generations behind the most forward-looking ones. The maker Kruspe in the later nineteenth century offered a 'bassoon of newest construction', roughly an Almenräder system, as well as a 'bassoon of older construction', having perhaps nine keys in a simple system. Other German bassoon makers active in the later nineteenth century are many in number, although only a few have been studied carefully.[59]

Many bassoons by Joseph Franz Seidel (fl. 1846–68) of Mainz resemble J. A. Heckel's bassoons, showing a different but analogous rod-axle key work. Friedrich Kulow, who worked as a journeyman under Wilhelm Heckel, founded his own business in Magdeburg in 1879. His surviving bassoons have many features of the Almenräder system, but have a double-headed B♭ key.[60] Some bassoons by Heinrich Joseph Haseneier (1798–1890), an instrument maker from 1840 in Koblenz, have double-headed vents for both A and B♭; no B♭ key for RT; a covered F vent; and double vents for F#. Novel features are sometimes present: restyled key touches; a conical bell bore; a very large vent for B1; rod-axle keys on the wing; and a ring for R2 that opens an additional vent into the down bore if R3 is depressed.

Not all innovations in German bassoons emanated from Almenräder or the Heckels, however. The Bohemian player Wenzel Neukirchner brought an influence from Prague to Stuttgart in 1829. His bassoon, produced by C. A. Schaufler and illustrated in Neukirchner's method of 1840, was based on the model of W. Horák of Prague. Three wing keys had spatulas arrayed in Central European order ('inverted', so that the spatula for A4 was furthest north). Despite the broadly flared bell finial, the bell's bore usually included a choke (as did at least some bells by Wiesner, Greve, and Stiegler). Novel features included keys for B1, C#2, Bb2/Bb3, and Eb3/Eb4. Schaufler patented his own design in 1847. On a Schaufler bassoon in the Waterhouse collection, the minor axis of the boot is thick, allowing all chimneys extra depth. The spatulas of the three wing keys are again reversed (a fourth wing key was sometimes present) (Ill. 38). A twenty-key Schaufler bassoon in the collection of Heckel, Biebrich, includes points of interest probably inspired by Weber or Almenräder, including a spatula and key for R3, a raised chimney for C#3/C#4, and keys for C#2 and B1. It has a spatula and open-standing key for both R3 (A2/A3) and L3 (D2/D3) mounted on a thickened wall of the wing joint. In 1853 Schaufler signed the rights of his 1847 patent over to Jakob Helwert. Later makers who adopted some elements of the Neukirchner system included Heinrich Berthold (Stuttgart), and Anton Kraus (Augsburg).[61]

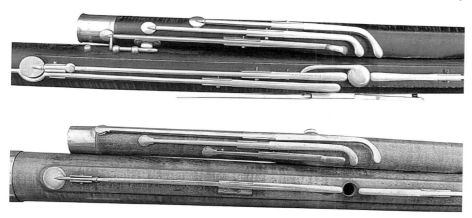

38. The LT wing keys of a bassoon by Wiesner (top) show the customary arrangement of spatulas. On a bassoon by Schaufler, the spatulas are reversed, in the Central European style. Waterhouse Collection.

J. H. G. Streitwolf (1779–1837) of Göttingen invented a 'unique, coil-shaped O-bend in wood' bearing keys for F and A♭. His bassoon also had a bell of larger than usual bore.[62] Wilhelm Hess, a bassoon maker of Munich, published a chart c.1850 for his own fourteen-key bassoon. As shown on the chart, the short-belled instrument had a closed B1 vent near the top of the long joint, opened by a spatula for L4. An 11-key bassoon by J. K. Felchlin of Bern (fl. a1836–55) survives.[63]

Saxony in 1850 counted some 380 wind-instrument makers employing 712 workers. But the production centre of German bassoons soon shifted from Saxony to the Vogtland. A French writer observed in 1861 that 'Neukirchen is to Germany what La Couture is to France. There are made this great quantity of wind instruments, [with] which Germany floods the neighbouring countries'.[64] A survey of the musical instrument industry of the Vogtland (Markneukirchen, Klingenthal, Adorf, Schöneck) in 1871–2 found 164 woodwind makers. Among the firms founded in the region were Gebrüder Mönnig (1876), G. H. Hüller (1878), and Oscar Adler (1885).[65]

Belgium

Charles Sax (1790–1865) of Brussels was a bassoon maker by 1815. In the Brussels collection are two of his bassoons – one of seven-key classical design, and one with sixteen keys, showing some Almenräder-like features. Infected by the scientific spirit, Sax elaborated his own acoustic theory on the division of the woodwind air column. In 1825, he exhibited in Haarlem a bassoon with a covered system and relocated tone holes. This bassoon is lost, along with a revised model built c.1840, but Sax's ideas are revealed in his application for a patent, which was granted in 1842.[66] Adolphe Sax continued his father's experimentation, producing a bassoon of brass; its lengthened boot joint carried all the finger touches, complemented by shorter bell and tenor joints.[67] He received a patent in 1851. Sax exhibited his bassoon in London in 1851 and 1862, but the instrument was never put into production[68] (Ill. 39).

Willent-Bordogni, professor at the Brussels Conservatory, wrote in 1844 that C. G. Bachmann had made 'a new bassoon after my ideas', which Willent-Bordogni passed on to Adolphe Sax, presumably for study or reproduction. The bassoon has not been traced, and its unique features, if any, are unknown.[69] Other makers in Brussels during this era included E. Albert, Jacques Albert, and Mahillon (the brother-in-law of Bachmann).

The Franco-Belgian author François-Joseph Fétis wrote in 1834 that 'the bassoon will not be in tune until its bore has been well calculated and the holes put into their true places'. While praising the workmanship on a bassoon by Adler of Paris, Fétis warned that its defects of tuning and equality would be remedied only by a complete reconstruction of the instrument. He labelled the chimneys 'acoustical monstrosities', demanded 'mathematical exactitude' in dividing the air column, and called for all tone holes to be covered.[70]

A traditional role of the bassoon is debated

From the 1830s, newly developed valves allowed brass instruments to play chromatically in the bass and tenor registers. These louder and newly capable instruments were suddenly a threat to the bassoon's ancient role in wind bands, especially in France. The *Bassonore*, a wide-bore bassoon invented in 1834 by Winnen, was designed to produce greater volume in both military bands and symphony orchestras. 'His new proportions have brought some changes in the nodes of vibration', Fétis wrote, invoking acoustical jargon, 'so that he has had to make some changes of fingering'. With new fingerings ('learnable within fifteen days') and a stronger reed, the player could supposedly obtain an intensity of sound quadruple that of the bassoon.[71] Savary jeune in 1834 offered 'grands pavillons' for bassoon.[72] The clarinetist and bassoonist Frédéric Berr headed the newly founded Gymnase Musical Militaire in 1836; in his bassoon method of the same year he illustrated a sixteen-key bassoon by Savary.[73] F. G. Adler exhibited a 'basson militaire' in 1839, and a bassoon with brass bell in 1844.[74]

Adolphe Sax moved from Brussels to Paris in 1843. The Paris Conservatoire in 1844 offered an incentive prize for 'the most improved bassoon of a new system',[75] probably a sign of anxiety over the bassoon's projection and chromatic fluency. In a public competition held 22 April 1845, Michele Carafa (director of the Gymnase Musical Militaire from 1838) led a band of 45 traditional instruments, including 4 bassoons, played by the professors and best students of the Gymnase. A band of 38 played Sax's patented instruments, including a family of saxhorns, in some of the same compositions. A commission judging the results found that while Carafa's band offered a great variety of timbres, Sax's band offered a more powerful and homogenous sound. The commission recommended that infantry bands henceforth contain two bassoons (with metal bells) and two saxophones, among other instruments.[76] Thirty-four other wind-instrument makers formed a committee to seek legal relief, including the bassoon makers Adler, Buffet Crampon, Triébert, and Winnen.[77] The eventual demise of bassoons in most French military bands was delayed by legal and political skirmishing, but the the single-reed saxophone, powerful and fully chromatic, was the ultimate victor.

This upheaval caused both economic and aesthetic ripples. In 1846, the bassoonist Jean Cokken became professor of tenor and bass saxophone at the Gymnase Musical

a)

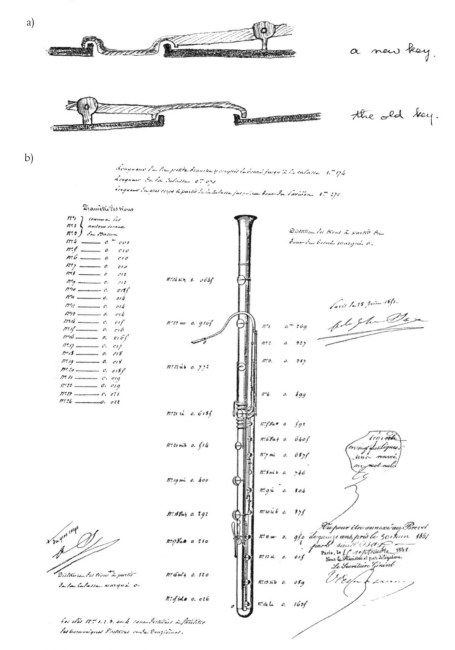

b)

39. (a) Drawing showing (above) a key designed by Charles Sax to eliminate the effect of closed chimneys and (below) a traditional key; (b) patent drawing of a bassoon by Adolphe Sax, 1851, showing mathematically determined tone-hole locations. Langwill Archive.

Militaire. But by 1850 he was mentioned as a bassoon professor there, and no prizes in saxophone were given.[78] The Parisian firm of Galander, a supplier to the Gymnase, in 1850 offered the *Galandronome*, a bassoon in B♭ (a whole tone lower than normal) with a dramatically flared metal bell for military use. In his saxophones and saxhorns,

Sax was creating families of homogenous timbres, enabled by the newfound principles of acoustical science. This sonic ideal, championed by Fétis as a revival of renaissance precedents, ran counter to the classical woodwind scheme of contrasting timbres (flute vs. oboe vs. clarinet vs. bassoon).[79] In fact, the homogenous scale of the saxophone was itself an affront to the contrasting registers of the bassoon.

Leading French composers had long taken an interest in military music. Meyerbeer helped select students for the Gymnase in 1837, while Berlioz in 1846 longed for its directorship.[80] Auber, director of the Conservatoire, auditioned Cokken and other aspiring professors for the Gymnase in 1846. Spontini c.1845 wrote a monograph on the reorganization of France's military music.[81] Adam composed a march to be played by both bands in the competition of 1845.[82] Colas noted that the orchestration of Halévy's *Le Juif errant* (1852) pointedly contrasted the timbres of old (Carafa's) and new (Sax's) bands.[83]

The bassoon in France

The most distinguished upholder of the status quo in France was Savary jeune, who ignored most of the more radical reforms described below. His early bassoons, dated 1820–3, have as few as eight keys; flat flaps cover the tone holes. Berr's chart of 1836 showed 'one of the latest instruments' of Savary', its sixteen keys mounted on a mixture of saddles and pillars. His latest known bassoon, dated 1853, has fifteen keys and domed key cups.[84] Savary added rollers to key spatulas and offered tuning slides (normally on the wing, although one surviving bassoon has five slides on three joints). He also added a closed-standing B1 to some of his bassoons and, to some, a crook key operated by the LT wing keys. But in bore and tone-hole placement, his later instruments remained essentially classical bassoons. Jean Kochen (Cokken), the future Conservatoire professor, received a Savary bassoon as first prize there in 1820. By 1836 Savary was a supplier to the Gymnase Musical Militaire; a prizewinner there in 1850 received a Savary bassoon.[85]

Theobald Boehm's conical ring flute was another influence on bassoon makers. Produced in Paris from 1837, the Boehm flute included rod-axle keys and brilles (open finger rings operating remote key covers). Jean-Louis Buffet patented alterations to Boehm's flute in 1838; he added his wife's name to his firm in 1844, so that it became known as Buffet Crampon. Jancourt credited the firm with adapting rod-axle keys to the bassoon by 1845.[86] Paul Goumas, the husband of Buffet's niece, joined the firm in 1851, becoming a partner in 1855. On the death of Jean-Louis Buffet in 1865, Goumas succeeded him, the next year introducing steam power at the Buffet Crampon factory in Mantes.[87]

Louis-Marie-Eugène Jancourt (1815–1901) toured with Charles Triebert during 1843–66, performing oboe/bassoon duets. In his method of 1847, he praised the bassoons of Savary, Adler, Buffet Crampon, and especially Frédéric Triebert (brother of Charles), whose bassoon achieved more fullness in the middle range without new fingerings.[88] His method showed an 'older' seventeen-key bassoon and an 'improved' sixteen-key bassoon; the latter had rings for R1 and R2 and a fork fingering for B2 and B3, as on clarinet. Both bassoons had a L1 key for E5 (Ill. 40). In 1848–9, Jancourt served two semesters as bassoon professor in Brussels, later returning to Paris to resume his chamber and orchestral career. He and Frédéric Triebert in 1850 relocated the A2/3

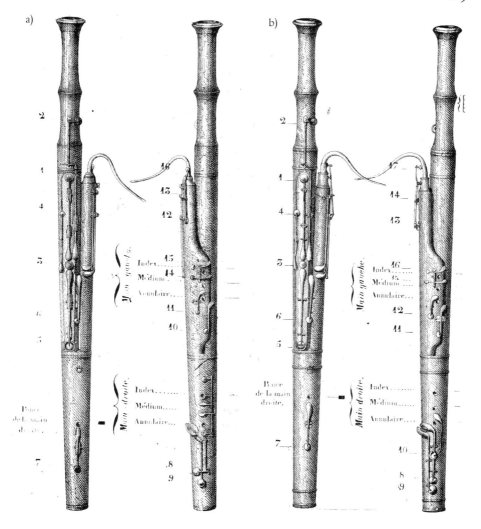

40. (a) Bassoon with sixteen keys; (b) bassoon with seventeen keys. Jancourt, *Méthode théorique et pratique pour le basson* (Paris, 1847).

vent (whose old location was 'mathematically vicious', Jancourt wrote), adding a spatula for R3.[89] Four later sources summarize Jancourt's efforts to improve the bassoon in collaboration with three firms: Buffet Crampon, Triebert, and Gautrot.[90]

Frédéric Triebert in 1853 entered into a business partnership with Angelo Gaëtan Philippe Marzoli, who was also a working bassoonist. In 1855 the firm produced a bassoon in collaboration with Boehm himself (described below). By 1856 a key operated by L1, producing F5 and facilitating trills, was added to the conventional Triebert bassoon. A new key for RT allowed 'an easy passing from F#2 to G#2, which was formerly nearly impossible, especially at speed'. For draining water from the boot, a removable cork replaced the fixed cork. A new double mechanism closed the tone holes for Bb1 and C2, but also opened the B1 tone hole.[91]

In 1859, the French government adoped the *diapason normal*, a new tuning standard of A-435, intended to remedy the existing motley of tuning pitches, ranging from A-441 to A-452.[92] The new, lower pitch standard made many older bassoons obsolete, as Cokken explained:

> As a result of the adoption of the diapason normal in France, the bassoon had to be reconstructed in new proportions. This furnished an opportunity to improve it and to add the means of more extended execution. It was therefore necessary to publish a new chart of fingerings, as well as exercises for familiarization.[93]

The chart showed a bassoon with a crook key for L4. Also present was an engraving of a bassoonist, showing rod-axle construction for many keys (Ill. 41). Cokken noted that the redesigned bassoon was adopted at the Conservatoire, where he was professor. Cokken was also principal bassoonist at the Opéra, which purchased four bassoons from Triebert in 1860 to accommodate the new pitch standard. Circa 1862, a price list of the Triebert firm acknowledged the assistance of Cokken. Among the four models illustrated, model 26 had rings or plateaux for L1-3, operating four speaker keys in the

41. French bassoon player and detail of reed. Cokken, *Méthode de basson* (Paris, c.1860).

absence of a L4 key. Marzoli left the Triebert firm and worked on his own during 1864–5; a bassoon bearing his mark alone contains this LH mechanism.

The firm Gautrot aîné published charts bearing Jancourt's name for a nineteen-key bassoon (before 1866) and and a seventeen-key bassoon (1866–9). Both had rings for L2, R2, and R3. According to the earlier chart, the mechanism for closing the crook hole was intended 'to give more sonority and surety to the low notes, which can be attacked without fear, loud or soft, from Bb1 to C3; it is also very useful for the following notes – G3, Ab3, F#4, G4, Ab4 – which are often rebels'. The hole, closed either by L4 or by a linkage to the LT wing keys, was open on C#3; D#3 through F#3; Bb3 through F4; certain fingerings for F#4 and G4; and B4 through F5.

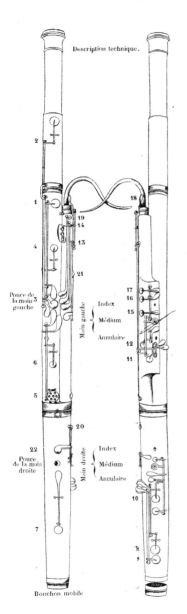

In 1875 Jancourt succeeded Cokken as professor in the Paris Conservatoire. He and Goumas reformed the bore of the bassoon, making it more 'mathematically regular'. This model, also marked by rings for L2 and R2, R2 key for C#/D#, and RT key for F#/G#3 trill, was adopted at the Conservatoire. To mark this, Evette & Schaeffer in 1876 published his *Étude du Basson Perfectionné à anneaux mobiles, plateau et 22 clés*, op. 58; a chart for this bassoon (later known as the système Jancourt) was soon published (Ill. 42). In 1885 Paul Goumas retired, selling the firm of Buffet Crampon to Evette & Schaeffer, who used both trade names at times. Around that time, Jancourt published his 'Perfectionnements apportés au basson', op. 98, echoing his commentary of 1876.

After Triebert's death in 1878, his firm was sold in 1881 to Gautrot aîné. Gautrot was sold in 1883 to Couesnon, who kept both the Triebert and Gautrot names in use. After Jancourt's retirement in 1891, Eugène Bourdeau was appointed professor at the conservatoire. By 1895, the rings and the RT key for G# of the Jancourt system were dropped on the 'modèle du Conservatoire' offered by Triebert.[94]

42. Bassoon with Jancourt system of c.1876. *Tablature du basson perfectionné à anneaux mobiles, plateaux et 22 clés Système Eugène Jancourt* (Paris, c.1876).

In 1861 the woodwind industry in France, headed by about 40 masters employing about 600 workers, produced 900 bassoons per year, as compared with 200 oboes, 3,000 flutes, 5,000 clarinets, and 350 serpents, among other instruments.[95] Other French bassoon makers in the middle third of the nineteenth century included Godfroy aîné (Paris); Cuvillier aîné (St. Omer); Lindemann (Strasbourg); and Proff (Tours). Other Parisian makers of the later nineteenth century included Georges Schubert and Thibouville-Lamy.[96]

Technology came to the aid of the bassoon reed maker in the form of a gouging machine, which eventually replaced traditional methods of hand-gouging cane. In 1834, Fétis reported on machines for oboe and bassoon reeds developed by the oboist and maker Henri Brod. The machine was refined and shown at the 1839 Paris Exposition.[97] Jancourt in 1847 described a gouging machine for bassoon by Triebert, preferring it to Brod's machine; an illustration in the 1862 price list closely resembles the gouging machines of the twentieth century. Triebert offered bassoon reeds by the dozen.[98]

Italy, Spain, Catalonia

Until unification in 1859–60, the northern states of Italy were Habsburg possessions; Austrian military bands were stationed in several Italian cities, and passed through many others.[99] As a result, many surviving bassoons in Italian collections are by Central European makers. A ten-key bassoon by 'F. Koller in Trieste' is marked with the Habsburg eagle and has a flared metal bell.[100] Of two bassoons in the De Wit catalogue stamped P. Piana/Milano, one is a Savary model (nine domed keys), the other is a Grenser model (eight flat keys). An eight-key bassoon by Giacomo de Luigi of Milan (1762–1840) survives in a private collection.[101] The firms of Maino & Orsi and Maldura produced bassoons after the specifications of professors at the conservatory of Milan.

Judging by instruments surviving in Iberian museums, many bassoonists used instruments by French makers. A nine-key brass bassoon by J. Vidal of Barcelona is reported.[102]

Austria and Central Europe

Bassoons made in Central Europe (the Habsburg Empire) during this era remained simple systems, only occasionally showing signs of the Western European trend toward acoustical reforms. They are usually distinctive in appearance, with slender and almost delicate bodies. On many, a trumpet-like metal finial atop the bell was intended to magnify the instrument's sound, although the effect was minor, according to Nagy[103] (Ill. 43). As in the French system, the low B key was usually closed-standing. Tone holes for Db2 and Eb2 were sometimes mounted on the thumb-side table of the long joint, connected to spatulas for L4 or LT.

The boots were often made tall above R1, evidently to locate the characteristic RT key for C# in an acoustically desirable place (the reverse strategy of Almenräder's lengthened wing joint). The holes for R3 and RT were left uncovered and the connection of the bores remained primitive, with no metal U-tube. A ring-like handle, sometimes installed on the plug, allowed easy removal for drainage. In a distinctive strategy for coping with awkward F#-G# passages, Stehle and Uhlmann sometimes added a L4 touch for G# – a long lever mounted in a groove in the boot joint, which was left thicker to accommodate it. Central European makers adopted distinctive key shapes:

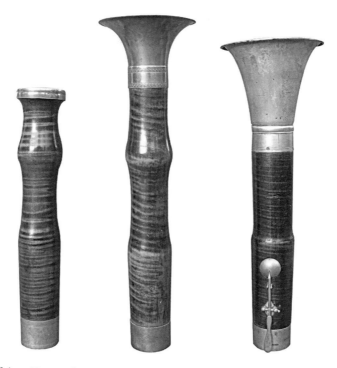

43. Bells of three Viennese bassoons. From left: Tauber, Rorarius, Uhlmann. Waterhouse Collection.

spoon-shaped spatulas, narrow but deep shanks, and domed cups. On Uhlmann's bassoons, the keys are often complex sculptural objects: waisted oval touches are soldered onto the levers.

The wing joints are noticeably shorter (to match the longer boot joints) and smaller-bored, and tone holes 1–7 are smaller in diameter than on Tauber's classical models. As on the bassoons of Horák and Schaufler, the ordering of wing spatulas for left thumb is opposite the French or German style. Tuning slides on the wing joint were common. On a bassoon by Ziegler of Vienna, a key for L4 operates a register key mounted just below the receiver (rather than on the crook).[104]

Firms (often multi-generational) active during the late classical period into the romantic period included Koch, Küss, Rorarius, and Uhlmann, all of Vienna, Alois Doke of Linz, and Eduard Piering of Graz.[105] Bassoon makers documented in the mid-century included Hell, Schemmel, Stecher, Stehle, and Ziegler, all of Vienna; Laussmann of Linz; Horák of Prague; Gerhardt of Ofen (Pest); and Scripsky of Košice.[106] Viennese makers late in the century included Leopold Uhlmann, Wenzel Bradka, and Franz Koktan.[107] In the second generation, the D2, C2, and B♭1 keys begin to be linked. Modernizing tendencies included pillar mounting of keys; double F# keys (the finger-side one linked to F2); mounting of E♭2 and D♭2 vents on the finger side of the bass joint; and up to three touches for C#3/C#4. Later instruments from the firms look increasingly similar, and decorative elements are toned down, reflecting their factory-type production.[108]

At the Vienna World Exhibition of 1873, Carl Stecher showed three bassoons, including one of palisander. Wenzel Bradka showed an ebony bassoon with two wings, in Parisian and Viennese tunings. Goumas of Paris showed two bassoons among other instruments. Reed makers for bassoon included Carl Mayer (Austria) and Sobeck of Luditz, Bohemia.[109]

After the importation of foreign players to the Vienna Hofoper c.1880, Dresden-style oboes and Boehm flutes supplanted traditional Viennese models. Viennese-made bassoons were soon replaced by German bassoons made by Berthold and Heckel. The transition was evident by 1885, when Karl Mayer, a bassoonist in the Hofoper of Vienna, issued charts for both Almenräder and Viennese systems.[110] Despite efforts to compete by Stecher, Koktan, and Leopold Uhlmann – borrowing features from the styles of Almenräder or Wilhelm Heckel – the Central European bassoon vanished from professional Viennese orchestras by the early twentieth century.[111]

Two instruments stamped by American makers show possible Central European influences. A five-key bassoon stamped by C. G. Christman, New York, has an exaggerated bell rim and baluster,[112] while a nine-key bassoon by Guetter of Bethlehem, PA, has a Tauber-like bell and Central European alignment of the two wing keys.[113]

England and Scotland

London makers of bassoons during the second quarter of the century at first maintained the traditional look, with stout boot joints, A♭ tone hole high on the bore, and E♭2 key located to the left of the D2 key. Tones holes 1 through 6, however, now tended to be relatively small in diameter. The flared wooden bell, seen earlier on some English bassoons, assumed variant shapes in some exemplars by Bilton, D'Almaine, Key, Metzler, and Millhouse. D'Almaine sometimes extended the LT table westward to accommodate the E♭ key in its traditional position. But influences from the continent were increasingly evident: some makers now located the key in the French position (right of the D spatula). A C# key for RT became common, although a C# key for L4 was sometimes seen. Two or three register keys were seen at times on the wing, sometimes with spatulas in inverted order.

By mid-century the trend was toward pillar-mounted keys of German silver, with domed key cups and spatulas (sometimes with rollers). Up to fifteen keys were commonly seen, including a covered D2 vent and a closed-standing key for B1. Other makers included Gerock, Pace, Prowse, Wood & Ivy, and Wrede.[114]

In 1839 Glen of Edinburgh bought from Ivy of London half a gross of 'rings for bassoon reeds'; these were probably stiff rings of iron, used as the upper binding on reeds before more flexible wires came into use. In 1840 Glen bought eight bundles of Spanish cane in two sizes from Barnett Meyers in London.[115]

London was often host to immigrant performers and important trade expositions. Bassoons by Savary caught the fancy of leading English players, including two famous sets of bassoon-playing brothers: William and Thomas Wotton, and E. F. and Wilfred James. Many prominent English players and teachers used original Savary bassoons throughout the later nineteenth century, and most English makers eventually offered at least one bassoon model explicitly based on Savary. Alfred Morton, who had reportedly worked under Savary, was by c.1875 making bassoons for the dealer Lafleur of London. These were inspired by Savary's bassoons, even though Morton offered a lining of ebonite and other refinements.[116] Palisander or rosewood was often an option to maple. Other makers of Savary models included Boosey & Co.; Chappell; Howell; Mahillon (Brussels and London); Rudall, Carte & Co.; and Samme.[117]

English players were exposed to bassoons by English, German, French, and Viennese makers at commercial exhibitions held in London in 1851 and later. But only the English and French instruments were received with favor. Geoffrey Rendall, who had tracked the sales of used bassoons through auction records, wrote: 'The field is held almost entirely by Morton, Savary, Triebert, [and] Buffet, with Morton maintaining the highest prices.'[118] The records of Rudall, Carte during the years 1870–7 show sales of bassoons by Albert, Marzoli, Gautrot, Triebert, and Goumas, mostly to military bands, some of these serving in Africa and Asia. In the Royal Military Exhibition of 1890, the 'modern' bassoon was represented by Rudall, Carte's conservative French system, made wholly or partly in ebonite with seventeen keys, including a L4-operated piano (crook) key. Similar key work was seen in an 1890 price list issued by Hawkes & Son, which showed 'perfected models' of two qualities, both of rosewood.

Boehm-inspired bassoons

Two important acoustical reforms often attributed to Theobald Boehm were anticipated (with more or less rigor) by Gottfried Weber, Almenräder, and Charles Sax: (1) making the bore of the instrument more rational or regular, and (2) giving the tone holes theoretically correct locations and sizes. Another long-lasting bassoon reform, more mechanical in nature, is traceable to Boehm's innovations. A single rod-axle key, which efficiently transmitted finger motion over long distances, was seen on a Boehm flute of 1829.[119] Almenräder, J. A. Heckel, and Buffet Crampon embraced the new key design by the 1840s, although all three were content to leave some keys as traditional levers. A fourth reform, the fully keyed system, was seen in the 1825 bassoon of Charles Sax (and earlier in the ophicleide, a brasswind instrument). It figured in the radical prototypes described below, in contras, and in related instruments (see chapters 9 and 10), but not on mainstream bassoons.

Applied in pure form, acoustical reforms of the bassoon tended to denature its familiar timbre; the resulting instruments sounded more like a baritone oboe, sarrusophone, or saxophone, according to the choices made by the reformer. Lacking the deep chimneys that vent the traditional bassoon's primary octave, they lacked, in varying degrees, the traditional bassoon sound. Many lacked the traditional fingerings as well. Boehm-inspired reformers often preferred the clarinet- or flute-style fingerings for B♭, B, E♭, and E in the second and third octaves, and they were quick to add unfamiliar keys to their bassoons. These high-concept prototypes epitomized the 'acoustically correct' bassoon, untempered by practical considerations of price, complexity, or maintenance. None was a commercial success, and they had little pedagogical impact. For all the early nineteenth-century complaints about the bassoon, its characteristic sound could not easily be 'improved'.

44. Detail of Ward-Tamplini bassoon, showing raised chimneys. Waterhouse Collection.

Giuseppe Tamplini was impressed with Boehm-system oboes and clarinets he had encountered in Paris. After settling in London in 1847, he persuaded a well-known maker of Boehm-type flutes, Cornelius Ward, to produce a Boehm-inspired reform bassoon, which they showed at the London World Exhibition of 1851. Ward took out a patent in 1853, and the instrument was marketed by Rudall, Carte. Tamplini's instrument was an elegant compromise between innovation and tradition. The locations and diameters of the tone holes were logically determined and the system was fully covered. Yet the holes debouched through chimneys raised on the body's exterior (Ill. 44). Tamplini reordered the sequence of keys for R4 and RT, while C#2 was opened by the third phalange of L2, an elegant but unfamiliar design. B♭2/B♭3 was originally fingered 123 4, a change that Tamplini later reconsidered. The lengths of the various joints were revised to accommodate the new key work. In voicing the pitches, Tamplini and Ward chose judiciously: L1 was only slightly wider than modern, and the diameter of the low B2 vent was c.16 mm, far less than on some other reform models.

Tamplini admitted that the sound was not that of the traditional bassoon. 'But it is not without sweetness and power, and blends well with other instruments and tone colours in the orchestra.' When his model did not find favor with players, Tamplini blamed ignorance, prejudice, habit, and private interests.[120] But in fact he had produced an expensive instrument (four times the price of Rudall, Carte's cheapest bassoon) with a fragile mechanism and several new fingerings. It sounded something like a baritone oboe, and its glued-in tone-hole chimneys were liable to leak, if not carefully maintained.

Boehm himself attempted to generalize the acoustical lessons of his 1847 flute to the bassoon:

By 1850 a trial metal tube, fitted with plugged tone holes, had been tested. He entrusted its construction to Triebert in collaboration with Marzoli. Their first instrument was not quite ready in time for the Paris exhibition of 1855, but Fétis published in his report full details of its bore and tone-hole specifications.[121]

On Marzoli's fingering chart, published in 1862, B♭2 was fingered as 123 4 and B2 as 123 5, as on a Boehm clarinet. Krakamp published another chart, somewhat simplified, in his bassoon method of 1872.[122] At the London Exhibition of 1862, the Triebert-Marzoli-Boehm bassoon, now made in wood, was awarded a prize. Pauer, reporting

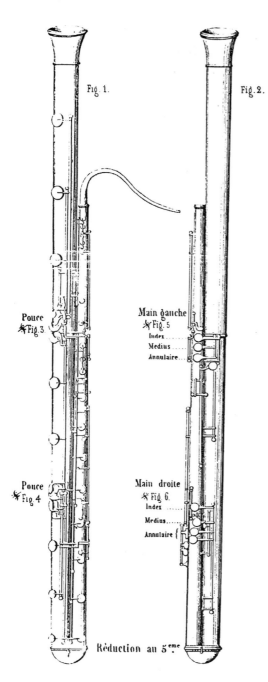

on the exhibition, praised the instrument's octave intonation, its pure, noble tone, and its easy-speaking low register and staccato. But 'the instrument was so complicated that one saw on it more keys than wood'. Its advocate Marzoli died in 1865, prior to the next Paris exhibition (1867). Meanwhile, the instrument had cost 1,200 francs, as compared with 280-320 francs for an ordinary bassoon.[123]

The five surviving specimens differ slightly in key work. On the Waterhouse exemplar, the key work is intricate and the body unswelled by thickenings or raised chimneys, so that it has the appearance of a giant folded oboe. All tone holes are keyed. L1 has a diameter of approximately 11 mm, the holes increasing in theoretically correct diameters to more than 24 mm for B1. The broad up-bore and shallow tone holes give a much more open sound than a conventional bassoon, old or new (Ill. 45).

Rossini, Auber, and Meyerbeer, hearing Boehm's bassoon in 1855, found the sound 'too metallic, blaring, and dissimilar to the ordinary bassoon'.[124] Jancourt admired the ingenious mechanism, but he wrote that 'two very essential points – quality of tone and simplicity of fingering – marred its success. It is therefore of fundamental importance to preserve the bassoon's timbre and character in any modifications or alterations.'[125] Like the composers named and like his counterpart Weissenborn, Jancourt treasured the traditional bassoon timbre and wanted it preserved.

45. Bassoon by Triebert-Marzoli-Boehm, showing fully covered system and proportional spacing of tone holes. Triebert, *Nouveau Prix Courant* (Paris, c.1862).

46. Bassoon attributed to Gautrot aîné, with clarinet-like fingering. Waterhouse Collection.

In the Heckel Collection, Biebrich, is a unique Boehm-influenced bassoon by Heinrich Joseph Haseneier (1798–1890) of Koblenz. On the fully keyed system, the tone holes are larger than usual and deep chimneys are absent. Some fingerings are borrowed from the Boehm flute or clarinet. Langwill reported that 'the instrument blows very freely with a harder, more open tone than the French bassoon'.[126]

Wilhelm Heckel had worked in Brussels in the 1870s for E. Albert, and he later visited Paris. Aware of the Boehm reform attempts, he built one or more fully keyed bassoons himself.[127] Models built according to principles of Boehm, with all finger holes covered by keys, suffered from 'hissing' and had less 'euphony' than the normal bassoon, Heckel observed. He voiced a craftsman's objection to the fully keyed system: 'the keys can lead to water problems, and they always add resistance'. Even if certain practical problems could be addressed, Heckel wrote, 'such an instrument would not be advantageous, because the essential character of the bassoon is lost, as the efforts and attempts of Triebert attest'.[128]

The Waterhouse collection includes a unique bassoon attributed to Gautrot aîné, c.1875. 'All tone holes are at logical intervals and covered, the fingers controlling remote spatulas.' Fingerings for Bb2, B2, and Eb3 are clarinet-like, and the keys for L4 and R4 also resemble those of the Boehm clarinet. 'It is the only bassoon ever made allowing the RT to stay idle.' The LT keys are traditional French bassoon system[129] (Ill. 46).

During his journeyman years Friedrich W. Kruspe worked in Munich, where he met Boehm. In 1860, he worked in Paris for Triebert. He patented his own reformed bassoon in 1892. Three exemplars are known, crafted in three joints with profuse key work borrowing ideas from both the Buffet and Heckel systems. All tone holes are covered by cups, plateaux, or brilles, although most diameters are close to conventional. The traditional chimneys are shortened; 'the bore is somewhat larger and the overall length somewhat shorter than a standard short bore modern Heckel'.[130] An extended boot joint is elegantly carved into a duplex tube and RH épaule. A short tenor joint carries only the two wing keys, while the combined 'long/bell' joint carries vents for D2 through B1 (open-standing). Touches for D2 and Eb2 are duplicated for RT. Long, clarinet-like trill keys were operated by R1, third phalange.

Without going as far as Boehm and his followers, many makers attempted to improve the ordinary bassoon through modest mechanical or acoustical innovations. On a bassoon by Adler of Bamberg, the conventional tone-hole lattice was retroactively covered by keys.[131] On a fully keyed bassoon by Esposito of Naples, dated 1881, tone holes are sited along the major axis of the boot, fully covered by keys; most appear to be of conventional diameters.[132] The 27-key system was reportedly designed by Luigi Caccavaio, a bassoonist of Naples.

Some makers (including Schaufler and Reinhold Lange) covered the L3 vent and moved it lower on the bore, by analogy with the covered R3 vent that Almenräder had pioneered. A contrary tactic was probably also catalyzed by the inquisitive spirit of the time: some makers lengthened the chimneys of certain conventionally sited tone holes. Schaufler and his followers thickened the boot joint. Haseneier and Schaufler often raised the tone-hole seat of B1 above the surface of the bell joint, adding depth. Around the turn of the twentieth century, several makers produced all-metal bassoons: Arsène-Zoé Lecomte (Paris), Andrés Vidal (Barcelona), and Martin Lehner (Munich).

Pedagogy and players

In his *Fagottschule* (1843), Almenräder stressed the necessity of understanding rests, paragraphs and periods in a musical work. The student should breathe only at punctuation marks, and without shortening long notes. Using varied articulations (soft and hard tongue strokes), the bassoonist should introduce diversity into his performance, supplementing the spare notation sometimes found. Bassoonists cannot double-tongue, Almenräder declared, because the bassoon reed intrudes into the oral cavity. He recommended instead a two-slurred, two-tongued pattern which, performed with extreme softness and delicacy, could simulate double-tonguing.[133]

The student may be in possession of an excellent instrument, but 'if he plays on a bad reed he is its slave, and cannot free himself', Almenräder wrote. 'He must learn which type of reed to make – broad or narrow, short or long, here to carve it thin, there to leave the wood thicker, etc. . . . a reed which works on one bassoon, sounding completely pure, may be completely false on another.' For shaping of the cane, a simple metal template was used.

Almenräder's student quickly encountered tenor clef, scales to B4, and exercises to F5. Like Ozi, Almenräder gave examples of passages first plain, then ornamented; his suggestions differed, however. Among the ornaments mentioned was a portamento, achieved by gradually sliding fingers off or onto tone holes or keys, suitable in cantabile movements when the line moves stepwise. *Beben*, a fingered vibrato (also mentioned by Jancourt, Neukirchner, and Hürth), was appropriate only on occasional long tones. Other permissible variations included varied dynamics and octavated passages during repeated sections. Help for impracticable passages included added fingers, fork fingerings, and sliding between spatulas. Almenräder mentioned duets by Blasius, Dumonchau, Ozi, and Jacobi, and concert works by Bärmann, Hummel, Jacobi, Koch, Lindpaintner, Mühling, and Weber. He complained of the vapid potpourris and fantasies then in fashion: every sixteen measures a fermata embellished with wide 'goat leaps', every thirty-two bars a new theme; 'through so many tempi rubati the coherence – such as it exists – is so torn apart, that neither rhythm nor phrase structure is to be felt'.

Almenräder addressed the bassoonist's instrument-specific needs: room acoustics, coupled with the choice of reed; maintaining the tuning pitch; problems of water in the bassoon bore, etc. He discussed remedies for defective bassoons, including re-reaming of the bore or tone holes of the wing and boot. Like Neukirchner, Almenräder described the U-joint of the bassoon as a metal 'drain'; the two authors also discussed care of the bassoon's key work. Later charts for Almenräder-system bassoons were published by Hofmann (Leipzig, 1874), Heckel (Mainz, 1881), and Schmidt (Dresden, 1887).

Neukirchner's method (1840), intended for his own new bassoon design, was published in Leipzig. Novel fingerings included half-hole venting of G3, G#3, G4, and G#4; keys for Bb2/Bb3 and Eb3/Eb4; and a third wing key to be opened for C#5, D5, and D#5. Conservative aspects included the occasional closing of the E2, F2, or G2 vents as pitch correctives; and the optional use of fork fingerings for Bb2/Bb3, C#3/C#4, and D#3.

Neukirchner advocated the abandonment of the crook hole. Schilling, on the contrary, described the crook hole in 1838 as a given (with no discussion of closing it). It is perhaps unsurprising that he also gave the natural range of the bassoon as from D2 to Bb4, the tones outside this range 'speaking with difficulty'.[134] Almenräder in 1843 claimed that new bassoons needed the crook hole, but that it could be closed on a well-made, well-played bassoon. Gontershausen seemed to confirm Almenräder's opinion:

> The little hole, seldom missing from the crook of newer bassoons, must always be drilled with a very small bit. . . . If, through good conservation, after assiduous use of the instrument, the pin hole [can be] closed, then all tones acquire more fullness and delicacy, without the purpose of the hole, the slurring of tones, being lost.[135]

Wilhelm Heckel's new models inspired a new method from C. J. Weissenborn, from 1857 principal in the Leipzig Gewandhaus Orchestra, and the earliest bassoon professor at the Leipzig Conservatory (from 1882).[136] In his method (Leipzig, 1887), he illustrated the Heckel bassoon model of 1885 and introduced some new fingerings. His extensive charts also contained traditional fingerings, however, for both Almenräder and simple-system bassoons. Weissenborn discussed flicking technique (momentary opening of speaker keys); small circles appeared in the exercises above notes to be flicked. He rejected the oblique embouchure.[137] Other charts and methods for Wilhelm Heckel's models included Lange (Wiesbaden and Offenbach, 1892) and Satzenhofer (Leipzig, St. Petersburg, Moscow, Riga, and London, 1900). Methods and charts for simple-system bassoons by Fröhlich (1810/1878), Streitwolf (1830), Hess (1850), Streck (1861), and Ozi (1894, in German and English) were published in Germany.

The Paris Conservatoire, dominating music instruction in France, lent its professors a weight of personal authority not equalled in other large countries. During this era the bassoon professors were F. Gebauer (1824–38), Barizel (1839–48), Willent-Bordogni (1849–52), Cokken (1852–75), Jancourt (1875–91), and Bourdeau (1891–p1925).

Their careers illustrate the varied posts and travel typical of the century's bassoon-ists. After winning a first prize himself at age sixteen, Willent-Bordogni performed in London, New York, and Philadelphia, as well as Paris. He was professor at the Brussels Conservatory 1842–8 before returning to Paris.[138] His successor, Cokken, served from ages twelve to eighteen as a military musician before entering the conservatoire for study. Jancourt, after beginning on the flute, was 'seduced by the timbre and character of the bassoon, becoming the favourite student of Gebauer' (Ill. 47). Jancourt became first bassoon at the Opéra-Comique in 1840; he played in London during vacation of 1841 for Drury Lane concerts; from 1843 to 1877 he played chamber music in Paris and the western provinces. He composed repertory for his own appearances: fifty solos (twenty-six of these on opera motifs), three sonatas for bassoon and piano, fifteen duos with oboe, and sixteen transcriptions, for two to four bassoons, of Mozart, Beethoven, Kuhlau, etc. He played in the leading Parisian orchestra (Société des concerts du conservatoire) c.1839–69, also serving twelve years on the governing committee. Eugène Bourdeau, after beginning work in the Opéra-Comique orchestra, continued his studies of the organ, becoming maître de chapelle of a religious order in Paris. He composed two solos de concours for bassoon, as well as Masses and motets.[139]

Professor Willent-Bordogni and his three successors each published a method for bassoon.[140] Berr, director of the Gymnase Musical Militaire, also wrote a bassoon method, dedicating it to Barizel. Each new method retained something of Ozi's substance and language, even as keys were added and fingerings evolved. Willent-Bordogni and Jancourt, for example, continued to advocate the oblique embouchure[141] (Ill. 48). Yet the methods also reflected evolving practices: rather than from a coat button, for example, the player should suspend the bassoon from a neck-strap. While retaining most of Ozi's reed-making instructions of 1803, Willent-Bordogni doubled Ozi's gouging specification to 'one-half line of thickness', equivalent to c. 1.1 mm.[142]

47. Eugène Jancourt, as portrayed in his *Méthode théorique et pratique pour le basson* (Paris, 1847).

CHAPITRE 3.me

DE L'EMBOUCHURE ET DE LA FORMATION DU SON.

L'embouchure est la manière de tenir l'anche dans la bouche, et de porter dans l'instrument le volume de vent suffisant pour en tirer le son et former les tons de son étendue ; la qualité du son dépend de la manière de contenir l'anche avec les lèvres. Il est essentiel de la tenir un peu obliquement. Ex : au moyen de cette position, le vent passe librement en quantité suffisante, et le son acquiert de la force et de la rondeur. Il ne faut pas tenir l'anche sur l'extrémité des 2 lames, ni à plat sur les lèvres, cela empêcherait la vibration et lui ôterait toute force dans le haut comme dans le bas ; l'on entendrait alors une espèce de sifflement, qu'on appelle un son de peigne, parcequ'il ressemble assez au bruit que l'on ferait en passant avec vitesse une lame de couteau sur toutes les dents d'un peigne. Ce son est tou_ jours très désagréable. Si, au contraire, on avance trop l'anche dans la bouche le son devient dur et rauque.

La seule position vraiment bonne est donc celle que j'indique afin de bien gouverner son embouchure et de parcourir avec assurance toute l'étendue du Basson, et, comme la lèvre inférieure est celle qui presse l'anche, il faut que la plus forte partie du roseau soit tournée en bas.

48.   In his method of 1847, Jancourt instructed the bassoonist to use an oblique embouchure.

Willent-Bordogni distinguished four types of articulation: coulé (slurred), détaché (tongued; like string staccato), piqué (tongued lightly and dryly; like string pizzicato), and louré (tongued legato).[143]

Jancourt remarked that vibrato occurs naturally in the voices of orators and singers. As the bassoon resembles the human voice, vibrato must be employed there as well. The effect is to be obtained, however, by *tremblement* of the right hand above the four open finger holes; the left hand has less effect, but can also be used. The notes susceptible of this fingered vibrato are B2, C3, C#3, D3, E3, F#3, G3, C4, and D4.[144] Cokken called for half-opening L1 to vent A♭3.[145] His crook key, linked to both the wing keys, 'serves to link more easily the notes from A4 to D5'. Willent-Bordogni gave two generous pages of fingerings for correcting intonation on individual pitches, and four pages of instructions for trills.[146] Jancourt praised Triebert's 'improved bassoon with sixteen keys' for simplifying fingerings on A2, E4, F4, and G#4. He noted that 'the facility to link [slur] notes depends a great deal on the reed; and suggested that the C# key could serve as a flick key for G4. 'There are some rebel notes for which one is forced to employ the C5 key of the wing joint', Jancourt wrote. He recommended relaxing the lips on lower notes to facilitate downward slurs, and he devoted five pages of discussion to trill fingerings.[147]

Jancourt noted among the functions of the bassoon: strengthening the viola; reinforcing orchestral staccatos; and doubling respectively the bass line, the viola, clarinet, flute, and oboe. Jancourt slightly expanded Ozi's list of convenient tonalities. For solos: C, D, F, G, B♭; A and D minor. For slow movements, A♭ and E♭ may be added to these; for andantino movements, A major and E minor may also be added.[148] Among Berr's *Progressive Studies* (1836) is no. 16, the bassoon solo from Rossini's *Barber of Seville* overture, in E major, a key that bedevilled earlier bassoonists.[149]

After the symphonie concertante passed from fashion, conservatoire students were instead heard in performances of chamber works, including Beethoven's quintet for piano and winds (1842), a wind quintet by Reicha (1843), a septet by Vogt (1844), the Aubade à 12 by F. Bazin (1851), and chamber symphonies by Prumier fils (1852/3).[150] Between 1835 and 1865, most of the *concours* (examination) pieces were also by Gebauer, Barizel, Berr, Willent, and Cokken. Weber's concerto was an examination piece in 1865, as were Mozart's concerto in 1877, and Weber's Andante and Hungarian Rondo in 1896. From 1898, however, concours pieces were newly commissioned from professional composers, beginning with the *Solo de concert*, op. 35, by Gabriel Pierné. At times pupils for the bassoon were scarce; the competitions in 1831–3 had no entrants on bassoon. There was no *concours* in 1871, in the wake of the Prussian siege of Paris.[151]

Early conservatory professors of bassoon in Belgium included Borini (Brussels, 1832–41),[152] Bacha (Liège, 1827), and Walravens (Leuven, 1860). Johannes Meinardus Coenen studied at the royal music school in The Hague; 'he was bassoonist 1840–2 in the court orchestra of King Willem II and gave solo recitals until 1851', when he began a successful career as a conductor. He wrote a bassoon concerto, a sonata for bassoon and piano, a quintet for piano and winds, and a woodwind quintet.[153]

Perfetti recognized four important centers of bassoon playing in nineteenth-century Italy: Parma, Bologna, Naples, and Milan. Luigi Tartagnini in 1819 became principal bassoonist in the ducal orchestra at Parma, where he also taught bassoon and singing. His pupils included Marzoli, later active in Paris as a bassoonist and maker.[154] Luigi Orselli, professor of bassoon in the Regia orchestra of Parma (c.1862), wrote that Verdi had raised the level of the bassoon to that of the oboe, clarinet, and cello; its voice was so homogenous that it could blend with the human voice, sounding in unison [or octaves] with soprano, tenor, and other voices. Reflecting his operatic orientation, Orselli's examination included sight-reading a piece of medium difficulty, transposing up or down, one tone or semitone.[155] His course of study included reed-making as well as methods and studies by Ozi, Gatti, Krakamp, Willent-Bordogni, Orselli, Neukirchner, and Tartagnini. His students learned compositions by some of these authors, and by Jacobi, Tamplini, Lassei, and Gebauer. In his bassoon method (c.1874) Orselli expanded on Ozi's precepts. The embouchure was to be 'relaxed' from Bb1 to G2, 'natural' from A2 through G3, and 'pinched' for A3 and above. The cheeks should not be inflated, which would cause a loss of force of sound. The little hole in the crook should be closed on all the low notes to obtain a more mellow sound and to sustain the note; also on B2, for a more beautiful sound. Orselli described the *portamento di voce* or *strisciamento*, an effect obtained by advancing or withdrawing the lips on the blades and shading the finger holes and keys.[156]

Tartagnini taught at Bologna in his early years (1813–16). Successors there included Nazareno Gatti (taught 1864–84), author of a method and exercises.[157] Emmanuele Krakamp, a Neapolitan flutist, wrote methods for many wind instruments; his method for bassoon (1872) was revised for modern use by Enzo Muccetti in 1959. Luigi Caccavaio taught in the Naples conservatory during 1866–1913. His chart for bassoon with 18 keys shows holes 1–6 and 8 uncovered, with several closed keys added. He later designed a reform bassoon with Esposito (mentioned above).

Giuseppe Buccinelli taught at the Milan Conservatory from 1808 to 1827. He was succeeded by Antonio Cantù (taught 1827–68), who served as first bassoon at the Teatro alla Scala 1831–62, performing in the premieres of several early Verdi operas. He was succeeded by his pupil Antonio Torriani, who taught 1868–1908. Principal in the opera orchestra from 1864 to 93, Torriani performed in the premiere performances of Verdi's *Requiem, Otello*, and *Falstaff*. Besides original compositions and arrangements for bassoon, he published a translation of Ozi (Ricordi, 1985) 'that is still a standard textbook in Italian conservatories . . . it gives the measurements of the reeds made by Cantù, appreciably larger than modern ones'. Maino & Orsi (est. Milan, 1880) produced bassoons with the 22-key Jancourt system to Torriani's specification.[158] Other professors included Giuseppe Cremonesi (another Cantù pupil) and Alberto Orefici, author of three books of studies for bassoon.[159] From 1885 Alessandro Maldura of Milan manufactured the Cremonesi system of bassoon.[160] Other Italian charts and methods were published by Gambaro (1835), Corticelli (1840), Willent-Bordogni/Cattaneo (1844), and Gatti (1880).

A continuing French influence was observable in Spain. The bassoon method of Blumer (Paris, 1840) had parallel French and Spanish texts. D. Camilo Melliez, a native of Carcassone, was professor of bassoon at the royal conservatory of music in Madrid during 1846-71.[161] He was also first bassoonist in the royal chapel and royal theater and the dedicatee of a bassoon method, written and published c. 1875 by the clarinettist Romero y Andia. Hough cited a Valencian tradition of wind playing and large symphonic bands prior to the foundation of a full-time opera company in Spain (Madrid, 1856) and symphony orchestra (Madrid, 1859).[162]

Theobald Hürth was noted as a soloist in Zürich in 1822, where he performed the *Grande Sonate*, op. 3, by Anton Liste, with the composer at the piano. By 1827 Hürth was principal bassoon in the Vienna Hofkapelle. After a solo appearance, a reviewer noted that Hürth's unusual bassoon had 'more structure, an unfamiliar sound, and improved mechanism, and thus a noticeable attractiveness to the enunciation'. This may have been an Almenräder bassoon; a letter from Hürth to Schott, dated 10 November 1830, sent greetings to 'Allmenröther'. Shortly after taking up his duties at the conservatory, Hürth wrote to the governing committee to request that four further keys be added to the school instruments: B1, Eb2, G#, and a second octave key.[163] Hürth's teaching materials survive in a manuscript copy by a pupil, Gustav Ibener. His preferred duo format allowed two or more students to play at once in a lesson, observed and corrected by the teacher. Nagy viewed Hürth's method as specifically Viennese, given its emphasis on *Volltönigkeit* (tonal fullness), *Beben* (a fingered vibrato), and *Schattierung* ('shadowing' through dynamic variations).[164] Bassoon methods were published in Vienna by Joseph Fahrbach (1840) and Andreas Nemetz (1844).[165] In 1847 Vojtech (Adalbert) Gross succeeded Bettlach as professor at the Prague conserva-tory. Gross was succeeded in 1886 by his former pupil Ludwig Milde.[166] Both Gross and Milde also taught at the conservatory in Bucharest.[167] Imre Weidinger (1792–1859), a blind Hungarian bassoonist, toured as a soloist throughout Europe, winning general praise. He performed in St. Petersburg in 1828 and in Deberan, Hungary, in 1830, selling only twelve tickets for the latter concert.[168]

London's musical vitality drew continental bassoonists to tour or sojourn there, including Willent-Bordogni (1824–31), Frédéric Baumann (1832–45), Jancourt (1841), and Tamplini (1847–88). Chamber music at the Musical Union Concerts, St. James's Hall, included the bassoonists Baumann (1845), Snelling (1855), Raspi (1862), Winterbottom (1864), and Hutchings (1864).[169] Professors at the Royal Academy of Music included George W. Trout (1880–3) and William B. Wotton (1883–1912). Wotton was also the original bassoon professor at the Royal College of Music (1883–1905). Original tutors were published in England by George Mackintosh (c.1840), Carl Boosé (c.1850), J. A. Kappey (c.1880), and Otto Langey (1885), while tutors from abroad increasingly contained parallel texts in English. Hawkes & Son in 1890 offered reeds of four brands: Trout's Best, Tromba, Snelling's, and Hawkes & Son's Excelsior (these last forty percent more expensive than the first three). Reeds were offered by the dozen or by the gross.

Austrian military bands included two bassoons around 1810, according to Fahrbach; their function was largely confined to accompaniment, and sometimes even to after-beat figures. In 1846, Nemetz quoted from Austrian marches that included two bassoon parts and contra.[170] When an Austrian regiment arrived in Florence in 1824, the tuning pitch of the Teatro della Pergola (A-427.5) rose to A-455. (After the Austrian occupation ended in 1859, the pitch was lowered to 440 by a decree of the Tuscan government.)[171] In 1841, the band of the Collegio in Florence included four fagotti and one flarmonica (a metal double-reed contrabass) among fifty-one players.[172]

Wilhelm Wieprecht, director of Prussian military music, in 1845 conceded that oboes, bassoons, and contrabassoons were not powerful in outdoor use, but argued that 'if our infantry music is to preserve its highest artistic significance, we must not force out these instruments'.[173] He held the line, and at the Paris World Exhibition of 1867, a combined Prussian military band including four oboes, six bassoons, and four contras played Wieprecht's arrangement of Weber's *Oberon* overture and his fantasy on motives from Meyerbeer's *Le Prophète*. Wieprecht's 'Normal-Instrumental-Tableau' of 1860 required oboes, bassoons and contrabassoons in Prussian infantry bands; with the unification of Germany in 1871, Wieprecht's model became standard for all infantry bands in the Reich.

Bassoons also persisted in the British military. Tamplini, who arrived in London in 1847 to play in the royal theater, became a bandmaster in a British regiment in 1853. He published *The Bandsman* (c.1859/60), a method for military bands, giving a table for simple-system bassoon. Circa 1872 he was appointed examiner at the Royal Academy of Music for the class of military music.[174] Meanwhile, the Royal Military School of Music (Kneller Hall) was founded in 1857; bassoon professors there included C. F. Mandel (from 1857) and J. T. Snelling (1859).[175]

Continued dispersion from Western Europe

Seeking opportunities, bassoonists from Italy, Germany, Austria, and France travelled across the globe. Italians performing in the east included Gallina (St. Petersburg, 1844) and Gatti (Odessa, 1851-2).[176] Leone Leoni (1847–1882) played in the orchestra of

Cairo.[177] Among the prominent performers in St. Petersburg who also taught at the conservatory were Satzenhofer (active 1875–1901, from Munich; Ill.49),[178] Platsatka (active 1877–1915, from Austria),[179] and Kotte (active 1893–1924, from Dresden).[180] In Moscow, Alexander Alyabyev (Aljabjew; 1787–1851) wrote a one-movement quintet for winds, left in manuscript.[181] During a soirée of the Russian Musical Society there in 1876, Mozart's Quintet, K. 452, was performed by the pianist Nikolay Rubinstein and the bassoonist K. F. Oeser, among others.[182] Oeser (or Ezer, 1832–85) taught at the Moscow Conservatory.[183] Vasily Sergeyevich Kalinnikov (1866–1901), composer of a noted symphony, was trained as a bassoonist at the Moscow Philharmonic Society Music School (a separate institution) under Ilyinsky and Blaramberg, p1884–1892.[184]

In 1824, the bassoonist Anton Reiff left Mainz for the United States, visiting Boston and Baltimore before settling in New York. He was a founder in 1842 of the New York Philharmonic, the first professional orchestra in the country. Willent-Bordogni performed in New York in 1824 and again in 1833–4.[185] In 1830, Hürth considered leaving Vienna, hoping for better opportunities in the United States.[186] German-born Paul Richard Eltz taught bassoon at New England Conservatory in 1875 and was the original principal bassoonist in the Boston Symphony Orchestra, 1881-3.[187] Italian-born Camillo Formentini (b.1854) taught bassoon and double bass at the conservatory of Montevideo, Uruguay, of which he later became director.

The first bassoons to arrive in English colonies were likely in the hands of regimental bandsmen. By 1871, however, bassoons probably figured in some or all of the philharmonic societies established in Adelaide, Barbados, Dunedin, Madras, Melbourne, and Sydney.[188]

Repertory

The glib, conversational, galant style of the classical period lived on in French wood-wind chamber music. Parisian groups performing woodwind quintets or other works, often with strings and/or piano, included the Société de musique (from 1847) and the Société des quintettes harmoniques (from 1869).[189] Contemporaneous with this conservative chamber music were the path-breaking symphonic and operatic works of Meyerbeer and Berlioz. Berlioz often wrote three bassoon parts, the bottom one doubled. In his *Grande messe des morts* (1837), *Symphonie funèbre et triomphale* (1840), and the cantata *l'Impériale* (1856) eight bassoons are specified, mostly in two voices but sometimes four. Berlioz also wrote four independent parts in the 'Waverley' overture (1828) and *Huit Scènes de Faust* (1829, Brander's Song).

In his orchestration treatise Berlioz noted the 'pale, cold, cadaverous timbre' of the bassoon's mid-register, citing the Resurrection of the Nuns in Meyerbeer's *Robert le Diable*, iii (1831). For quick legato passages, Berlioz cited the bathing scene from Meyerbeer's *Huguenots* ii (1836). Berlioz wrote for woodwinds in three octaves in the development section of the *Symphonie fantastique*, i (1830), and again in the repeat of the clarinet theme, iii.[190] Berlioz warned in his orchestration treatise that notes above B♭4 were dangerous on the bassoon, but he wrote to B4 in the *Waverley* overture.

Eingeführt am Kaiserlichen Conservatorium in St. Petersburg.

Neue praktische

Fagott-Schule

Method for the Bassoon.

Zum

Selbstunterricht

geeignet
von

J. Satzenhofer.

Professor am Kaiserlichen
Konservatorium in St. Petersburg

Teil I   2 M. netto.
Teil II 2 M. netto.   Teil III (Duette) 2 M. netto.
Komplett in 1 Band 4 M. netto.

Verlag von Jul. Heinr. Zimmermann.
LEIPZIG. ST. PETERSBURG. MOSKAU. RIGA. LONDON.
Im gleichen Verlage erschien:
Petrow, J. A. Tonleiter-Schule für Fagott 2 M. _ netto.

49. Title page of Satzenhofer's tri-lingual method for the bassoon of Wilhelm Heckel (1900).

From the time of *Rigoletto* (1851), Verdi began to use the bassoon for its individual timbre. In *Falstaff* (1893), he used the bassoon's staccato liberally in support of the comic plot. He treasured its lyrical powers too, however, and scored with great imagination for four bassoons in *Don Carlo* (1867), the Requiem (1874, 'Libera me'), *Otello* (1887), and *Quatro pezzi sacri* (1898).[191] In 1995 a manuscript containing an early work by Verdi, probably a three-movement capriccio for bassoon and orchestra, was discovered. It may be identical with a work for bassoon and orchestra performed in Busseto on 25 February 1838.[192]

Wagner wrote for three bassoons in *Lohengrin* (1850), often in a masterly texture of three separate parts. In *Tristan und Isolde* (1865), he began to take the third bassoon as low as A1, requiring an extended bell joint. In *Das Rheingold* (1869), Wagner featured the bassoons ever more prominently, but in modular motives – splashes of tone color (often dark), with two or three bassoons often moving in thirds, notably in the motives called 'Erda', 'Scheming', and 'the Ring'. In the square-cut prelude to *Die Meistersinger* (1868), the bassoons' running staccato eighth notes are marked 'sehr kurz gestoßen' (very shortly tongued). This effect is reminiscent of Berlioz's *Symphonie fantastique*, Grieg's 'In the Hall of the Mountain King' (from *Peer Gynt*, 1876), and Dukas's *Sorcerer's Apprentice* (1897).

Tchaikovsky's Symphony no. 2 ('Little Russian', 1872) begins with a motto played solo by the horn; the composer chose the bassoon to provide an echo, preserving the motto's dignity while heightening its pathos. The composer's Symphony no. 4 (1878) includes several unforgettable solos for bassoon in the upper-middle register; he closed the troubled slow movement by recalling a theme from the first movement, this time ending *pianissimo morendo* on the bassoon's open F3. Tchaikovsky chose to open his Symphony no. 6 (1893) with a *pp* solo in the bassoon's low register, a foretaste of the *pppppp* the composer wrote a few minutes later, leading into the movement's exposition.

Among the earliest attention paid to the instrument by Richard Strauss was *Der Zweikampf*, 'an amusing little trifle' for flute, bassoon and orchestra, composed in 1884.[193] In his *Don Quixote* (1897), the hapless title character is introduced by a fanfare – heroic if awkwardly dissonant – by two bassoons soli. In Variation 8, portraying an adventure in a magic boat, the three bassoons and contra take up a flowing theme in four-part imitative counterpoint, carrying on in learned fashion for forty measures.

No less significant than passages conceived expressly for bassoon were composers' increasingly automatic assumptions that the bassoon could match the demands placed on other instruments. In his overture to *Tannhäuser* (1845), Wagner wrote to E5 for the bassoon, doubling the string line. Like Mendelssohn's Symphony no. 4 (1833), *Tannhäuser* demanded triple tonguing on a single pitch from the bassoonist. Rimsky-Korsakov's *Scheherazade* suite, op. 35 (1888), required the bassoonist to match the virtuosity of the clarinetist in a famous solo cadenza of fevered intensity. In the *Valse* movement (iii) of his Symphony no. 5 (1888), Tchaikovsky wrote a solo for the bassoon including a sequence of slurs outlining descending sevenths. The passage tests the legato powers of the player, because shifting to a lower mode of response is always more delicate than jumping higher, especially if no crook key is present.

Chapter 7

A tale of two systems, 1900–1990

By the dawn of the new century, the flood of radical innovation had receded. The nineteenth-century reform bassoons were commercial failures, but they served to air the question of what was desired from the bassoon during the romantic era. Apparently the desired instrument would still be 'majestic in the bass, touching in the tenor, full and serious in the middle', as Jancourt had written in 1847.[1] In other words, its scale would not be homogenized into the uniformly metallic timbre heard from most of the reform bassoons. It would not match the penetrating power of the treble woodwinds, especially in an orchestral context. In order to produce the irreplaceable colors to which composers and listeners had become accustomed, it would preserve the chimneyed tone holes that offended the 'mathematically' minded purists. To this day, most Heckel-system bassoons have five deep, uncovered holes for the fingers, while French-system bassoons generally have six. The bassoon's lattice of open-standing holes does not proceed in strictly increasing diameter in correspondence with the conical bore. And yet by 1900 it was clear that this sort of modestly evolved bassoon timbre was the preference of composers and conductors.[2] Meanwhile, players accepted certain additional plates, rings, and keys that made their lives easier. They rejected the idea of a fork fingering for B2/B3, along with other fingerings or keys borrowed from Boehm clarinets or flutes. The fork fingering for E♭3 survived, still an obstacle to finger technique and sonority. The new fingerings for E4 and above were seldom simpler than the classical fingerings they replaced, although the resulting pitches often had more power and evenness.

Further development of the bassoon became more a matter of smoothing out minor imperfections, and of tweaking rather than transcending the traditional sound. Reliable chromatic response over more than three octaves, a full range of available trills, and manageable intonation at all dynamic levels were still a tall order for any wind instrument. And these are only the audible qualities — makers and players also had to confront questions of wear, moisture, stability, and cost. To all these issues twentieth-century makers devoted themselves.

In 1900 three traditions of bassoon making survived: the German system, the French system, and the English. The English bassoon, based on the older Savary model, was already under challenge from the newer Buffet models, while a fourth tradition — that of Central Europe — was recently deceased, even though some older bassoons were still in use in non-professional circles. It does not follow, however, that bassoon players thus produced three or four immediately distinguishable regional sounds. The world's many players, no matter their choice of bassoon, had a range of different ideas about tone production, in which pitch standards, mental concept, reed style, embouchure, and training all played a part. As a result, bassoon playing in the new century was richly varied from one country to another.

Within each of the two types of bassoon that prevailed during the twentieth century, design changes were subtle and often invisible (though not inaudible). For bassoon makers and players, more consequential changes occurred in the social and economic fabric of modern industrial society. New trends in transportation, communications, and global expansion had broad and meaningful effects on the bassoon's cultural role.

1900–1914: New concerns and production techniques

Many European makers adopted techniques of mass production, which allowed them to produce hundreds of bassoons per year. Advertising brochures sometimes boasted of steam or electric power, showing an iconic factory with smokestack. A stratified product line was often seen, with three or more levels of quality and price. Some makers, however, took an opposite tack by stressing the artisanal tradition of their work. Wilhelm Heckel advertised in c.1907 that hundreds of pattern instruments and tools were preserved in fireproof vaults at his shop, and invited lovers of music and art to visit his private museum of early woodwind instruments. His historical consciousness reflected much thought about the essential qualities of the bassoon.[3]

In an era of increased international commerce and travel, both makers and players had to cope with a multiplicity of pitch standards. Archie Camden described the situation in England c.1896:

> All professional orchestras were usually flat pitch by then. . . . It was, however, quite a different matter in the field of military and brass bands and amateur societies. All their instruments were built to the high pitch and no one was anxious to incur the expense of buying new. . . . [O]rchestral wind players . . . not only were burdened with two instruments on their travels but . . . had to accustom their ears to the constantly changing pitch. Those players with perfect or absolute pitch were in misery.[4]

In a catalog of c.1907, the Heckel firm noted six 'most-used tunings', ranging from A-435 to approximately A-460. Another concern of makers and players was management of low-register response. Soon after 1905, Hermann Ficker lined the bassoon's bass joint with felt, in an evident attempt to mute the bass response.[5] In another strategy, both Heckel and Gustav Mollenhauer offered a 'mute-mechanism', in which small pairs of holes replaced most of the normal single tone holes on the bass joint; the player could choose to open only one vent of the pair, thereby obtaining a muted response. Under this option, the bell joint was also narrowed to a minimum internal diameter of 1.0 cm.[6]

A simpler approach to the management of low-register response was management of the crook vent. Crooks were commonly made with venting holes (often located up to three inches above the receiver top, unlike the half-inch spacing of today) (Ill. 50). But closing the crook vent for smoother response in the low register was not a universal practice, while closing the vent for G4 and G#4 was only occasionally recommended in charts before World War II. By the late nineteenth century, a short key was sometimes mounted on the crook itself; it could be converted manually from open to closed position. This system required quickness or compromise at times, but apparently served the needs of players for many years. Eventually, on most German-system bassoons, a crook key mounted on a long rod-axle was operated by LT.[7] On French-system instruments, the key was normally operated by L4, although a second spatula for LT was often optional.[8]

Makers addressed the needs of military bands, which were sometimes posted to tropical corners of various European empires. In a 1910 catalogue, Hawkes & Son advised military bandmasters that 'bands stationed in hot climates should invariably have the wing joint in ebonite'. In 1902 Boosey & Co. offered the entire bassoon in either ebonite or rosewood. A Mahillon bassoon in ebonite was 'specifically recommended for military bands in India and the Colonies'. For all German-system bassoons, a lining of the down bore with hard rubber became standard. All these strategies helped stabilize the dimensions of the bore against humidity changes.

In 1900, many British and Belgian players still favored the bassoon design of Savary jeune (d.1853). Makers in those countries obliged, supplying instruments with seven open finger holes and no duplicated touches; a low B key and a crook key were optional. Their bells echoed the distinctive Savary profile. Hawkes & Son advertised in 1910 that the firm had acquired the tools of Alfred Morton, who had supposedly worked for Savary in the mid-nineteenth century, becoming his successor in spirit in London after 1872. The catalogue stated that: 'of the many past makers – Almenräder,

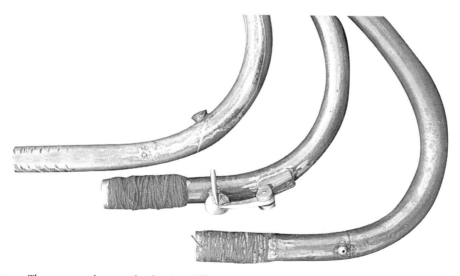

50.   Three pre-modern crooks showing different strategies for the vent. Waterhouse Collection.

Savary, and Cornelius Ward – it is only Savary whose old models are still sought for and possess some value'. Hawkes & Son bassoons were tested and tuned by E. F. James, principal bassoon in four London orchestras as well as festivals in Birmingham, Leeds, Gloucester, Worcester, and Hereford; an English bassoonist could be highly mobile in an age of abundant rail service.[9] On display at the Board of Trade in London, 1905, were samples of cane for oboe and bassoon reeds, available from farmers in Godella, Spain (near Valencia).[10]

In 1908 bassoons of the Mahillon firm had a Savary-style bell and a crook key for L4; better models offered more rod-axle keys, including low B1, and covered vents for R3 and RT. Mahillon, with a factory in London until World War I, had a strong presence in the British market. In Brussels, meanwhile, Mahillon offered a model endorsed by Josse Boogaerts, who was professor at the Brussels Conservatoire, 1899–1937. The Boogaerts model had a simple RT and covered R2 and R3. His chart called for the crook key to be closed on B3 and C4, unlike French charts of the time.

Meanwhile the major French maker of bassoons had embraced new ideas. In an Evette & Schaeffer catalog of 1912, all bassoons had the Buffet Crampon logo, a crook key for L4, the longer keys on rods, a low B key, and a covered R3. On the twenty-key 'système Evette & Schaeffer' model, a RT key allowed for an F#/G# trill. The twenty-key Jancourt model had brilles (rings) for L2 and R2. The nineteen-key Conservatoire Model of 1911 lacked these features, but had a C# key for R1. All models were offered in maple or palisander, with maillechort (German silver) keys; brass keys were optional on most models. A wing lining of caoutchouc (hard rubber) was recommended: it 'renders the bore of the small branche absolutely smooth, favoring the emission of sound; also, being waterproof, it conserves the exact proportions of the bore'. Recommended accessories included the bassoon method by Bourdeau, Buffet Crampon reeds, gouged cane, reed-making tools, and charts by Jancourt, Coyon, and Letellier.

The dealer H. Schoenaers-Millereau of Paris offered both a Conservatoire model with twenty-one keys and two rings, and Savary models with thirteen to nineteen keys. Ullmann of Paris c.1907 offered bassoons with fifteen to seventeen keys; the cheaper models had only lever keys. In Italy, Leopoldo Bucci, a professor at the Milan conservatory, worked with Maino & Orsi to revise its French-inspired bassoon design.[11]

Makers in Germany were eager to sell bassoons to players of the French system. An early catalog by Oscar Adler offered Heckel and French models, as well as a French-looking model with German fingering patterns on the boot (Ill. 51). In a similar vein, Heckel's catalog of 1907 noted:

The following bassoons are made with bore and joints like the well-known and commonly used Heckel bassoons. The outer form of the instruments, the layout of keys and spatulas is as with French bassoons, so that a transition from those instruments to a genuine Heckel bassoon comes very easily. The fingerings of these instruments are the same as those of Parisian bassoons, except for a few pitches in the high register.[12]

a)   b)

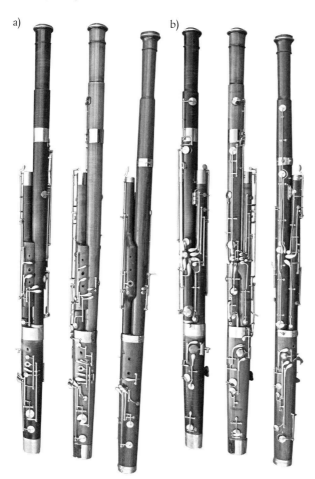

51. Three bassoons combining attributes of the French and German systems: (a) finger side; (b) thumb side. From left: Heckel (1907), Heckel (1921), Honi & fils (Paris, c.1900). Waterhouse Collection.

In Italy, Cirio Stadio advocated the Heckel bassoon in his method of 1908. His pupil Sanguinetti succeeded him at the Milan Conservatory, but most Italian players held to the French/Italian system until after World War II. J. Satzenhofer, professor at Imperial Conservatory, St. Petersburg, pictured Wilhelm Heckel's system in his method of 1900.

Conductors' tastes played a role in the choice of bassoon type. Hans Richter, a prominent leader of Viennese and German orchestras, became conductor of the Hallé Orchestra of Manchester, England, in 1899. 'Not happy with the quality of English bassoon playing', Richter brought two Viennese players of Heckel bassoons to the orchestra in 1903–4.[13] Preferences were not simple chauvinism, however. Despite his own German birth, the immigrant Walter Damrosch in 1905 recruited five prominent French and Belgian wind players, including the bassoonist Auguste Mesnard, to be principals in his New York Symphony Orchestra. Wilhelm Gericke, conductor of the Boston Symphony Orchestra, had installed a French player, Albert Debuchy, as his principal bassoon during 1901–5.

An obituary for Wilhelm Heckel in 1909 noted that the maker had cultivated relations with conductors of the largest Kapellen.[14] Among the congratulants during the firm's seventy-fifth anniversary in 1906 were Richard Strauss, the conductor Felix Mottl, and the head of the Prussian Army musical establishment, Professor Roßberg. A Heckel catalog of c.1907 cited Heckel players in 'the most important army and marine bands in the largest cities of the world'.[15] Military bands accounted for the majority of Rudall, Carte & Co.'s bassoon sales, as shown in the firm's order books for 1869–1942. Alfred Hays of London, c.1905 'sole agent for Buffet Military band instruments', offered the Jancourt, Evette & Schaeffer, and Conservatoire systems, plus a model in metal.

Early in the new century Wilhelm Heckel abandoned the table on the long joint and offset the C2 vent, giving this joint the appearance it has today. In 1901, Heckel patented a mechanism for the R3 key, a rod through the boot replacing the old linkage that wrapped around the boot.[16] In 1902, Heckel and his son August patented a boot key 'for clear-sounding high G3', that is, the brille mechanism for R2 and the F key.

Kruspe of Erfurt in 1909 still advertised its 'C. Kruspe System' model in three pieces, with some added keys and relocated tone holes. But experimentation often had more modest or even retrospective goals; a patent application of 1906 by Oscar Adler revived the fork B♭, using a new linkage and vent.

1914–1939: War, peace, and microphones

As always, war thinned the ranks of bassoon makers, who tended to be young and male. Hans and Fritz Mönnig, owners of the family firm, served in the German military during World War I. Among the makers killed in the war were August Heckel, Hans Willy Hüller, and many of the Hüller firm's employees.[17]

In peacetime, the existing concerns of bassoon makers and players continued. J. N. Mollenhauer of Fulda in 1925–7 lamented the collapse of the A-435 pitch standard established in 1859; writing again in 1931–3, he blamed radio broadcasts of orchestral concerts for the upward pressure.[18] A new standard of A-440, supposedly universal, was established in 1939.[19]

Some makers increased their manufacturing capacity and targeted new markets. In 1928, Hüller employed 100 workers and produced 11,527 woodwind instruments; 'seventy percent of the production went overseas'. Lein noted that the Gebrüder Mönnig firm exported to the U. S. market during the 1920s.[20] V. Kohlert of Graslitz claimed to have sold 1,233 bassoons in 1928–30; the firm in 1933 offered four German models and three French models.[21] A visitor to the Heckel factory in 1937 noted that the bassoon's bell was turned after a mechanical pattern, while the boot was turned on an oval-cutting lathe. Holes were drilled by a complicated copy machine designed by W. H. Heckel. The firm's guest book at the time included signatures in Arabic and Japanese.[22] A visitor to J. Mollenhauer & Söhne, Fulda, in 1937, noted a 'copier-machine' similar to Heckel's.[23]

Makers also offered more options to customers. Whisper-key locks appeared as options in Heckel's 1931 catalogue.[24] Kohlert options in 1933 included an A1 bell, nickel or silver plating, a French model with L4 piano key, and finger holes lined with

hard rubber. Some later models had long and wing joints of equal length for convenience in packing (this design, long seen in many French-system bassoons, was later
called the 'gentleman's cut'). The German-American repairman Hans Mönnig claimed
to have invented 'water tubes' (silver liners for the five finger holes, projecting into the
bore to divert condensation) as an after-market option in the 1920s.[25] Exploring a
different strategy, Edgar Pätz of Leipzig in 1932 patented a design that covered finger
holes 1–5, moving the vents to the thumb side; this was apparently not produced. The
Boehm influence surfaced again in 1931, when a Heckel catalog showed 'an instrument with touches and mechanisms on the boot joint that was decidedly similar to
that found on a Boehm system clarinet. . . . Bb2/Bb3 could be played as 123 4 and B2/
B3 as 123 5'.[26] But this bassoon was a unique exemplar made in response to a customer
request.

W. H. Heckel told of building a metal bassoon in order to compare its sound to his
modern Heckel bassoon model. It was well in tune with itself, he reported, but the
tone color was incoherent and dull, lacking the 'soul' analogous to the male voice.[27]
Nonetheless, metal bassoons were offered by Heckel (1931) and Mönnig (1932/3), and
patented by Wunderlich of Siebenbrunn (1936). Mönnig built bassoons of Plexiglass
in 1937, as did Meinel & Herold in 1937/8, intended for use in extreme climates. The
Mönnig model was used by German army bands in North Africa.[28]

On a less visible level, W. H. Heckel had been experimenting with aspects of the
bassoon's proportions, while hardly changing its key work or appearance. After many
slight adjustments to the location and diameter of tone holes, he ended up shortening
the sounding length of a standard bassoon by a large fraction of an inch, while
increasing the comparable bore width, in places, by tiny fractions of an inch.[29] The
eventual result, usually dated from around 1920, was the 'short bore' bassoon, which
had noticeably increased pitch flexibility and projection. It made new demands on the
player, however: in order to preserve good intonation, the short-bore bassoonist
needed a flexible embouchure, a flexible reed, and a good ear. The new model also
posed risks for the maker, as Alan Fox wrote in 1968:

> From the manufacturer's standpoint, the short bore instrument is more difficult to
> control. The bore dominates the tones holes . . . [especially] in the middle and
> upper register notes. . . . In the long bore instrument, most of the tones holes domi-
> nate the bore. The bore deviations show up as differences in resistance and tone,
> rather than pitch, with variations being less severe than in the other type.[30]

After abandoning Almenräder's double-headed vent for A2/A3, Wilhelm Heckel had
drilled a single hole into the up bore; this vent now became dual once more (an oval
hole into the up bore, plus a small round hole into the down bore). The vents for Bb2/
Bb3, formerly two holes under one pad cup, now became triple. Locations and diameters of Heckel's tone holes show continuing tweaking over time, as do the main
bores. The wall thickness was increased slightly during the 1930s, especially in the
boot joint. The chimney of the G vent was made perpendicular (thus shallower).
Meanwhile, long-bore and 'World System' Heckel models were still built at times, and
the firm continued to respond to personal requests from customers.

The French bassoon remained a narrower-bored instrument than the German, especially in the bell. Compared with a variety of Heckel bassoons, a Buffet from 1930 shows the following visible differences: tone holes L1–3 and R1–2 are larger; tone holes L3 and R1 are significantly further apart; most keyed tone holes on the boot joint are smaller and higher on the bore; the A and B♭ vents are single holes; and tone holes on the long and bell joints are significantly narrower.[31] In an acoustical comparison of Buffet and Heckel bassoons (vintage unspecified), Krüger found that the Buffet had a strong additional formant around 2,500 Hz, accounting for the generally brighter tone perceived by many listeners.[32]

The 1922 Buffet Crampon catalogue showed little visible innovation over the 1912 catalogue of its alter ego, Evette & Schaeffer. Orsi of Milan offered what was outwardly, at least, a Buffet Crampon imitation. Boosey's new 'Regent' Bassoon, pictured in a 1923 catalogue, offered a 'Creation key' for LT, allowing easy alternation between E4 and G4, as demanded in the aria 'Auf starkem Fittige', no. 15 of Haydn's oratorio.[33] Before its merger with Hawkes & Son in 1931, Boosey & Co. had produced 724 bassoons and contras. As a legacy of the merger, four 'Morton' bassoons were made in 1931, keeping the Savary ideal alive still.[34] Rudall Carte & Co. dropped the Savary model name by 1931, while continuing to offer similar bassoons under unchanged model numbers.

Cecil James (1913–99), a stalwart of the French bassoon in London, noted the shifting tastes of English bassoonists during this period:

> In my early days of bassoon playing most players used the 'Buffet' bassoon, except for a few who used the French system made by Mahillon in Belgium and Morton in England. . . . [Around 1930] began in London the first real stirring of interest in the German system bassoon, triggered off I believe by a visit of the New York Philharmonic and their excellent bassoon department, all playing Heckel bassoons. . . . I have a feeling that the French system bassoon is a little more particular about the selection of reeds if one is to avoid that awful 'buzz' sound; to my ears this is most objectionable, but in those days, sadly, it seemed to satisfy so many players in England – and, dare I say it, in France! [35]

A Boosey & Hawkes catalogue from after 1931 offered the 'Model H', a German system:

> This model has achieved a remarkable degree of popularity with performers in this country and America; it possesses many advantages over the ordinary models, due mainly to the duplication of certain key work which affords greater facilities for the execution of rapid passages. . . . A further advantage is the open bell key which tends to improve the tone of the lowest register.

In fact the B1 tone hole of the Buffet and other French models is engineered to remain open on C1 and C#1 as well, though not on higher notes.

In the United States, C. G. Conn of Elkhart, an importer of bassoons since 1880, offered both systems c.1924. The 'Professional Model' (French System, seventeen keys) was 'considerably cheaper than the Heckel system and for this reason is chosen often by the beginner', according to a sales brochure. The 'Symphony Model' was a Heckel System; 'professionals choose this model, as it enables them to play difficult passages with greater ease, being quick in response and surprisingly agile'. The Cundy-Bettoney Company of Boston offered a 'Paris Conservatory model, maple wood, hard-rubber lined throughout' in a 1927 catalogue. Its bassoons were made 'for the first time in this country' for use by U. S. Army bands, the catalogue stated, making it 'no longer necessary to rely on Europe for these rather uncommon instruments'. (Harry Bettoney, the English-born head of the firm, was evidently unaware of the American-made bassoons of the classical period.) H. & A. Selmer, Inc., the Elkhart branch of the French firm, in 1931 offered the H. Selmer (Paris) Full Conservatory system model and two models branded Barbier (Paris): the Heckel System, lined or unlined, with automatic crook key; and the French Conservatory System.

The electrical era of music begins (1925)

Archie Camden described the days of acoustical (pre-electrical) recording:

> For orchestral works there was an enormous horn-like microphone in a central position, and any player with a prominent solo had to creep up near to it to achieve the right balance – and then go back to let someone else have a go.[36]

The bassoon was sometimes used to play or double the cello line, probably because its strong overtone structure would register on the acoustical-era recording equipment.[37]

The electric microphone, introduced to commercial recording in 1925, captured a wider range of dynamics and frequency, a particular advantage to the bassoon and other low-to-midrange instruments. Camden's 1926 performance of Mozart's K. 191 occupied five 78 rpm sides, with Senaillé's *Allegro spiritoso* on the sixth. The earliest concerto recording of a bassoon, it caused a stir in the global woodwind community:

> [The conductor Hamilton] Harty came back from America and said all the bassoonists, and most of the woodwind players, had got it. The same story kept coming back to me from other parts of the world – the Senaillé had acquired quite a public of its own, and (I was told officially) had the greatest sales in America – and Japan!

The bassoon may have been chosen for this early test because of its low tessitura and uncommon timbre. The Columbia Gramophone Company's studio in Clerkenwell 'wished to know how the solo bassoon sounded'.[38] Despite the improvement, early electrical microphones did not do full justice to the bassoon sound. Sol Schoenbach reported that:

> . . . the advent of sound movies helped the German bassoon gain dominance over the French because the German bassoon recorded better than the French bassoon

on the equipment they had in those days. The engineers would complain that they couldn't pick up the French bassoon clearly on their microphones.[39]

The electric microphone also opened the door to live radio broadcasting. Recordings and broadcasts, which allowed performers to hear themselves and even distant colleagues, would eventually transform the musical economy. Live musicians were suddenly optional – the new electronic media allowed performances remote in place or time.

Victor Bruns entered the Rimsky-Korsakov Conservatorium in 1924, where he was one of five bassoon students under Aleksander Wassilliew, principal bassoonist of the Leningrad Philharmonic. He recalled:

> In this time silent films arrived, which was wonderful for the students, who were engaged to play twice a day to play, including the most difficult excerpts like *Scheherazade*, receiving higher wages than at the Opera.[40]

The silent-film work that sustained Bruns and his fellow students was doomed by the arrival of the electrical microphone, even though the new sound films created recording opportunities for a few bassoonists. W. H. Heckel sensed the socio-economic shift under way in 1933 when he praised 'live' music:

> It brings people closer to people and stimulates them to go to a concert hall, and not always to forsake people, sitting alone in a little room with a warmed-up cup of coffee, half-sleeping while hearing a radio symphony. [41]

Hearing other bassoonists on radio, or oneself on a recording, abruptly raised the consciousness of players, raising issues like low-register response and vibrato. Benjamin Kohon, a prominent New York bassoonist, wrote in 1932:

> I consider the bassoon a very difficult instrument to learn – due mostly to the reed problem. The attack is difficult, particularly on the lower notes, especially in trying to play very softly. . . . I think a little vibrato is also not amiss, but this must not be exaggerated, and when playing these sustained notes, they should be practiced at times evenly, and at times with a little vibrato – the vibrato being produced by the throat.[42]

Bassoonists recording for films and phonograph records had to meet raised expectations. In 1939, Schoenbach recorded the opening solo of *Le sacre du printemps* for the Disney film *Fantasia*. 'He later reported that it took forty-five repetitions before [conductor Leopold] Stokowski was satisfied.'[43] (Tape editing still lay a few years in the future.) The film also gave new life to Dukas's *L'apprenti sorcier* (1897), providing a generation of the broad public with an iconic earful of the bassoon and contrabassoon. The timbre and volume sought by artistic bassoonists had always been influenced by the need to project the sound into a concert hall. The recording studio lessened this need. Don Christlieb described an abrupt shift 'to a darker set-up', spurred by the attractive dark tone of a colleague, the hornist Dennis Brain.[44]

Radio broadcasting exposed players and other listeners to varied styles of music, past and present. Between 1936 and 1939, Gwydion Brooke, who was principal bassoonist of the BBC Scottish Orchestra, also broadcast regularly as a member of the groups Rhythm and Reeds, and Rhythm Classics, playing virtuosic arrangements of waltzes, schottisches, and novelty tunes. Brooke had begun on the tenor saxophone in 1923 at the age of eleven, striving to imitate the novelty recordings of the saxophonist Rudy Wiedoft, issued 1917–34.[45] He was later one of the earliest English bassoonists to use vibrato. The bassoon made an early appearance in jazz and dance-band recordings by the orchestras of Fats Waller (1928, played by Garvin Bushell) and Paul Whiteman (1929, played by Red Mayer or Frankie Trumbauer).[46] Bushell was inspired by Herb Johnson, a saxophonist/bassoonist who was playing in the Sam Wooding 'symphonic jazz' orchestra in New York in 1923–4. Bushell doubled on bassoon at times at the Apollo Theater (1934) and Cotton Club (1936) in New York. Johnson had studied at 'the conservatory in Boston', and Bushell would later study with Simon Kovar and Eli Carmen, prominent bassoonists in New York.[47]

War, state management, and internationalization of taste, 1939–1989

Another war caused new disruption for makers and players of the bassoon. Bassoonists joining the British forces included Cecil James, Gwydion Brooke, and Anthony Baines.[48] Among the American players who interrupted their careers were Stephen Maxym, Frank Ruggieri, Sol Schoenbach (who later 'battled' to reclaim his former position), Leonard Sharrow, and Sherman Walt. Raymond Allard reportedly played in a U.S. Army band.

Viktor Bruns, playing at the Leningrad State Opera in 1937, was deported on three days' notice, along with other German citizens. Bruns ended up in the Volksoper orchestra of Berlin, but was drafted into the German military in 1944.[49] The maker Albert Mönnig died in a bombing raid, while his brother Willy Mönnig was a prisoner of war until 1947.[50] Hermann Hüller was taken to Buchenwald and never returned. In 1939, the Püchner firm was ordered to switch production to aircraft components. Later in the war, the Hüller firm was required to begin producing armaments.[51] At the Heckel firm, only three old men, two apprentices, and one handicapped man were active, producing only one hundred bassoons during the war. Materials were hard to come by, as were buyers.[52]

Bassoons were out of production at Strasser Marigaux Lemaire during the entire war for lack of suitable wood. Even before the Buffet Crampon factory in Mantes was damaged by bombs, materials and workers were lacking.[53] In the United States, mass production of bassoons began in 1940, when C. G. Conn of Elkhart advertised its custom-built drilling machine, which would produce tone holes in bassoon bodies of American maple.[54] In 1942 the factory was diverted into making items for defense; female workers replaced the male workers who left to join the armed forces. Bassoon production apparently resumed from 1947 to 1966.[55]

After the war ended in 1945, the production, sale, and purchase of bassoons took on a geopolitical dimension. Traditional woodwind-making centers, formerly in western Bohemia, were now divided by national borders. Markneukirchen, Schöneck, and Klingenthal were in the DDR (East Germany), while Graslitz (Kraslice), part of the Sudetenland, was annexed to Czechoslovakia; ethnic Germans there were repatriated to East Germany on short notice. Bassoon factories in both countries were either expropriated or subjected to state management, under strong influence of the USSR. Adler, Mönnig, and Hüller were directed to handle foreign sales through Demusa, a DDR office located at Leninstraße 133, Klingenthal, founded in 1960. Production slowed because of bureaucratic delays. Orders in hard currencies were given priority, although American traders were barred from importing bassoons from the DDR. They circumvented this obstacle by assigning invented brands to unstamped imported instruments. The first postwar shipments of reparations by the DDR went to the Soviet Union, according to Lein, including bassoons from Hüller. By 1947 Oskar and Wilhelm Hüller were dismissed from the family company by the state-appointed managers.[56]

The West German town of Nauheim became a magnet for makers displaced from the Sudetenland. The Vinzenz Püchner factory in Kraslice was expropriated by the Czech government under the Beneš decrees of 1945. Its former production foreman, Wenzel Schreiber, emigrated to Nauheim in 1947, where he founded his own woodwind-making firm. A year later, Joseph Püchner also emigrated to Nauheim, establishing a new firm under his own name. Unable at first to obtain suitably dried wood, the factory at first produced music stands, rubber mouthpieces, and motorcycle horns, and repaired woodwind instruments until, after a few years, wood was obtained.[57]

The heavy hand of state management continued to shape the destinies of the DDR bassoon makers. 'In 1972 all the companies were completely nationalized, and Hüller was called VEB-Woodwind Instruments Schöneck'; other firms were similarly renamed. From 1975, Lein noted, 'Hüller was allowed to produce only bassoons, Adler only oboes and bassoons'. Between 1975 and 1989, most of the Mönnig factory output went to countries of the Eastern bloc. Willy Mönnig recorded that the company produced 15,897 bassoons between 1925 and 1993.[58]

Even long-established firms in West Germany suffered a delayed recovery from wartime disruption. Johannes Mollenhauer of Kassel, nearing age seventy after the war, resumed production in the kitchen of his private home, along with two co-workers. His firm later contracted some routine assembly tasks to individuals in the Czech Republic, where wages were lower.[59] Wilhelm Herman Heckel wrote in 1947 that 'My factory is indeed in operation, but it works only in much reduced volume'.[60]

Franz Groffy, a trained engineer, headed the Heckel firm after the death in 1952 of his father-in-law W. H. Heckel, overseeing subtle changes in the firm's designs. Burton noted that in a sample of twenty-six Heckel bassoons, those manufactured during the 1960s 'were generally longer than those of the preceding four decades'.[61] Other observers noted that under Groffy's supervision, the wall thickness increased and tone holes on the long and bell joints were no longer undercut (Ill. 52). Burton and Hähnchen noted some of the variations in bore and tone-hole diameter found in selected bassoons by Schreiber, Conn, Polisi, and Mönnig.[62]

Radio broadcasting and electrical recording affected the livelihoods of professional bassoon players, creating new opportunities for those in chosen ensembles, while triggering a grand decline in the live-performance economy. After World War II, the

52. Edith Groffy Reiter, a qualified instrument maker in the fifth generation of the Heckel firm. Langwill Archive.

broad adoption of tape recorders enabled producers and engineers to edit the captured sounds into a finished product virtually free of such musical flaws as wayward intonation, cracked notes, and rhythmic imprecisions. As listeners became accustomed to such technical perfection, their expectations of performers rose. Conductors and players, including bassoonists, began to worry most about intonation and strict fidelity to the printed score. Rhythmic flexibility and personal expression began to wane. Prewar recordings sounded like a live performance, one wit observed, whereas postwar live performances sound like a studio recording, with few technical flaws. This new literal style, audible in recordings by elite professional orchestras, later became the goal of amateur players as well.

Easy long-distance travel shrank the world further, exposing bassoonists to the sounds and tastes of their counterparts from abroad and sharpening the rivalry for a universally accepted bassoon model. The visit of the New York Philharmonic to

London in 1928, mentioned above, inspired some English players to change to the Heckel system. Cecil James, who adhered to the French system through this era, claimed to have no trouble blending with second bassoonists who played German instruments. James commented in 1987:

> ... Some years earlier [1936] I had changed to a Buffet, saying good-bye to my Boosey & Hawkes; the Buffet, I found had a bigger weight of tone. ... The French bassoon has many faults – weak notes, and doubtful intonation on many of them – but these weaknesses can be overcome with extra keys, and with fingerings that are not to be found in the standard fingering charts. But with a good reed on a good day, one can sing like a bird on the French system bassoon.[63]

James in 1953 co-signed a letter to *The Daily Telegraph* of London praising the French bassoon. This drew an answer from Archie Camden, who claimed that 'in addition to the players in all Austrian, German, and Dutch orchestras, almost all of the leading players in this country and America now use the German instrument'. The year 1953 also saw the fadeout of the French instrument in the United States, as the French-born Raymond Allard retired from the Boston Symphony Orchestra.

Worldwide use of the French system was in moderate decline since World War I. Many leading Italian players had adopted the German system after World War II, and within a generation it was firmly ensconced. In Belgium, an enclave of German-system players already existed in Liège (close to the German border) when Leo van de Moortel, professor at the Royal Conservatory in Brussels, exchanged his Mahillon for a Heckel in 1958.[64] French-system professors who retired in Mons and Ghent (c.1975) and Antwerp (1985) were succeeded by German-system professors.

The prospects of the French instrument took a startling plunge in 1969, when the bassoon section in the Orchestre de Paris changed over to German models. André Sennedat, principal in the orchestra since 1967, had reportedly been contemplating a change for some years. After the death in 1968 of the orchestra's founding music director, the Frenchman Charles Munch, Sennedat effected the change under Munch's successor, the Austrian Herbert von Karajan.[65] It was suddenly clear that under jet-setting, non-French conductors, even the most emblematic Parisian ensembles were no longer sanctuaries for the revered French instrument.[66] Meanwhile Pierre Boulez, perhaps the most eminent French conductor of the later twentieth century, preferred the Heckel bassoon.

Maurice Allard, professor of bassoon at the Paris Conservatory from 1957, was a consultant to Buffet and the warrior-in-chief in this *guerre des bassons*. In the Allard era, a 'fagott' (as the French called it, reserving 'basson' for the French instrument) was not allowed into the Conservatory building, let alone the bassoon class.[67] Allard in 1974 founded an advocacy group, *Les Amis du basson français*, whose *Bulletin* (later renamed *Le Basson*) 'served as the spearhead to respond to the attacks point by point'.[68] Allard had only to look to Spain to see new defections. The French system prevailed in Spain until 1971, when influential players changed over to the German system. 'By around 1980 all the bassoonists in Spain had changed to Heckel system instruments', Hough reported.[69]

The French-system players mounted a show of force at the Geneva Concours of 1974: among the thirty entrants were fourteen Buffet Crampon players (eleven from France; one each from Switzerland, Japan, and Belgium).[70] Meanwhile, alumni of the Paris conservatory – Noel Devos in Rio de Janeiro and Alain Lacour in São Paulo – anchored all-French system sections in prominent Brazilian orchestras. (The Brazilian front was breached in 1987/8, when Aloysio Fagerlande, a player in the Orquestra Sinfônica Brasileira in Rio, converted to the German system.[71])

Fernand Corbillon, a Buffet player who was doubtless mindful of his professional prospects, took up the German Fagott alongside his Buffet in 1974. In 1980, he chose to return to the French system, but he now viewed his Buffet through new eyes: 'Ah! If it had a little of the breadth in the low register and above all if it had the double B♭ spatulas of the fagott!'[72] A tour of the Buffet Crampon factory, reported by François Carry in 1978, provided valuable insights into the concerns of French players and the methods of the major maker.[73]

The building pressure on the French school of makers and players was evident when Buffet's model 35RC (named after Robert Carrée, who worked with Allard to develop it) was introduced in 1980 as 'a challenge to the Heckel-bassoon'. It offered four new added keys, among other improvements, to improve resonance or tuning or both.[74] Carrée began as an apprentice at Buffet Crampon in 1921, became technical director in 1953, and retired in 1974, but remained a technical advisor until his death in 1982. (Selmer, dormant as a bassoon maker since World War II, resumed production in 1980.)

Allard and the general director of Buffet Crampon, Roland Kurz, began a campaign to show the French instrument in the most favorable light. A phalanx of eight French bassoonists, all taught by Allard, traveled to the first European meeting of the IDRS, held in Edinburgh, 12–15 August 1980, where they performed in sub-groups and as a whole. Buffet exhibited the new 35RC model and contra alongside oboes and bassoons from makers in both hemispheres. If one counted Allard, two Belgians, and the North American French Bassoon Quartet (Heckel players who doubled on the Buffet), there were fifteen players of the French bassoon among the two hundred oboists and bassoonists attending.[75] The following February, Buffet Crampon sponsored a recital by a Buffet player, Philippe Berthemont, in London.[76] In 1982, Buffet Crampon promised to award prizes totalling 10,000 francs to 'the three best laureates playing the French system' at the International Bassoon Competition in Toulon.[77]

Observers agreed that the new Buffet produced a larger, darker sound.[78] Comparing the French and German models, Roger Birnstingl noted that 'the two instruments can be played well or terribly badly. The two present delicate problems (and not always the same), but the greatest artists succeed in minimizing them.'[79] Arthur Grossman, a Heckel-playing American, in 1981 lamented the passing of regional differences among orchestras of the world 'due to the internationalism of conductors, who want orchestras everywhere to have the same sound'. His complaint extended to the vanishing regional variations among Heckel players.[80]

Career paths were often limited by one's instrument. In the 1970s the Antwerp Philharmonic and Antwerp Opera orchestras advertised auditions as 'German system only'.[81] Alain Chantaraud identified a 'paradox' in 1986: 'French players win orchestral auditions, then quickly change to the German bassoon if they want the position.'[82] Waterhouse reported in 1989 that under the conductor Barenboim, 'only players able and willing to play the German instrument would be re-engaged' at the Opéra.[83]

By 1989, Buffet Crampon offered an updated model with a revised bore, a new linkage for the high A and C keys ('improving the high register'), and new *pointage* on the long joint. Despite this thoughtful tweaking, sales of Buffet bassoons were on the wane: after production of 106 bassoons in 1979 and 139 in 1980, production figures for 1987–90 came to 53, 18, 19, 45.[84]

The postwar economic boom in the United States created a powerful demand for bassoons; school and amateur musicians needed low-priced instruments in quantity. The German manufacturers had capacity and needed customers. From 1954 to 1963, Conn sold German-system bassoons assembled from imported parts by its subsidiary in upstate New York, the New Berlin Instrument Co. Meanwhile, the German maker Schreiber was by the 1960s producing about 1,300 moderately priced bassoons per year, many of which were exported to the United States. Up to ninety per cent of Kohlert's postwar annual production was exported during the period 1945–65.[85] During the 1960s, the Polisi Bassoon Corporation of New York marketed bassoons produced by Kohlert or Schreiber, with many added keys and touches.

Amid this thriving international trade, some bassoons were made on American soil. In 1950, the Lesher Woodwind Company began producing bassoons in Elkhart. The Linton Manufacturing Co. produced bassoons in Elkhart (c.1960–70; later purchased by Armstrong). C. G. Conn, acquired by H. & A. Selmer in the 1960s, continued to offer bassoons under the Selmer-Bundy brand.[86] Frank Aman (or Alman; 1881–1966), who had apprenticed under Wilhelm Heckel c.1892, worked in Elkhart to develop prototype bassoons for H. & A. Selmer.[87] This was by 1970 the Selmer division of The Magnavox Company.[88]

Hugo Fox, principal bassoonist in the Chicago Symphony Orchestra 1922–49, began to produce long-bore bassoons after the Heckel model in 1951. From 1963, the company was headed by Alan Fox, son of the founder. By 1968, the firm offered a short-bore design as well. After Hugo Fox's death in 1969, the firm produced its first contrabassoon (1970) and in 1971 introduced the Renard line of student bassoons in wood, polypropylene, or plastic. Annual production during the late 1980s reached 800–1,000 bassoons and two dozen contrabassoons.[89]

A 1985 trade publication showed twenty-one bassoon manufacturers in the world. Five of these were in West Germany (Heckel, Kreul & Moosmann, Mollenhauer, Püchner, Schreiber), four in the USA (Armstrong, Buescher, Fox, Selmer-Bundy), two in Czechoslovakia (Amati, Lignatone), two in East Germany (Hüller, Mönnig), two in France (Buffet-Crampon, Selmer), two in China (Hsinghai, Lark), and one each in Austria (Zuleger), Italy (Orsi), Holland (Schenkelaars), and Taiwan (Flügel/Chu-Seng). Omitted from this list were Sonora/Adler and several boutique makers.

The old high pitch/low pitch dichotomy was ancient history by the later twentieth century, but there was incremental upward pressure on the supposed standard of A-440. Waterhouse reported various high tuning pitches: Hamburg 1972 = 448; Munich Concours 1972 = 446; Turin 1973 = 442; piano of Queen Elizabeth Hall,

London 1973 = 442; Munich Concours 1975 = 443 or higher. While some makers began to tune their bassoons to 442, players at the upper end of this range had to resort to shorter reeds or crooks, or even to enlarging tone holes.

Revisions after World War II to the basic designs of the Heckel and Buffet bassoons had comparatively subtle effects. A few manufacturers experimented with refinements of the key mechanism. Buffet introduced a 'correction key' to narrow the octave between G#2 and G#3, and a 'croissant' key to provide half-hole venting for L2. The Cuçiureanu System, which added four separate mechanisms on the boot and long joint for the purpose of improving trills and connections in the low register, was offered by Hüller and by Fox.[90] Like many other ingenious additions to the existing Heckel key mechanism, it was rarely built.

Widely adopted innovations in reed-making changed the lives and sounds of bassoon players.[91] Christlieb wrote that Emil Hoffman and Frederick Moritz, 'the only performers in [1930s] Los Angeles who knew anything about the art' of bassoon reed making, shrouded their methods in 'guild-like secrecy'. Christlieb's chance experience of working in a machine shop during wartime service opened the door to a new-found precision in the making of bassoon reeds and reaming of bassoon bores:

> Once I saw the equipment I knew we in music were living in the dark ages. It was at that time that I found a way to measure the thickness of cane at all stages of the reed-making procedure. . . . From this knowledge I made a dial indicator that was practical and refined for measuring assembled reeds. It was a matter of adapting a needle to slip inside of a reed. . . .

Christlieb published details of his dial indicator, an electrically powered profile cutter for reeds, and an internal measuring device for bassoon bores. By 1996, he claimed to manufacture 1,000 pieces of profiled bassoon cane per month, using his machine profiler.[92]

Electrically powered reed-making machines remained rare, but other, simpler inventions arose to benefit bassoonists. The cane profiling machine, a specialized planer that processed the cane of the reed-to-be, produced finely graduated blades; it brought symmetry and a higher degree of completion to a task that had earlier been performed by hand. Georg Rieger, a toolmaker of Gaggenau, Germany, took up playing the bassoon in 1953; in 1954 he built his first gouging and profiling machines for bassoon reeds.[93] Among other early makers of such machines were Sassenberg of Berlin, Alfred Klopfer of Zwickau, and Fred Pfeifer of New York. The principle of the plane-type profiler eventually inspired a 'tip profiler' machine. Used after the reed was formed and opened, it brought all-but-final dimensions to the tip region of a reed. Meanwhile, dial indicators after Christlieb's idea became common. These machines and indicators removed ever more guess-work from the reed-making process, aiding both commercial and individual users. In 1949, Waldemar Bhosys published an article calling for the reed maker to grade cane according to hardness, in order to obtain consistent results.[94] To a much greater degree than before, bassoonists of the postwar era could hope to play on reeds that responded well in all registers, allowing them to

concentrate on cultivating musical expression, as string, brass, and keyboard players
had long been doing.

New approaches arose for supporting the bassoon in comfortable positions for
playing. A seat strap was favored in some countries, while other players attached
spikes reaching the floor or braces resting on the knee. The Buffet Crampon Model
RC had a balance hanger (also available on many German bassoons) to be used with
a right-shoulder strap. The traditional angle of the crook bend remained most popular,
but Buffet's Model RC adopted an almost perpendicular bend. Many players explored
less-acute bends, which altered the angle of encounter between reed and embouchure,
and between the embouchure and the player's hands. For almost the first time, makers
began to give serious attention to the needs of smaller players, extending spatulas and
adding solid or perforated plateaux in place of open brilles. Women had become
common as bassoonists in many countries after World War II. Both men and women
with smaller hands were now able to consider the bassoon as an option, rather than
passing it over in favor of other woodwinds.

Pedagogy and players, 1900–1989

Robert Philip provided an overview of orchestral bassoon playing in 1923–52, based
on a selection of early sound recordings. Vibrato was only occasionally present in the
1920s, seeming to go hand in hand with flexible phrasing. First heard among French
and American bassoonists, a fast vibrato of the 1930s gave way to a slower vibrato by
the 1940s. In Britain, early recorded bassoonists of both systems played with a harder
and less flexible tone and without vibrato. In the 1940s, some British bassoonists on
record could be heard emulating the vibrato and supple phrasing of 'French and
French-influenced examples, such as Goossens on the oboe and Gilbert on the flute'.
Bassoonists recorded in other European countries 'were mostly sparing in the use of
vibrato, with the exception of the Concertgebouw Orchestra in the 1940s. Even in the
1950s vibrato was not heard from bassoonists in German or Viennese orchestras, and
their phrasing tended be broad rather than intricate.'[95]

A survey made in 1926 confirmed that methods and studies by French-system
writers predominated in the conservatories of Paris, Brussels, Bologna, and Madrid.
In Berlin, Vienna, and St. Petersburg, methods and studies for the German system
predominated.[96] Early books of orchestral studies were edited and published by
Adrien Bérendès (Berlin, 1900), Johannes Böhm (Vienna and Leipzig, 1910), and
Gumbert-Wiegand/Wilhelm Knochenhauer (Leipzig, n.d).

A closer look at pedagogy and attitudes is available in a 1927 article by Léon
Letellier, professor of bassoon in the Paris Conservatoire, with co-author Edouard
Flament.[97] The prescribed methods (Berr, Bourdeau, Cokken, Jancourt, Ozi, Willent-
Bordogni) and exercises (Bourdeau, Espaignet, Fuente, Gambaro, Jancourt, Orefici,
Orselli) were all written by French-system players, most of them French-born.
Recommended concertos and solos were generally by French composers.

Letellier and Flament described many alternate fingerings for the bassoon; normally
the standard one was clear or expressive, while the alternate fingering was muted or
technical. The latter were sometimes forked, including Bb2 and Bb3. The authors

described a form of triple-tonguing (tu-tu-ku) for rapid triple rhythms, but no analogous double tonguing. In fact, they recommended that the conductor relax the tempo in Beethoven's Symphony no. 4, iv, at the bassoon solo. They also described a detailed team approach to both reed making and pianissimo response. This included warnings to composers (and also to conductors, no doubt): the second bassoon, a specialist in low notes, could play F2 to Eb4 *pianissimo*, Db2 to F#4 *piano*, Bb1 to F#4 *mezzo-forte*. 'To write for our first bassoon, we employ the contrary procedure, and we don't forget that strong reeds will never play piano in the low register, while the high register, on the contrary, will speak with great facility.' The first bassoon could play Bb1 to C#5 *forte*, D2 to Bb4 *mezzo-forte*, F2 to F#4 *piano*, and A2 to D#4 *pianissimo*.

A note of chauvinism sometimes colored the authors' comments. Among German bassoonists, 'it is rare to encounter musicians playing as well on their instrument as the French, first because they don't know how to trim their reeds perfectly ... then because the bore of their bassoon gives a sonority that is very inferior to ours'. Letellier and Flament credited touring French ensembles with having 'made our instrument appreciated in Germany' – namely Taffanel's Chamber Music Society (including Letellier and Bourdeau), and the Colonne and Lamoureux orchestras.[98]

The Paris curriculum had broadened only slightly in 1957–84, as reported by the professor, Maurice Allard. At the Hochschule für Musik und darstellende Kunst, Vienna, in 1982, the curriculum had expanded to embrace Ozi, Orefici, Dubois, Giampieri, Bitsch, and Gatti alongside the German-system studies. Concert works studied in Vienna still inclined toward German-speaking composers, although there were more exceptions than in Paris.[99]

Montanari returned to Italy from Brazil in 1946 as principal of La Scala Theater Orchestra, and playing a Heckel bassoon.[100] He converted his pupils at the Milan Conservatory to the Heckel system, including Dall'Oca, Menghini, Danzi, Meana, and Pari, all of whom became teachers at major Italian conservatories. Montanari's co-principal Enzo Muccetti was another convert in 1951.[101]

Bassoonists in the major American orchestras were overwhelmingly foreign-born until well into the twentieth century. Germans predominated in the early decades of the New York Philharmonic, the Chicago Symphony, and the Philadelphia Orchestra. In fact, the French system was unknown in some parts of the United States. During an American tour in 1944, 'my Buffet caused quite a stir among the younger American bassoon players – most of whom had never seen a French bassoon!' Cecil James wrote.[102]

And yet the French system was common in parts of the United States.[103] New York was a city of mixed usage. The short-lived New York Symphony and its conductor, Walter Damrosch, favored the French instrument, played by Auguste Mesnard and Louis Letellier. The two also taught at the Institute of Musical Art, founded by Frank Damrosch (brother of Walter).[104] Philip found Mesnard's playing to be 'in a very French style, with a warm, reedy tone, and a fairly fast, subtle vibrato, which gives flexibility to the phrasing'. Students in New York secondary schools were normally taught the French system; Leonard Sharrow and Stephen Maxym began thus, later changing to the Heckel system.[105] The Juilliard School, which absorbed the Institute of Musical Art, for a time maintained teachers of both systems.[106] Although the New

York Philharmonic traditionally employed German-system players, Auguste Mesnard was a member from 1913 to 1924; he also played in the Chicago Opera from 1910 to 1913.[107]

An 'American school of wind playing' has been identified with principles of phrasing and tone production codified by the French-born Marcel Tabuteau, who was principal oboist in the Philadelphia Orchestra 1915–54. Tabuteau's style was partly a matter of individual insight, partly a merging of French and German practices. Schoenbach noted that Tabuteau changed his oboe playing to fit with the louder-sounding German bassoons. Meanwhile, Walter Guetter, Tabuteau's colleague in Philadelphia, 'played his Heckel bassoon with some of the warmth of the French style, and his fast, shallow, slightly variable vibrato also sounds quite French, rather like the flute vibrato of William Kincaid in the same orchestra'.[108] Schoenbach, who succeeded Guetter, described his own accommodation to Tabuteau's style. 'There is no relationship between the way I play now and the way I played originally. The vibrato is completely tamed down, the basic tone has changed, and so on.' Schoenbach called Tabuteau 'the greatest musical influence in my life'. 'I modeled my approach on his, I thought everything out carefully, and presented it with confidence.' Tabuteau's well-documented teachings were one conspicuous strand of a broader French influence. The flutist William Kincaid (who 'had a lot to offer along the same lines as Tabuteau', Schoenbach wrote) had studied with Georges Barrère, another Frenchman recruited by Walter Damrosch in 1905. On an important point of technique, Schoenbach wrote:

> Mr. [Ralph] McLane, the clarinetist, once pointed out to me that I had a tendency to mouth each note. He explained that by changing the embouchure for each note, I was missing the opportunity to have a genuine line of articulation.[109]

McLane had studied with the French clarinetist Gaston Hamelin. At the elite Curtis Institute of Music in Philadelphia, bassoonists studied with Guetter, Ferdinand Del Negro, or Schoenbach. Many also had chamber music classes under Tabuteau.

After Raymond Allard retired from the Boston Symphony in 1953, the French bassoon was in eclipse in major American orchestras, until Gerald Corey revived it in the Baltimore Symphony in 1971.[110] During the 1980s, Charles Holdeman revived the French bassoon in the Delaware Symphony. Both players used either the Buffet or the Heckel-system bassoon according to the repertoire, and always at the sufferance of the conductor.

Louis Hugh Cooper, who taught bassoon at the University of Michigan from 1945 to 1997, was renowned for his knowledge of the bassoon's acoustics. He collaborated with the Püchner firm to manufacture bassoons for the American taste, and he in 1949 began a 'Bassoon Clinic Series' of writings for *Étude* magazine. Among other writings on bassoon and reed acoustics, he published, with Howard Toplansky, an encyclopedia of bassoon fingerings with commentary.[111]

Like Britons and Americans, Czech players absorbed ideas of timbre, vibrato, and phrasing from French bassoonists. František Herman claimed that 'the Prague bassoon school attempts a musico-technical symbiosis of the two systems . . . a special way of playing the Heckel instrument, recognizable through a timbral brightness and through lightness in the playing'. Herman cited Karel Bidlo, for thirty years principal in the Czech Philharmonic, as a representative of the Prague school.[112]

During most of the twentieth century, two bassoon teachers provided pedagogical continuity in Vienna. Karl Strobl played in the Vienna Opera and Philharmonic from 1903 to 1936 and taught at the Vienna Conservatory. During 1938–88, Karl Öhlberger was professor of bassoon in Vienna, training more than 200 students in a carefully preserved tradition.[113] Sallagar noted in 1978 that Viennese reeds were distinguished by a strong arch – nearly round in cross-section under the wires – and long blade – first wire to tip normally 30 mm.[114] Öhlberger's successor Michael Werba summarized attributes of the Viennese school: a timbre rich in overtones, finely developed legato, and a homogenously blending tone (with only occasional vibrato). Singular reeds allowed for a wide dynamic range and unusually short articulation. The *Pianomechanik* (whisper key) remained closed, except in the highest register, and 'long' fingerings were used for C#4 and D4. The C# key for LT was used at times as a speaker key.[115] Koblitz added that double-tonguing was discouraged as detracting from timbre, and that speaker keys were held open on A3, Bb3, B3, and C4; he conceded that the special fingerings were technically difficult and problematic in intonation.[116]

The Italian bassoonist Sergio Penazzi codified several avant-garde techniques (including quarter-tones, multiphonic chords, and timbral enhancements) in two method books (1971, 1982)[117] (Ex. 7.1). Thom de Klerk, a former principal bassoonist in the Concertgebouw Orchestra, from 1959 conducted the Dutch Wind Ensemble, founded by Amsterdam Conservatory pupils. After his death in 1966, the group, later known as the Netherlands Wind Ensemble, revived much of the harmonie repertory, performing, touring, and making numerous recordings.

Mordechai Rechtman left Hitler's Germany with his family in 1933. In 1938, at the age of fifteen, he obtained a place in the Palestine Opera Orchestra. 'Israel was a bassoon-less land', he observed. From 1946 to 1991 he was principal bassoonist in the Israel Philharmonic and a member of the Israel Woodwind Quintet, for which he made many effective transcriptions.[118]

Prominent bassoonists in Russia included Ivan Kostlan (Bolshoi Theater Orchestra; Moscow Conservatory, 1922–63) and Dmitri Erëmin (Leningrad Philharmonic; Leningrad Conservatory, 1946–72).[119] Valery Popov, professor at the Moscow Conservatory from 1971 and principal in the USSR State Symphony orchestra, was the dedicatee of more than twenty compositions – concertos, sonatas, and chamber works.[120]

The roots of the western orchestral tradition in China date to 1879, when European residents formed an ensemble in Shanghai. Chinese musicians joined the orchestra in 1927, which was renamed the Shanghai Symphony Orchestra in 1956.[121] Russians fleeing the Bolshevik Revolution founded the conservatory of Shanghai and the orchestra of Harbin.[122] Orchestral activity ceased with the Cultural Revolution of 1966. When the Philadelphia Orchestra toured China in 1973, helping to thaw international relations, its conductor Eugene Ormandy was invited to lead a rehearsal of the Central Philharmonic Society. The principal bassoonist, Liu Qi, recalled in 2008 that 'most of the members had been workers or cultivated fields since the Cultural

DITEGGIATURE ALEATORIE
PARTICOLARMENTE RICCHE
DI POSSIBILITÀ SONORE

ALEATORY FINGERINGS AFFORDING
NUMEROUS SOUND POSSIBILITIES

Esempio 91

Con lo spostamento delle labbra dalla parte superiore alla
parte inferiore dell'ancia nonché stringendo o allargando
molto, oppure usando i denti, si ottengono armonici supe-
riori e inferiori, accordi omogenei o disomogenei.

Example 91

*By moving the lips from the upper to the lower part of the
reed, and from the very wide to the very tight position, or
by squeezing the reed between the teeth, high or low
harmonics may be obtained, as well as homogeneous or he-
terogeneous chords.*

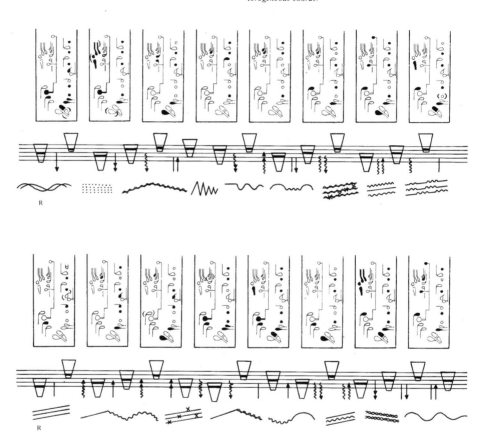

Ex. 7.1. Penazzi, *Metodo per fagotto* (1982), p. 130.

Revolution began in 1966. Our instruments were chipped and glued together, and the score we played was hand-copied.'[123]

Before the Cultural Revolution and after its end in 1976, Chinese bassoon playing was closely linked to Eastern bloc countries. Liu Qi had toured the Soviet Union and Eastern Europe in 1951, playing in a Chinese youth ensemble.[124] The Czech bassoonist Rudolf Komorous taught bassoon and chamber music at the Beijing Conservatory 1959–61.[125] In 1979, the woodwinds of the Central Philharmonic Ensemble created a tone 'reminiscent of a good East European Orchestra', Christopher Weait observed.

The bassoons Weait saw in Shanghai and Peking (Beijing) in 1979 were made in Eastern Europe or sometimes after an Eastern European model (Liu Qi counted five bassoon factories in China then). Of about 100 male and female bassoonists in Peking, twenty served in army ensembles.[126] Beginning in the 1980s, many Chinese bassoonists pursued bassoon study abroad outside the Eastern bloc.[127] The first China National Bassoon Conference, held in 1984 at Shanghai Conservatory, offered a program of recitals, lectures, and competitions. A second milestone came in 1993, when Zhu Yuangping presented a solo bassoon concert in Beijing Concert Hall, accompanied by the China Central Philharmonic orchestra.[128]

A pioneering symphony concert series in Tokyo, 1925, was staffed with Russian players from Harbin, according to Narusawa. The New Symphony Orchestra, a full-time professional group, was founded in 1926; Masashi Ueda was bassoon soloist in Mozart's Sinfonia Concertante in a 1930 performance.[129] The Tokyo National University of Fine Arts and Music enrolled students majoring in wind instruments beginning in 1931. The bassoon instructor between 1954 and 1975 was Heihachiro Mita.[130] Oshi Nakanishi published a bassoon method in Japanese (1978). By the 1960s, Japanese players were active in Europe and the United States as students and as professional orchestral bassoonists.

The American bassoonist James Hough told of his personal role in introducing woodwind chamber music to Taiwan in 1971, along with the American oboist Jerol Clark.[131] When the Korea Bassoon Association held its first bassoon camp in 1982, the guest artist was Otto Eifert. He found 'excellent technical prowess' in the students, who were playing mostly Schreiber bassoons.[132]

Garvin Bushell, the pioneering jazz bassoonist, continued to record with Will Bill Davison (1947), Wilbur de Paris (1960–1), John Coltrane (1961), and Gil Evans (1964).[133] A bassoon was included in the dance bands of Artie Shaw (1946) and Paul Whiteman (late 1940s).[134] Karen Borca, a trained bassoonist closely associated with the jazz pianist Cecil Taylor, was also a saxophonist. The opposite situation was more common: jazz saxophonists who played bassoon at times included Errol Buddle, Bob Cooper, Bob Gioga, Illinois Jacquet, Daniel Jones, Yusef Lateef, Ray Pizzi, Karl Porter, Josea Taylor, and Frank Tiberi.[135] Arrangers of jazz and popular music who wrote prominent bassoon parts included Dick Cary and Bill Douglas (himself a bassoonist).[136] The bassoonists Alexander Alexandrov, Lindsay Cooper, and Brian Gulland gave the instrument a presence in rock bands during the 1970s.[137]

Repertory

Composers increasingly valued the bassoon for its distinctive voice, often at new heights of pitch. In the minimally spare orchestration of *Kindertotenlieder* (1901–4), i, Mahler assigned the bassoon a simple but poignant half-step motive. At letter 6, he transposed it up nearly two octaves, reaching D5 in a brief soli passage with flute and two horns (Ex. 7.2). Debussy's *Iberia* (1909) includes an exposed melody in unison with solo violin, starting on A#4 and ascending to D5, marked 'lontain et expressif'. Clearly he preferred the exact timbre of the high bassoon (in a challenging passage) to a treble woodwind (for which the passage would have been routine). Debussy's

Ex. 7.2. Mahler, *Kindertotenlieder*, 'Nun will die Sonn' so hell aufgeh'n', excerpt (1901/4).

arabesque melodic style and tonal freedom demanded fluency in extreme tonalities and whole-tone scales. The opening to Stravinsky's *Le sacre du printemps* (1913) conjures the asymmetrical and embellished melody of a Russian reed-pipe (dudka) (Ex. 7.3). The composer apparently chose the highest register of the bassoon for its unfamiliar timbre; even some composers present at the premiere wondered if they were hearing a saxophone. Louis Speyer, the first oboist in the Ballets Russes orchestra, recalled that his colleague 'Abdon Laus, who later became first bassoon of the Boston Symphony Orchestra, under Monteux, was the first to attack this difficult solo; he had to find fingerings, which was a terrible experience'.[138]

The bassoon's middle register also attracted composers, including Stravinsky, who chose the bassoon to introduce the Berceuse in his *Firebird* (1910). In a slow interlude in Sibelius's Symphony no. 5, i (1915), the bassoon intones a mournful chromatic plaint over a chorus of quietly rustling strings. It is not a proper melody, only a brushful of freely chosen orchestral color (Ex. 7.4).

Composers frequently stretched the limits of the bassoonist's technique, taking it for granted that the player could match the fluency of other winds. Maurice Ravel's *Rapsodie espagnole* (1907) features a flamenco-like duo-cadenza for bassoons, echoing a duo-cadenza for clarinets. Two passages well known to bassoonists – the pentatonic ascent to E5 in Ravel's Piano Concerto in G (1920) and the bassoon's solo turn in *Boléro* (1927) – are echoes of prior solos by other instruments. In the first bassoon part of his Octet (1923), Stravinsky freely wrote ungrateful trills on upper-register pitches (F4, A♭4, and A4, for example). The bassoon artist of the twentieth century was expected to learn by rote such non-intuitive trills, which often involve moving two or

Ex. 7.3. Stravinsky, *Le sacre du printemps*, opening (1913).

Ex. 7.4. Sibelius, Symphony no. 5, first movement, excerpt (1915).

more fingers, sometimes in opposite directions. Composers began to pose more severe challenges: Edgard Varèse's *Octandre* (1924) demands rapid slurs between B1 and A4, as well as a flutter-tongued G#4, attacked *piano* and swelling to *sfff*.

Mahler was attracted by the bassoon's gift of arid staccato (attributable to the rich overtones of its low register). The scherzo of his Symphony no. 9 (1909), a grotesque dance, is riddled with trills and sequential melodies for bassoon, contra, and lower strings, all joining in a ponderous staccato. Prokofiev used the dry staccato of four bassoons in his *Humorous Scherzo* (1916) and of two bassoons, this time in the upper register, in his Symphony no. 1 ('Classical', 1916–17). In his *Peter and the Wolf* (1936), the bassoon assumed a familiar character role as the grandfather: gruff, halting, and complaining. Sensing that low B1 is the driest and most inflexible note on the instrument, Prokofiev featured it prominently. The bassoon's staccato fascinated Stravinsky. In *Symphony of Psalms* (1930) a bassoon passage is heard staccato; upon repetition, the staccato is thrown into relief by the second and third bassoons, marked legato, which double the first at the lower octave. Stravinsky reached an obsessive extreme in *Mavra* (1922, rev. 1947), where he sometimes marked the bassoons 'excessivement court et sec'. He frequently included the bassoon in his innovatively scored chamber works, including *Renard* (1915–16), *l'Histoire du Soldat* (1918), and *Pastorale* (1924).

Respighi featured the bassoon prominently in his *Trittico Botticelliano* (1927/8), opening the second movement with a tender cantilena in the upper register. He at times spotlighted the bassoon's third octave in exposed trumpet-like themes – as in the first movements of the *Trittico* and *The Pines of Rome* (1924). In his Symphony no. 9 (1945), Shostakovich cast the bassoon as protagonist in a quasi-operatic scena; supported by hushed tremolando strings, the bassoon ascends phrase by phrase to an anguished high Db5. In a second outcry a few bars later, the bassoon ascends to D5, then descends without haste into apparent stasis, only to segue into the beginning, pianissimo but staccato and scherzo-like, of the symphony's final movement.

Barber's *Summer Music* (1957) opens with a high-register plaint for bassoon solo, followed by register-crossing slurs; finely etched staccatos and abruptly changing dynamics demand a nimble tongue. Britten's *Nocturne* (1958) makes analogous demands; the second movement ('The Kraken') includes a long stretch of virtuosic staccato in the tenor register (up to C5), albeit at a slightly more stately tempo than Barber's (Ex. 7.5).

The bassoon was only rarely a concerto soloist during this era of enormous orchestras.[139] When it was, composers usually matched the solo bassoon's modest volume with a reduced accompaniment. Examples include: Wolf-Ferrari, Suite-concertino (with chamber orchestra, 1933); Villa-Lobos, *Ciranda da sete notas* (with strings, 1933); Jacob, Concerto (with strings and percussion, 1935); Strauss, Duet Concertino for clarinet and bassoon (with strings and harp, 1948); Jolivet, Concerto (with strings, harp and piano, 1954); Gubaidulina, Concerto (with low strings, 1975); and Panufnik, Concerto (with small orchestra, 1985). Hindemith included the bassoon among multiple soloists in concertos for trumpet, bassoon, and orchestra (1954) and for flute, oboe, clarinet, bassoon, harp, and orchestra (1950).

By the early twentieth century, the bassoon was no longer found in most marching bands. Some schools and military units maintained concert bands, where one or two bassoons were often present. Chamber ensembles involving bassoon were often ad hoc affairs, although some led a semi-permanent existence; early examples included the Reed Club and the Georges Barrère Wind Ensemble in New York, the Wind Instrument Chamber Music Society of London, and Taffanel's society for wind-instrument chamber music in Paris. Chamber repertoire for winds was written by composers of stature, including Auric, Berio, Françaix, Holst, Ibert, Jacob, Janáček, Ligeti, Milhaud, Nielsen, Poulenc, Schoenberg, Stockhausen, Schuller, and Zemlinsky.

From 1898, concours pieces at the Paris Conservatoire were generally by living French composers. Many required the player to demonstrate contrasting moods, usually slow and lyrical versus fast and athletic. Among the most memorable was Saint-Saëns's neo-baroque Sonata, op. 168 (1921), dedicated to Léon Letellier. Saint-Saëns wrote to his publisher: 'I saw in the method that I could ascend to E5; otherwise I would never have dared.'[140] Many later solos de concours ascend to E5 or even F5,

Ex. 7.5. Britten, *Nocturne*, second movement ('Kraken'), excerpt (1958).

including the notable examples by Dutilleux (*Sarabande et Cortège*, 1942, dedicated to Gustave Dhérin) and Françaix (Concerto, 1979, dedicated to Maurice Allard).[141] Saint-Saëns wrote his op. 168 as part of a cycle of sonatas for woodwinds and piano. Debussy planned a sonata for bassoon and harpsichord, never realized. Poulenc, a third French composer with cyclic intentions, worked on a sonata for bassoon and piano, now apparently lost.[142]

Edward Elgar learned to play the bassoon while working in his father's music shop. A photo shows the young bassoonist in an ensemble with colleagues, for which he composed several wind quintets (two flutes, oboe, clarinet, and bassoon) in 1878–9. His *Romance*, op. 62, (1910), dedicated to E. F. James, swells with swashbuckling rhetoric. In *Falstaff* (1913), the bassoon portrays the title character; Elgar considered this 'symphonic study' his orchestral masterpiece. Paul Hindemith was another friend (and capable player) of the bassoon. His sonata for bassoon and piano (1938) is in the style of two other works involving bassoon: *Kleine Kammermusik*, op. 24/2 (1922), and Septet (1948). Sonatas by Etler (1951) and Gould (1951) reveal debts to Hindemith. Other notable works for bassoon include solos or duos by Cascarino, Castelnuovo-Tedesco, Denisov, Hovhaness, Koechlin, Mignone, Poulenc, Rautavaara, Skalkottas, Tansman, and Wilder.[143]

Chapter 8

The bassoonist's world since 1990

A tremor of change in geopolitics and economics came on 9 November 1989, when the wall separating East Berlin from West Berlin was dismantled. With the ensuing reunification of Germany came a reordering of the Eastern European musical world, including the professional lives of bassoon makers and players. Meanwhile western-style orchestras and conservatories flourished in many Asian countries, always using the Heckel-system bassoon; use of the French system continued to wane even in its European strongholds. Octave and tenor bassoons were revived in several countries for the teaching of young children.

Changes in the bassoon itself during these years were mostly internal and subtle. Much more consequential for the twenty-first century bassoonist was the explosive development of communications media, allowing words, music, and pictures to be recorded and transmitted with great speed and ease. New digital media – recording and editing, web-based distribution, and portable music players – largely supplanted the old recorded-music economy, weakening or bankrupting numerous record labels specializing in classical repertory. This economic loss was offset, in an artistic sense, by the enfranchisement provided by new recording technology: entrepreneurs (or performers themselves) could produce sound or video recordings of impressive technical quality without major investment, distributing the results through digital media, including internet downloads. The outcome was a proliferation of available recordings, and a breakdown of the compensation and royalty structure that sustained the recording industry for most of the twentieth century.

A continuing homogenization of performing styles was evident; the sound and performing styles of bassoonists from nation to nation and continent to continent continued to converge. Even as the French bassoon itself became rare, the new international style of bassoon playing (on Heckel-system instruments) owed much to French ideas of phrasing and vibrato as heard and taught in the 1920s and 1930s.

A countercurrent evident during preceding decades acquired momentum: the use of early bassoons (usually reproductions of instruments used before 1850) in repertory from the sixteenth through the nineteenth centuries. While still uncommon in jazz and pop music, the bassoon gradually gained in acceptance in those domains, as barriers between musical genres and styles continued to erode.

The French bassoon

The domination of the Heckel-system bassoon in modern symphony orchestras was already decisive in 1990. After the battle for the Buffet had essentially been lost, a number of German-system players spoke up to praise it.[1] Meyrick Alexander, a British player of the German system who also cultivated the Buffet, offered a valuable snapshot as of 1993:

> The principal bassoonist of the Paris Opéra holds a very special position; the present incumbent is Gilbert Audin who is also Professeur at the Conservatoire and chief design consultant at the Buffet factory. His co-principal, Jean-Pierre Laroque, holds a similar post with the other manufacturer, Selmer. . . . In Paris, three orchestras play French system – the Opéra and the [two] Radio France orchestra[s], while the Orchestre de Paris and the EIC [Ensemble internationale contemporain] are on the German type. Only French is taught at the Conservatoire, and bands outside the capital are fairly evenly divided. Outside France, the French system is in use in Switzerland, Belgium and Spain and possibly South America.[2]

By 2001 there were professors of both French and German systems at the two 'national' conservatories in France, Paris and Lyon.[3] Circa 2009, the Buffet was still used by three players (among seven) at the Paris Opéra, and a recruitment advertisement for the Garde Républicaine band specified the French instrument.[4] Two players in the Belgian National Orchestra upheld the Buffet tradition in 2010, alone among professional players in Belgium.[5]

A Buffet bassoon sold new in 2009 had a raised chimney for L3 and the 'croissant' key (a plateau for L2 creating a half-hole vent for F#4 and G4, available on the RC model since the 1980s). The whisper key was linked to the A4 and C5 vent keys. A player who had previously played the Buffet RC model commented that a selective widening of the bore seemed to contribute to a darker overall sound, with more embouchure pressure required[6] (Ill. 53).

The French bassoon is the first instrument of a decreasing number of players, yet many players of the Heckel-type bassoon have chosen to take up the French bassoon for occasional use. Such usage is often historically inclined: for example, the New Queens Hall Orchestra, which attempted to recreate the sound of London orchestras as heard in the year 1900.[7]

The Heckel-type bassoon

Even before the reunification of Germany (3 October 1990), changes were evident in the organization of the VEB Brasswind and Signal Instrument Factory, which included the bassoon makers Adler, Hüller, and Mönnig. In early 1990, Lein reported, the divisions of VEB 'were privatized into a limited liability company, the Vogtland Musical Instrument Factories, Markneukirchen (GmbH). . . . There were many offers from companies in the West to form joint ventures with various of the Vogtland firms.'[8] Gerhard Hüller, scion of the venerable bassoon-making family, chose to remain with

Le nouveau basson Buffet Crampon

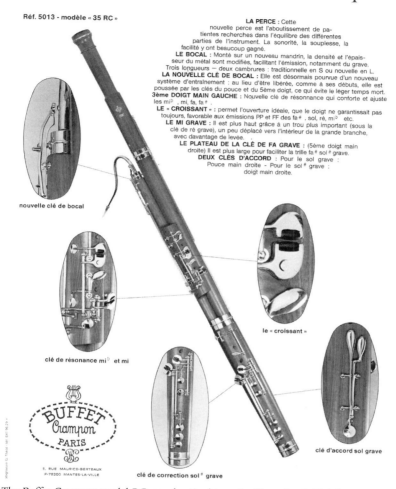

Réf. 5013 - modèle « 35 RC »

LA PERCE : Cette nouvelle perce est l'aboutissement de patientes recherches dans l'équilibre des différentes parties de l'instrument. La sonorité, la souplesse, la facilité y ont beaucoup gagné.

LE BOCAL : Monté sur un nouveau mandrin, la densité et l'épaisseur du métal sont modifiés, facilitant l'émission, notamment du grave. Trois longueurs — deux cambrures : traditionnelle en S ou nouvelle en L.

LA NOUVELLE CLÉ DE BOCAL : Elle est désormais pourvue d'un nouveau système d'entraînement : au lieu d'être libérée, comme à ses débuts, elle est poussée par les clés du pouce et du 5ème doigt, ce qui évite le léger temps mort.

3ème DOIGT MAIN GAUCHE : Nouvelle clé de résonance qui conforte et ajuste les mi♭, mi, fa, fa♯.

LE « CROISSANT » : permet l'ouverture idéale, que le doigt ne garantissait pas toujours, favorable aux émissions PP et FF des fa♯, sol, rè, mi♭ etc.

LE MI GRAVE : Il est plus haut grâce à un trou plus important (sous la clé de rè grave), un peu déplacé vers l'intérieur de la grande branche, avec davantage de levée.

LE PLATEAU DE LA CLÉ DE FA GRAVE : (5ème doigt main droite) Il est plus large pour faciliter la trille fa♯ sol♯ grave.

DEUX CLÉS D'ACCORD : Pour le sol grave : Pouce main droite - Pour le sol♯ grave : doigt main droite.

nouvelle clé de bocal

le « croissant »

clé de résonance mi♭ et mi

clé d'accord sol grave

clé de correction sol♯ grave

53. The Buffet Crampon model RC, as advertised in 1981. Photo by G. Théol.

the VEB firm. By the end of 1991, the firm's management laid off him and all the Hüller bassoon makers, bringing the brand to an end. VEB continued to produce the Amati brand of bassoons and contras. The Gottfried Meinert firm began to produce bassoons under the supervision of Frank Meinert, who had trained at Hüller and Adler. One veteran of the Kohlert firm, Rudolf Walter, founded his own firm. Some of the West German manufacturers of bassoons – Heckel, Püchner, Mollenhauer, Moosman, and Schreiber – absorbed displaced workers from the Vogtland. Schreiber, still based in Nauheim, in 1991 employed ten workers in a rented facility in Erlbach in the Vogtland, where unemployment was high and wages were lower. In 2001 Schreiber moved all woodwind production to nearby Markneukirchen, not far from the Schreiber family's ancestral home in Graslitz.[9]

At the beginning of the year 2000, the Gebrüder Mönnig and Oscar Adler & Co. workshops were consolidated under new ownership. Mönnig models were more expensive, while the Adler models were less so. Contrabassoons were produced under both names. In 2009, the flagship Mönnig model 214 was made of unstained curly maple, 'specially coated' so that the down bore was not lined. Adler began to offer a truncated bassoon to C2 with simplified mechanism for children. The Leitzinger firm of Hösbach, Germany, offering bassoon crooks since 1989, introduced a bassoon model in 2004. All the large bassoon makers of Germany offered bassoons in several price ranges; even the elite house of Heckel introduced a model at a reduced price called the Heckel Crest.

In marketing efforts, many makers avoided substantive discussion of their bore and tone-hole dimensions, instead emphasizing the number of keys and rollers offered. Exceptions included Yamaha and Fox Products Corp., both of which explicitly compared some of their bassoons to certain Heckel models. The Yamaha firm offered two models, based on Heckel models of prewar and postwar vintages. Fox offered both long-bore and short-bore designs, each available in professional models with a choice of conventional or 'thick' walls (implying deeper chimneys, in general). The idea of a thicker-wall body had been explored by Heckel and other makers, but the customer had seldom been offered a choice.

Student bassoons in wood, polypropylene, or plastic were offered by Fox under the Renard brand. Nearly a quarter of the firm's bassoons were exported in 2008, when annual production stood at 2,200 bassoons and 20 contras. The J. H. Linton Co. of Elkhart continued to offer bassoons made in plastic; these were claimed to be 'the lightest bassoon available'. B. H. Bell of Lakefield, Ontario, Canada, began offering professional-quality bassoons on the Heckel pattern by 1992. Three bassoon factories in China were reported in 2010: Hsinghai (Xinghai) and Chang Yu, both in Beijing; and Lark, in Shanghai. Their products were sold under many brand names.[10]

The three wing keys for left thumb (A4, C5, and D5), originally conceived as vents for the bassoon's third and fourth octaves, are not ideally located for the secondary purpose of 'flicking' – facilitating attacks in the second register. The bassoonist Arthur Weisberg addressed this problem in collaboration with the repairman James Keyes by developing a 'double automatic octave system' controlling two newly drilled holes on the wing joint.[11] Makers offered many other ingenious new key mechanisms as options, but the average player's mechanism remained little changed from the early twentieth century, except for the now-standard whisper key.

The mechanization of reed making continued. Gougers, profilers, and tip finishers were available from European and North American makers, as well as machines for ever more specialized tasks: pre-gouging, tube scoring, and tube wrapping. Devices for cane selection were brought to market, including a torsion tester (measuring stiffness), indention meters (measuring hardness), and pycnometers (measuring density).[12] Several makers developed digitally controlled cutting machines for the commercial processing of cane.

The early bassoon

The revival of early wind instruments began as a trickle during the 1950s and 1960s. Among the first generation to play early bassoons in concerts and on recordings were Otto Fleischmann, Hans-Jurg Lange, the brothers Peter and Werner Mauruschat, Otto Steinkopf, and Walter Stiftner. Most of these pioneers used surviving instruments, although Steinkopf manufactured his own reproduction of a baroque bassoon by J. C. Denner. During the 1970s, a broader second generation of players and makers addressed themselves to rediscovering the forgotten technique of early bassoons, and to making suitable reeds, crooks, and reproduction instruments. During the digital recording age in the 1980s, great swathes of seventeenth- to nineteenth-century repertory – familiar or not – were recorded, giving a great boost to the popularity of dulcians and of baroque, classical, and even romantic-era bassoons.[13] Curricula in early bassoon were offered in conservatories in The Hague and Basel, soon followed by others. Since 1990, period-instrument orchestras have arisen in most large European and North American cities, and some in Latin America and Japan. By the twenty-first century, summer courses including the early bassoon proliferated, while an increasing number of conservatories and universities offered degrees in early music performance, often including bassoon instruction. Books and articles addressed the needs of early-bassoon players.[14]

Boutique makers supplied the market with historical bassoon reproductions in an increasing number of models, mostly at the revival pitch standards of A-415 (for baroque music), A-430 (classical), A-392 (early French baroque), and A-435/440 (romantic music). Several dozen reproduction bassoons were sold in the world annually, compared with several thousand Heckel-system bassoons. Makers of reproduction early bassoons in 2010 included Mathew Dart, Eric Moulder, and Tony Millyard in England; Olivier Cottet and Laurent Verjat in France; Peter de Koningh and David Mings in the Netherlands; Guntram Wolf in Germany; Pau Orriols in Barcelona; and Robert Cronin and Leslie Ross in the USA.

Internet-based commerce brought a global revolution to the marketing of antiques, including old bassoons. Sellers were connected with a vast pool of buyers, many of them living far away from traditional market places. Collectors witnessed a coming of age in the field: antique bassoons, while still cheap compared with violins and the like, rose in monetary value enough that counterfeits began to appear.

Internationalization

The bassoon's spread, still rippling out from a European origin after five centuries, increasingly reached Asian cultures. As more symphony orchestras and conservatories were founded, Western bassoonists sometimes performed and taught in Asia, while Asian-born bassoonists often received at least part of their education in the West, sometimes obtaining employment and remaining.

The Hong Kong Academy of the Performing Arts was founded in 1984. Korea National University of Arts in 1993 opened the first conservatory-type school of music in Korea.[15] Not only players but even a conservatory could be transnational: Yong

Siew Toh Conservatory opened in Singapore, 2003, as a joint initiative between the National University of Singapore and The Peabody Institute, an American conservatory. The bassoon professor was Zhang Jin Min, a Chinese who had studied in Beijing, Paris, and Geneva.

Stephan Weidauer, an orchestral bassoonist and professor from Saarbrücken, participated in a tour of five Chinese conservatories in 2006. Sponsored by the Püchner firm, the tour teamed Weidauer with three Chinese bassoonists, one of them resident in Vienna. Weidauer reported that the conservatories – in Beijing, Shenyang, Shanghai, Xian, and Chengdu – each enrolled from 3,000 to 16,000 students. He found the bassoon professors to be young and mostly foreign-trained, and the students to be preoccupied with technical issues rather than expression or style.[16] A second tour in 2007 included visits to conservatories in Changchun and Urumqi.[17]

In May 2009 the Central Conservatorium of Music, Beijing, hosted an international bassoon symposium and festival. Featured soloists came from Australia, Austria, China, Germany, Hong Kong, Singapore, Taiwan, and the USA. Seeking to convey the global reach of the event, one ad hoc ensemble was billed as the Universal Bassoon Ensemble. When the Asian Double Reed Society was formed in 2010, the governing board included, among others, American bassoonists employed in the Guangzhou and Bangkok Symphony orchestras, and a Chinese bassoonist employed in the Hamburg Camerata.

Pedagogy and performing styles

Marcel Tabuteau's teachings, identified with an 'American school' of wind playing, lived on. Terry B. Ewell sought to adapt for bassoonists one of Tabuteau's distinctive techniques: 'drive', a sort of intensity, which Ewell analyzed as dynamics, timbre, vibrato, and other factors.[18] *Sound in Motion*, a book for players of all instruments by the bassoonist David McGill, proceeded from a similar basis.[19] Yet this once-distinctive style, initiated by a transplanted Frenchman, was not always easy to distinguish from an increasingly homogenous international style, heard in professional orchestras on every continent. Joseph Polisi, a bassoonist and president of the Juilliard School in New York, attributed the homogenization largely to jet-setting conductors, who imposed their personal interpretations on even the briefest wind solos in orchestral works.[20]

Two traditions of bassoon playing remained unassimilated, if not wholly unchanged: the French and the Viennese. The sound of the late Maurice Allard was described by a sympathetic player as 'trop clair' (overly bright) for modern orchestras. Later French players 'evolved a sound which has turned the tables completely'. Aided by the newer Buffet and Selmer instruments, a highly resistant reed, and an oblique embouchure, leading French players began to produce a smooth, dark sound that was equal in suavity to that of elite German-system players, while remaining recognizably distinct.[21]

Eleanor Froelich, an American who studied in Vienna under Karl Öhlberger, commented in 2006:

The Viennese have a much wider palette of articulations than Americans or Germans. They have a staccato that is incredibly short, on one end of the range, and one that is almost like glue on the other end. For example, the short one sounds rather peculiar to American ears unaccustomed to Viennese playing. . . . Vibrato is technically a taboo in Vienna but nevertheless has managed to sneak in. Even Öhlberger said that one can't play *Le sacre du printemps* or *Boléro* without it. But it is something which can, and must, I think, be turned on and off as well as up and down in speed when needed. . . .[22]

Before 1990, advertisements for conservatories, university music departments, and summer courses were rare in *The Double Reed*. Ads for American and Canadian educational programs have since become common. Opportunities in professional orchestras are no match for the stream of trained bassoonists issuing from the world's conservatories and music schools. The result is fierce competition for the few chairs becoming vacant each year. Workshops are offered and articles written on the narrow but crucial topic of 'Preparing for Auditions', while commercial recordings of 'Orchestral Excerpts for Bassoon', played in a model style, are sold and imitated.

A diachronic view of performing styles

Classical musicians sometimes make reference to 'schools' of performance, and to perceived lineages extending from teacher to student. The base level of such connections is the individual teacher and his/her studio. A questionnaire distributed to attendees of the International Double Reed Society conference in Birmingham, UK, in 2009, for example, sought to document 'a double reed family tree based on teaching lines'. At another level, the 'school' may be regional or national in scope. Sound recordings from c.1900–45 make clear that sharp differences existed among national schools of bassoon playing; these audible differences faded during the increasingly international twentieth century. We may take a still broader view, asking: what stylistic characteristics did the world's bassoon players have in common c.1900, and how much did that characteristic style change by 2010?

The oboist Bruce Haynes described three broad styles of performing Western art music. One of these was briefly described in chapter 7: the Modern style, marked by metronomic strictness, continuous vibrato, 'long line' or climactic phrasing, and careful control over pitch and expression.[23] It arose partly because of the new constraints of recording; both the producers and consumers of sound recordings were intolerant of errors and waywardness. The preoccupations of twentieth-century bassoonists like Benjamin Kohon (quoted in chapter 7) with intonation, low-register response, and vibrato are markers of the Modern style, which was entrenched in many orchestras by the end of World War II and is still the dominant style.

Preceding this in time was what Haynes called the Romantic style, marked by free tempos, portamentos, and overt expression. It is evident on most recordings made before World War II. Haynes observed:

Tempos in Romantic style are usually slower than anyone would consider using today. In the case of dances, they are so slow and 'cantabile' that their characteristic rhythms are difficult to perceive, and they become unrecognizable as dances. The usual impression given by romantic music is of an unrelenting heaviness due to too many accents. The beat hierarchy, so important in Baroque style, and which continued to be preached until the late nineteenth century, had clearly waned: while good beats are emphasized, so are bad beats, and every other kind. Pickups are often played loudly into their downbeats. . . .[24]

In the orchestral repertory, the plain or even blocky phrasing of early recorded bassoonists is one manifestation of the lingering Romantic style.[25] A recording of the Bach Orchestral Suite no. 1, conducted in 1943 by the eminent bassoonist Fernand Oubradous (1903–86), shows the beat-heavy phrasing described by Haynes.[26] But the portamentos taught by Almenräder and Orselli had evidently faded from use before the era of recording.

A third style, which Haynes called Eloquent or Period style, is heard today only in certain performances of baroque music. Based on baroque-era declamation rather than the 'machine-like regularity' of the Modern style, the Eloquent style, as defined by Haynes, is marked by gesture, dynamic nuance, inflection (individual note-shaping), tempo rubato, agogic accents and note placing, pauses, and beat hierarchy.[27] For the bassoonist, the Eloquent style raises questions of tuning (often below A-440; equal vs. earlier temperaments), vibrato, alternate fingerings (for color or phrasing), articulation, crook venting, reed choice, and embouchure (flat vs. oblique).

Repertory

Even while the bassoon culture was spreading to new populations, its growth was stagnating in some Western cultures. In symphonic and chamber music concert programs, the repertory remained largely that of the Viennese classics through World War II. Alongside the conservative mainstream, however, new music continued to be written for both solo bassoon and ensembles containing bassoon. Some compositions called for new or extended techniques, and sometimes for amplification or sound processing. A generation after Bartolozzi's writings, Riedelbauch and Méndez explored the production and use of multiphonic tones.[28] The bassoonist Johnny Reinhard, founder in 1981 of the American Festival of Microtonal Music, published a microtonal fingering chart for bassoon.[29]

Luciano Berio's *Sequenza XII* for solo bassoon was written for Pascal Gallois, receiving its premiere in 1995. The longest of Berio's Sequenzas for various solo instruments, no. XII can last from eighteen to twenty-six minutes. In a monumentally paced opening glissando from G#4 down to C2, intensity is managed through pitch tremolos (sometimes alternating notes more than two octaves apart) and color tremolos, in which bright and dark timbres of the same pitch alternate. The descending line, sometimes suggesting the Dopplerian drone of a propeller airplane, gains force through its breadth of pitch and its continuity (achieved through circular breathing).

Ex. 8.1. Berio, *Sequenza XII*, excerpt (1995).

Harmonics, chords, and staccato tonguing effects open a door into little-explored possibilites of the bassoon[30] (Ex. 8.1).

Additions to the repertory for solo bassoon and orchestra included a bassoon concerto (1992) by Ellen Taafe Zwilich, the Strathclyde Concerto no. 8 (1993) by Peter Maxwell Davies, *Five Sacred Trees* (1995) by John Williams, 'Concert Piece' by Libby Larsen (2008), and *Winterlight* (2008) by Martin Lodge. Eric Ewazen composed a concerto for bassoon and wind ensemble (2002). Works for bassoon and piano were written by André Previn (sonata, 1999), Graham Waterhouse ('Diplo-Diversions', 2002), and George Perle ('BassoonMusic', 2004). Performance art pieces included 'Dead Elvis', by Michael Daugherty (1993), and Peter Schickele's 'Sonata Abassoonata' (1996), both requiring acting from the bassoonist.

Bassoon quartets and other ensembles took on increased popularity in the late twentieth century. These groups (which sometimes include a contrabassoon playing or doubling the lowest part) often played transcribed music. Original compositions have also become common, including breezy quartets by Peter Schickele (*Last Tango in Bayreuth*, 1974) and Daniel Dorff (*It Takes Four to Tango*, 1997), where the perceived conservatism of the bassoon and its players is sent up via languorous rhythms and suave counterpoint. *Hell's Angels* (1998–9), by Daugherty, featured a solo quartet of bassoonists with orchestra. A publication by Helge Bartholomäus provided an intro-duction to the repertory as of 1992.[31]

Players began to give attention to electronic pickup and amplification of the bassoon's sound. Lex van Diepen described his use of extra microphones to capture the bassoon's tone, which emanates from so many tone holes.[32] Michael Rabinowitz described four competing microphone pickup devices: one positioned in a tone hole of the wing; another inserted into a hole drilled in the crook; a contact pickup attached to the crook; and dual microphones floating above the bell and F2 vents. He found that 'a keyboard or a guitar amp with at least a fifteen-inch speaker supports the large range of bassoon best'. Rabinowitz pointed out that 'once you start using a pickup, any guitar effect will work with the bassoon', including Mutron, Chorus, Harmonizer, and Digital Delay.[33] Joanne Cameron discussed using a computer inter-face to give the bassoonist access to such signal-processing tools as pitch shifters, delays, spatial effects, flangers, filters, distortion and granular effects, and real-time sampling.[34]

As barriers fell between genres of music, performers were increasingly likely to use the bassoon in jazz and popular music. Among the most active jazz players were Rabinowitz, Paul Hanson, Javier Abad, Alexandre Silverio, James Lassen, Alexandre Ouzonoff, and Sara Schoenbeck.

The bassoon in the media and professional associations

By 2008, the International Double Reed Society (IDRS) claimed over 4,400 members from 56 countries; approximately forty per cent of these members were bassoonists. In 2010 the formation of an Asian Double Reed Society was announced; its governing board included oboists and bassoonists born or active in China, Hong Kong, Japan, Taiwan, and Thailand. Other double reed organizations from around the world in 2010 included the British Double Reed Society, Deutsche Gesellschaft für Oboe und Fagott e.v., Japan Bassoon Society, Vereniging Nederlandstalig Dubbelriet Genootschap, FagotClub Nederland, Finnish Double Reed Society, Mägyar Fàgottos tarasag (Hungary), Association Bassons (France), Fou de Basson (France), Chinese Association of Bassoon, Australasian Double Reed Society, and Midwest Double Reed Society (USA). The publications, websites, and discussion groups of these associations allowed bassoonists contact with their colleagues around the globe. Two independent magazines, *Oboe-Fagott* (Wiesbaden, from 1984) and *Oboe Klarinette Fagott* (Schorndorf: Hofmann, from 1991), addressed readers of German.[35] One enthusiast maintained an internet radio channel devoted entirely to recordings of the French-system bassoon.[36]

Chapter 9

The contrabassoon

In the broadest usage, a contrabassoon is a conical, double-reed instrument capable of doubling the bass line of a composition at the lower octave.* (Beginning in the nineteenth century, a more restricted definition is followed; see below.) Octave doubling by winds was known to Michael Praetorius, who wrote in 1620:

> Given an ample number of instrumentalists, the tutti sections produce a magnificent sound if one assigns to the bass part an ordinary or bass sackbut, a great bass curtal or shawm, and a violone, which all sound an octave lower, as the sub- or contra-basses on the organ. This is quite common in Italian concertos nowadays and is sufficiently tenable.[1]

This frequent role of octave doubling makes for difficulty in tracing the use of contrabassoons. If the player was able to play by reading an ordinary bassoon or string bass part, then the decision to use a contrabassoon was often in the hands of a local conductor, not necessarily the composer. Scattered evidence suggests, however, that octave doubling, one of several uses of the contrabassoon, was common.

In any era, a bassoonist taking up a contra instrument was most comfortable if the fingerings were similar to those of his bassoon. Most contrabassoons throughout the centuries have answered this demand, at least through written D4. Doubling at the lower octave was a simple matter if the contrabassoon was pitched an octave lower than the bassoon. But if the contra was pitched a fourth or fifth lower, then the player had to learn a new correspondence of fingerings to the staff, or else have a transposed part written.

Early contrabassoons were essentially upsized dulcians and bassoons. Even more than on the standard bassoon, the player needed to have a hand span of average or larger breadth. In time, efforts to increase dynamic range and portability led to contrabassoons that diverged from the bassoon's design archetype.

Curtals or dulcians pitched below C2

In organ terminology, a stop that sounds as written is called an eight-foot stop; one sounding the lower octave while using the same fingerings is called a sixteen-foot

---

* Pitch names in this chapter refer to written pitches, sounding an octave lower, unless otherwise specified.

stop.[2] Such doubling on the organ was established by 1458, well before contrabassoons appeared.[3] Early evidence of dulcians pitched lower than eight-foot C dates from 1590, when the Hofkapelle of Archduke Karl II of Styria (Graz) owned 'ain groß fagat, ain Quint nieder'.[4] In 1609, the Frauenkirche of Nuremberg owned quartbass and octavebass dulcians, both made by Jörg Haas.[5] In Vienna, 1613, Christoph Straus scored for 'fagotto grande' in a sacred concerto.[6] The Barfüsserkirche in Frankfurt by 1626 owned an octavebass, a quintbass, one 'ordinary' bass, and two unspecified dulcians.

Octave doubling may have been the original impetus for developing large Pommers and dulcians, including the quart- and quintbass sizes. Many vocal compositions do not descend below written G2 or F2; even occasional exceptions might have been octavated, as they are by string bass players today.

Praetorius presented the two common Doppelfagott sizes as a matter of convenience for the player:

> We should notice at this point that there are two kinds of Doppelfagott – one called Quintfagott, which descends to F1 like the great bass shawm, and the other called Quartfagott, which can go down only to G1. It is best to use the first for pieces with B♭ in the signature, and the second for those with B-natural. It is very convenient if both sizes are available to the performer, since the semitones can be better pitched with fingers, rather than keys, over the holes.[7]

The Kassel Hofkapelle, familiar to Praetorius, owned both a quartbass and a quintbass by 1638.[8]

Dulcians were also used in the consort culture of the sixteenth century. Three, four, or five players played as many parts using consorts of instruments built in pitches a fifth (or occasionally a fourth) apart. The consort might elect, however, to vary the tessitura by simply switching from an eight-foot consort of dulcians to a twelve-foot, or a sixteen-foot consort of instruments. A quintbass, Choristfagott, and tenor would have lain in Praetorius's prescribed relationship of fifths. Wiemken explained:

> Taking the Augsburg Stadtpfeiffer as an example, consorts of dulcians at both eight feet, or concert pitch, and sixteen feet were available for their instrumental proffering of motets, chansons, dances, etc. Michael Praetorius, again, speaks directly to this practice. He states that when consorts of sackbuts or dulcians played a four- to six-voice composition, they transposed that music down a fourth, a fifth, or even an octave, especially if that piece sported *chiavette*, or 'high clefs'.[9]

In 1626, the Stadtpfeifer of Nuremberg owned an octavebass, two quartbasses, seven basses, and several smaller dulcians.[10] Wiemken described a third possible use for contrabass dulcians: playing a bass part that lies low in the bass range, but comfortably within the semi-contra range.[11]

Four octavebass dulcians survive, along with five quartbass dulcians, all but one in the basic 6 + 4 configuration of the bass dulcian.[12] Both sizes presented makers with the challenge of boring side-by-side holes over a length of four to six feet. One of the two octavebasses at Sondershausen shows the dangers of this method: the planing of the body (or subsequent reaming) exposed one of the bores to the surface. The maker inserted a neatly mortised patch and marked it with his maker's stamp.[13]

Made in one piece each, except for detachable bells, the Sondershausen octavebasses are both marked 'JB', apparently Johann Bohlmann of Frankenhausen; one bears the date 1681. They originally belonged to the court orchestra at Arnstadt, where they would have been used under Adam Drese, Kapellmeister from 1683 to 1701. J. S. Bach, who was organist at Arnstadt 1703–6, would likely have heard these instruments in use.[14] The octavebass at Augsburg has the mark HIERO.S, denoting Hieronymus (Jeronimo) Bassano. He avoided drilling such long bores by making his octavebass in three sections, attached end to end. The topmost section, moreover, now consists of left and right halves, evidently a repair. All these sections are glued permanently together, so that the instrument is not dismountable.[15] The unmarked fourth contrabass, now at Schloss Pillnitz, Dresden, is in one piece and is apparently unsigned (Ill. 54). Both Angerhöfer and Lyndon-Jones described it as a masterly creation, given its long bore and slender body.[16]

A surviving quartbass, now at Linz, is stamped 'GK' or possibly 'CK'. This may be the instrument referred to in an item in Kremsmünster monastery accounts, 7 June 1628, 'for adjusting the crumhorns, together with some reeds for the Quart-fagott'.[17] P. B. Lechler, the chorus master there, in 1645 wrote a canzona for two violins, viola and three dulcians, 'of which the lowest is designated as fagotto grosso'.[18] Three

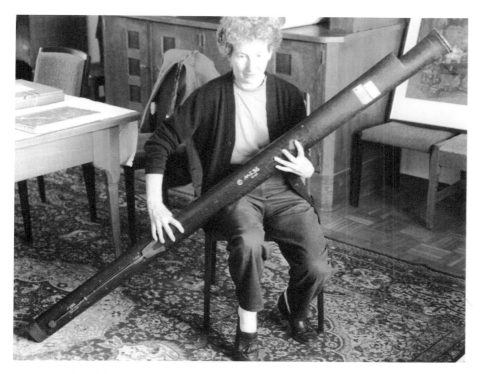

54. Octavebass dulcian. Pillnitz Collection, Dresden.

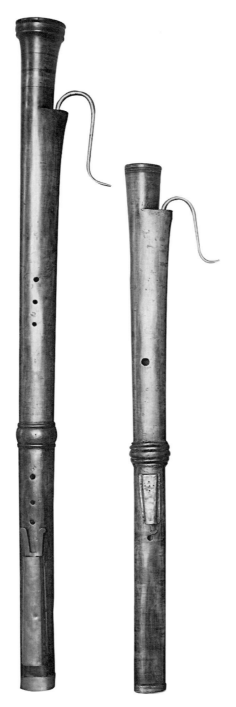

55. Quartbass and bass dulcians by HIER.S (Hieronymus or Geronimo Bassano). Sammlung alter Musikinstrumente, Vienna.

surviving quartbass dulcians bear Hieronymous Bassano's mark. All are of two-piece construction (Ill. 55).

The baroque contrabassoon

In 1683, Jacques Danican Philidor played 'gros basson à la quarte et à l'octave' in the royal chapel of France. This terse label is significant. No prior evidence of octave doubling by wind or string instruments in French churches is known; regular use of a sixteen-foot string instrument in French opera arose only c.1701.[19] While the primary role of the gros basson was evidently to double the bass line at the lower octave, a trio sonata dating from 1685 also called for the instrument: 'Pièce à double trompette et de différents tons et le gros basson', by André Danican Philidor, older brother of Jacques.[20]

Philidor's gros basson was not a dulcian; such instruments are unknown in French court use, and in any event the pitch change of 1664–8 had entailed a general replacement of woodwind instruments at the court. No further description of Philidor's 'gros basson à la quarte et à l'octave' is available, but we may reasonably guess that his octave contra roughly resembled the three-key, four-piece contra by Andreas Eichentopf, which is described below. Jacques was listed again as player of the 'gros basson à la quarte et à l'octave' in 1708, and (after Jacques's death) André Philidor was listed similarly in 1712. No other French player is connected with the instrument, suggesting that the Philidor family were the owners and possibly the makers of the only known gros bassons. (Jacques was documented as a maker of oboes.)

A contrabassoon was known in England around this time; the Talbot Manuscript, dated to the period 1690–1700, briefly mentioned the 'pedal or double basson, FFF, touch as basson'. This was evidently a quartbass in the style of the French basson, with similar fingering.[21] French oboists who performed in England in 1673–85 may have begun the introduction of French instruments.[22]

Octave doubling in large church spaces was recommended in 1706 by Martin Hermann Fuhrmann, a Kantor in Berlin. He regretted that the bombardone (great bass shawm) had been displaced by the French basson.[23] Fuhrmann evidently had no contrabassoon at his disposal. But there is scattered evidence of their use in Germany, and two three-key contrabassoons survive. These two-meter-tall instruments are essentially giant bassoons, descending to written B♭1. (The configuration is 6 + 5.) The one now in Leipzig, signed by Andreas Eichentopf of Nordhausen and dated 1714, was used in the orchestra of the imperial counts of Stolberg; its specific repertory is not documented (Ill. 56). The other contra, externally similar to the Eichentopf but not signed, is now at Sondershausen. It was used under Kapellmeister Balthasar Freislich, who served at the court from 1718 to 1731. Individual scoring appears in one Christmas cantata by Freislich, but the contrabassoon probably doubled the bass line in many other works, including cantatas of G. H. Stölzel.[24] Another octave contra, now lost, was listed in an inventory from Rudolstadt, dated to 1714 or before.[25] Telemann's motet 'Danket dem Herrn' called for fagotto grosso plus basso continuo.[26] A funeral cantata composed by Georg Österreich for use in the ducal chapel at Gottorp, Schleswig, in 1702 called for Contrafagott in tutti passages.[27] The term bassono grande appears in a manuscript continuo part of Vivaldi's concerto for multiple instruments, RV 576, written for the Dresden Kapelle. Michael Talbot believed this referred to a contrabassoon.[28]

At the Marienkirch in Lübeck, a great bass shawm was used from 1685 until the early eighteenth century, under Dieterich Buxtehude (d.1707). A quartbass bassoon by J. H. Eichentopf of Leipzig appears to have replaced the shawm, possibly around 1730.[29] The bassoon, though nominally a quartbass, reportedly sounds only a major third below A-440; this suggests that the organ pitch was at approximately A-460.

J. S. Bach's Saint John Passion, performed in Leipzig, 1723, calls for bassono grosso, with range C2 to F4. A surviving continuo part shows late autograph annotations of various tacets and pianissimo markings.[30] Bach's use of the contra was squarely in the tradition of the German Kapellmeisters mentioned earlier.[31]

In Italy, the Milanese woodwind maker Anciuti invented a strikingly original contra measuring 2.14 m in height. The bell, in the shape of a dragon's head, produces B♭0 (written B♭1). At the bottom of the boot, a novel connection, carved in a visible U-shape, continues the illusion of a coiled serpent. The down bore is on the player's left, facilitating the player's access to finger holes 1 through 3, while open-standing keys cover holes 4 through 11. The layout is 6 + 5. Anciuti's unprecedented keys for the right hand (and low C) cover tone holes ranging from 12 to 36 mm in diameter. The chimney-less, semi-covered system is nearly a century in advance of similar efforts

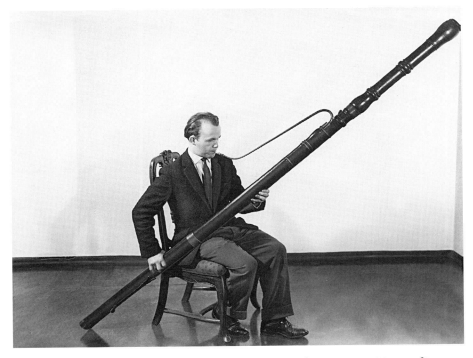

56. Gunther Angerhöfer with contrabassoon by A. Eichentopf. Inv. no. 3394, Museum für Musikinstrumente der Universität Leipzig.

by the Saxes and Boehm. Pride of invention is evident in a plaque affixed at the U-joint, which reads: 'Invenit et fecit Ioannes Maria Anciuti Mediolani 1732'.[32] The spike supporting the instrument is original, although the original crook appears to be missing. This late example of a serpent-form instrument seems intended for use on a theater stage or projecting from an orchestra pit, its growling low pitches further suggesting a fierce sea monster. The serpent's head has a movable tongue, while the wide bore and tone holes emit a powerful sound.[33]

In England, Thomas Stanesby Junior announced in a 1739 newspaper advertisement the construction of two contrabassoons.[34] One or both were used for octave doubling in Handel's *L'Allegro, il penseroso ed il moderato* (1740) and *Music for the Royal Fireworks* (1749). A contrabassoon, marked 1739 and likely one of these instruments, survives in 6 + 5 configuration, measuring 2.53 m high. For a twenty-fifth anniversary commemoration of Handel's death in Westminster Abbey, John Ashley played the Stanesby contra. The contra was placed front and center, between the conductor and the audience. One observer remarked, perhaps hyperbolically, that it could not be heard.[35] This and later published reports of a weak low register (possibly attributable instead to ill-suited crooks and reeds) are contradicted by David Chatterton, an expert player familiar with both the surviving original and a reproduction of it.[36]

Departure from the bassoon pattern: Contrabassoons of the classical period

Quartbass and quintbass instruments were occasionally made in this period, in a bassoon-like 6 + 5 format. A five-key quintbass (187 cm tall) survives by Heinrich Grenser of Dresden (1764–1813).[37] An inventory at the maker's death included models for both Quintfagott and Quartfagott contras.[38] An unfinished semi-contra (178 cm) survives in Antwerp (Vleeshuis 219). Its bell and body have a French or Belgian appearance.

A new pattern of octave-bass instruments seems to have been preferred, however, with the low register abbreviated to reduce height and weight. In place of the bassoon-like 6 + 5 configuration embraced by Stanesby and both Eichentopfs, classical octave contras were typically more compact (6 + 3), extending only to D1 (written D2). The long joint was truncated for the player's convenience in handling. Instead of the immense crook and wing joint seen on the early eighteenth-century instruments, the classical contrabassoon was redesigned in sections, for the maker's convenience in boring. In early classical contras, a relatively short crook was inserted into a brass pipe leading upward to a miniature wooden boot joint above the player's head. The down bore resumed with a short wooden connector, entering the short wing joint proper only a little above the player's left hand. Sometimes the wing was sectioned again, beneath the third finger hole on the épaule. In most later exemplars, the three-piece lead pipe was replaced by a single brass 'hairpin', the ancestor of today's metal lead-pipe.

Questions of chimney depth and wall thickness would preoccupy many contra makers throughout the classical and romantic periods. On a standard bassoon of the period, the entire eight-note scale – F2 to F3 – vented through deep chimneys, which were traditional on the LH épaule and the boot. As makers experimented to reduce the weight of octave contras, they often pared wood away from non-critical exterior regions of the boot. Tauber, Rorarius, and many other makers left standing a right-hand épaule projecting c.2 cm above the finger side of the boot joint, giving these three chimneys a depth of up to 4.5 cm (Ill. 57). Meanwhile, the vents for G2 and F2 also remained greater in depth than diameter.[39] Overblown pitches vented mostly through these eight deep chimneys, which contributed greatly to the instrument's familiar sound (enhancing its characteristic filtering effect). Holes on the long joints of classical contras often opened through a table raised above the otherwise cylindrical body; the table sometimes added depth to the chimneys. At the Metropolitan Museum of Art, New York, is a contra attributed to Uhlmann. In place of a long table, the thumb side of the long joint is sculpted into two elegant hillocks to provide chimneys for the E and E♭ vents.

Makers of contrabassoon during the classical period were centered in the existing Habsburg Empire. A Viennese newspaper carried an article about the maker and player Theodor Lotz in 1785:

[H]e has also constructed a large octave bassoon. Although an octave deeper, it is nevertheless played with just as gentle breath and with the same sort of reed and fingerings as the usual bassoon. With this instrument Herr Lotz had the highest

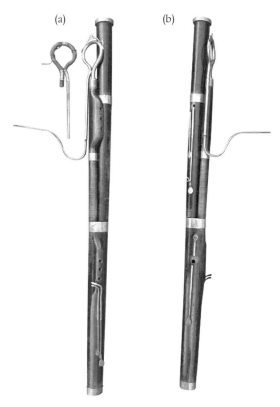

57. Octave contrabassoon to D by Rorarius: (a) finger side, showing raised chimneys for the right hand; (b) thumb side. Waterhouse Collection.

honor of appearing before his majesty the Kaiser, while performing in a great musical academy in the royal and imperial national theater with the royal imperial chamber harmonie ensemble, receiving applause from the public. Connoisseurs and amateurs alike admired the good effect this instrument has in the wind ensemble, and also in the strongly constituted orchestra.[40]

Lotz's estate in 1792 included '3 alte grosse Fagott'.[41] His employee Tauber went on to become a prolific maker of contras.[42] Makers active in Vienna also included Wolfgang Kies or Küss, Martin Lempp, and Augustin Rorarius. Other regional makers included Carl Doke (Linz), H. Mayer (Lienz), Schöllnast (Pressburg), Truška (Prague), and Wenzel (i) Horak (Prague).[43] Closed keys for A♭2 and E♭3 were standard; the latter was typically operated by a spatula for LT, in the Viennese fashion. Later models by Central European makers sometimes had widely flaring metal bells, in an attempt to increase projection. Two surviving contras by Martin Lempp show a re-engineered boot joint: atop a short vestigial boot, side by side, are a down-bore épaule section for R4–6 and a plain up bore section (see below for later examples).[44]

Octave contras from Germany and France are less common during the period. A seven-key contra by Finke (fl. Dresden, a1813–1874), now in Huddersfield City Museum, shows several unusual features: a range to written C2 (2.02 m tall), an ovally coiled lead-pipe, a flaring wooden bell and, in place of the conventional boot joint, two long billets strapped together and connected by a metal U-joint. The musical instrument factory of B. Schott Söhne, Mainz, opened in 1818. A six-key contra bearing the firm's stamp survives in Brussels, measuring 170 cm. In addition to the familiar keys (for D, F, Eb, F#, and G#), the A vent (R3) is covered and relocated lower on the bore.[45] Almenräder, an advisor to Schott, wrote nothing about the contrabassoon, but this covered A vent possibly reflects his thinking. Meanwhile, another Schott contra is an eight-key instrument with an uncovered A2.[46] In 1826 the firm advertised a nine-key contrabassoon.[47]

A surviving five-key contra by the Tuerlinckx firm of Malines, Belgium, was reportedly inspired by a contrabassoon used by bands of the occupying Austrian army in 1785.[48] Charles Sax exhibited 'a new contrabassoon, improved by the exhibitor', in Brussels, 1830.[49] The improvements presumably included his novel countersunk key flaps of 1825, which when closed occupied the already shallow chimneys, subtracting their effect from the vibrating air column. Pezé of Paris c.1825 reportedly built a contrabassoon, while Jean-Jacques Baumann, another Parisian maker, advertised a contrabassoon in 1825.[50] Frédéric-Guillaume Adler (fl. 1808–54) exhibited a contrabassoon in Paris, 1844.[51]

Peter Appelberg in 1772 supplied a *contre-basson* to the Danish court.[52] A contra survives by the Swiss maker Rudolf Seelhoffer (fl. 1813–42).[53]

Classical repertory

Traditional uses of contrabassoons continued during the later eighteenth century. F. M. Sandmayr, a Salzburg court bassoonist from 1768 until 1804, also played 'groß Quart-fagot' in the Salzburg cathedral, presumably doubling bass lines at the octave.[54] Meanwhile, John Ashley played contrabassoon in festival orchestras in London (1784) and Worcester (1788), and William Jenkinson played in Worcester (1803).[55]

The emergence of large harmonie ensembles provided a new role for the octave contrabassoon – having the same fingerings, it could double the second bassoon line with little difficulty.[56] The casual addition of a contrabassoon to sextets or octets was probably known in Vienna before it was documented c.1783.[57]

In Mozart's *Mauerische Trauermusik*, K. 477, a wind harmonie (two oboes, clarinet, three basset horns, contrabassoon, and two horns) functions in virtual independence of the strings. The 'gran fagotto' doubles the third basset horn line. Curiously, there are no bassoon parts, and the upper two basset horn and gran fagotto parts were added later to the autograph.[58] Theodore Lotz played in the premiere in November 1785 at Mozart's masonic lodge.[59] The death inventory of the Viennese maker Jakob Bauer in 1797 included 'quite unknown concertos and variations for "Pedal, kleinen Fagot . . . dann auch 9 stimmigen Harmonien mit dem pedal Fagot"'.

Suitable instruments and players began to attract composers of orchestral music. Haydn scored for contrabassoon in three oratorios for Vienna.[60] In *The Seven Last Words* (1795–6), the contra was used in a harmonie-like intermezzo for twelve winds. In the aria no. 22 of *The Creation* (1796–8), the low register of the contra and two bassoons evokes the 'Tiere Last' (heavy beasts). Elsewhere, as in *The Seasons* (1799–1801), the contra part selectively doubles the string bass or the second bassoon, and occasionally has an independent voice. The Viennese contra's vogue continued into the new century. Schubert's funeral composition *Eine kleine Trauermusik*, D. 79 (1813), was scored for a wind nonet, including contra. One contrabassoon was documented in the imperial orchestra (1807), two in a performance of Handel's *Timotheus* (1822), and four in performances of *The Seasons* (1839) and *The Creation* (1843).[61]

In the premiere performance of his symphony no. 8 on 27 February 1814, Beethoven conducted an orchestra that included two contrabassoons, probably reading from a spare double bass part. Beethoven also scored for a single contra in his fifth and ninth symphonies, his *Missa solemnis, King Stephen* (1811), two overtures, and five short works for 'Militärmusik' (wind band). Three of these, WoO 20–22, were labeled 'Turkish music'.[62] 'Turkish' marches with contra are heard in *The Ruins of Athens* (1812) and in the ninth symphony (1824) finale. In his opera *Fidelio*, Beethoven used the contra to reinforce the cellos and basses in a hushed and suspenseful duet of jail-breakers (no. 12); at the moment when a heavy stone is rolled free, the contra joins the strings in an outburst outlining a diminished-seventh chord.[63]

An Augustinian monastery near Brno in October 1817 ordered a contrabassoon from Schöllnast in Pressburg. Its delivery in February 1818 caused the choir director 'immense joy'. Written contra parts occur in dozens of surviving harmonie arrangements in the monastery's library, including several Turkish pieces.[64]

Except in the military, evidence for contra use in France during the period is scarce. Instead of a contrabassoon, a contrabass oboe (described in chapter 3) was played by a bassoonist at the Paris Opéra for a brief period during the 1780s. A plan to form a contrabassoon class at the Paris Conservatoire in 1794 came to nothing.[65] Choron, writing in 1813, described the contra as being no longer in use.[66] Nicolò Isouard's *Aladin* (1822) included an important part for contra;[67] acts 3–5 were completed by A. M. Benincori, who had resided in Vienna, 1800–3. The contra mostly doubles the bassoon part in Berlioz's overture to *Les francs-juges* (1828), and is specified in Auber's opera *La muette de Portici* (1828).[68]

Continuing the classical pattern, 1831–1879

Five- to ten-key contras were slow to evolve. Surviving examples sometimes have new keys added and/or alterations made to accommodate changing pitch standards. The familiar Central European style was continued by Peuckert & Sohn (Breslau), Joseph Horalek (Warsaw), Wenzel Schamal (Prague), Emanuel Kohlerth (Graslitz), S. Koch (Vienna), Carl Weber (Graz), and C. Lange (St. Petersburg).[69]

Incremental innovations appeared. A nine-key contra from the shop of I. Ziegler (Vienna) has a covered A vent, as does a contra by Horák (Prague).[70] An instrument by C. W. Moritz (Berlin) has a sectioned boot as well as covered A2, B2, and D3.[71] No surviving contras bear the mark of Almenräder u. Heckel. Contras bearing the stamp Heckel/Biebrich, apparently dating from after 1845, are 'hairpin' models to D2, furnished with rod-axle key work and a double-headed A vent seen on the Almenräder-Heckel bassoon. Two exemplars have a covered D (L3) and F (RT), and

E♭ operated by L4, but in other respects show conservative, non-duplicated key work: C# for RT, B♭ for R3, F# for RT, G# for R4[72] (Ill. 58).

The contrabassoon in the orchestra, 1831–1879

The Gewandhaus Orchestra of Leipzig purchased a contrabassoon especially for the performance of Mendelssohn's overture *Meerestille* in 1834.[73] During this period, Wagner wrote for contra in his Symphony in C (Prague, 1832); *Rule Britannia* overture (Riga, 1837); *Liebesmahl der Apostel* (Dresden, 1843); and Grosser Festmarsch (Philadelphia, 1876). The use by Berlioz in his *Symphonie funèbre et triomphale* (Paris, 1840) is a borrowing of music from his overture to *Les francs-juges* (1828). Glinka scored for contra in his *Russlan and Ludmilla* overture (St. Petersburg, 1842/1858).

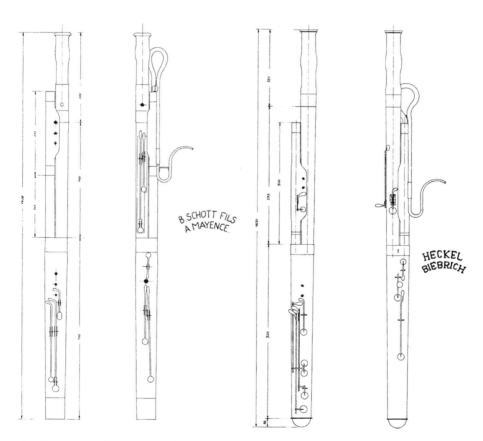

58. Octave contrabassoons to D by Schott and J. A. Heckel (probably shortened below the left-hand épaule). Wilhelm Heckel GmbH.

Verdi in *Macbeth* (1847) scored for contra 'as part of a small off-stage ensemble (two oboes, six clarinets, two bassoons and contra) which furnishes a sort of adagio march' to accompany the apparitions of the eight kings. About six weeks before the Paris (second) version was performed, Verdi wrote to Arrivabene (Genoa, 5 March 1865) that 'they've sent to Milan to get one [contrabassoon]'.[74] In Verdi's *Don Carlo* (Paris, 1867), the contra helps announce the entrance and exit of the Grand Inquisitor.[75]

Brahms specified contra in his *Triumphlied* (Bremen, 1871), Variations on a Theme of Haydn (Vienna, 1873), and symphonies no. 1 (Karlsruhe, 1876) and no. 3 (Vienna, 1883). Dvorak's Serenade for Winds, op. 44 (Prague, 1879), pointedly refers in its opening (and closing) march to the harmonie tradition; the contrabassoon or double bass part has a role in that traditonal texture.

Military music and rivals to the contrabassoon

In 1820 a typical Austrian military band included one contrabassoon (together with two bassoons and twenty-one other instruments). The Viennese bandmaster Philipp Fahrbach in 1845 still prescribed one contrabassoon and two bassoons, amid greatly expanded clarinet and brass sections. But with the development of valved brass instruments, bassoons and contrabassoons were vulnerable to replacement:

> Our contrabassoons are a buzzing evil; the full, round, mellow bombardon [tuba], if well played, is the most beautiful bass for military musicians and puts the broad, buzzing, incomprehensible contrabassoon by a wide stretch into the background. . . .[76]

Nemetz had already reported in 1844 that contrabassoons were losing ground in Austrian military bands to Stehle's new 'Harmonie-Bass'; other bass brasswinds soon appeared, made by Červený (Königgratz, 1845), Pelitti (Milan, 1846), and Adolph Sax (Paris, 1846).[77] (See chapter 10 for discussion of these instruments.) After the middle of the nineteenth century, traditional bassoons and contrabassoons were almost completely displaced from the Austrian military.[78]

In 1825, all French infantry and royal guard bands had two or three contrabassoons, Letellier reported.[79] Kastner wrote in 1836 that the contrabassoon was often used in military music, but rarely in the orchestra.[80] By 1845, when a public competition was staged on the Champ de Mars, Paris, between Carafa's traditional band and a band containing Sax's new brass instruments, the contrabassoon had already been replaced by the ophicleide.

Under Wilhelm Wieprecht, Prussian infantry bands in 1838 each had two bassoons and two contrabassoons.[81] When various military bands met in competition at the Paris Exposition of 1867, only those bands from Prussia, Russia, and Spain contained contrabassoons; they were absent from bands from Baden, Bavaria, Belgium, France, and the Netherlands.[82] As in Austria, tubas began to replace the contrabassoon in Prussian military bands; an orchestration manual of 1883 lamented its scarcity.[83] The records of the London firm Rudall Carte show the sale of a 'maple contra fagotto brass key' to the 213th Regiment in 1873. The source was 'Coulson', apparently a dealer.

Verdi claimed in 1865 that the contrabassoon (of whatever description) 'is known even in Busseto, where I wrote marches for the instrument thirty years ago'.[84] Verdi may have been thinking of a conventional Central European contra – these were common in Italy, to judge from the number preserved in Italian collections today. In 1845, Pelitti of Milan exhibited a 'metal contrabassoon' at the Istituto Lombardo competition. This had 'the same fingering as the bassoon', although other particulars are unknown.

Rejecting the classical pattern: New ideals and new technologies

One of Boehm's inventions was simple, ingenious, and seminal. He converted the traditional key-work pattern, long levers mounted on short axles, into a new pattern of short levers mounted on long axles. He engineered this by rotating the axle of the simple key lever ninety degrees, so that it ran along the length of the instrument. The key spatula and key flap became short levers projecting, usually at a perpendicular angle, from opposite ends of the axle.

The liberating effect of this new technology on the contrabassoon was revolutionary. The rod-axle key allowed control of any tone hole from a finger spatula mounted at any remote location. Makers were now free to remodel the instrument's torso, reducing its awkward height while locating tone holes at acoustically desirable positions. The rod-axle key simultaneously eliminated the constraints of both human finger spans and old-fashioned key levers (which cannot jump easily from tube to tube of a folded instrument). Using the new key systems, octave contras to written C2 or lower became standard; they could be relatively compact and fingered much like the standard bassoon. Semi-contra bassoons, with their attendant problem of transposition, fell out of favor.[85] Isolated late examples, like that of Samme (London, c.1850), used a simple system, which was relatively cheap to produce.[86]

Much development of the contrabassoon during the nineteenth century was driven by the requirements of military bands, which sought bass and contrabass instruments with increased power and portability. Woodwind makers explored two routes to increased power: a wider bore and wider tone holes. They pursued portability by adding more folds to the instrument's bore. Haseneier's Contrabassophon was the logical result of these trends. Though made of wood, it made use of rod-axle keys and was folded to a height of 1.4 m for military use. The layout was [od +] 3u + 5d + 2u. Because it lacks deep chimneys (a defining characteristic of the bassoon and contrabassoon), the Contrabassophon is discussed in chapter 10. But its influence is sometimes seen in the more conservative contras discussed in this chapter.

True contrabassoons are defined here as having a relatively narrow bore; chimneys for holes L1 through L3 or more; and the traditional bassoon/contra fingering schema. Most instruments lacking these characteristics are discussed in chapter 10, regardless of the names applied to them by makers or earlier writers.

During the nineteenth century, the true contrabassoon was developed in three broad categories: (1) the traditional two-tube Viennese pattern, typically 6 + 3 but sometimes extended to 6 + 4 or 6 + 5; (2) the ultra-compact pattern (three tubes of approximately equal length) inspired by the Contrabassophon pattern (Stritter/Heckel 1877, Bradka, Berthold, Moritz, Samal); and (3) the 'modern' pattern of two long tubes plus one shorter tube; a fourth tube was later added to the modern pattern to produce written B♭1 or A1. (The lead pipe does not count as a tube in these descriptions.)

Few contras were built in Paris during the mid-nineteenth century. According to Pierre, Triebert and Marzoli made a copy 'after a German model' of contra around 1849.[87] This may have been the instrument acquired by the Société des Concerts du Conservatoire in 1863. Another contra reportedly built in Paris during these lean years was by Paul Goumas, who was associated with Buffet Crampon from 1851 to 1885.[88] In 1890 Pierre complained of the slow speech, disagreeable buzzing, and intonation of older contrabassoons then in use in France:

> [They] date back at least fifty years and . . . consequently have not benefited at all from progress in manufacture; they are old German instruments more or less modified, of which the mechanism and the bore are not conceived after rational principles and, as they have been constructed before the reform of the concert pitch, the repairs they have undergone to lower them have only added to their faults.[89]

The 'pitch reform' was the promulgation of the 'diapason normal' (A-435 Hz) in 1859, replacing a variety of higher pitches.[90]

Both Jancourt and Pierre had praise, however, for a new model introduced between 1885 and 1890 by Evette & Schaeffer.[91] Made in wood with fifteen keys mounted on rods and spatulas for the covered finger holes, 'which allows them to be drilled with more justness than before', it descended to C2.[92] Pierre regretted that Evette & Schaeffer maintained the vertical format, 2.4 m high, projecting 60 cm over the heads of the performers, 'like a tall factory smokestack towering in the sky'.[93] This was an extension of the classical 6 + 3 pattern to 6 + 4. Pierre approved of the quick response, although he thought that the sound lacked brilliance [éclat]. Still, he acknowledged 'real progress on the instruments in use at the Opéra and the Société des Concerts', apparently this model.

Pierre also approved of the more innovative contra of Thibouville, evidently a revision in brass (by 1890) of a model developed by 1888 at the request of Lucien Jacot of the Opéra-Comique. It was folded into 'four parallel tubes' (here meaning three plus the lead pipe) standing 1.5 m in height, with nineteen keys and six plateaux, fingering as the bassoon. 'The sound,' he wrote, 'stronger than that of a contrabassoon in wood, is perhaps less handsome than one will wish (it has some analogy to that of a sarrusophone).' Also of metal are ultra-compact contras in the Kampmann and Joppig collections; the Kampmann exemplar, engraved with the name of Evette & Schaeffer, has six plateaux and twelve keys and stands 1.29 m tall. The tone holes are broad and shallow, yet it has the narrow bore of a true contrabassoon.[94]

When English sources after 1874 mentioned a 'contrabassoon', they were often referring to a Contrabassophon, as made by Morton in London. Yet more traditional contras were known, and models by the Paris makers were available, if perhaps still uncommon. Rendall referred to 'a big rosewood contra with brass keys with rounded cups c.1850' in the possession of A. D. Royan.[95] Buffet Crampon maintained a branch office in London under the names of P. Goumas, 1876–85, and Evette & Schaeffer, 1885–1927. Tamplini exhibited a contra fagotto by Marzoli (d. 1865) and Triebert in London, 1885.[96]

Sometimes all three of the century's contra patterns are seen in the output of a single maker. From 1845 or earlier, the firm of J. A. Heckel had made the traditional 6d + 3u model. A contrabassoon appeared in 1877 bearing the marks of both 'Heckel Biebrich' and 'System Stritter' (Ill. 59). The makers were inspired by the ultra-compact configuration of Haseneier's Contrabassophon,[97] but rejected its extremely wide bore in favor of a conventional contrabassoon bore. The normal hand positions were inverted (left hand was held at bottom and the right hand at top). The assignment of fingers and thumbs to particular pitches was little changed; the inversion was dictated by the maker's efforts to reduce the height of the instrument to a minimum, for convenience in marching. The layout was 5u + 3d + 2u. Like the left hand, the right hand was provided with an épaule and chimneys for some pitches (B2, C3). But the traditional boot joint was absent, and with it the chimneys through which lower pitches had traditionally vented. One apparent innovation was the octave speaker key, sited on the lead pipe and operated by LT. It was made in both high- and low-pitch

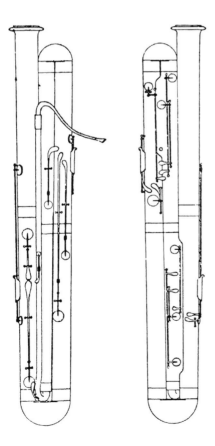

59. Ultra-compact contrabassoon of 1877 by Stritter and Heckel. Kaiserliches Patentamt, Patentschrift no. 1131.

models. On one exemplar, the middle C# key was operated by RT, while hole R1 remained uncovered by a plateau or key cup.

The ultra-compact, right-hand-uppermost model was short-lived. In 1879, the firm introduced the taller, left-hand-uppermost model familiar to players today, albeit at first only to written C2, in a layout of 3u + 4d + 3u. Early examples are marked 'Heckel', but carry the additional mark of 'System Stritter'.

Friedrich Stritter (1849–1922) had joined J. A. Heckel in 1870 as his then sole employee, later becoming foreman. After Heckel died on 13 April 1877, his son Wilhelm Heckel, aged twenty, took over direction of the firm. On 24 October 1877 (soon after German patent legislation took effect), Stritter received a patent for an ultra-compact, left-hand model contrabassoon. After this early design was revised in 1879 as a right-hand model (essentially the type known today), the revision was also acknowledged as his work. An early fingering chart for the 1879 contra was subtitled 'System F. Stritter'; Heckel's name was mentioned only in the quoted endorsement by Richard Wagner.[98] Continuing his work with Heckel, Stritter received 100 marks as royalty on each contra; he was presented with a gold watch on his twenty-fifth anniversary with the firm in 1895. In 1900, however, he was dismissed after a dispute with Heckel. From 1901 he worked for Reinhold Lange, a rival of Heckel who in his advertising resurrected the issue of Stritter's 1877 patent. In 1901–2 Stritter was involved in an unsuccessful lawsuit against Heckel over patent infringement.[99]

Der Fagott, published in 1899 by Wilhelm Heckel, made no mention of the 1877 model. In a 1931 revision of *Der Fagott*, Wilhelm Hermann Heckel presented the model as an 1876 invention by his grandfather and father, omitting any mention of Stritter.[100] This dismissive view, later amplified in books by Langwill and Jansen, is contradicted by the evidence summarized above.[101] That Stritter had a role in designing the 1877 and 1879 models is apparent, even if the conventional 'Heckel' label is used below.

During the nineteenth century, the firm C. W. Moritz of Berlin likewise built a succession of models, from hairpin contra to written D2, to ultra-compact contra and, by 1898, a taller contra to written C2,[102] similar to the W. Heckel model of 1879. The firm of Wenzel Bradka (fl. Vienna, 1862–1911) offered an ultra-compact model, while some models by Samal (fl. Prague, later nineteenth century) and Berthold (fl. Speyer, 1894–twentieth century) had a degree of contraction somewhere between the ultra-compact and the modern models.

The early modern contrabassoon

Heckel's model of 1879 was significantly taller than the 1877 model, abandoning the compactness that Haseneier and the military had sought. The revised model was more convenient, however, for a seated player resting it on the floor, the weight supported by a spike. Wilhelm Heckel took a significant step away from the acoustical design of the 1877 model: he dispensed with the épaule for the right hand, evidently having judged three open-standing chimneys sufficient to preserve the bassoon-like character of the contra. Tone holes 4 and 5, thus made larger and shallower, could contribute to a more powerful sound of both fundamental and overblown notes.

In August 1896, Hans Richter (conductor of the Bayreuth Festival) endorsed a version of the Heckel contra descending to low Bb1. A trade journalist in 1899 praised the 'elegance and neatness' and 'absolute purity of tone' of the new three-tube contra, contrasting it with the 'monstrous bulk' and 'powerful but raw tone' of Haseneier's Contrabassophon. He noted that a special model to C2 had a down-bent metal bell suitable for marching, which reduced the contra's overall height to 1.23 m.[103]

By 1899, Wilhelm Heckel advertised his contra's wooden construction, bassoon-like fingerings, and its 'extraordinarily smooth, full, strong, organ-like tone'.[104] In 1901 the firm announced the addition of a second octave vent key. Use of the lower key prevented a 'buzzing tone' on A3, while use of the upper key allowed pitches from written C4 to F4 to be fingered 'exactly as in the middle register'.[105]

The contrabassoon in repertory, 1879–1900

Richard Wagner endorsed the new bassoon and contra models of Wilhelm Heckel, who had visited Bayreuth for several days in 1879, at the invitation of the Wiesbaden conductor Wilhelm Jahn. Wagner praised its ability to make slurs on very low pitches.[106] He scored for contra in *Parsifal* (1879–82), and he reportedly allowed Hans Richter to introduce it into his earlier works.[107]

After 1880, serviceable contrabassoons (of various descriptions) and players were available in many cities, and composers increasingly wrote parts for the instrument. Mahler wrote contra parts for symphonies premiered in Budapest, Cologne, Munich, Prague, and Vienna. Thomas, Saint-Saëns, Reyer, Vidal, and Erlanger wrote contra parts for productions in Paris. Richard Strauss wrote demanding chromatic parts for contra as early as *Don Juan* (Weimar, 1889), and brief solo passages in *Also sprach Zarathustra* (Frankfurt, 1896). The contra figured in English oratorios, including Sullivan's *The Martyr of Antioch* (Leeds, 1880) and *The Golden Legend* (Leeds, 1886), and Elgar's *The Dream of Gerontius* (Birmingham, 1900). The English composer Frederick Corder in 1896 lamented the state of contrabassoon playing in London: 'Although much improved of late years, it is a disagreeable affair and is only tolerated because of the necessity of reinforcing the thin bassoons in large orchestras.'[108] In 1904, the Parisian composer Charles-Marie Widor preferred the sarrusophone to the contrabassoon.[109]

A new era of contrabassoon playing

In time, the Heckel design was accepted or adapted in all markets for contrabassoons. Flament and Letellier reported that the performance of Strauss's *Salome* in Paris (1905) introduced the new contrabassoon of Evette et Schaeffer (later Buffet Crampon): 'A perfect instrument, of a marvelous sonority and very sweet throughout its range. The fingering is the same as that of the French bassoon; its scale is almost three octaves (low Bb1 to high G3)' (Ill. 60). Selmer of Paris also made wooden contras with bassoon fingering.[110] Both these instruments were adaptations of the 1879 or later Heckel designs to the French fingering system. In 1922 the upright Evette & Schaeffer contra, with removable Bb bonnet, had been adopted by the Opéra, Société des

Concerts du Conservatoire, Concerts Colonne, Concerts Sechiari, and Concerts de Monte-Carlo.[111] Mahillon of Brussels in 1908 offered a fully keyed contra in wood, with bassoon fingerings, range from C2 to G4. Evident differences from the Evette model included location of the low C# vent on the non-detachable bell and the retention of levers for some LT keys. (The Mahillon bell still bore the distinctive Savary-inspired profile.)

German makers who imitated the Heckel contra model during the early twentieth century included Oscar Adler of Markneukirchen, V. Kohlert of Graslitz, J. Mollenhauer & Söhne of Fulda, G. Mollenhauer & Söhne of Kassel, Moritz of Berlin, and Zimmermann of Leipzig and Markneukirchen.

In a catalogue of c.1907, Heckel stressed again the contra's 'fingering system like the Heckel bassoon, so that every bassoonist can play immediately, without special study'. New features included the F#–G# interlocked trill,[112] a tuning-slide on the lead-pipe to regulate the pitch, and single-reed mouthpieces for both bassoon and contra. He offered a choice of bells, noting that those with wooden bends (to Bb1 or A1) sound 'somewhat more covered' than the straight bell to C2. Another option was a down-folded metal bell to Bb1; this reduced the contra's height to near that of a standard bassoon. A down-folded metal bell to A1, advertised in 1931, was somewhat

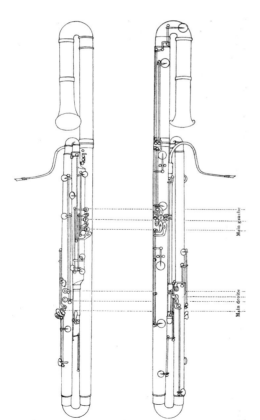

60.   French-system contrabassoon by Evette & Schaeffer. Couppas, *Tablature du contrebasson Système Evette & Schaeffer* (Paris, c. 1906).

taller. Metal replaced wood on the smaller U-bends, apparently between 1927 and 1931. Heckel in 1931 noted that the bore had been revised and improved over the years, and later gave fingerings as high as written A#4.[113] After 1945, a second F# key for R4 was advertised.[114]

English makers and dealers offered a variety of instruments under the contra name – French system, German system, standard bore, wide bore. The two opposite selling propositions were 'familiar and identical to bassoon fingerings' (true contras) and 'easily learnt' (reed contrabasses). Higham of Manchester c.1909 offered 'perfected contrabassoons to C or Bb, suitable alike for military and orchestral music, magnificent tone, English or Continental fingering . . . low pitch instruments made to order'. Rudall Carte's catalogue in 1928 included 'maple contra fagotti, with same fingering as French-system bassoon, at high or low pitch'.[115] Boosey & Hawkes during the 1930s–40s offered a contra to Bb1 in French or German systems.

Composers of the early twentieth century began to include contrabassoon parts routinely in large orchestral or operatic works. By 1908–9, in *Das Lied von der Erde* (v) 'Abschied', letter 6, Mahler used the contra as an important solo voice, weaving a chromatic obbligato with the flute (Ex. 9.1). Prominent contra solos, brooding but not clumsy, figure in Strauss's *Salomé* (1905) and *Elektra* (1909), the latter descending to written B1. Of Ravel's numerous uses of the contra, the most memorable is perhaps the evocative solo in *Ma mère l'oye*, where the contra represents the ponderous but ingenuous beast. Holst and Sibelius scored memorably for contra in several tone poems; Elgar and Shostakovich in several symphonies; Berg in his two operas. Stravinsky scored for contra in *Firebird* and *Petrushka* and for two contras (one of them alternating with bassoon) in *Le sacre du printemps*. Schoenberg called for contra not only in large tone poems and an opera, but also in modestly scored works like his two chamber symphonies.

The advent of electrical sound recording and radio broadcasting created a new, unwritten demand for the contrabassoon. Its overtone-rich sound was often added to the string basses for greater clarity in recording. Elgar's own recording of his Symphony no. 2 (1925) is one instance, and the 1926 catalogue of the Heckel firm also mentions the practice.[116]

In a preface to a new edition of Widor's orchestration manual, the composer Gordon Jacob rebutted Widor's earlier complaints, at least for England in 1945:

In this country the double bassoon is of far more frequent appearance than the sarrusophone. The modern instrument is fairly flexible and agile, and in the hands of a good player who has specialized in its use it is capable of a good deal more execution than Widor gives it credit for.[117]

Notable later contra parts occur in Britten's Symphony for Cello and Orchestra, op. 68 (1963), and works of Michael Tippett.

By the mid-twentieth century, contras not built on the Heckel pattern (or the Evette model, itself a Heckel adaptation) were rarely encountered. Standards of performance rose, if only gradually. As in past centuries, the typical player was a doubler, trained as a bassoonist but often lacking specific instruction on the contra. Players were more

Ex. 9.1.   Mahler 1908/9, *Das Lied von der Erde*, 'Abschied', excerpt (1908/9).

likely to purchase ready-made reeds than to make their own, and only dedicated specialists were likely to master fine points of difference between bassoon playing and contra playing, including divergent fingerings above written F4 (and occasionally below),[118] a more open vocal tract to bring pitches into tune, and confident production of the third octave and above.

Methods and texts appeared, including those by Piard (1952), Biggers (1977), and Angerhöfer and Seltmann (1984). By 1984, the curriculum of the Hochschule für Musik in Vienna included studies of orchestral contrabassoon parts.[119]

A 1980 advertisement by Buffet Crampon cited problems of the French-system contra: the low register was generally flat, the high register sharp, and the sonority often restricted in the middle and high registers. It listed the following recent improvements: resiting the lower tone holes to raise the flat low register; enlarging the bore of the wing joint to obtain a fuller and better-tuned middle register; relocating the hole for written G2 to the tenon; relocating the vents on the lead pipe; adding a correction hole for the high-note key; adding a tuning slide to the lead pipe; a new bore for the crook; abandonment of the wooden C bell; and fixing of the metal bell.

Other makers of contras after the Heckel pattern added refinements. Püchner began, in the late twentieth century, to offer an optional model with special keywork to accommodate players with smaller hands. Fox Products, in collaboration with Arlen Fast, offered a model with improved high-register venting, facilitating the response and intonation of the third octave. At least three makers – Buffet Crampon, Wolf, and Adler – rotated the contra's last U-joint by ninety degrees, thereby removing an obstacle from the player's field of vision. In 2001, Guntram Wolf of Kronach introduced the contraforte, a radical redesign (in cooperation with Benedikt Eppelsheim) of the contrabassoon, employing a wide bore and a four-tube layout. (See chapter 10.)

As the twentieth century matured, a spirit of competition spurred increasing numbers of players to cultivate the contrabassoon in its own right, and the instrument began to appear in new and prominent roles. Erwin Schulhoff's *Bass Nightingale* (1922) was written for solo contra. In 1953 Jiří Novak's *Fairy Tale Suite* combined contra with piano, while the Andante & Rondo, op. 52 (revised as op. 63) of Willy Hess combined contra with a string quartet. The jazz artist Garvin Bushell played contrabassoon on the track 'Spiritual' with the John Coltrane Group in a 1961 recording.[120] Valentine Kennedy performed Ralph Nicholson's *Impromptu*, a solo with the Guildford Orchestra, in 1969. Other works for solo contrabassoon and orchestra included *Leviathan* (1969) by Ruth Gipps, *Musik* (1976) by Burt Rudolph, and concertos by Gunther Schuller (1977), Donald Erb (1984), and Daniel Dorff (1991).[121]

By 1994, more than a hundred works specifying the contrabassoon in chamber music were listed in bibliographies of bassoon repertory, including works by György Ligeti, Wolfgang Rihm, and Iannis Xenakis.[122] The contra also became a frequent member in quartets with bassoons, playing transcriptions and some original compositions.

Chapter 10

The bassoon idea: relatives after mechanization

The invention of the rod-axle key mechanism c.1829 was an important catalyst for large woodwinds, opening the door to fully keyed (or 'covered') systems, which usually produced a fully chromatic scale. The astonishing variety of sixteen-foot register instruments during the nineteenth and twentieth centuries sometimes had double reeds and conical bores, but at other times they had single reeds, tuba-type mouthpieces, or cylindrical bores. Only those with double reeds and conical bores are mentioned here.*

Among keyed-system instruments (a matter of external mechanics), some also had a 'closed' fingering system (a matter of acoustical behavior). A closed system results when the tone holes approach the diameter of the instrument's bore; when a tone hole is this large, the lower part of the bore is effectively 'cut off', exerting little effect on the sounding note. On a closed system, most or all keys stand closed, and only one tone hole is opened at a time. Closed, unkeyed systems had long been common on small, cylindrical instruments like some bagpipe chanters, but not on large, conical instruments, where such large tone holes would have been larger than the player's finger tips. Boehm's rod-axle technology, which had resulted in flutes where all diatonic keys are open-standing, soon gave rise to bass woodwinds where nearly all keys were closed-standing – such was its revolutionary sweep.

The nineteenth-century quest for a contrabass wind instrument that was sufficiently loud for outdoor performance led many inventors to larger tone holes and sometimes onward to the closed fingering system. To the unpracticed eye, such instruments are not immediately distinguishable from conventional woodwinds, but they in fact comprise a distinct sub-family by reason of their fingering differences. The trained bassoonist had no equity in this fingering system, which in principle resembled a monophonic keyboard instrument. Piano-like keys were occasionally fitted, but most makers retained conventional woodwind spatulas. The novelty of the new system is obvious from engraved labels giving pitch names, seen on the spatulas of bass and contrabass instruments made by Stehle and later makers.

Another concern for makers was the physical height of traditional contra-register woodwinds, which was often 1.7 m or more. In broad terms, the trend was from a two-tube configuration to a three-tube configuration (the lead pipe is not included in

---

* Written pitch names in this chapter sound an octave lower, unless otherwise noted.

these counts). In the following discussion, the various instruments are presented in five groups, in order of historical appearance. First we consider two-tube instruments having closed systems (the Harmonie-Bass and early Tritonicon). Next developed was the influential Contrabassophon (three tubes, open system, very wide bore), followed by the revised Tritonicon and its imitations (three tubes, closed system, very wide bore), the sarrusophone (three tubes, open system, moderately wide bore), and the rothophone (two tubes, open system, narrow bore). The one latter-day instrument here is the contraforte (four tubes, open system, moderately wide bore). Emphasis is placed in this chapter and in the following selective table on the bass and contrabass members of each type.

Name	Tubes	Layout	System	Bore
Harmonie-Bass	2	6 + 3	closed	moderately wide
Tritonicon (1844)	2	6 + 3	closed	moderately wide
Contrabassophon	3	3 + 5 + 2	open	very wide
Tritonicon (1856)	3	6 + 2 + 1	closed	very wide
Sarrusophone	3	3 + 2 + 2	open	wide
Rothophone	2	6 + 1	open	narrow
Contraforte	4	3 + 3 + 3 + 3	open	moderately wide

Many of these double-reed bass instruments have been called Contrafagott, contra-fagotto, or contrabassoon by makers, players, or band masters. Berlioz even heard a player of the Russian bassoon call his cupped-mouthpiece instrument a 'contre-basson'.[1] In such loose usage, the term implied nothing more than a low-pitched instrument having tone holes. Instruments discussed in this chapter lack at least one of the following defining characteristics of the true contrabassoon: traditional narrow bore; deep, narrow chimneys for holes 1–3 or more; an open fingering schema; and a double-reed mouthpiece.

The two-tube Harmonie-Bass and Tritonicon

When inventors began to develop new contra-register double-reed woodwinds during the nineteenth century, the status quo was the Central European contrabassoon, a two-tube instrument to D1 standing c.1.7 m high. Its 'hairpin'-style lead pipe and flaring brass bell were often retained on inventive new two-column instruments, even while its wooden body, uncovered finger holes, chimneys, and open-system fingering were often abandoned.[2] Another significant inspiration was the ophicleide, an adaptation in metal of the bassoon's two-tube pattern.[3] This brasswind instrument was about 1 m high; a coiled crook led to its cup mouthpiece. The inventor, Halary of Paris, produced a seven-key version in 1817; he patented a nine-key version in 1821. The folded tube was reasonably portable, and the player's thumbs could control many of the keys. In the ophicleide's fingering schema, however, the highest tone hole was opened by R1. Aside from one open-standing key (the lowest), the others were closed-standing. Moreover, because of the great size of the tone holes, the fingering system was semi-closed: one or a few of the keys were opened to produce a chromatic series of fundamental pitches, from B1 to Bb2 (sounding as written) on an ophicleide in C. The layout was 2 + 5.

Johann Stehle of Vienna in 1836 patented a 'brass wind instrument on the pattern of a contrabassoon', descending to C and having 'each tone hole in its rightful place'. At least some tone holes were unkeyed (covered only by the fingers), while a tuning slide allowed water to be emptied and the pitch to be lowered by a quarter tone. It supposedly produced a more powerful tone than a wooden contrabassoon, while being lighter and more convenient to handle.[4] The instrument does not survive, but the patent offers some details of description.[5]

In 1838 Stehle patented a new instrument having larger tone holes and a completely covered system, though nominally based on the 1836 instrument. He exhibited it in Vienna, 1839 and 1845, as the 'Harmonie-Bass'.[6] Its conical brass body was bent once like an ophicleide, but it was taller: about 1.65 m (Ill. 61). This was close to the height of a traditional hairpin contra to D, as made by Stehle and others.[7] Like the ophicleide, the Harmonie-Bass was fingered according to a mostly closed system; one key at a time was opened, except that the lowest key was open-standing. But in its number of closed keys (fourteen) and mapping of fingers to the basic scale, the Harmonie-Bass was unlike the ophicleide. It also had a semi-helical bend in the middle of the down bore, which allowed Stehle to bring the simple lever keys within easy reach of the

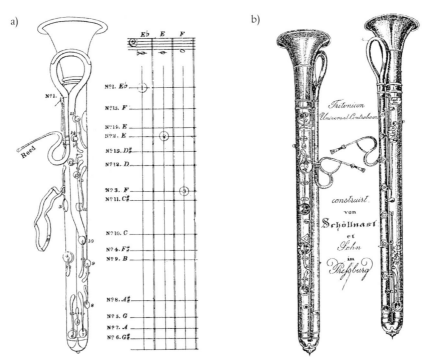

61. (a) Detail of fingering chart for Stehle's Harmonie-Bass; only one key was opened per pitch; (b) Tritonicon by Schöllnast, after 1844. *Niemitz's Method for Musical Instruments Used in a Military Band* (London, p.1844); Mestské múzeum Bratislava.

player's fingers. Like the traditional hairpin contrabassoon, the Harmonie-Bass had a fundamental scale from D2 to F3, overblown from F#3 upwards without aid of octave-keys. Although the fingering system was closed, it bore a vestigial relationship to that of the classical contrabassoon: the highest note of the fundamental scale (F3) was governed by L1, the scale descending to end on written D2, the lowest hole being closed by LT. The layout was 6 + 3.

With its closed fingering system and lack of chimneys, this instrument was hardly a true contrabassoon. That did not stop many commentators from labeling it as such, even though its inventor preferred a trade name – Harmonie-Bass – that emphasized its utility in wind ensembles. In his method for the Harmonie-Bass, Andreas Nemetz was quick to praise the instrument:

> But of late the use of the double bassoon is greatly lessened by the spread of the new brass wind instrument (invented by the instrument-maker by appointment to H.I.M., Herr Stehle in Vienna), called Harmonie-Bass and played with a double-bassoon reed; for who would not gladly exchange the rattling sounds of the double bassoon for the full and strong tones of the Harmonie-Bass?[8]

Nemetz observed that notes above (written) F3 were produced without any octave key, simply by overblowing the fundamental scale at the octave, or (for written F#4 and G4) at the double octave, with altered embouchure.[9]

On 5 May 1839, the 'Tritonikon', a brass instrument newly invented by Schöllnast & Sohn, was announced in the press.[10] In an illustration printed for advertising, Schöllnast himself styled it the 'Tritonicon Universal-Contrabasz'.[11] The instrument differed from Stehle's Harmonie-Bass in two significant ways. Rod-axle keys allowed Schöllnast to use a simple column for the down bore, dispensing with the semi-helical bend of Stehle's Harmonie-Bass (although simple lever keys were still employed on the up bore).[12] Both the Harmonie-Bass and the tritonicon were carried at a near-horizontal angle when marching, judging by the bend of their crooks.[13] Schöllnast described a 'compass from D2 to F3 or even up to C4 (with exceptionally good players) with dynamic range from piano up to sextuple loudness of a contrabassoon'.[14] In 1845 Ferdinand Hell of Vienna exhibited two tritonicons, presumably similar to the instrument by Schöllnast. The one known surviving instrument of this type bears the mark of Gebrüder Placht, a dealer.[15]

Leopold Uhlmann of Vienna produced a double-reed, two-tube instrument of brass pitched in F. Its bore appears to resemble that of the traditional hairpin contra, but all the tone holes (without chimneys) were covered by closed-standing keys (five lever keys and six rod-axle keys). An example preserved in Parma was dated by Kiefer to the middle 1840s. Labels on the spatulas indicate that the fingering is a closed system.[16]

Innovative contra instruments of metal also appeared in Italy, apparently beginning in 1840, when Giovacchino Bimboni obtained a privilege for his new 'contrabbasso a fiato', according to a newspaper announcement published in 1842.[17] Tosoroni later referred to this instrument as the flarmonica or contrabbasso d'armonie. Despite the similarity of this last name, the flarmonica did not finger like Stehle's Harmonie-Bass, as the following comments by Tosoroni make clear:

> This instrument is pitched in F; it was made in Florence by the distinguished professor of trombone Giovacchino Bimboni. . . . He made two for his band, and although made of tin-plated iron [latta], they produced a very great effect. It is sounded with a reed [bocchetta] like that of the bassoon, but larger. For a bassoon player it is most easy to play, as the fingering conforms in all respects to that instrument. Its note is at the unison with that of the contro-fagotto; like it, it sounds the low bass well. For bands, and for large ensembles [grandi masse] and for a prodigious effect, it sounds well all tonalities and [their] relatives.[18]

Tosoroni also described a second instrument, the contra-fagotto or fagottone, descending to Bb1, thus a lower instrument than Stehle's. 'Its construction being very heavy, it only sounds the low bass, but with very good effect, especially in bands and in wind harmonie ensembles. It sounds well in all tonalities, and their relatives.'[19] Given the names, it is a surprise to learn that a contrabass horn (with cup mouthpiece and no valves) survives, with a maker's plaque engraved "Contrabasso/Pelittone/ Fagattone" [*sic*].[20]

The Pelitti firm of Milan sought to enter the Austrian market for military instruments, creating several diffent versions of a 'contrafagotto di metallo' in preparation for a Milan competition of 1845; Pelitti patented versions in both Vienna and Milan in 1846.[21] By 1847 Pelitti had developed a revised instrument having twelve keys and pitched in F.[22] A two-tube instrument by Pelitti survives.[23]

Haseneier's three-tube Contrabassophon

Heinrich Joseph Haseneier of Koblenz in 1847 began to develop a wide-bore contra-register instrument in wood. The body was tightly folded into a package the height of a standard bassoon, with an eye toward military use (Ill. 62). Haseneier 'reportedly met Boehm at Bad Ems, where the latter was taking a cure'.[24] Making use of the creative freedom allowed by rod-axle keys, he reconfigured the contra into an ultra-compact form of three parallel tubes (plus lead pipe) of nearly equal length, descending to written C2. The former 'hairpin' or lead pipe was folded downward, yielding a layout of [od +] 3u + 5d + 2u. Haseneier's application for a patent in 1850 was unsuccessful; this was a great irony, given the Contrabassophon's later influence.

Models were made in C (concert pitch) for orchestral use and in Bb for military use. The instrument combined an open but completely keyed system with a compact folding and a wide bore. A Contrabassophon pitched in Bb, now at Cologne, stands 1.38 m high ('only an inch taller than the usual bassoon', as Lenz noted in 1850; vs. c.1.7 m for the Harmonie-Bass or a typical hairpin contra); its bore increases from c.5.1 mm at the crook tip to c.20 mm in the first joint, to c.100 mm at the bell opening.[25] While the wooden seats of the broad tone holes projected from the body of the Contrabassophon, the depth-to-diameter ratio was modest, as was the filtering effect. Combined with the wide bore, this gave the instrument a powerful sound.

62. Contrabassophon by Alfred Morton. Langwill Archive.

Blackman noted the immense size of the keys: low C# is 68 mm wide, versus 32 mm on a standard contra; the bore for the low C# tone hole is 70 per cent broader than the modern contrabassoon, though still not as broad as on the tritonicon.[26]

The Contrabassophon used a fingering system congenial to bassoonists; a band master reviewing it in 1850 stated that every bassoonist could master the instrument 'after a few days' practice'. The third mode of the seven-finger scale produced an in-tune twelfth, rather than the sharp response of the bassoon. The fingerings were thus like an idealized bassoon, not a real one. 'The range is just over three octaves from a low C2 up to a high D5', Blackman reported:

> In order to play the lower notes, the large keys need considerable strength to ensure that no air escapes under the larger pads. . . . In order to help impart more force, six of the main keys . . . have a larger saddle shape that is meant to be used by the stronger middle phalanges of the fingers. . . .
>
>   However, the effort is worthwhile when the notes of the middle to upper registers generate such magnificent resonance . . . perhaps starting to take on characteristics of a tuba in tone and volume. One weakness of the design, which perhaps was one of the elements in its demise, was the instrument's inability to play softer dynamics with ease. This is especially the case in the lowest half-octave, where a pianissimo is virtually impossible to produce.[27]

Several other makers imitated the Contrabassophon, including Alfred Morton of London (Ill. 62). Lafleur's 'new contrabassoon in C', a Morton copy offered in a catalogue of c.1875, cost 70 pounds, almost three times the cost of a Morton bassoon.[28] Between 1874 and 1879, Morton worked with W. H. Stone to introduce minor refinements. Constant Pierre was familiar with the Morton instrument, and admired its bassoon-like layout of key spatulas. Because of the great expense of the instrument, however, only three had been sold by 1890, all to the British military. Of those, two had been abandoned, he was told, for the reed contrabass of Mahillon, apparently because the Contrabassophon's bulk and weight were 'too considerable for a marching musician'.[29]

An imitation of the Morton model was patented in France by Fontaine-Besson in 1890; it descended to Bb and had a water key at the first U-joint.[30] Other makers included Geipel of Breslau, Doelling of Potsdam, and Bradka of Gumpoldskirchen (Vienna). An exemplar signed by Schultze of New York is probably a German import.[31]

Much use was by military bands, as Haseneier had anticipated. But Stone, a talented amateur bassoonist, played the Contrabassophon in various English orchestras. Langwill reported that a higher pitched model in F was made at the request of Sir Arthur Sullivan for use in the orchestra of the Savoy Theatre, London. Morton's son played the Contrabassophon with the Hallé orchestra, at the Crystal Palace, at Richter's concerts, and at the Opera (Covent Garden).[32] Anthony Baines briefly used a Morton model in the London Philharmonic Orchestra in c.1939.[33]

Keyboard basses with two, three, or four tubes

The new fingering schema of the Harmonie-Bass and similar instruments allotted up to six keys to the four fingers of the player's hand. In chromatic passages, cross-fingering was not an option, and the player was sometimes presented with awkward slides between spatulas. The bandmaster and inventor Wilhelm Wieprecht addressed this problem in 1845 through a piano-like keyboard, which freed the player to use almost any finger on any key.[34] His '16 füssiger Orgelbass' had a double-reed mouth-piece and a one-octave keyboard for the right hand.[35] Fourteen closed holes divided the total length 'according to acoustical laws' in a layout of 7d + 7u. His patent application was unsuccessful (Ill. 63).

A few years after the appearance of Haseneier's three-tube Contrabassophon, Wieprecht worked with his longtime collaborator Carl Wilhelm Moritz to develop a four-tube 'keyboard contrabassoon' (Ill. 64). In a patent application submitted jointly with Moritz's widow on 29 May 1856, Wieprecht credited his late partner with having executed his (Wieprecht's) idea, which other makers had called an impossibility.[36] He noted the difficulty of balancing a very heavy instrument while trying to finger it; his entire key work was operated by the right hand, 'so that the left hand could be devoted unhindered to supporting the instrument. . . . The difficulty or ease of technique was equal in all tonalities.' [37] In the patent drawing eighteen tone holes are visible in a layout of 5d + 5u + 5d + 3u. An octave key on the crook was operated by the left hand.[38] The bore of the keyboard contrabassoon was similar throughout to Stehle's. By 1873, the instrument was no longer in use, due largely to its high cost.[39]

Wieprecht and Moritz, exploiting the rod-axle technology, severed all connection to the traditional contrabassoon fingering. While Stehle's Harmonie-Bass had a closed system, its lever-key spatulas still connected the closest fingers to the respective tone holes, with the highest pitches activated by L1. In the Wieprecht/Moritz instruments, the highest pitches were activated by R1, while the lowest pitches were activated by L4, as on the piano keyboard. This was a new archetypal schema for the fingering of woodwinds.

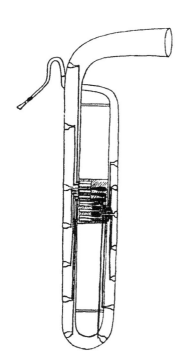

63. *16 füßiger Orgelbass* by Wieprecht. Geheimes Staatsarchiv Preussiches Kulturbesitz.

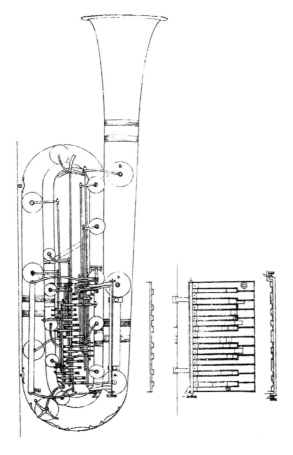

64. *Klaviatur-Kontrafagott* by Wieprecht. Geheimes Staatsarchiv Preussiches Kulturbesitz.

The piano-like keyboards of Wieprecht and Moritz were short-lived, but the same ordering was preserved for traditional-looking spatulas, as described below. As the names 'organ bass' and 'keyboard-contrabassoon' implied, these instruments were as suited to keyboard players as to traditional contrabassoonists. Playing in remote keys was 'hardly more difficult than simple keys', the makers advertised.

Wieprecht wielded an international influence on military music, organizing the military music of Turkey (1847) and Guatemala (1852) on the Prussian model. In 1855, fighting an upward tendency of pitch standards, he wrote a memo to the general intendant of Berlin theaters.[40]

The three-tube tritonicon and related instruments

Červený, who had worked for Schöllnast in 1839, produced two versions of the tritonicon. On the two-tube model, illustrated in a leaflet of 1853, rod-axle keys were fitted to tone holes on the down bore, and lever keys to those on the up bore. On one such instrument, the conventional-looking spatulas were reordered into a Wieprechtian piano keyboard schema.[41]

At the request of a military bandmaster named Hájek, Červený in 1856 reconfigured the tritonicon into a new compact, three-tube pattern.[42] Its pitch was raised in 1868 from D2 to Eb2 in order to reduce weight and make fingering more convenient.[43] The oldest Červený tritonicon in the Prague collection, no. 1790, is of brass with a silver crown and decorative engraving, 107 cm tall. The mechanism consists of fifteen keys and vents, eleven (closed-standing) for the fingers and two (open-standing) for LT. Behind are touches for RT vent keys. The diameter of the rear tone holes is 73 and 70 mm; the diameters of front vents varies from 33 to 63 mm. No octave-key was present.[44] The layout of a three-tube tritonicon is 6u + 2d + 1u.[45]

Mendel reported in 1873 that the revised tritonicon was favored by Austrian and some Prussian military bands, and Schafhäutl wrote in 1882 that the tritonicon was 'beloved of military musicians in Austria'.[46] This model, with piano-like assignment of spatulas, would be produced, with only minor variations, from 1856 into the twenty-first century, often under the names reed contrabass, contrebasse à anche, contrabasso ad ancia, etc. (See below.)

Červený planned the development of a complete family of tritonicons as a family of 'metal bassoons', as shown in a surviving note sheet from the company archives with notated compasses from the subcontra to the alto sizes.[47] One smaller instrument survives, a bass in Bb with 22 keys.[48] The 'Subkontrafagott', introduced in 1867 but now lost, was pitched an octave lower than this. Despite later misunderstandings of its range, this instrument reached to Bb0 (written Bb1), which is in fact the typical bottom note for conventional Heckel-type contrabassoons. A later version, exhibited by Červený at Paris in 1889 and illustrated by Pierre, had revised keywork to accommodate two octave keys.[49]

The contrebasse à anche or reed contrabass

V.-Ch. Mahillon's 'contrebasse à anche', introduced in 1868, was a lightly revised three-tube tritonicon. The positions of the holes for G2, F#2, and F2 were shifted to simplify the mechanism.[50] By 1874, Mahillon added two octave-keys for the left thumb.[51] An English catalogue from 1908 or later described this instrument under the name 'the double bassoon or contra fagotto':

> A brass instrument with seventeen keys specially recommended for military band use. Its reed . . . does not require the same nicety in the pressure of the lips . . . [and] allows the player to acquire great proficiency with only a few days' practice. The fingering is simple in the extreme, no matter in which key the music may be written. In military bands the instrument will be found invaluable; it softens the harshness of the brass instruments and owing to the depth of its tone, renders unnecessary the use of a string bass, the introduction of which has been so often condemned.[52]

Both Boosey & Co. (1902) and Besson offered a reed contrabass, styled as an 'Eb contra bassoon in brass with seventeen keys' (Ill. 65). Other makers included E. Albert

65. Reed contrabass by Besson.
Waterhouse Collection.

(Brussels); Gautrot (Paris); Maino & Orsi (Milan); and Rampone (Milan). Angerhöfer reported an unpublished method for the instrument by Nazareno Gatti.[53]

As recently as 2008, Orsi offered a 'contrabasso ad ancia' as a special-order item. Eppelsheim identified an instrument in the Brussels collection as a protype for a smaller 'basse à anche' in B♭2. Only 58 cm high, with a bell diameter of c.191 mm, the instrument stands a fifth above the contrabasse à anche.[54]

The bass and contrabass sarrusophones

Gautrot patented his three-tube bass sarrusophone in 1856, deriving the trade name from the bandmaster Pierre Auguste Sarrus, who had reportedly inspired its invention. Gautrot exhibited it at Bayonne in 1864 and again at the Paris Exposition of 1867, for which occasion Gounod wrote his *Chorale et musette* for sarrusophone sextet.[55] The sarrusophone's open fingering system had much in common with traditional woodwinds. Simpler to finger than the bassoon, it employed the thumbs only for one low pitch and for the octave keys. The lowest-pitched sarrusophones approach the ultra-compact folding seen in the contrabassophone. The larger sizes – the bass in B♭ and contrabasses in E♭, C, and B♭ – have the layout 3 + 2 + 2. The bass in B♭ stands 92 cm tall, the contrabass in E♭ 120–7 cm, and the contrabass in B♭ 132–46 cm[56] (Ill. 66).

The upper range of the sarrusophone extends two octaves and a sixth above the seven-finger note. Modern versions have a lower extension of two semitones; older versions reportedly extended only a semitone below.[57] The sarrusophones, lacking the chimneys of the bassoon, produce a penetrating tone that has been compared to that of a reedy saxophone. Leruste listed a series of disadvantages, including harsh notes not suitable for pianissimo, a difficult note production in the second octave, difficult descending slurs, and a recommended confinement to eight major keys, plus their relative minors.[58] A commercial rival, the contrabassoon maker Wilhelm Heckel,

66. Contrabass sarrusophone in E♭ by Conn. Waterhouse Collection.

disparaged the sarrusophone tone: 'This instrument shows what a hard, sonorous tone results from following theoretical-acoustical principles.'[59] The English composer Frederick Corder dismissed sarrusophones as 'large coarse oboes, more suitable for the open air'.[60] Yet in 1904, the Parisian composer Charles-Marie Widor preferred the sarrusophone to the contrabassoon.[61]

In military use, the sarrusophone was outstripped by the saxophone. During the years 1903–25 Evette & Schaeffer produced 17,000 saxophones versus 115 sarrusophones in nine sizes (the E♭ contrabass was most popular).[62] C. G. Conn reportedly produced 148 contrabass sarrusophones in E♭ for the U. S. armed forces between 1921 and World War II. Other makers of the early twentieth century included Boosey & Hawkes (UK), Cabart (France), Laviña (Spain), and Rampone and Rancilio (Italy). Orsi of Milan in 2008 offered sarrusophones in all sizes as special-order items, while Schenkelaars & Brekloo (Eindhoven) and Benedikt Eppelsheim (Munich) offered selected sizes.

In 1867 Gautrot published a sarrusophone tutor by Emile Coyon, who had played the E♭ contrabass in the Garde Nationale of the Seine under Jancourt, who served as bandmaster prior to joining the Conservatoire as bassoon professor in 1875.[63] Leruste in 1926 claimed to have written a method himself.

Saint-Saëns allowed the contrabass sarrusophone to replace the contrabassoon in *Les noces de Prométhée* (1867), and he made the gift of a sarrusophone to the Lyon Opera for the performance of his *Étienne Marcel* (1879). Massenet scored for sarrusophone in *Esclarmonde* (1889) and Dukas in *L'apprenti sorcier* (1897). According to Leruste, the sarrusophone was also used in performances of works by Bach, Haydn, Mozart, and Beethoven.[64] In 1907, scoring for the instrument reached a notable peak when it was specified in orchestral works by several prominent composers, including Ravel (*Rapsodie espagnole*, 1907–8, and *L'heure espagnole*, 1907–9). Paderewski's Polonia Symphony op. 24 (1907) called for three sarrusophones, while Joseph Holbrooke scored for two sizes in *Apollo and the Seaman* (1907).[65] Two years before this, however, Evette & Schaeffer had already introduced a French model of contrabassoon based on the Heckel design. Orchestral conductors and players generally came to prefer the new contrabassoon, evidently feeling that the sarrusophone surrendered too much of the iconic contra tone. Later demands for the contrabass sarrusophone included Delius's *Eventyr* (1917; performed London, 1919), Boito's *Nerone* (first performed 1924) and Stravinsky's *Threni* (Venice, 1958). The sarrusophone was reportedly used in the Pittsburgh Symphony during the 1940s to play contrabassoon parts.

Hough reported that the E♭ contrabass sarrusophone was used in Spanish municipal bands until about 1900, when 'band directors preferred the sound of the contrabassoon'.[66] During the 1903 season, an E♭ contrabass was used in the Sousa Band.[67] The University of Illinois band collection includes seven sizes of sarrusophone played during 1924–43, including contrabasses in C and E♭.[68] *NGDMM2* alluded to 'evidence that the entire sarrusophone family was used in French, Italian, and Spanish bands'.[69]

Some latter-day orchestras and opera houses have followed composers' specifications, reinstating the sarrusophone as specified in works of Dukas, Ravel, Paderewski, Lili Boulanger, Delius, and Stravinsky. Gounod's *Chorale et musette* has been revived in recent years by Thomas Kiefer's sarrusophone ensemble. Recent scoring for sarrusophone includes works by Bruce Boughton, Barney Childs, Alan Silvestri, and Gareth Wood.

The contrabass was heard in the Paul Whiteman dance orchestra during the 1920s–30s. Sidney Bechet recorded a jazz number on contrabass sarrusophone in 1924.[70] In the 1980s, a sarrusophone was heard in the Roscoe Mitchell New Chamber Ensemble, a jazz group.[71]

The bass rothophone and saxorusophone

In 1912 the inventor Friedrich F. Roth brought out a double-reed variation of the saxophone with a slightly narrower bore, intended for use in wind bands. A family of five sizes was patented in 1912 by Fratelli A. & N. Bottali of Milan, who supplied it to Italian bands until 1937. After the demise of Bottali, the successor Orsi marketed the instrument under the name 'saxorusophone'.[72] The bass in B♭ has the layout 6 + 1.

The four-tube contraforte

In 2001, Guntram Wolf of Kronach introduced the contraforte, a radical redesign (in cooperation with Benedikt Eppelsheim) of the contrabassoon, employing a wide bore and a four-tube layout. Descending to written A1, the contraforte has a layout of

3 + 3 + 3 + 3. The lead pipe (rubber-lined) and all U-joints are made of wood; a novel design uses O-rings to enhance sealing between joints. The tone holes are not chimneys, although the ebony tone-hole seats project from the maple body. Bassoon-like fingering is preserved in the first two octaves, and simplified in the third octave. Wolf claims that written F5 is easily possible on the instrument. A new half-holing mechanism and automatic octave venting set the mechanism apart from that of the Heckel-type contra.[73] One or two harmonic keys on the crook are activated by a steel cable linkage. A wick of compressed felt continually drains moisture away from the lead pipe. The wide bore, large tone holes, and many technical innovations give the contraforte a broad dynamic range, effective in both pianissimo and fortissimo. Given time, this thoughtful invention, which seems to draw on strengths of both the Heckel pattern and the Contrabassophon, may be accepted in the conservative world of contra players.

Chapter 11

Smaller sizes of bassoon

The original reason for folding the standard bassoon was the superhuman length of its bore. In the smaller sizes this need is absent or reduced. An octave bassoon's bore is short enough – about four feet – for it to present no great awkwardness if unfolded. The tenor bassoon would be roughly six feet long (including crook) if straightened. Meanwhile, the lowest tones of a small bassoon are not always required, especially in consort use. Hand spans are less a factor than on the standard bassoon; the chimneys are present in smaller bassoons mostly from convention. Yet it is sometimes said that the smaller sizes, despite their chimneys, surrender some of the quintessence of the standard bassoon's tone.

Thus the notion of smaller bassoons is largely derivative, perhaps a product of an enduring penchant for sized consorts of musical instruments.[1] Yet smaller bassoons, made in most eras of the bassoon's history, were more manageable for children, players on horseback, and other players with small hands or space constraints. After more than a century of virtual extinction, they made a comeback in the late twentieth century. Whereas the standard bassoon, because of its length and weight, is usually held obliquely across the player's body, with the bell tipped away, this need is largely absent for the smaller sizes. The smallest sizes can be held almost parallel to the body, and the crook is therefore bent more slightly. Rather than weight, mobility of the fingers is often the main consideration in deciding how to support the instrument.

Smaller dulcians

There is little doubt that potentates of the sixteenth and seventeenth centuries were conscious of the appearance of their musical instruments. Among the 'absolutely beautiful and excellent instruments as would befit any eminent lord or potentate' described by Hans J. Fugger in 1571 were treble, tenor, bass, and greatbass dulcians. He described the smallest of these, made of exotic tulipwood, as 'more beautiful than any precious stone'.[2] Even when not specially decorated, the smallest instrument present in a dulcian consort was likely to draw attention.

Praetorius showed the discant dulcian only in a keyless 6 + 4 layout; R4 and L4 controlled tone holes on the up bore. But most surviving small dulcians show a conventional 6 + 4 layout with two keys. Of the three surviving descant or soprano dulcians, two carry the marks of SELM and MTNZ. One of the surviving five altos is keyless 6 + 3, matching the illustration of Praetorius; it carries the mark associated with the Bassano family. Three others are marked MELCHOR R.S. [Rodriguez]. Surviving tenors carry marks associated with the Bassano family, with 'CR', and with MELCHOR R.S. The surviving smaller dulcians from Spanish makers are international in their features, lacking the ring mounts and usually the estrangul of surviving bass bajones.[3]

In the dulcian era, the smaller sizes often took middle or upper lines in a consort. Such consorts sometimes played in isolation, as explained in chapter 2. At times one or more small dulcians accompanied or doubled singers in vocal music. Pietro Flaccomio called for 'basoncico alias fagotto piccolo' to double the alto line in his *Concentus in duos distincti choros* (Venice, 1611).[4] In Spain, bajoncillos were often in pairs, usually with a standard bajón underneath, as in works by Arze-Latin, de Carrión, Comes, Muelas, and Vaquedano.[5] In a three-choir sacred work by Miguel de Irízar (1635–84), the third choir consists of two bajoncillos, a tenor voice, and a bajón.[6] At other times, they might form a four-voice choir (treble, alto, and tenor bajoncillos with bajón).[7] Spanish players were sometimes also shawmists. In Madrid, 1655, it was noted that 'two tenor shawm players [are] also able to play vajón … [and] two alto shawm players [are] also able to play the vajoncito …'.[8] Rabassa in 1724 wrote that the contralto and tenor baxoncillos were no longer in use.[9]

The smaller sizes of dulcian were sometimes used in mixed consorts. Four Christmas responsories by Pedro de Esperança, composed c.1615 for the Santa Cruz monastery, Coimbra, call for fagotilho, violin, baixão and gamba. 'The fagotilho part lies in the range C4 to F5 and could be played only on a discant bajoncillo in c (range G3 to G5)', Kilbey noted.[10] Many small sizes of dulcian may lie hidden beneath other forgotten nuances of terminology.

The baroque era

Surviving octave bassoons from this era carry the marks of I. C. Denner, C. A. Grenser, Kuteruf, Müller, and Scherer. A tenor bassoon by C. Schramme survives[11] (Ill. 67).

The abbé Denis De Coetlogon wrote in 1745 that 'the best bassoon I ever heard was one Le Breton, bassoon of our Lady at Paris, who invented a counter-tenor to the bassoon'. This bassoonist may be identifiable with the 'Le Breton' listed in 1692 by Du Pradel as a 'master for the playing and making of wind instruments'.[12] Before he

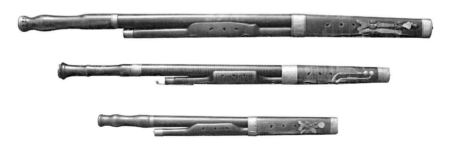

67.   From bottom: octave bassoon by Scherer; tenor bassoon by Savary jeune; bassoon by G. Wietfelt. Waterhouse Collection.

was recorded as a bassoon maker, Charles Bizey in 1711 held the title of valet de chambre in De Coetlogon's household.[13] His apprentice during 1747–53 was Prudent Thierriot; an after-death inventory of Prudent's property included 'plusieurs octaves de hautbois et de basson'.[14] (A baritone oboe by Prudent survives, but no small bassoons.)

Use was sometimes in like consorts, as in the Danish royal oboe band, where eight bassoons in different sizes (probably octave, tenor, and standard) presented a matched appearance. The composer Keiser noted in 1720 that 'the king of Denmark has eight such bassoons and bassonets in his Grenadier Guards, which are extremely pompous (solemn) and pleasing to hear'.[15] Oboists were forced to play the smaller sizes, to their reported displeasure. Whether the oboists found the small bassoons unsatisfactory or simply unfamiliar, we don't know, but appearance was clearly a guiding principle.

Surviving at the Musikhistorisk Museum, Copenhagen, are octave bassoons by C. A. Grenser of Dresden (E 140), and Jeremias Schlegel of Basel (E 132). One wonders whether the large numbers of bassoons reportedly owned by some players during the period included smaller sizes.

Keiser in a letter of 3 November 1720 offered the court of Württemberg two suites he had recently composed for bassoon octets, saying that 'when the men are all drilled on this instrument, such a harmonie makes a special effect'.[16] While his offer was not accepted, a 1718 inventory at Württemberg included a quint bassoon.[17] Between 1700 and 1713, inventories of the Kapelle instruments at Gotha included one Quintfagott and one *Stimmwerck* or set. Ahrens conjectured that the Stimmwerck included four instruments, presumably of two or more sizes.[18] These may have been four-piece bassoons, or they may have been dulcians. Friedrich Zachow (1663–1712) of Halle wrote for two bassonetti in his cantata 'Dies ist der Tag'.[19] The notated ranges are F4–C6 and D4–A5.[20]

The use of small bassoons by young pupils, documented in 1792 (see below), was almost certainly known earlier. 'Georg Gotthelf Liebeskind was born on 22 November 1732 at Altenburg, where his father served as a bassoonist. Georg learned bassoon from his father at an early age, and by the time he was eight had developed considerable skill on the instrument.'[21]

The classical era

Surviving octave bassoons from this era carry the marks of Bühner & Keller, Collings, Custodi, Delusse, H. Grenser, Jacoby, M. Lot, G. A. Rottenburgh, and J. Schlegel. Surviving tenor bassoons carry the marks of Adler, G. Babb, Blockley, Cahusac, J. B. Eisenbrandt, Gerock, H. Grenser, Hirsbrunner, I. Kraus, Peale, Saxton, Tauber, Tölcke, Tuerlinckx, and Wussinger.[22]

Joshua Collin(g)s, describing himself as 'musical instrument-maker and turner from Manchester', immigrated to Annapolis, Maryland, by 1773. An octave bassoon surviving in an English collection presumably predates his immigration. John Hiwell, Inspector and Superintendent of Music in the Continental Army during the American Revolutionary War, later (1785) advertised his services as a teacher of the bassoon and tenoroon, among other instruments.[23] The 'alto fagotto' developed by George Wood of London, with a wide flaring bore and a clarinet mouthpiece, was not really a bassoon. It was based on the 'Caledonica', invented about 1825 by the Scottish bandmaster William Meikle.[24]

Records show that the firm of Tuerlinckx in Malines, Belgium, offered octave and tenor bassoons during the period 1782–1830.[25] Caspar Tauber, active in Vienna 1794–1829, made small bassoons and contras.[26] Scholl advertised a newly improved octave bassoon in Vienna, 1803.[27]

The virtuoso bassoonist Carl Bärmann (1782–1842) was first taught by Ritter on the tenor bassoon at the age of ten.[28] Another use, nowadays hidden from view, has been suggested: that conventional bassoon solos were at times played on the tenor bassoon. Klaus Hubmann proposed that the tenor bassoon was sometimes used without being explicitly specified, the generic term Fagott being understood to mean 'the appropriate size of bassoon'.[29] Mozart's K. 292 is a possible example: the bassoon part never descends below F2 (the tenor bassoon's lowest note). Meanwhile, three bassoon sonatas by Dürnitz, Mozart's associate, contain high notes (A4, B4) that would be difficult and surprising writing for conventional bassoon in otherwise easy compositions. Works by Ritter, Malzat, Stamitz, and Pfeiffer are likewise playable on either standard bassoon or tenor bassoon. Hubmann and Weidauer offered additional evidence.[30] This hypothesis implies that tenor bassoon players would have learned to play at concert pitch, rather than having a part transposed for them.

Beethoven left an incomplete 'Romance cantabile in E minor', probably intended for the Westerholt-Gysenberg family.[31] Among the family, Count Friedrich played the bassoon. The bassoon part, descending only to F#2 but ascending to B4 repeatedly, is easily playable on tenor bassoon, but would be challenging on standard bassoon. Beethoven's Trio Concertante in G major, WoO 37, written in Bonn between 1786 and 1790 for piano, flute, and bassoon, was also dedicated to the Westerholt-Gysenbergs.[32] Moore noted that the writing

> ... is uncharacteristically difficult, if not impossible, for the classical bassoon ... the opening passage of the second movement contains turns on high A4 and ascends to high C5. In addition, this work was written for amateurs; therefore it is very tempting to suggest that it was intended for the tenor bassoon.[33]

Count Friedrich possibly played both these works on a tenor bassoon.

Meanwhile, some surviving tenor bassoons may turn out to sound a semitone higher than a quint bassoon. Using such a *Hochsext* bassoon, the player could read a treble-clef part as if it were bass clef; after adjusting the key signature, the resulting pitches would sound an octave lower than written. The octave bassoon, so much higher in pitch, would not have been needed for even high-lying bassoon parts; possibly it was used most often in bassoon ensembles.

A composition for an octet of bassoons survives in Zwickau (Ratschulbibliothek no. 738). The title page of the manuscript calls for two horns, two 'fagotti-octavo', two 'fagotti-quarto', and two fagotti. The musical style, with its 'drum bass', is clearly that of the classical period. The composer's name was first reported as G. M. Trost.[34] But

Ventzke in 1977 argued that the name should instead be read as G. M. Frost, and noted that one J. G. M. Frost, a court *Pfeifer*, was documented in Dresden, 1786.[35]

The tenor bassoon is occasionally visible in military bands during this era. In the Kapelle of the archducal regiment of Schwerin, Ludwigslust, 'bassonets' were used; they were replaced by bassett horns in 1789.[36] A composition calling for tenor bassoon was published by T. Olmsted in Albany, New York, in 1807. 'Gov. Sullivan's March', by U. K. Hill, is scored for two clarinets, tenoroon, and bassoon. The tenoroon part extends from C3 to G4, written at concert pitch.[37]

Jakob Baur offered sheet music for 'kleinen Fagot' in Vienna, 1780–97.[38] The court bassoonist Cžeyka performed his own variations on a tenor bassoon in the imperial court theater in Vienna on 21 March 1815. A review described the instrument as being 'smaller than the regular bassoon and having a sonorous and pleasant tone'.[39]

The romantic era

Surviving octave bassoons from this era carry the marks of Dupré, Hawkes & Son, Leiberz, Proff, Savary jeune, Stehle, and G. Wood.[40] Surviving tenor bassoons carry the marks of Evette & Schaeffer, Gautrot, Hawkes & Son, Kies [Küss], Marzoli, W. Milhouse, Morton, de Rosa, and Savary jeune.[41] Douglas B. Moore cited a tenoroon by Pelitti of Milan (brown wood, twelve brass keys).[42]

During this era, the smaller bassoons are apt to be confused with certain English horns having a folded bore, especially if a lower extension is also present. One example by Andrea Fornari of Venice is labeled 'fagottino' in the catalogue of the La Scala museum collection, where it is preserved.[43] Its lower register is extended by a fifth (to Bb2), all these lower pitches being governed by keys for L4, LT, and RT. The layout is 8 + 3. But the bell rises only to half the instrument's height and the L3 tone hole is doubled oboe-style.[44] A further source of confusion is that corno inglese parts by Rossini were often notated in the bass clef, sounding an octave higher.[45]

A tenoroon in the Waterhouse collection, stamped both 'A. Marzoli' and 'TMB' (for Triebert Marzoli Boehm), has a plateau and two brilles for the left hand operating register vents, but an uncovered right hand[46] (Ill. 68). Evette & Schaeffer exhibited three models (in Eb, F, and G, with 15 keys) in 1889.[47]

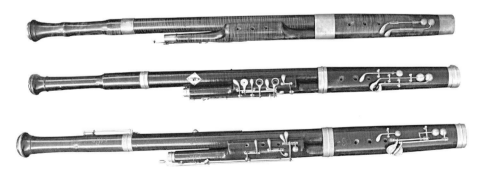

68. From bottom: tenor bassoons by Gautrot aîné, Triebert-Marzoli-Boehm, and Savary jeune. Waterhouse Collection.

Almenräder noted:

> One can begin teaching young students early using a Quartfagott, suited for small hands, until the time a larger instrument suits their hands. I have done so with ten-year-old students, who learn two to three years on a Quartfagott and then shift to a regular bassoon. The result was a favorable one, in which the student made astonishing strides on the second instrument.[48]

Waterhouse reported that 'the same practice was reported in the Foundling Hospital of London and more recently in the band of a Sicilian orphanage'.[49] Satzenhofer gave a close paraphrase of Almenräder's comment in 1900, but later added that the quart tenor bassoon is 'hardly ever used now, at any rate not in Russia and in Germany'.[50] An eleven-key tenor bassoon in the Victoria & Albert Museum collection is stamped by R. de Rosa, who was a military bandmaster, later a dealer in musical instruments.[51]

Use of the tenor bassoon as a solo instrument continued. Pierre cited the examples of Reickmans and Espaignet at Bordeaux beginning in 1833, and of Jancourt, who played an instrument in *mi bemol* by Savary in recitals in Paris during 1839–40.[52] Tosoroni c.1850 described a 'piccolo fagotto or fagottino, this modern and gracious instrument (also called quartino di fagotto). . . . It is particularly adapted for playing the solo with a very beautiful effect in song; its favored tones are B♭, E♭, A♭, and related keys.'[53] Presumably he was referring to the true tenor bassoon, not the English horn. Pagnocelli of Naples reportedly gave concerts c.1870 on a tenor bassoon in G in Italy and France with success.[54] In London, E. F. James 'occasionally played solos on a rosewood Morton tenoroon with brass keys'.[55] The catalogue of the dealer Lafleur offered a Morton tenoroon c.1875.[56]

1900 to present

By 1887 Weissenborn described the Quartfagott as being 'no more in use. . . . It seems never, or very rarely, to have been used in orchestras.'[57] He mentioned no other small sizes. Such comments by Weissenborn and Satzenhofer, together with a lack of surviving instruments by German makers of the later nineteenth century, suggest that the vogue for smaller bassoons faded there sooner than in England and France.

Without amounting to a revival, brief flickers of interest appeared. The firm of Wilhelm Heckel, in a catalogue of c.1907, advertised product no. 40, a 'Heckel-fagottino in F with E/F# trill and D# key on the wing, and an automatic G ring; fingering as that of the Heckel-Fagott'. The accompanying picture showed a slightly simpler system than usual on Heckel bassoons, and the lowest tone hole located on the long joint.[58] An Evette & Schaeffer catalog of 1912 noted: 'We also make bassoons in F and G, but with simple mechanism. These bassoons, being of small dimensions, lack the space for a complicated mechanism.'[59] Douglas B. Moore cited a 'tenoroon' by D. Rancilio (fl. Milan c.1914–31; twelve keys).[60]

The smaller instruments seem to have lain mostly dormant until the late twentieth century, although an exception is reported. 'It has also been used in military bands, in particular when the players were mounted on horseback. John Burness (retired, BBC SO) recalls having witnessed this in a French military band on horseback at the Edinburgh Tattoo in 1951.'[61]

William Waterhouse used a tenor bassoon by Savary jeune to play a transcription in a London recital in 1980. In 1989 his former pupil Richard Moore commissioned a tenor bassoon with modern German system from the maker Guntram Wolf, who was reportedly building small bassoons since 1986.[62] After taking delivery of the instrument, Moore performed in 1992 at both the Ysbreker Festival (Amsterdam) and the International Double Reed Society conference (Frankfurt). He had commissioned a trio for tenor bassoon, bassoon, and contra from Viktor Bruns, and incidentally inspired the Sonatine for Tenor Bassoon and Piano, op. 96, by Bruns.

Moosman (Waiblingen) in 1990 introduced a quart-bassoon in F.[63] In 1999 T. W. Howarth & Co of London introduced a 'Mini-Bassoon', pitched a fifth above the bassoon and built by Wolf. The idea caught on with British teachers wishing to start students at the age of seven or eight years. Most teachers preferred their students to read from transposed parts, thus learning the fingerings they would later use in making the transition to a standard bassoon.[64] Vonk offered the following rule of thumb: 'You can move on to a standard bassoon when you're just the same height as it is.'[65]

Wolf introduced simple-system tenor bassoons and octave bassoons, sometimes decorated with bold tiger stripes, in order to heighten the appeal to young players. Festivals or symposia for fagottinos or mini-bassoons were held in German cities 2001–10. In 2003–4 the University for Music and Theater in Vienna established a project called 'New Music for Young Bassoonists'.[66] Other European firms began to produce small bassoons for young players, including Amati-Rodewald (Koblenz), Walter Bassetto (Frauenfeld, Switzerland), and Kauda (Longué-Jumelles, France). The various instruments offered varied from a standard German system and full range, to a simplified system and a bottom range of written C2. Ter Voert, Müller, and Rüdiger published methods for children beginning with quart or quint bassoons.[67]

Epilogue

Viewed from a long and global perspective, the bassoon's history is a series of three radiations from European origins: the dulcian from Italy, Spain, and Portugal (sixteenth and seventeenth centuries); the baroque bassoon from France (late seventeenth and eighteenth centuries); and the Heckel-type bassoon from Germany (1880s and later). This view is reductive, of course; within each of the three waves, imitators abroad eventually began exporting, while holdovers, cross-currents, incremental developments, and revivals further complicated the reality. Rather than belaboring this point, it may be more productive to ask what needs (physical, musical, and conceptual) each of these iterations of the bassoon idea evidently filled.

The dulcian (or fagotto or bajón) was portable, loud enough for outdoor use, and both flexible and agile in the bass register. But beyond these issues of mere utility, the specific scoring practices of Castello, Monteverdi, and Schütz make it clear that composers had begun to value the dulcian for its individual tone color. Both the written repertory and comments by Praetorius indicate that the average player was not expected to exceed an upper limit of D4; this was within a bass singer's vocal range and, to speak in terms of the bore's acoustics, within the second mode of response.

The design of the baroque bassoon, made in four separate pieces, allowed a new degree of control over the shape of the interior bore; makers began to take advantage of their newly improved access to tweak the bore's shape. While remaining mostly conical, the bore now sometimes included intentional changes of slope, including short cylindrical sections, and sometimes even an inversely conical section in the bell. By such means makers succeeded in taming the power of the lowest bass notes, keeping finger holes within reach, and obtaining a secure tenor register to G4 or higher (requiring the third mode of response). It is perhaps notable that the basse de cromorne, an unfolded predecessor with a more open sound, enjoyed only a sparse production, while the widely adopted baroque bassoon incorporated the chimneys of the old dulcian, at least for holes 1 to 8. The chimney, born of necessity, had become a recognized virtue.

Composers of the late seventeenth century, including Delalande and Kusser, began to assign occasional tenor lines to the bassoon. By the late eighteenth century, composers were so taken with the bassoon's tenor voice that it became a mainstay of the Viennese classical style of orchestration. No other instrument was chosen so often to double a singer, violin, or treble woodwind at the lower octave as the bassoon; its bland yet supple tenor was the satin pillow on which composers displayed many of their melodic jewels. This aural construct, spreading far beyond Austria and the classical era, is still a tool in the kit of composers and orchestrators.

A narrower bore and (eventually) register vent keys made the overblown notes of the classical bassoon more secure, while its thinner walls gave all registers a more penetrating sound, the benefit being felt most significantly in the tenor. Chromatic keys were not a new discovery – they had been known on the musette chanter since the seventeeneth century – but makers and bassoonists suddenly deemed them desirable, because they gave a brighter, clearer sound; in extreme tonalities (increasingly popular), the new keys also relieved the awkwardness of long chains of cross-fingerings.

Around the end of the classical period, some instrument makers began to discover the new science of musical acoustics. Under Almenräder in Germany and Jancourt in France, bassoons were developed with larger tone holes more proportionally spaced (mostly from hole 6 downward), and with a proportionally longer up bore. Although these trends ran counter to the artisanal design of the traditional bassoon, they were accepted in some measure by many other German and French makers.

Almenräder seems to have appreciated that the bassoon's distinctive tonal character resulted from two design features: the chimneyed finger holes (abhorrent to Weber and later theorists) and the unusually long extension bore (ignored by the theorists). Almenräder made judicious compromises, enlarging and relocating the A vent (controlled by R3) and making the extension bore more regularly conical, especially in the bell. His added chromatic keys reduced the number of pitches that had to be cross-fingered. But Almenräder preserved the eight traditional chimneys, even while he enlarged the vents on the up bore. He dealt with the perturbing influence of the extension bore in a practical way, providing 'double venting' for A♭, A, and B♭.

Some observers found his bassoons (and those of his onetime partner J. A. Heckel) lacking in the traditional warmth associated with the bassoon. In other words, the bassoon idea by now occupied a privileged place in the ear and mind of listeners, which the Almenräder/Heckel bassoon was filling only imperfectly.

Under Jancourt, Cokken, Triebert, and Buffet Crampon, the French bassoon underwent a milder reform. It retained its narrower up bore (including a slight choke in the bell) with smaller vents, and its open finger hole for RT. The A vent (R3) was lowered only about 6 cm on the bore, compared with about 10 cm on the Almenräder bassoon. Among the significant German innovations spurned by the French were double venting (for A♭, A, and B♭) and thumb spatulas for C♯ and B♭. Perhaps the most significant French innovation in key work was the mechanism for LT, which produced three pitches (B♭1, B1, and C2) using a linkage of two spatulas.

During the later nineteenth century, four distinct traditions competed in the marketplace – the Almenräder/Heckel design, the successive conservatoire systems in France, the Savary-inspired models of England and Belgium, and the Central European models. Late in the century, the bassoon was widely expected to have a fully chromatic scale over more than three octaves; this demanded that the fourth and fifth modes of response be available and musically useful. The bassoonist was required to be comfortable in all tonalities and in imitation of all other melodic instruments, imposing new demands of intonation, response, and dynamic range.

In the 1880s, Wilhelm Heckel replaced his father's Almenräder-based designs with his own far-reaching innovations. He redesigned the bore as a broader and more regular cone, and further lengthened its ascending portion. His final revisions in the bassoon's key work are essentially those used today. But Heckel accepted the bassoon's chimneys and its traditional contrasting timbres in upper and lower registers. These considered choices led to the third great wave of design export in the bassoon's history.

The Central European model faded first, replaced by Heckel's new designs. During the early twentieth century, the English/Belgian model was replaced in most individual cases by the French model, now most closely associated with the synonymous marks Buffet Crampon and Evette & Schaeffer. French-system bassoons had a vogue of their own, albeit shorter: they were also manufactured in Belgium, England, Italy, the United States, and even in Germany (the last intended for export).

Wilhelm Heckel's ambition to export his models to all markets was clear in the terrestrial globe shown in his advertising. Other makers in Germany quickly imitated his models, followed by makers in the Netherlands, Central Europe, England, and the United States. Complaints by listeners of a 'tubby' or dull sound were sometimes voiced against the Heckel or German bassoon prior to mid-century. But as players from non-German schools of playing took up the instrument, a fruitful cross-fertilization took place; they drew from the Heckel bassoon a French-influenced sound: a range of colors, often enlivened by supple phrasing or vibrato. During the entire twentieth century, the German bassoon, subtly revised in the hands of Heckel's successors and imitators, gained influence. By the twenty-first century, it drove the French model, despite its undoubted virtues, to the brink of extinction.

John Backus (1911–88) was a distinguished musical acoustician, a conductor, and an amateur bassoonist. His complaint about the bassoon, written c.1969, echoed an old strain:

> The bassoon demonstrates woodwind deficiencies especially well. Practically every note of this instrument is out of tune and needs to be pulled into tune with the lips; in fact, some notes can be varied as much as a minor third. This situation, together with the half-holing required for some notes, makes the bassoon an uncooperative instrument and difficult to play. Except for having keys added, it has changed little in several hundred years, has been aptly called a 'fossil', and badly needs an acoustical working-over. (The author is a bassoonist and hopes to do this working-over if he lives long enough.)[1]

The bassoon has outlived Professor Backus, just as it outlived all the nineteenth-century reformers. Few players have found the intonation quite as problematic as Backus did. And since he wrote these lines, it must be said, well-made instruments and reeds have become increasingly common. Their impressive quality stems not from an 'acoustical working-over', but from largely traditional designs, now manufactured to tolerances at a micrometric level. The instrument's finger technique is still notoriously complex, due not only to half-holing technique, but also to the bassoon's extended upper range and its innate resonance curve. But through efficient pedagogy and assiduous practice, many of today's players surmount virtually all technical obstacles. (Indeed, this mastery is now common on reproduction baroque and classical bassoons as well.) The instrument's origins are circumstantial, its design conservative and perhaps unlikely. But the conservative design has withstood nearly 200 years of positivistic debate and experimentation, a clear sign that composers, players, and listeners treasure the bassoon's iconic voice.

Notes

Acknowledgements

1. The Langwill and Waterhouse archives are now housed at the Edinburgh University Collection of Historic Musical Instruments.
2. See Waterhouse 1993:ix–xii for a full account.
3. Waterhouse 1993.
4. Langwill 1965.
5. Waterhouse 2003.

Introduction

1. The archetype of the contrabassoon eventually diverged from that of the bassoon; see chapter 9.
2. Veazey 1988:44–8.
3. The overtones heard in each of the bassoon's pitches occur in a harmonic ratio (aside from the starting transient or multiphonic sounds); overblowing is a separate phenomenon. See Kopp 2007.

Chapter 1. Early names, precursors, the bassoon idea

1. Kilbey 2002:105.
2. Ibid. 28.
3. Ibid. 127; 135.
4. Ibid. 144; 168.
5. Brossard 1703:13.
6. Prizer 1982:114.
7. Ibid.
8. A 1706 inventory of the Vienna Hofkapell included 'nine dolcini, like fagoti, of dark wood, red and inlaid with white bone'. Stradner 1987:54.
9. Baines 1950:20. Dating after Woodley 2001:499. Tinctoris was employed at Cambria, Orléans, and Chartres before entering the service of King Ferrante I in the early 1470s.
10. Cited in Boydell 1982:398. Zacconi's fagotto had a range of C2 to Bb3 (cited in Kilbey 2002:20).
11. Boydell 1982:412; 401.
12. See Myers 1983:358–60; Foster 2005:48–9.
13. Foster 2005:49–50.
14. Boydell 1982:388–9.
15. Ibid. 37; 389.
16. Boydell 1982:390; redacted by Collver 1996:101 to 'dolziana'.
17. 'Dal bel monte': Boydell 1982:53; Brown 1973:100. 'In bando intene': Brown 1973:99; redacted by Collver 1996:186 to 'dolziani'.
18. 'Tratte del tristo abisso': Brown 1973:102

19. Boydell 1982:392–3, citing Galpin 1940–1:66–7.

20. Boydell 1982: 307; 296.

21. *L'Amico fado*, 'O noi lieti': Collver 1996:185–6 (redacted from dolzaine; cf. Brown 1973:107).

22. 'La Pellegrina': Kilbey 2002:29.

23. Boydell 1982:399.

24. Ibid. 401.

25. Ibid. 402.

26. Klitz 1971:113.

27. Masel 1995:1381–2.

28. Some otherwise helpful writers, including Weaver 1961 and Collver and Dickey 1996, chose to redact the original term 'dolzaina' to 'dolcian' or 'dolziana', introducing a new layer of obscurity.

29. Ambrogio 1539:37; 179.

30. Cocks 1959: 57–9.

31. Afranio was a canon in the service of Cardinal Ippolito d'Este. After Ippolito's death in 1520, he entered the service of Duke Alfonso I. Cavicchi 2002:43–4.

32. Kilbey 2002:18. Federico Gonzaga wrote to Statio Gadio on 15 October that Isabella had decided to take the instruments for Francesco. Prizer 1982:112, n. 101.

33. Galpin 1940–1:63–4.

34. Without invoking Ravilio's name, Cavicchi 2002:45 raised a similar hypothesis.

35. Brown 1975:238; 241.

36. Galpin 1940–1:58.

37. Ibid. 60.

38. Reproduced in Galpin 1940–1, on insert following page 72.

39. Galpin 1940–1:69.

40. Moser 1966:21; 176. ' . . . et in illo mirabiliori, quod nuper Monachus excogitat, quod fistulos nullos habet, sed quosdam concavitates in latum lignum excisos, in modum serpentum ambulantes, quod sonorum admodum edit contentum.' English translation by William Waterhouse.

41. Baines 1977:263.

42. Mersenne 1636:305.

43. Mersenne 1636:298–300 also referred to the smooth-skinned but multi-bored *courtaut* and *cervelas* (racket) as 'fagots'.

44. Herbert 2006:57.

45. Powell 1996; Cheape 2008:4; 141; 143.

46. Mersenne 1636:305. Propositions 33–4 are on Mersenne's page 298. The 'corollary' label is apparently borrowed from Ambrogio.

47. 'It is quite easy to add the skin and bellows to them . . . like the Fagot of Afranio. . . .' Mersenne 1636:305, citing Ambrogio 1539:179; 37.

48. He described each of the phagotum's chanters as a fagot, and also as a 'basson'. Galpin 1940–1:59.

49. Trichet c.1640 included a faithful redrawing (omitted in Lesure's edition of 1959). Wasielewski published an incomplete re-drawing in 1878, and Forsyth reproduced the original image in 1914.

50. Tevo 1706:12 abandoned the 'phagotum' spelling, along with any distinction it conveyed.

51. Walther 1732:238.

52. Gerber 1812/14:20. The page number from Albonesi suggests that Gerber had seen the picture of the phagotum. By this time, however, the bassoon was made in joints, giving a new (if limited) plausibility to the 'bundle of sticks' etymology.

53. F. J. Fétis, *Rm* 1828, tome 2:219, repeated the Afranio 1539 story. He referred there to earlier discussion in *Rm* 1828, tome 1:273.

54. Willent-Bordogni 1844:2.

55. Stone 1879:151.

56. Waterhouse 1993:359.

57. Gerber 1812–14:107.

58. Langwill 1965:41–2.

59. Wasielewski 1878:74.

60. Lavoix 1878:111–12.

61. Langwill 1965:45.

62. Praetorius 1618–20, transl. Crookes, 48.
63. Klitz 1971:116.
64. Valdrighi 1884:301.
65. Lescat and Saint-Arroman 1999:72, citing Diderot and d'Alembert 1751.
66. Boydell 2001:717.
67. Euting 1899:26; Kleefeld 1899/1900:266.
68. Forsyth 1914:487–90. The reference is probably to Lavoix, who misspelled Schnitzer as 'Scheltzer'.
69. Galpin 1940–1:71–2.
70. Langwill 1965:vii.

Chapter 2. The dulcian family

1. Kilbey 2002:13–14 gives further details, including variant designs and construction methods.
2. Surviving exceptions to this description include a quartbass (Linz 217; 7 + 3), a bass (Lisbon MX-1, MIC-0173; 6 + 3), and an alto (Augsburg 3017; 6 + 3). For further details, see Young 1997:188; Kilbey 2002:229–30; 196.
3. See Bowles 2001 on these and other processional occasions.
4. Waterhouse 2001a:877.
5. John Hanchet, personal communication 2008.
6. Ongaro 1985:391.
7. Kilbey 2002:13 cited apple, beech, box, cedar, cherry, ebony, jujube, oak, olive, pear, plum, rosewood, rowan, spruce, tulipwood, walnut, and yew; some of these woods were used only for smaller sizes.
8. A letter by Robert Cronin in *DR* 10/3 (1987):58–9 discusses the specific advantages in detail.
9. Quoted in Kilbey 2002:113.
10. In comparisons, the baroque bassoon was often described as being softer in tone than the dulcian. See Kilbey 2002:82; 89.
11. Ibid. 60–1; 64.
12. Borràs i Roca 2008:110–15. Further research may one day show that some surviving non-Spanish dulcians share the Dorian tuning;
13. Kilbey 2002:136.
14. Ibid. 117.
15. Speer 1697:241.
16. `Ein großer Fagott ins C, octaf' and 'ein großer Fagott ins B, octaf' appeared in a Kassel inventory of 1613. But in 1638, another Kassel inventory listed 'ein groß Quintfagott ins C octaf' and 'ein Quartfagott', possibly the same instruments. Kilbey 2002:131–2; 138. If those reported in 1613 were octave-bass instruments, they were possibly acquired after Praetorius's first two visits, thus escaping his notice.
17. Borràs i Roca 2008:300.
18. Van Heyghen 2005 gives a detailed account of the Praetorian scheme of wind consort practice, including transpositions.
19. Kilbey 2002:121. The 'descants' mentioned here were possibly altos in D3. In shawm consorts, at least, the ensemble was equipped with a spare player and instrument, who played alternately, 'for reasons of endurance'. This 'supernumerary' principle, explained in Duffin 2007:70, may figure in the described sizes of historical consorts.
20. Kilbey 2002:128–9.
21. Spohr 2004:47–8.
22. Choreographed steps were particular to well-known tenors. McGee 2005:154–5.
23. An early practice for dealing with occasional low tessitura was transposition of the work up a fifth. See Gilbert 2005:112.
24. `The Venetian ensemble for which Giovanni Alvise arranged motets by Busnois and Obrecht in the mid-1490s was six-part, as was the band at this time in Siena. The additional player was usually a fourth double reed player. . . .' Polk 2005:23. '[T]otal ranges expanded from slightly more than two octaves to a potential three octaves or more.' Ibid. 22.
25. Waterhouse 2001:880, probably based on Knebel 1899:60.
26. Kilbey 2002:18–19.

27. Ibid. 31–2, quoting Marucini 1577.
28. `Colonia Bassanese descritta', unpublished sketch by Almorò Albrizzi, 1741; cited by Ruffati 1998:351.
29. Ongaro 1985:391.
30. One dance in this collection is entitled 'Fagot', although this is not an indication of orchestration. A similar dance name occurs in a collection by Phalèse, 1549. Edwards 2001 lists hundreds of sources of manuscript or printed music for two or more instruments prior to 1630. Many of these are suitable for dulcian.
31. Herbert 2006:90–6 described the early trombone's unwritten and written repertories.
32. Claudio Monteverdi in 1611 located a musician able to play recorder, cornett, trombone, flute, and bassoon – all of these instruments were demanded for the fifth part in Francesco Gonzaga's wind band in Mantua. Kilbey 2002:21. Earlier, a list of *Tromboni Natale* in Venice dated 26 March 1557 comprised 'un bason da sonar, una copia di fifari, un trombone, 3 trombette'. Ibid. 19. For other instances, see ibid. 25, and Stradner 1987:54. Players of both instruments at San Marco, Venice, in 1603 and 1619 are noted below.
33. Collver and Dickey 1996:101.
34. *Communiones totius anni* (Venice, 1611).
35. Newman 1972:117.
36. Kilbey 2002:241.
37. Large artillery pieces in the fifteenth and sixteenth centuries were sometimes known as *bombardes*; smaller ones were sometimes known as *curtals, courtauts,* or *serpentoni*. The buttafuoco – a *Luntenstock* or artillery tool – gave its name to a type of double clarinet (or string drum). Van der Meer 1999:48.
38. Kilbey 2002:119, my italics.
39. Ibid. 140, my italics. For Emperor Mathias's visit to the Saxon court in 1617, Schütz was instructed to ensure that 'His Electoral Grace's ensemble . . . acquit itself with honor and glory before the visitors'. Spagnoli 1993:164.
40. See Kilbey 2002:227–8; 250–51.
41. An inventory of Raymund Fugger's collection, made in Augsburg, 1566, included 217 wind instruments in twenty-six consorts. Among these were 'ten fagotti with two cornetts, in a case covered with black leather; eight shawms and one fagotti [*sic*], each in its own case; one doltzana, in a square decorated case; two fagotti belonging with the ten mentioned above, each of these in a sack; and one small doltzana made in Venice'. Tremmel 1993:67–8; Kilbey 2002:110.
42. Kilbey 2002:20.
43. Ibid. 22.
44. Rosand 1993:78.
45. Outside Venice, a fagotto was in use at the church of S. Maria Maggiore in Bergamo in 1610. Bonta 1989:18; 27.
46. Selfridge-Field 1994:336.
47. Ibid. 156. However, according to Bonomo 1992:96 and Federhofer and Saunders 2001:249, Sansoni was 'di Venezia' but served 1613–19 at the court of Archuke Ferdinand Joseph in Graz, moving to the Viennese Hofkapelle when the archduke became emperor in 1619.
48. Selfridge-Field 1994:337. Dulcian players included Giovanni Battista Rossi, c.1640; Joseph Bonincontri, 1666–a1696; and Pietro Aut[en]garden, 1674–96. Kilbey 2002:143.
49. Bonomo 1992:109–17.
50. Selfridge-Field 1994:100.
51. Ibid. 296.
52. Bonomo 1992:109–17.
53. Selfridge-Field 1994:45; Giron 2006:121–2.
54. Selfridge-Field 1994:18.
55. Selfridge-Field 1994:23 listed other liturgical uses for ensemble canzonas and sonatas, broken down by multi-decade eras.
56. The fagotto was specified in sacred works published in Venice, 1620–56, by Berettari, Cornetto, Freddi, Grandi, and Zavaglioli. Ibid. 25–8.
57. Selfridge-Field 1994:129.
58. Ibid. 122. Bonomo 1992:109–17 listed six Italian collections of sonatas for one or two fagotti and nine Italian collections of ensemble sonatas.

59. Ibid. 125.
60. Ibid. 112.
61. Wagner 1976:38–41 offered a possible explanation based on a clash of pitch standards. Bonomo 1992:144 and other writers posited that Selma owned a dulcian with an atypically lengthened bore. Selma's father Antonio had made three-keyed bajones in 1616 and 1638, although the function of the third key was not specified. Kilbey 2002:62; 66.
62. Bonomo 1992:130–40.
63. Selfridge-Field 1994:148.
64. Kurtzmann and Koldau 2002: section 12.7.
65. Selfridge-Field 1994:167.
66. Ibid. 38–9. The little-known opera survives at the Biblioteca Marciana, Ms Cod. Ital. IV-447. Weaver 1961 provides an introduction to the sixteenth-century traditions of orchestration in opera.
67. Kilbey 2002:47.
68. Knebel 1899:60.
69. Waterhouse 1993:32.
70. Bouterse 2000:243–50.
71. Spiessens 2000:15.
72. Kilbey 2002:177.
73. Two engravings from Galle c.1590 seem to portray two- or three-piece dulcians. But the two instruments as drawn are nonsensical enough that no safe conclusions can be drawn. See Kilbey 2002:177–9.
74. Denis van Alsloot (Antwerp, 1616), [The] Onze-Lieve-Vrouw-Zavel.
75. Spiessens 2000:16.
76. Kilbey 2002:180.
77. Decobert 2001:699. Henry Dumont's Motets à II, III et IV parties (Paris, 1681) included one symphonie and several motets scored for two violins, viola, baroque bassoon, and continuo.
78. Nicolaus à Kempis, Symphoniae (Antwerp, 1644 and 1647).
79. Fritz Heller, personal communication, 24 September 2010.
80. Kilbey 2002:47 cited other possible evidence – in each instance ambiguous – from 1524, 1530, and 1553. See Kreitner 1999:537 on the evidence from Palencia, 1553. Kilbey also noted that 'a prolonged visit to England by the Madrid Capilla Real from 1554 to 1555 seems to have generated many instrument orders for the Bassanos'; that is, various wind instruments for cathedrals in Ciudad Rodrigo, Burgos, Huesca, and Salamanca. Ibid. 34–5; 43.
81. Kilbey 2002:47–74.
82. Borràs i Roca 2008: 28–130; the sources included Lorente 1672, Tosca i Mascó 1707, Nassare 1723, and Valls 1742.
83. Borràs i Roca 2008:101–17.
84. Ibid. 251–3.
85. Ibid. 224–6.
86. Kreitner 1992:537; Comstock 1999:33; Kenyon de Pascual 1995a:69; Kilbey, 2002:71.
87. Ibid. 44.
88. Ibid. 97; 46; Comstock 1999:38.
89. Kilbey 2002:100. Kilbey noted another possible meaning: gedackt instruments, which are otherwise known only by German makers.
90. Kenyon de Pascual 1995a:67–8.
91. Kilbey 2002:50; 57.
92. Baade 2001:99.
93. The chapel of the Duke of Lerma in 1615 included a book of canzions (still extant today) used by black slaves 'when they were learning to play their instruments'. Kilbey 2002:60.
94. Baade 2001:102–3.
95. Colleen Ruth Baade, unpublished conference paper, 1998. http://222.arts.uci.edu/sscm/archives/1998abstract.html.
96. Kenyon de Pascual 1984:73–4. The Catalan term 'baixó' can mean dulcian or bassoon.
97. German princes in the mid-seventeenth century maintained 'agents in European cities to recruit musicians for the court'. Spagnoli 1993:169. Venetians recruited to the Munich court included Andrea Gabrieli, Francesco Guami, and Giovanni Gabrieli. Italians recruited to the imperial

court in Vienna included Buonamente, Bertali, Bertoli, Sances, and Cesti. Germans studying in Venice included Hassler, Rosenmüller, and Schütz.

98. Tremmel 1993:67–8.
99. Kilbey 2002:119; 121; 124–5.
100. `By about 1580 ... the dulcian was widely accepted as a primary choice for the bass. Its flexibility in the lowest octave was its strength, and its tone quality particularly effective with a combination of cornetts and sackbuts. In short, by the end of the century, for the low bass part the dulcian in many contexts completely took the place of the bass size of the trombone.' Polk 2005:23.
101. Kilbey 2002:118–19.
102. Ibid. 124.
103. Ibid. 150–67; Frandesen 2006:455–80; Collver and Dickey 1996:75–184.
104. Bonomo 1992:118–19
105. Kilbey 2002:17.
106. For documentation of Italians in the chapel in 1653, see Spagnoli 1993:168.
107. Sacred concertos calling for a single dulcian number in the hundreds: for a selection, consult Kilbey 2002; Collver and Dickey 1996; and *NGDMM 2* under the following names: Ahle, Bernhard, Bollius, Buxtehude, Daser, Kindermann, Knüpfer, Megerle, Praetorius, Scheidt, Schütz, Selich, Selle, Staden, Straus, Weckmann, and Zeutschner.
108. Snyder 2001:705.
109. Instrumental ensemble works specifying dulcian survive by Albrici, Becker, Bleyer, Böddecker, Buchner, Capricornus, Draghi, Ferro, Forcheim or Furchheim, Förster, Gremboszewski, Harnisch, Höfer, Jarzebski, Kertzinger, Knüpfer, Mielczewski, Moritz von Hessen, Nicolai, Petsch, Poglietti, Pohle, Prentzl, Rosenmüller, Scherer, Schmelzer, Speer, Spiegler, Theile, Thieme, Valentini, Vierdanck, Weckmann, and Zumbach van KoesFieldt. The Teresi database contains details: http://www2.music.indiana.edu/s/dteresi/.
110. McCredie 1964:175–8; Kilbey 2002:165.
111. Collver and Dickey 1996:68–9.
112. Kilbey 2002:107.
113. Page 2001:623.
114. Spagnoli 1993:175.
115. Kilbey 2001:122.
116. Ibid. 189.
117. Waterhouse 1993:396.
118. `Ecce nunc benedicti domini', cited in Kilbey 2002:132.
119. Howey 1991:65.
120. Speer 1697:241–56. The sonatas were intended to exemplify writing for the dulcian. An earlier edition (1687) does not contain this material.
121. Kilbey 2002:121.
122. Waterhouse 1993:94–5.
123. Translated in Dreyfus 1990:108–10.
124. The variant spellings are original. Kilbey 2002:135–7.
125. Kilbey 2002:139–40. Staden learned dulcian and other instruments in Augsburg from Jakob Pauer, who had played under Lassus in Munich, 1591–6, presumably using the Vagott ordered from Venice in 1588.
126. Kirnbauer 1989:429.
127. Schlosser 1920:12–13. Geroldi and his successors were apparently dealers, rather than makers.
128. Kilbey 2002:126–7.
129. Ibid. 123; 130.
130. Ibid. 128.
131. Piwkowski 1970:17, citing Chybiński 1949 and Feicht 1966.
132. Wagner 1976:23; Collver and Dickey 1996:140; 143.
133. See Bonomo 1992:94; 146, n. 76, for further discussion of such links.
134. See Collver and Dickey 1996:15–18 for a review of collections containing manuscript sources.
135. Kilbey 2002:107. Schütz reportedly sent instruments from Venice to Dresden in 1613.
136. Kilbey 2002:125; Frandsen 2006:457–80. Bonomo 1992:118–19 describes two Schütz works for multiple dulcians: SWV 476 and SWV 49.
137. Kilbey 2002:129; 144.

138. Kilbey 2002:165. Both works also call for 'fagotto piccolo' and 'fagotto commune'.
139. Federhofer and Saunders 2001:249 contradicts Selfridge-Field's assertion (1994:337) that Sansoni was employed at St Mark's in Venice in 1614–19.
140. Frandsen 2006:180–1.
141. Pyron 2001.
142. Spitzer 2004:46.
143. Kilbey 2002:25.
144. Ibid. 229–30.
145. Ibid. 96.
146. Vasconcellos 1870:96.
147. Illustrated with commentary at http://www.dulcians.org/iconography.html.
148. Anthony Bassano held a court appointment as instrument maker in 1538. From 1539 he and four brothers constituted a court recorder consort; from before 1544 they had instrument-making workshops in the Charterhouse, near London. Waterhouse 1993:20.
149. Kilbey 2002:35.
150. Ibid. 126.
151. Ibid. 38.
152. Ibid. 37.
153. Ibid. 38.
154. Ibid. 36.
155. Ibid. 39.
156. Bermúdez 1999:149.
157. Kilbey 2002:45–6.
158. Bermúdez 1999:150.
159. Starner 2006:105–20.
160. Bermúdez 1999:156.
161. Starner 2000:77.
162. Bermúdez 1999:150.
163. Stevenson 1968:162–3. The original terms mentioned were 'dolzainas' and 'orlos'.
164. Kilbey 2002:70; Mauleón Rodriguez 2010:184–90.
165. Bermúdez 1999:157–8.
166. Sepp (1655–1733) studied under Melchor Gletle in Augsburg and sang in the Imperial Choir in Vienna. Sepp complained in 1692 of having bought in Spain, 'at an excessive price, musical instruments which were inferior to those made in Germany'. Kilbey 2002:77.
167. Fucci 1992:3.
168. Starner 2006:118.
169. In Cuzco during 1644–73, for example. See Baker 2004:359.
170. Bermúdez 1999:153.
171. Ibid.
172. Ibid. 152.
173. Ibid. 158.
174. Mendoza de Arce 2006:23.
175. Starner 2000:73.
176. Ibid. 74–5.
177. Starner 2006:105–20;
178. Kilbey 2002:59; 72; 74; Koegel 2001:141; Kilbey 2002:80–2.
179. Ibid. 86.
180. Ibid. 213. A bass-sized dulcian missing all its metal fittings was recently acquired by the Metropolitan Museum, New York. Its body is of a tropical wood, perhaps suggesting a Latin American origin.
181. Ibid. 88.
182. Starner 2000:77.
183. Bermúdez 1999:158.
184. Baker 2004:365.
185. Castagna 1999:641.
186. Justi 1995:62, note 16.
187. Vasconcellos 1663:120.
188. Justi 1995:65.

189. Ibid. 63.
190. Irving 2010:106.
191. Lindorff 2004:408.
192. Morley-Pegge 2001.
193. *Réunion des sociétés des beaux-arts des départements dans la salle de l'hémicycle de l'École des Beaux-Arts en 1892* (Paris: 1892): 359.
194. Kopp 2002:66–8.
195. Mersenne 1636:278.
196. Kopp 2002:107.
197. Kilbey 2002:144.
198. Rifkin 2001:830–1.
199. Silbiger 2001:199–200.
200. Jensen 1992:186–7; 183.
201. Ibid. 186–9. In Trondheim, 1744, Johann Daniel Berlin called the four-key bassoon 'Dulcian or Fagott, or Bass-Fagott'.
202. These are available online in the Düben Collection: http://www2.musik.uu.se/duben/Duben. php
203. Kilbey 2002:144.
204. `6 Stucks Esdoren Hout bas dulsians. Coor mes'. Bouterse 2000:245–6.
205. Kilbey 2002:146.
206. Ibid. 140; 142.
207. Ibid. 147; Nickel 1971:181–2.
208. Kilbey 2002:148.
209. Illustrated ibid. 149.
210. Ibid. 82.
211. Kenyon de Pascual 1994:26.
212. Borràs y Rocca 2008:319–49.
213. Kilbey 2002:90.
214. Kenyon de Pascual 1995b:143–4.
215. Kilbey 2002:91–2.

Chapter 3. *The bassoon idea: early relatives*

1. Masel 1995:1373; 1351.
2. A keyless cylindrical instrument designed to overblow at the twelfth will have a scalar gap between the uppermost fundamental note and the lowest overblown note. In some instances, the gap was bridged by the addition of upper-extension keys, as on the musette chanter and the chalumeau.
3. Myers 1989:383–4.
4. Masel 1995:1356.
5. Baines 1984:369.
6. Galpin 1940:70.
7. Masel 1995:1353.
8. Hanchet estimated that these shawms were made between 1525 and 1625. Typescript notes on shawms, dated August 1993. See Myers 2000:390 for a discussion of early evidence of large shawms.
9. Prunières 1909:230, n. 2.
10. Reproduced in Boydell 1982, plate lxvi.
11. Jurgens 1974:374; 37.
12. Collver and Dickey 1996:48; 57–8; 62; 71; 74.
13. Brossard 1703; Jürgen Eppelsheim, 'Pommern tiefer Lage (Bombardi, Bombardoni, Bomharte) als Bestandteil des Basso continuo-Instrumentariums', *Bachwoche Ansbach . . . Eröffnungsgottesdienst* [concert booklet 2005], 11–23, at 17.
14. Measurements include the body without pirouette. Waterhouse 2001b:720.
15. Ibid.
16. Mersenne 1636:300; 302; Köhler 1987:372.
17. In the Paradin woodcut of 1551, the drone contained three or more bores. See Kopp 2011:243–4.
18. Schlosser 1920:12; Masel 1995:1389.

19. The Praetorius racket assortment included two descant, three alto/tenor, one bass, and one great bass. Praetorius 1618–20:29. An inventory from Kassel, 1613, listed 'two bass, two tenor, and three soprani'. Baines 1951:30; Masel 1995:1389.
20. Masel 1995:1386 argued that Praetorius's kortholt had two upper extension keys and discrepant labeling.
21. Ibid. 1387.
22. Ibid. 1383.
23. Praetorius 1618–20:49; plate 12.
24. An inventory after the death of the harp player Romain Poille (24 January 1632) listed a courtaut. Jurgens 1974:36–7.
25. Mersenne 1636:299; 300.
26. Masel 1995:1383–4 hypothesized that the Sorduen-bas's bore was conical, making it 'a type of dulcian'.
27. Weber 2006:260 ascribed this racket-bassoon to Denner's son, giving no explanation.
28. Ibid. 261.
29. Ibid. 260; Waterhouse, 2001b; Masel 1995:1390.
30. Ibid.
31. Bouterse 2005:10.4.2 and 10.4.3 describes rackets by Wyne and an anonymous maker in detail, with photos.
32. Weber 2006:261.
33. Chouquet 1875:71.
34. Moutier 1766, 1:438–9.
35. Masel 1995:1392.
36. Weber and van der Meer 1972:23–4.
37. Joppig 1982:122.
38. Heyde 2007b.
39. Mersenne explained the quartet as comprising three sizes of 'hautbois de Poitou' and one cornemuse. But surviving payroll records mention the bass size only as 'basse de musette de Poitou' or 'basse-contre de musette de Poitou'. The dessus size existed in two versions: hautbois (presumably without windcap) and musette (presumably with windcap). See Kopp 2004:133–5.
40. Masel 1995:1383–4 found 'some similarity to the Sorduen-Bas', which he reckoned to be a conical instrument, 'although the specifics of construction and range differ'.
41. Kopp 2004:141–3.
42. Mersenne 1636:307; other uses are documented in Kopp 2004:129.
43. The instruments are pictured in Mersenne 1635:86–8; the same three illustrations appear in Mersenne 1636:298; 300; 302. Most later writers have relied on Mersenne's French, which contains a lengthier discussion of the proto-bassoons, but is less clear on some details.
44. The right-hand instrument in Mersenne 1636:298 and the second instrument from the right in Mersenne 1636:302 are called both 'fagot' and 'basson'; the left-hand instrument in Mersenne 1636:300 is called both 'basson' and 'tarot'.
45. Mersenne 1635:86; Mersenne 1636:298; Kopp 2002:101–3.
46. Mersenne 1635:87; Mersenne 1636:300.
47. Mersenne 1635:88; Mersenne 1636:302.
48. Jurgens 1974:37.
49. Trichet 1640:286; 367.
50. Masel 1995:1377; Robin 2004:23–4.
51. *Almanach musicale* 1781:212–13
52. Schmidt 1994:105–11.
53. Eppelsheim 1986:56–77; Vincent Robin, 'Contrebasse de hautbois, ou cromorne? Éléments de recherche pour l'identification du cromorne français aux XVIIe et XVIIIe siècles', thesis, Conservatoire supérieur de Paris, May 1995; 9.
54. Borjon de Scellery 1672: frontispiece.
55. Robin 2004:25.
56. `Recueil de plusieurs vieux airs . . . recueillis par Philidor l'Aisné en 1690`. Paris, Bibliothèque nationale, Ms 83104, fol. 39–46.

57. Laborde 1780 mentioned 'the cromorne, which was formerly bass to the hautbois' before the bassoon's development. Quoted in Haynes 2001b:44. Haynes cited Lully's use of two cromornes in *Thésée* (1675) and three cromornes in *Atys* (1676); ibid. 38. See chapter 4.
58. Garsault 1761:627; 660; plate xxxvi; Robin 2004:24.
59. See Finkelman 2001a:151; Girard 2001:67.
60. Ibid. 124.

Chapter 4. *The baroque bassoon*

1. See Smith 2010, Kopp 1999, and Bouterse 2000 for relevant evidence. Transitional instruments include the Mersenne proto-bassoons and a unique surviving instrument from Catajo Castle, now in the Vienna collection (SAM 189, formerly C201).
2. La Barre 1740, translated in Kopp 2002:75–6.
3. Praetorius wrote that 'flute makers' should construct instruments in sections to play in tune with church organs, which sound lower in winter than summer. Bouterse 2005:523. See Dart 2011, chapter 2, for a discussion of chambering and bore types.
4. This statement applies to three of Mersenne's proto-bassoons; the instrument shown at right in Mersenne 1636:298 was instead a 7 + 3 instrument.
5. Giannini 1987:10–11.
6. Haynes 2001:799.
7. Dart 2011:137.
8. Haynes and Cooke 2001:796.
9. Mattheson 1713:269.
10. Williams and Ledbetter 2001. Christian Stölzel was the brother of the Kapellmeister Gottfried Heinrich Stölzel. Ahrens 2009:59; 368.
11. Owens 2005:229–30. Kusser's *Erindo*, produced at Hamburg, 1694, contained an early use of two solo bassoons in opera: the aria no. 34. McCredie 1964:178.
12. Nösselt 1980:236.
13. Hutchings 1961:154
14. Giannini 1998:xiii.
15. Waterhouse 1993 passim.
16. Dart 2011:46–52.
17. A second post for bassoon was created by 1683, occupied by Jacques Danican-Philidor. Smith 2010:152–3.
18. Cessac 1988:435–6;438; 443–4; 448; 450; 454; 459; 462; 466; 469–70.
19. Spitzer 2004: 24; Holman 2005:252.
20. Lully's early scorings for five part double-reed band (1657–64) were probably played by 'a mix of hautboys and cromornes'. Haynes 2001b:60.
21. Ibid. 145–7; 157; 125.
22. H. 499; H. 520. Cessac 1988:454.
23. Sadler 1981–2:59–60.
24. Sadler 1992c.
25. `Initially the players evidently jibbed at some of the composer's technical demands. Jourdan states that "at the rehearsal of one of his first operas, I myself have seen [Rameau] on the point of losing his temper well and truly, because they demanded of him that he should change … certain notes in the bassoon parts that had never existed on the instrument …".' Sadler 1981–2:59–60.
26. Sadler 1992b.
27. Béthisy 1754 noted that some players could ascend to A4 and B4.
28. Act 1: iii or iv; Sadler 1992a.
29. The B1 was possibly obtained by lipping up the B♭1 or by half-closing the B♭1 key flap. The pitch also appears in the chorus 'Descendez, brillante immortelle' (Act 5, no. 3).
30. Borjon de Scellery 1672:3.
31. Haynes 2001b:51.
32. *Pièces à deux basse de viole basse de violon et basson* (Versailles, 1700).
33. Mellers 1987:213.
34. Béthisy 1754:305.

35. Kopp 2004:140–1.
36. Haynes 2001b:158–9.
37. Zohn 2009:570.
38. Rés. Vma Ms 500.
39. Haynes 2001b:412.
40. Maillard 1987:413; Stockigt 2008:98; 101.
41. Haynes 2001b:412.
42. Hodges 1980:248.
43. Bukoff 1985 49; 51.
44. Ibid. 51–2.
45. Benoit 1992:175.
46. Rapoport 2009:67–94.
47. Cotte 1979:315.
48. Baines 1948b:19.
49. Other French woodwind players had visited as early as 1673. Haynes 2001b:146–7. Jacques (5) Hotteterre, a French-born oboist and cousin of the bassoonist Nicolas II Hotteterre, worked at the English court by 1675. Giannini 1993:378–9.
50. British Library, Ms Harleian 2034, fol. 207b. This sketch is apparently an unpublished portion of Randle Holme, *the Academy of Armory . . . with the Instruments Used in All Trades and Sciences* (Chester: self-published, 1688).
51. See Dart 2011:42–4; 95–7.
52. Waterhouse 1993:11.
53. Heyde 2007:55–6.
54. Waterhouse 1993:46; Lasocki 2010:85; 88. Brown claimed to be of German origin.
55. Dart 2011:160–1.
56. Tilmouth 2001:563.
57. Térey-Smith 2001:408.
58. Spitzer 2004:275.
59. Haynes 2001b:288.
60. Stockigt 2008:99.
61. Sadie 1972:63; 174.
62. Page 2001:624.
63. Kilbey 2002:40.
64. Hicks 2001:800.
65. Page 2001:625:fig. 3.
66. Térey-Smith 2001:408; Hicks 2001:772; 779.
67. Stockigt 2008:96.
68. Hutchings 1961:329; Holman and Gilman 2001.
69. `Instrumentalists, Past & Present, 7: Bassoons'. *Orchestral Times* (February 1905):26.
70. Fiske and King 2001:452.
71. Johnson 1972:97; 48. An inventory dating from c.1728–62 included three bassoons, according to Gray 1933:232.
72. Sallagar and Nagy 1992:119; 113.
73. Lasocki 2010:94. 'A very fine bassoon made by Schuchart' was advertised for sale in New York in 1768. Ibid. 95.
74. Hirschstein stood godfather to an Eichentopf child in 1726. Heyde 1987:481.
75. Ibid. 482–3.
76. Dart 2011:120–4.
77. Haynes 2001b:137.
78. Hutchings 1961:115; see ibid. 16 for further description of German efforts to imitate Lully's Grand Bande.
79. Owens 2005:229.
80. Spitzer 2004:221.
81. Ibid. 222; Landsmann 1989:21; Haynes 2001:142.
82. Habla 1987:63.
83. Zohn 2009:562–3.
84. Landsmann 1989:26–7; Heller 1997:247; Talbot 1993:47.

85. Talbot 1993:124. Talbot 1979:561 and Selfridge-Field 1979:139–40 believed the term 'bassono grande' in RV 576 referred to a contrabassoon, available in the Dresden Hofkapelle.
86. Waterhouse 1993:145.
87. Dart 2011:211–23.
88. Haynes 2001b:427–8.
89. Spitzer 2004:431.
90. Dreyfus 1990:123–4; 248–9, n. 36; 125.
91. Ibid. 120 and n. 27.
92. An exception is seen in Cantata 63, where the bassono part is at chorton, perhaps because it functions, in Lullian fashion, 'as the bass member of the oboe group'. Ibid. 124.
93. Ibid. 123.
94. Pirro 1907:236, cited by Terry 1958:118–19. According to Langwill 1965:83, the bassoonist would have been C. F. Fischer or Bernhard George Ulrich.
95. Terry 1958:118–19.
96. Dreyfus 1990:117.
97. Spitzer 2004:431.
98. Haynes 2001b:431.
99. Dreyfus 1990:125.
100. Ibid. 117.
101. Dreyfus 1990:116 summarized the debate. 'In Leipzig ... [w]hen a player was available and could read from a normal continuo part, he may well have played every movement'. Ibid. 118.
102. Ibid. 117.
103. Dreyfus 1990:127.
104. Stockigt 2008:94–5.
105. Emery and Wolff 2001:312.
106. David and Mendel 1945:51.
107. Dreyfus 1990:100; Botwinick 2005:8–9.
108. McCredie 1964:184.
109. Ibid. 183.
110. Zohn 2009:561.
111. Zohn 2001:224–5.
112. Stockigt 2008:105–7.
113. Fleming 1726, quoted in Hofer 1992b:183.
114. Haynes 2001b:163.
115. Owens 1995:352–3, quoted in Haynes 2001b:286.
116. Stilz 1995:106.
117. Haynes, 2001b:426.
118. Fleming 1726:181, translated in Haynes 2001b:61–2.
119. Page 2001:624.
120. Haynes 2001b:164, citing Owens 1995:354.
121. Haynes 2001b:165.
122. Zohn 2009:571.
123. Ibid. 156. An anonymous, early eighteenth-century partita for lute, chalumeau, oboe, viola d'amore and bassoon survives at Kremsmünster, Benediktiner-Stift, Ms L77. Ness and Kolzcynski 2001:60.
124. Hubmann 1994:49.
125. Linz Mu36; the stamp is illegible. Young 1997:200.
126. Young 1997:195; 20; 22.
127. Page 2001.
128. Hubmann 1994:48.
129. Hubmann 2002:413.
130. Nagy 1987:90; 96.
131. Stockight 2008:90–1.
132. http://www2.music.indiana.edu/s/dteresi/. Some of the earlier sonatas may have been composed with the dulcian in mind.
133. Fasch was in the service of Count Morzin during 1719–22. Vaclav Kapsa, 'Missing Music? The Baroque Concerto in Bohemia', *Czech Music* (July 2009), online at: http://www.thefreelibrary.com.

134. Červenka 1992:22–3.

135. Hodges 1980:657.

136. Spitzer 2004:431; Hodges 1980:270; 274; 344.

137. Haynes 2001b 312.

138. Ibid. 307.

139. Salvetti and Keahey 2001:487–8.

140. Burney 1771:69–71.

141. Koenigsbeck 1994:39. An edition of this sonata by Waterhouse (Oxford University Press, 1963) attributed it to 'Jerome Besozzi', also described as 'Girolamo 1713–86'. Citing a Breitkopf & Härtel catalogue of 1778, Koenigsbeck 1994:39 attributed two bassoon concertos to 'Geronimo Besozzi (1712–86)'. Despite the disparate names and dates, each was presumably referring to the bassoonist Paolo Girolamo Besozzi (1704–78), as later described in Salvetti and Keahey 2001.

142. Salvetti and Keahey 2001. A sonata in C for oboe and bassoon, attributed by Sciannameo to Alessandro, was reattributed by Koenigsbeck 1994:39 to Carlo Besozzi.

143. Nimetz 1967.

144. Spitzer 2004:150; Haynes 2001b:404.

145. Ibid. 399.

146. Charles De Brosses, who visited the Pietá in 1739–40, heard girl students playing the bassoon. Neuls-Bates 1982:66. Boys were taught trades or assigned menial tasks instead. See Talbot 2004:87–8.

147. Talbot 2005:8.

148. Talbot 2004:80–1.

149. Heller 1997:28.

150. Giron 2006:121–2.

151. White 2000:89.

152. Fertonani 1998:428.

153. Selfridge-Field 1994:255–6.

154. Fertonani 1998:429–30.

155. Ibid. 433.

156. RV 487, i, mm 45–6. Ibid. 430.

157. In RV 477, finale, m 44 descends to B1; in RV 495, opening Presto, m 248 descends to B♭1. Ibid.

158. Selfridge-Field 1994:231.

159. Ibid. 259.

160. '1 franse Esdorenhout dulsian Basson in 4 Stucken'. Bouterse 2000:243–50. A painting showing a four-piece bassoon in the style of the surviving Haka bassoon was long attributed to Harmen Hals (d.1668), thus suggesting an early date for a Dutch bassoon in that style. But the attribution has been revised to 'imitator of Jan Steen', thus negating its chronological evidence. Fusenig 2006:248.

161. Bouterse 2005:68–9.

162. Ottenbourgs 1989:565; Waterhouse 1993:337.

163. *Larigot* 15:22.

164. Waterhouse 1993:430.

165. Aksdal 1982:83.

166. Jensen 1992:190.

167. Jensen 1992:185.

168. Ibid. 193.

169. Ibid. 203.

170. Ibid. 191

171. Kilbey 2002:145–6.

172. Hodges 1980:355.

173. Chybiński 1949, cited in Piwkowski 1970:31. Nine had Polish surnames.

174. Bula 1976:30.

175. Mooser 1948:91.

176. Ibid. 92; 97.

177. Kilbey 2002:450.

Chapter 5. The classical bassoon, c.1760–1830

1. Bailleux 1775. The E♭ key on a bassoon by Johann Georg Eisenmenger (d.1742) may or may not be original; see Young 1993:70.
2. Joppig 1987:253.
3. *The Harmonicon* 1830:193, signed by 'I. P.', possibly John Parry.
4. Joppig 1987:259–60.
5. Halfpenny 1957:33.
6. Krüger 1991:65–6.
7. Koch 1802:549–50.
8. Performance instructions for the cantata *Applausus*, Hob. XXIVa:6. Quoted in Landon 1978:148.
9. *Musikalischer Almanach* 1782:93. Unsigned article attributed by G. Angerhöfer.
10. Fröhlich 1829:149.
11. Haynes 2001b:418.
12. Spitzer 2004: Appendix. B. Spitzer's appendixes B–D give specifications of dozens of orchestras during the period.
13. Cugnier 1780:328–9; Griswold 1988:115.
14. Haynes and Cook 2001a:800.
15. Onerati 1995:290.
16. Heyde 2007a:32–7; Dullat 1984:100–1.
17. Thomas Lot's brother Martin and his cousin Gilles Lot were also bassoon makers. Waterhouse 1993:242.
18. Jeltsch 1997:143–4; Giannini 1998:xiii.
19. Framery 1788:116.
20. Cugnier 1780:334; 330–1.
21. Ozi 1787:3. The RT key was not used to produce F#2, but rather to tune G#2, Ozi wrote. Later makers and players disagreed, adapting it as a chromatic key for F#2.
22. Fétis 1856:1326–7.
23. Waterhouse 1993:374.
24. This sample is based on instruments in the Waterhouse Collection; broader research may yield different results.
25. Vichy Samedi 11 décembre 2010 [auction catalogue] (Vichy: Vichy Enchères, 2010):nos. 413; 405.
26. Cugnier 1780:335–6; translated in Griswold 1985:37.
27. Waterhouse 1993:194; 340; 346–7.
28. Waterhouse 1993:77–8; 197; 338.
29. F. J. Fétis, 'Exposition des produits de l'industrie . . . Basson à quinze clefs de M. Adler', *Revue musicale* (1828):217–24, at 220–1. R Saint-Arroman 2005, 1:167–9.
30. Francesco Petrini published two collections in Paris, 1778: one for bassoon and harp, the other for bassoon, violin, and harp. Koenigsbeck 1994:329.
31. Cugnier 1780:324; Griswold 1988:120–1.
32. Cugnier 1780:340.
33. Ibid. 332–3; Griswold 1988:122.
34. Cugnier 1780:333–4; Griswold 1988:121.
35. Ibid. 1780:335.
36. Ibid. 135–6. When rollers were introduced by Savary and other makers, the first keys to receive them were often the F and A♭ keys, in order to facilitate passages between G# and the historical fingering for F#3: -23 456F.
37. Harmonie music and the Institut were closely intertwined with Freemasonry. All the founding professors of clarinet, horn, and bassoon were freemasons. Griswold 1979:93–4. Eighteen bassoon professors with seventy-two students were at first proposed, along with one contra class, but the plans were ultimately reduced. Pierre 1895a:118.
38. Pierre 1900:637–40.
39. Ibid. 511; 513.
40. Ozi 1787:4–5, transl. in Griswold 1988:119.
41. Ozi 1803:6, 9, transl. in Griswold 1988:120.
42. bid. 27.
43. Ibid. 5.
44. Ozi 1787:5; 7.

45. Ozi 1803:4. 28 lines long, or $2\frac{1}{3}$ inches; 8 lines or $\frac{2}{3}$ inch wide at the tip; and 5 lines or $\frac{5}{12}$ inch wide at the first wire. Ibid. 142–4.
46. Ibid. 145
47. Macnutt 2001:579; Griswold 2001:835. Ozi was prosperous enough that his death inventory included a respectable cellar of wines. Pierre 1895b:100.
48. Castil-Blaze 1825:56–7.
49. Brook 2001:187.
50. Bartenstein 1974:43–4.
51. Ibid. 59; 61; 74; 75.
52. Faquet 2003:170–1.
53. Griswold 1979:101; 125.
54. The concertos were published 1785–1801. Griswold 1979:526–37.
55. Griswold 1988:118.
56. Mongrédien 1996:282.
57. White 2001:859.
58. Griswold 2001:836–6.
59. Humblot 1909:26–7. In 1790 Devienne purchased two flutes and a bassoon from Porthaux. Giannini 1998:9.
60. Pierre 1900:972; 479; 481; 486; 487; 500.
61. Griswold 2001; Montgomery 2001.
62. His uncle, Joseph Reicha (1752–95), wrote several partitas for all five winds, among other harmonie works for the court of Oettingen-Wallerstein. Koenigsbeck 1994:351.
63. Sirker 1968:25. Three quintets by Nikolaus Schmitt (d.c.1802), enumerated by Fétis and published by Pleyel, Paris, are lost. Fétis (b. 1784) was acquainted with the composer, who played flute, clarinet, and bassoon and was 'chef de la musique des gardes-françaises'. Ibid.
64. Hodges 1980:299–300; Sirker 1968:26–8.
65. Ibid. 33.
66. Ibid. 38. This conflicts with the traditionally cited date of c.1802, which is earlier than Reicha's earliest efforts.
67. Cucuel 1913:21
68. Ibid. 22.
69. Hofer 1992b:186; Griswold 1979:570.
70. Cucuel 1913:22.
71. Francoeur 1772; Lescat 1999:29–40.
72. Griswold 1979:75.
73. Ibid. 117.
74. Up to three women singers or musicians were permitted at the society's private meals and concerts. Ibid. 73. The makers Charles and Frédéric Triebert delivered clarinets, horns, and bassoons to their lodge c.1840, for use in ceremonies. Cotte 1979:316.
75. Griswold 1979:81.
76. Ibid. 570.
77. Koenigsbeck 1994:79.
78. Page 2001:625–7.
79. Waterhouse 1993:205.
80. Heyde 2007a:55, translation revised.
81. In 1775, Crone had ordered instruments from Paul Ludwig Lehnhold. Heyde 2007a:56–7.
82. Heyde 1987:484.
83. Young 1993:98–9.
84. Heyde 1993:598. Griesling & Schlott, a maker of bassoons and other woodwinds in Berlin, was running a manufactory of similar size c.1807.
85. Ibid. 599.
86. Ibid. 596–7.
87. Haynes 2001a:799.
88. Fröhlich 1829:148.
89. Young 1993:105–6.
90. Almenräder 1837:84–5.
91. Heyde 1993:600.
92. Ibid. 601.

93. Joppig 1987:258.
94. Ozi 1805; Ozi 1806; Joppig 1987:256.
95. Without mentioning Ozi by name, Fröhlich referred frequently to 'the Parisian method'.
96. Fröhlich 1810:52.
97. Ibid. 62
98. In staccato articulation, the player should avoid 'noises from the throat and movements of the chin'. Ibid. 62; 64–5.
99. Ibid. 52.
100. Ibid. 61. The table goes only to B4, and thus never itself calls for the C5 key.
101. Ibid. 58.
102. Ibid. 55. Fröhlich's characterization of the French reed as 'broader' contradicts his illustration.
103. Fröhlich 1810:56.
104. Fröhlich 1829:144–5; 146.
105. Ibid. 17.
106. Levin 1988:2–3; Griswold 1996:103–5.
107. Rhodes 1983:98.
108. Rhodes 2000: 496–502.
109. Rhodes 1983:100.
110. Ibid. 101.
111. Bärmann 1820:505–6.
112. Fröhlich 1829:147.
113. Kiefer and Waterhouse 1994:104–9.
114. Hodges 1980:671.
115. *AmZ* 1822:755.
116. Sundelin 1828:13.
117. Hodges 1980:139.
118. Rhodes 2000:497, n. 15.
119. Nösselt 1980:236; Hodges 1980:139.
120. Hofer 2006:26–31; Zohn 2009:570, n. 40.
121. Hellyer 1973:43–4.
122. Rhodes 1995:21–2.
123. Warrack 1976:135–6.
124. William Waterhouse, preface to Carl Maria von Weber, *Andante e rondo ungarese*, op. 35 (Vienna: Universal Edition, 1991).
125. Bartenstein 1974:113 cited other examples from Euryanthe and the Konzertstück in F Minor.
126. Stockigt 2008:97; 102.
127. Maunder 1998:181; Steblin 2008:48; Waterhouse 1993:232; 147; 243.
128. Steblin 2008:29; 30. 'As a foreigner, [Lempp] was charged 20 fl., twice the amount paid by Viennese-born musicians'. Members paid into 'a special treasury that was then used to support poor and sick members, as well as widows and orphans. The fees for those who performed in the inner city were substantially higher.'
129. Maunder 1998:183–5.
130. Ibid. 172.
131. Radant and Landon 1994:36–8.
132. Linz Mu 117; from Stift Hohenfurt. Young 1997:204–5.
133. Steblin 2008:44; 45.
134. Anton Schintler sold bassoon reeds to Esterháza in 1777–8. Maunder 1998:181–90.
135. Steblin 2008:47; Maunder 1998:181.
136. Poznan, Muzeum Instrumentów Muzycznych. Photo in the Waterhouse archives.
137. Hellyer 1975:50–1; 58–9; 56.
138. Ibid. 54.
139. Steblin 2008:53.
140. Keeß and Blumenbach 1830:2.
141. Steblin 2008:54; 56.
142. Szórádová 2000:374.
143. Waterhouse 1993:260–1; 322; 340; 304; 92; 438.
144. Nagy 1983; Nagy 1984:63–4.

145. Brief details of the lives of Esterházy bassoonists are given in Hellyer 1985:5–6, 14, 17, 20; 118–22; 178–80.
146. Spitzer and Zaslaw 2004:399–404; 421–8.
147. Hellyer 1975:50–1
148. Červenka 1992:21–2 counted 70–80 bassoon concertos written by Czech composers during the years 1720–1830, of which about thirty survive. He singled out those by J. A. E. Koželuh, Vanhal, and Rössler-Rosetti for musical merit. Ibid.
149. Sirker 1968:34–5.
150. Hubmann 2002:414.
151. Masier 1995:46.
152. Bartenstein 1974:43–4.
153. Eppelsheim 1995:266.
154. Jones 2009:177.
155. Stockigt 2008:100.
156. Zohn 2009:572.
157. On the first page of the manuscript source (British Library Add. Ms 32218), in an unknown hand, is the inscription: 'per il Sigr Griesbacher'. William Waterhouse, typescript notes dated 17 February 1997.
158. Ward 1949:21; 23.
159. Ibid. 8–9.
160. William Waterhouse, liner notes for Musicaphon SACD M56886. Leopold Mozart reportedly wrote a concerto for bassoon by 1757, now lost. Eisen 2001:271.
161. Sadie 1983:42; Girdlestone 1978:83; Ward 1949:25.
162. Hess 1957; Montgomery 1975:342–51.
163. K. Anh. 230 was possibly among Dürniz's three other 'Mozart' concertos, but all have disappeared, and the surviving catalog of Dürniz's collection lists none of them. Hess 1957:223–32. Hubmann 1990 and Hubmann 1992 give further details.
164. See Levin 1988.
165. Zohn 2009:573.
166. Ibid. 574–5.
167. Sadie 1983:98.
168. Translated in Gjerdingen 2007:452.
169. Albrecht 2008:15.
170. Albrecht 2006:72, n. 110.
171. Volkmann 1942:135–46.
172. Page 2001:625.
173. Blomhert 1996:91–102.
174. Huber 1999:85–90. 'Basson' stops were also seen on instruments by Adrien Lepine (1772), J. G. Gabrahn (1783), and Erard (1802); see Clarke 2009:114.
175. See Michael Struck-Schloen, 'Launiger Flöten-Vorgänger: Die Kölne Oper gräbt Wenzel Müllers Zauberzither aus', *Frankfurter allgemeine Zeitung*, 20 July 2004.
176. Lasocki 2010:96.
177. Ibid. 79–83; Waterhouse 1993:264–5; 35.
178. Lasocki 2010:89–90; 110; 80–1.
179. Nicholson 1821; Lasocki 2010:117; 129.
180. Waterhouse 1993:32; 54–5; 133; 292; 435.
181. Reissinger 2001:24; Koenigsbeck 1994:115.
182. Gärtner and Pauly 1994:190.
183. Hodges 2008:218.
184. Spitzer and Zaslaw 2004:404–13.
185. Hodges 1980:432.
186. Ibid. 435.
187. Jameson 1933:48–9.
188. Jones 2009:125.
189. Koenigsbeck 1994:19; Stockigt 2008:95–6.
190. Page 2001:624.
191. Stockigt 2008:105.
192. Weston 1997:44; Ashman 1998:9–10.

193. Curwen 1897:138.
194. Spiessens 1998:170–9.
195. Waterhouse 1993:404–5; Hodges 1980:636.
196. Hodges 1980:190–1.
197. Bernardini 1989:53.
198. Waterhouse 1993:29; 249; 32; 302; 151; 290.
199. Toschi 1998:96, no. 2.
200. Koenigsbeck 1992:361; Rostagno 2001:530.
201. Balthasar 2001:182.
202. Toschi 1998:93.
203. Gallino 1993:40.
204. Durran 2005:107.
205. Stockigt 2008:103.
206. Nicolò Paganini, *Tre Duetti Concertanti per violino et fagotto*, ed. Italo Vescovo and Flavio Menardi Noguera (Milan: Suvini Zerboni, 1997):vii–viii; Koenigsbeck 1994:320.
207. Waterhouse 1993:8; 118; 177; 199; 245; 354; 369; 390; 392.
208. Hodges 1980: 453; 462; 87; 259; 250; 484; 483; 196; 155; 279; 308.
209. Waterhouse 1993:286; 440; Borràs i Roca 2001:114; Borràs i Roca and Ezquerro 1999:1; 30.
210. Kenyon de Pascual 2001:824.
211. Hodges 1980: 113; 167; 448; 628.
212. Aksdal 1982:83.
213. Layton and Grimley 2001; Hodges 1980:104–5; Koenigsbeck 1994:161.
214. Hodges 1980:519–20.
215. Waterhouse 1993:10; 71.
216. Jensen 1992:196.
217. Hodges 1980: 327; 382; 459; 463; 518; 613; 647; Waterhouse 1993:432.
218. *QMMR* 1824:198.
219. Mooser 1948:368–9; Koenigsbeck 1994:66; Hodges 1980:158.
220. Mooser 1948:368–70.
221. Hodges 1980:92; 458; 533; 539; 669.
222. Translated in Ritzarev 2006:255, citing *Moskovskiye Vedomosti* 1791, no. 56:857.
223. Ritzarev 2006:180.
224. Tarr 2003:26.
225. Lasocki 2009:26; 27.
226. Ibid. 24.
227. Lasocki 2010:115; 113.
228. Waterhouse 1993:59, 257.
229. Ibid. 427; 118.
230. Sonneck 1907:15; 269; Shive 1996:409.
231. Zohn 2009:577.
232. Sonneck 1907:318; 144; 149.
233. Waterhouse 2001, Table 1.
234. Hodges 1980:499.
235. Shive 1996:412.
236. Ibid. 416.
237. Béhague 2001a:874.
238. Gesualdo 1961:100–6.
239. Béhague 2001b:135.
240. Justi 1995:85–7.
241. Cotte 1979:316.

Chapter 6. The scientific bassoon, c.1830–1900

1. Bärmann 1820:603; Weissenborn 1887:vii.
2. Haine 1995:77–83.
3. See Dullat 1984:100–2 on patents and the German Gewerbeordnung of 1830.
4. *Rm* 8/19 (11 May 1834):148.

5. Ventzke 1996:108. Kastner gave Neukirchner and his bassoon a favorable review, reprinted in Saint-Arroman 2005, 2:172.

6. Jackson 2006:132. Weber's optimism stemmed from recent progress in the manufacture of optical instruments, which worked with another sort of wave.

7. Weber 1816b:698–9; Weber 1816a:68; 72–3. He also called for a key enabling slurs from keyed B♭2/B♭3 to nearby notes, a coupling of the B♭1 key to the D2 key, and facilitation of C#2. These ideas were later elaborated in Weber 1828.

8. Almenräder 1823:1.

9. Rosemeyer 2003:328–9.

10. Schrieber 1938:174. The specific improvements by this date are not documented.

11. Weber 1825:138 attributed Almenräder's successful bassoons to the 'excellent craftsmen' employed at Schott.

12. Almenräder 1823:3; Weber 1825:130–1. See Heyde 1972:227–30 for a critical discussion of these innovations, including some precedents by other makers.

13. Weber 1825:125–8. Almenräder explained the rationale of the double boring in 1837; see below.

14. Ibid. 133.

15. Weber 1825:131–3. Heyde 1972:288 noted that J. F. Simiot had in 1808 suggested keys for B1 and C#2, but these had not come into use.

16. Weber 1825:132. Heyde 1972:228 noted that Grenser introduced this feature a few years earlier.

17. Ibid. 138–9.

18. Ibid. 129, fig.2.

19. Ibid. 129–30.

20. Fétis 1828c in Saint-Arrowman 2005, 1:169.

21. Weber 1828:128

22. Ibid. 128–9.

23. Ibid. 129. This key system (and later German and French systems) are presented in schematic diagrams in Vorhees 2003.

24. Weber 1828:130.

25. Fröhlich 1829:149.

26. Fétis, *Gazette musicale de la Belgique* 15 May 1834.

27. Waterhouse 1993:362.

28. Heyde 1977:122.

29. Rosemeyer 2003:336.

30. Namely Wölfing of Wiesbaden and Bachmann of Biebrich. J. A. Heckel, letter to Herrn Schott, 18 April 1839. The oft-quoted wording of Weissenborn 1887:vii is misleading: 'It was more than ten years – (from 1824 until 1835) before they [Almenräder and Heckel] could consider their arduous work [redesigning the classical bassoon] accomplished'.

31. Waterhouse 1993:6–7.

32. Almenräder 1837:80.

33. Ibid. 83.

34. Ibid.

35. Ibid. 82; 81. According to an editorial note on p. 87, the article was written in 1835.

36. The *Fagottschule* was underway by 1835 and possibly mostly complete by 1836; Schott delayed publication because of difficulties with the French translation. Rosemeyer 2002:96. Ventzke 1996:107 dated its publication to 13 September 1843, one day before the author's death.

37. Almenräder 1843, table V.

38. Ibid., table II.

39. '... das in Deutschland unter dem Namen Zuckerahorn bekannte amerikanische Holz – in Frankreich "bois de Palisander" genannt'. Almenräder 1843:129.

40. Rosemeyer 2003:338; Berlin Exhibition 1846:212.

41. Joppig 1981:347 cited a court decree of 1845 allowing two crowns on the stamp; the plain stamp is not explained.

42. Karl von Schafhäutl, *Bericht über die Instrument auf der Londoner Industrieausstellung 1851.* Transcribed by Fritz Marcus. Ms, Waterhouse archive. Zamminer's treatise, *Die Musik und die musikalischen Instrumente in ihrer Beziehung zu den Gesetzen der Akustik* (Gießen: Ricker, 1855) is discussed in Werr 2011:40.

43. Waterhouse 1993:167–8.

44. Biebrich, Heckel F-30. On the Heckel Museum's drawing is the annotation: '1. mal Fis-Gis Triller!' Before J. A. Heckel died in 1877, the butt C# key for R1 and a crook key were added, according to Carse 1939:198.
45. Carse 1939:198 wrote that Almenräder had provided a thumb-plate for B♭. This is not seen on Almenräder 1843, table V, nor on any surviving instrument.
46. In the French system, this tradition was upheld. Another early German departure was the E♭ key for L4, which predated Almenräder.
47. A just comparison between J. A. Heckel's bassoons and those of W. Heckel will be possible only when a corpus of precise measurements is available. Generalizations are complicated by the range of pitches in which surviving models were built.
48. Shown in Heckel's 1879 fingering chart and Heckel 1899 (laid-in illustration).
49. Altenburg 1899:340–1.
50. 'With many large orchestras, having three bassoons, two are Heckel bassoons to B♭, and the third is a Heckel bassoon to contra A.' Heckel 1899:15.
51. Heckel 1881. *Tabelle der Fagotte von Hofinstrumentenmacher J. A. Wilh. Heckel nach C. Almenräders Angabe. Modell 1879* (Biebrich: Heckel, [1879]).
52. Waterhouse 1993:168; Almenräder 1843:121 described relining in wood as a repair technique.
53. Altenburg 1898:340–1.
54. 'It occurred to R. Wagner at once [in 1879] that the hollow tone [Hollaut] of earlier instruments which he was accustomed to hear, had altered here to full tone [Wohllaut].' Altenburg 1899:340–1. Wagner, resident in Biebrich in 1862, had visited J. A. Heckel; his comments from that visit are unknown.
55. Krüger 1991:65–6.
56. Altenburg 1899:22.
57. Heckel 1931:18.
58. Heckel 1899:15.
59. See, for example, Ventzke 1996 on Stuttgart-made bassoons, Dullat 1990 on Berthold, Ventzke 2001 on Haseneier, Gillesen 1995 on Helwert, and Ventzke 1995 on Lange and Ficker.
60. Gillesen 1998.
61. Ventzke 1996:104; Dullat 1990:273–7.
62. Waterhouse 1993:389–90. Günter Hart, 'Musikinstrumentenmacher in Göttingen bis zur Mitte des 19. Jahrhunderts'. Ms, Göttinger Stadtarchiv B 498.
63. Waterhouse 1993:113.
64. Pontécoulant 1861:ii, 581.
65. Waterhouse 1993:268; 2; 186.
66. Charles Joseph Sax, patent application, 8 August 1842.
67. Preserved as Paris C. 1401; see Pilliaut 1894:23; patent drawing in Dullat 1990c:128.
68. Haine and De Keyser 1980:3; 78–81; Langwill 1965:63–4; Klimko 2009:215–24.
69. Willent-Bordogni 1844:3; Langwill 1965:64.
70. *Rm* 8/11 (11 May 1834):148.
71. Ibid.
72. Invoice dated 11 April 1834; photocopy in the Waterhouse archive.
73. Berr 1836:2.
74. Waterhouse 1993:3.
75. Willent-Bordogni 1844:3.
76. Kastner 1848:261–8; 273.
77. Waterhouse 1993:348.
78. Berlioz 2009:291, note 15; *Revue et gazette musicale de Paris* 17 (1850):348–9.
79. Colas 2007: 165–6.
80. *Le Monde dramatique* 3 (Paris, 1837):288; Berlioz 1969:533, 546.
81. Gerhard 2001:218.
82. Kastner 1848:261.
83. Colas 2007:168–71.
84. Young 1993:199–201.
85. Young 1993:200.
86. Jancourt 1885. The rod-axle key offered 'less chance that the position of the touch or the pad would be disturbed by a flexing of the shank'. In addition to ring or brille keys, other reforms

in key work included the needle spring, opposing springs, and the gradual replacement of brass keys by white bronzes (German silver, nickel silver). Bate and Voorhees 2001:554.

87. Waterhouse 1993:49–50.
88. Jancourt 1847:17.
89. Jancourt 1885.
90. Jancourt 1885, a two-page chronological summary of 'Perfectionnements Apportés au Basson', is more complete and historical than Jancourt's *Étude du basson perfectionné*, op. 58 (Jancourt 1876). Also of interest are his *Tablature du basson perfectionné à anneaux mobiles par Eug. Jancourt* (Paris: Gautrot aîné, a1866); and *Tablature du basson perfectionné à anneaux mobiles et 19 clefs* (Paris: Gautrot aîné, c.1866–9).
91. Jancourt 1885.
92. Burgess 2012 (forthcoming).
93. Cokken 1860:4.
94. See the advertisement for 'Bassons Triebert' in E. Guilbaud, *Guide pratique des sociétés musicales et des chefs de musique*, second edition (Paris: L'Instrumental):224 (reprinted in Fauquet 2003:105).
95. Pontécoulant 1861 ii:581.
96. Waterhouse 1993:139; 77–8; 236; 311; 363; 397–8.
97. *Rm*, 13 July 1834:221; Waterhouse 1993:46.
98. Jancourt 1847:17 also seemed to suggest that a machine finished the exterior of the cane: '. . . the exterior is also finished in an irreproachable manner; this last operation appeared to be impracticable by mechanical means before now, and the solution of this problem is a true service rendered to bassoonists by the inventor'.
99. Onerati 1995:268.
100. Perfetti 1989:40–1.
101. Langeveld 1992, nos. 22, 23; Waterhouse 1993:84.
102. Waterhouse 1993:413.
103. Michael Nagy, 'Zur Bau-Charakteristik von wiener Fagotten', unpublished paper from the symposium 'Zur Situation der Wiener Bläser', Vienna, 27–28 October 1983, p. 14.
104. Metropolitan Museum of Art, New York.
105. Waterhouse 1993:108–9; 218; 334; 407–8; 92; 303.
106. Ibid. 170–1; 352; 383; 384; 444; 226; 18; 113; Szórádová 2000:369.
107. Waterhouse 1993:407–8; 42; 213.
108. Nagy 1984:66.
109. E. Schelle, *Officieller Ausstellungs-Bericht heraus, durch die General-Direction der Weltausstellung 1873* (Vienna: K.K. Hof- und Staats-Druckerei, 1873). Ms extract by Fritz Marcus, Waterhouse archive.
110. Karl Mayer, *System C. Almenräder für deutsche Fagotte/Griff-Tabelle für Wiener-Fagotte (gewöhnliche Fagotte)*. Vienna: self-published, c.1885.
111. Nagy 1984:70.
112. Illustrated in Eliason 2001:109.
113. Illustrated in Carter 2001:72.
114. Waterhouse 1993:133; 289; 312; 435–6.
115. *The Glen Account Book, 1838–1853*, ed. Arnold Myers (Edinburgh: EUCHMI, 1985):42.
116. Langwill 1965:56.
117. Waterhouse 1993:40; 61–2; 184; 249–50; 338; 339; 343.
118. Kopp 2012:211.
119. Boehm 1847, fig. II; discussed in Bate 1969:117. An early French interest in acoustical science was voiced by Bernard Sarrette, founding director of the Paris Conservatoire, in 1796: 'Physics will explain, via acoustical rules, the means employed by the ancients to augment sound . . . it will obtain for portable wind instruments of low register the volume they lack'. Pierre 1895a:186–7.
120. Tamplini 1881:7–9.
121. Waterhouse 1983, no. 20. For contemporary reports of this instrument see Ventzke 1976:13–16. Boehm studied acoustics under Schafhäutl beginning in 1845. Bate and Böhm 2001. He later admitted that tone-hole locations on the bassoon were complicated by the modifying influence of the reed. Boehm 1922:173.
122. Ventzke 1976:16.
123. Ibid.

124. Tamplini 1888:9.
125. Jancourt 1876:2.
126. Langwill 1965:66; pictured in Dullat 1990c:126.
127. Heckel 1931:18. This is possibly the 'German bassoon, where all finger-holes are provided with keys [with] the same properties as the French "Boehm-system" bassoon', illustrated in the pictorial supplement to Heckel 1899.
128. Heckel 1899:13–14.
129. Waterhouse 1983, no. 22.
130. Klimko 1979:[6].
131. Biebrich, Heckel Collection, F-19A.
132. Langeveld 1992, no. 33, described it as 'Boehm system'; it is fully keyed, with tone holes spaced proportionally.
133. Almenräder 1843, chapters 5 and 9. Schott, based in Mainz with shops in Paris and Antwerp, published bilingual texts for their methods, including Almenräder 1823, Almenräder 1841/3, and Kuffner 1829.
134. Schilling 1838, art. 'Fagott', 647.
135. Gontershausen 1855:383.
136. Waterhouse 2007:40–1.
137. Weissenborn 1887:xvii. Spaniol 2009 contains commentary on the changing contents of the much-reprinted method.
138. Nutly 1858:338–9.
139. Letellier and Flament 1927:1591–2.
140. Other bassoon methods were published in France by Schiltz (1836), Berr (1836), and Cornette (1854).
141. Willent-Bordogni 1844:4; Jancourt 1847:15.
142. Willent-Bordogni 1844:102.
143. Ibid. 6.
144. Jancourt 1847:44. See also Berr 1836:21.
145. Berr 1836 called for half-holing both A♭3 and A♭4.
146. Willent-Bordogni 1844:8–9; 37–60 [recte 37–40].
147. Jancourt 1847:17; 28; 18; 32–6.
148. Ibid. 2–3.
149. Berr 1836:63.
150. Pierre 1900:973; 975.
151. Pierre 1900:511; 638–9.
152. Grégoir 1862.
153. Ten Bokum 2001; Koenigsbeck 1992:82; Grégoir 1864.
154. Lasagni 1999.
155. Perfetti 1989:28.
156. Orselli 1874 9; 10; 11; 86; 60.
157. Ms notes, Waterhouse archive.
158. Toschi 1998:95.
159. Ibid.
160. Waterhouse 1993:75.
161. Viñes, J. J. (2008). 'Don Pablo Sarasate y familias relacionadas', *Pregón siglo XXI* (31). http://www.pregon21.com/index.php/hemeroteca/articulo-del-numero-31/2008.
162. Hough 1998:123.
163. *AmZ* 1827:138, quoted in Nagy 1983:259; Albrecht 1999:30–1.
164. Nagy 1983:258–64.
165. Waterhouse 1992.
166. Masier 1995:46; McGill 2007: 71–5.
167. Masier 1995:46; McGill 2007:73.
168. Sallagar 1993:81–2; *Revue musicale* 3 (1828):189; Hodges 1980:652.
169. Carse 1948:37; Robin Chatwin, typescript notes, Waterhouse archive.
170. Habla 1998:160.
171. Onerati 1995:284; 269; Brixel 1996:127–48.
172. Onerati 1995:276.

173. Quoted in Habla 1998:155. Picchianti wrote in 1850 that German bands were mostly composed of Bohemian players; quoted in Onerati 1995:269.
174. *Musical Opinion* 1 (January 1889):166.
175. Ms notes, Waterhouse archive.
176. Gunther Angerhöfer, typescript notes 1999:3, Waterhouse archive.
177. Perfetti 1989:26.
178. Hodges 1980:579.
179. Tarr 2003:257.
180. Ibid.
181. Sirker 1968:43–4.
182. Tarr 2003:90.
183. Valery Popov, personal communication to William Waterhouse, 21 May 2000.
184. Spencer 2001.
185. Hodges 1980:666; Nutly 1858:335–6.
186. Nagy 1983:259.
187. www.stokowski.org.
188. Perfetti 1989:26–7; Lunn 1871:227.
189. Fauquet 2003:1840.
190. Bartenstein 1974:113; 114; 121.
191. Travis 1956:44–5.
192. There is some possibility, however, that it was not originally written for bassoon. See Rossella Lorenz, 'Lost Verdi Works Find a Voice', *The European Magazine* (21–27 December 1995):14.
193. Del Mar 1969:266.

Chapter 7. *A tale of two systems, 1900–1990*

1. Jancourt 1847:2.
2. In a visible archaism, most of the longest keys (for LT) of the Heckel-type bassoon are levers, not rod-axle keys.
3. *Verzeichnis über Künstler-Instrumente: Ausgabe 204* (Biebrich: Heckel, c.1907):1.
4. Camden 1982:101–2.
5. Waterhouse 1993:115.
6. *Verzeichnis über Künstler-Instrumente: Ausgabe 204* (Biebrich: Heckel, c.1907):3; Gustav Mollenhauer & Söhne, Cassel [catalogue c.1910].
7. In 1906, Heckel patented a closing mechanism for the side hole in the crook, the so-called Schliessmechanik. Ventzke 1991:541.
8. Many early crook keys, from Savary to Wilhelm Heckel, were closed by opening the high A key and C keys.
9. *Illustrated Price List of the "Hawkes" Military Band Instruments* (London: Hawkes & Son, [1910]).
10. 'Instrumentalists, Past & Present, 7: Bassoons', *Orchestral Times* (February 1905):26.
11. Stadio 1908:19.
12. *Verzeichnis über Künstler-Instrumente: Ausgabe 204* (Biebrich: Heckel, c.1907):3.
13. Camden 1982:23; James 1990:4–5, n. 6.
14. 'Wilhelm Heckel' [obituary], *ZfI* 29 (1909):445.
15. *Verzeichnis über Künstler-Instrumente: Ausgabe 204* (Biebrich: Heckel, c.1907), front cover.
16. Ventzke 1991:541.
17. Lein 1999:13; 15.
18. Waterhouse 1993:268–9; *Süddeutsche Musiker-Zeitung* 43 (22 October 1931); *Süddeutsche Musiker-Zeitung* 4 (16 February 1933).
19. Haynes 2001a:800.
20. Lein 1999:16; 14.
21. *V. Kohlert's Söhne Graslitz, Böhmen ČSR* [catalogue, c.1933]:53–4.
22. Kroll 1937:1–3.
23. Schönemann 1937:2–3.
24. Heckel 1931:29.
25. Swiney 1999:73; 71.
26. Klimko 1983:20.

27. W. H. Heckel, 'Holz und Metall als Baustoff für Musikinstrumente' *ZfI* 53/18 (15 June 1933). *R* Leipzig: Paul de Wit.

28. Waterhouse 1993:268; Ventzke and Weller 2005:16; Weller 1997:89.

29. Burton 1975:37; 61.

30. Quoted in Burton 1975:36.

31. See Hähnchen 2008:36–8 for a comparison of tone-hole diameters on long and bell joints of Selmer and Heckel-system bassoons.

32. Krüger 1991:65–6.

33. A similar key had been seen on bassoons since the Berr method of 1836.

34. White and Myers 2004:76.

35. James 1990: 4.

36. Camden 1982:109. Heckel reported that AG of Berlin had acquired a Heckel contra for the same purpose (catalog c. 1931:38).

37. Day 2002:11.

38. Camden 1982:110–11; 109.

39. Dietz 1987:49.

40. Bartholomäus 1992:188.

41. W. H. Heckel, 'Holz und Metall als Baustoff für Musikinstrumente' *ZfI* 53/18 (15 June 1933). *R* Leipzig: Paul de Wit.

42. Kohon 1932:12.

43. Waterhouse 1999:35.

44. Christlieb 1996:74.

45. Price 2006:7; obituary by Graham Melville-Mason, *The Independent*, 5 April 2005.

46. Porter 2002.

47. Bushell 1988:49–50; 97; 111; Schuller 1968:325n.

48. James 1999:28; John Cruft, 'Anthony Baines: An Obituary Tribute', *DRN* 39 (Summer 1997):37–8; 'Gwydion Brooke' [unsigned obituary], *DRN* 72 (Autumn):5–6.

49. Bartholomäus 1992:189.

50. Vonk 2007:33; Joppig 1986:48.

51. Lein 1999:19.

52. Vonk 2007:22; La Touche 2000:11–12.

53. Charles Strasser, letter to L. G. Langwill, 2 May 1949, Waterhouse archive; Vonk 2007:26.

54. 'How Conn Tooled Up to Make America's First Bassoon', *Musical Merchandise* (September 1940):9.

55. Margaret Downey Banks, personal communication, 15 February 2010.

56. Lein 1999:110.

57. Joppig 1997a:37; Lein and Lein 1997:25.

58. Lein 1999:19; 16; 20.

59. Lein 2003:80–1.

60. Wilhelm Hermann Heckel, letter to William Waterhouse, 17 October 1947. Waterhouse Archive.

61. Burton 1975:34.

62. Burton 1975: 67–8; Hähnchen 2008:36–9.

63. James 1987:4–5.

64. `Debased Bassoon', *Daily Telegraph* 19 September 1953; 'Waspish Bassoon', ibid. 21 September 1953; 'Leo Van de Moortel', *TWB* 3/1 (1972–3):2–3.

65. William Waterhouse, 'A First for France', *TWB* 1/3 (1970):5; David H. Carroll, 'Now It Can Be Told!', *TWB* 2/1 (1971):4. Corey 1975:28–9 and Birnstingl 1981:11–12 give further details of this tug-of-war.

66. Herman 1992:96 described a similar replacement of bassoons in the Orchestre de Paris under the conductor Daniel Barenboim.

67. Kopp 2010:52.

68. Chantaraud 1995:85.

69. Hough 1998:124.

70. *Les Amis du Basson Français* 1 (1975).

71. Ricardo Rapoport, personal communication, 28 December 2010.

72. *Le Basson* 1983:20.

73. Carry 1978:16–19.

74. Carrée 1982:17; Hilkenbach 1989:13–16; Joppig 1991:42–4.

75. Bertement 1981:4.

76. Kurz 1981:9.

77. 'Toulon 1982', *Le Basson* 8 (March 1982):4.

78. Laurence Taylor in *Le Basson* 7 (March 1981):13; Chantauraud 1995:85.

79. Birnstingl 1981:11.

80. Grossman 1981:12.

81. Luc Loubry, personal communication, 28 December 2010.

82. Chantauraud 1995:86.

83. `Willliam Waterhouse Column', *DRN* 6 (February): 5–6

84. *Le Basson* 7 (1981):24; Joppig 1991:44.

85. Lein and Lein 1990, note 27.

86. Morgan 1998:15–16.

87. Data sheet from AMIS committee, citing taped interview (1990) with Jack Laslie, a co-worker at Selmer. Waterhouse archive.

88. *Woodwind* (September 1970):4.

89. *The News-Sentinel*, Fort Wayne, Indiana, 10 January 1990.

90. Described in Cuçiureanu 1985.

91. More radical inventions included the 'logical bassoon' of Giles Brindley, in which key covers were activated by solenoid control, and the Edgar Brown/Zoltan Lukacs bassoon, a revised German bore with redesigned tone holes and fingering. Neither of these went into commercial production. See Brindley 1968; Brown 1998.

92. Christlieb 1945; Christlieb 1996:18–19.

93. Jirka 2003:144.

94. Bhosys 1949.

95. Philip 1992:133–9.

96. Antonio Romo, 'Historical Memoir on the Bassoon and Programme of Instruction in the Same', Ms (10 July 1926) translated by Lyndesay G. Langwill, pp. 26–8. Waterhouse archive.

97. Letellier and Flament 1927:1594.

98. Ibid. 1563; 1595.

99. Allard and Öhlberger 1984:35–9.

100. Toscanini reportedly bought four Heckel bassoons for the section at La Scala in 1946. Dietz 1987:44, quoting Muccetti.

101. Perfetti 1989:35–9; Corey 1977:5. Stadio 1908:19–20 lists Italian bassoon professors of the late nineteenth and early twentieth centuries.

102. James 1987:28.

103. The University of Illinois Band c.1920–1 included two French-system bassoons and contra. *DR* 11/3 (1988), cover; 3.

104. *New York Times* 1 June 1905; ibid. October 1905.

105. Mackey 2001:31.

106. Dietz 1987:48–9.

107. Ibisch 1978:5.

108. Philip 1992:135.

109. Dietz 1987:49–50.

110. Gerald Corey, letter to William Waterhouse, 30 May 1989.

111. Cooper and Toplansky 1968.

112. Herman 1992:95–6.

113. Kuttner 2002:10; Farmer 2001:35.

114. Strobl's reed measurements were: overall length 58 mm, blade length 32 mm, tip width 18 mm, diameter 8–9 mm (after forming). Sallagar 1978:2; 5. Sallagar reported a typical Viennese tip width in 1978 of 16 mm.

115. Werba 1993:16; Werba 1995:10–11.

116. Koblitz 2001; Atanasov 2006.

117. Penazzi 1971; Penazzi 1982.

118. Hansche 2000:120–1.

119. Kott and Haldey 2010b:71; Kott and Haldey 2009:89.

120. William Waterhouse, 'Valery Popov', *DRN* 7 (May 1989):4.

121. Stock 2001; www.chinaculture.org/

122. Hough 1999:75.

123. Chen Jie, 'Notes of Harmony' 351:1 (27 May 2009), online publication.
124. Weidauer 2007:181.
125. Schoenbaum and Backus 2001.
126. Weait 1979:5–6.
127. Hough 1999:78.
128. Yanhui Xu, personal communication, 31 December 2010.
129. Narusawa 2004:118. In 1951, this became the NHK Symphony Orchestra.
130. Krieger 1991:12.
131. Hough 1999:76.
132. Eifert 1982:22.
133. Bushell 1988:170; 173–6.
134. Schuller 1989:712; Bushell 1988:112.
135. Porter 2002; Beebe 2009.
136. 'Cary, Dick', *EPM*; 'Douglas, Bill', *EPM*.
137. Wilmer and Kennedy 2001; 'Anatoly Vapirov', *EPM*; 'Gryphon', *EPM*.
138. Kelly 2001:289. Mussorgsky's *Sorochinsky Fair* (1875–81) included a strikingly similar dudka melody for bassoon (pitched lower, however) in 'The Lad's Dumka', ed. Liadov. Taruskin 1996, 2:934–6.
139. See Cox 2000 and three articles by Kott and Haldey (2009, 2010a, 2010b) for discussion of works for solo bassoon and orchestra.
140. Finscher 1997:63–4.
141. Solos to 1984 are described in Fletcher 1988.
142. Schmidt 1995:467.
143. Sonatas and shorter works by Russian composers after World War II are surveyed in Kott and Haldey 2005 and Kott and Haldey 2008. Czech and Slovak Music for bassoon and piano in the twentieth century are surveyed in Edwards 2010.

Chapter 8. The bassoonist's world since 1990

1. See, for example, Koenigsbeck 1999:71.
2. Alexander 1993:12–13.
3. Turkovic 2001:3.
4. Charles Holdeman, personal communication, 25 May 2010.
5. Luc Loubry, personal communication, 28 December 2010.
6. Charles Holdeman, personal communication, 25 May 2010.
7. Meyrick Alexander, personal communication, 31 December 2010.
8. Lein 1999:21.
9. Lein 2010:82–3.
10. Yanhui Xu, personal communication, 25 December 2010.
11. Weisberg 1998; Weisberg 2001. After Weisberg's death in 2009, the project continued under the direction of Robert Jordan.
12. For a discussion of the pycnometer, see Schultze-Florey 2002.
13. This is spoken of as the CD (compact disk) era, although many digital recordings were also released on LP.
14. Weidauer 1989; Carroll 1999; Sherwood 1998.
15. http://www.karts.ac.kr/karts/main/html.
16. Weidauer 2006:145.
17. Weidauer 2007.
18. Ewell 1992.
19. McGill 2008. Storch 2008 gave exhaustive details of Tabuteau's career and teaching.
20. Kopp 2010:54.
21. Alexander 1993:13.
22. Quoted in Atanasov 2006:77; 79.
23. Haynes 2007:49–50.
24. Haynes 2007:54.
25. Philip 1992:135–8.

26. Odéon 123868–9 (XXP 7388-1, 89-1, 90-1). Released on CD as 'Fernand Oubradous bassoniste et chef d'orchestre joue et dirige Johann Sebastian Bach', Dante Productions LYS 412.
27. Ibid. 59.
28. Riedelbach 1988; Méndez 2003.
29. Johnny Reinhard, 'Microtonal Bassoon (chart)', *Pitch for the International Microtonalist* ¼ (1990).
30. See Rampley 2004.
31. Bartholomäus 1992.
32. Van Diepen 2007:111–12.
33. Rabinowitz 2007:108–10.
34. Ewell 2005:119.
35. Earlier entitled *Klarinette*. Later entitled *rohrblatt*.
36. Live365 Basson, operated by Guy Mallery of Stockton, California, 2005–10.

Chapter 9. *The contrabassoon*

1. Praetorius 1619. Transl. by Jeffrey Kite-Powell, 107. 'Italian concertos' were simply works for voices and instruments combined, a Venetian export described in chapter 3. In chapter 20, Praetorius again mentioned octave doubling by strings, double curtals and great bass shawms. Praetorius 1618–20, transl. Crooks, 54.
2. Organ stops are named after the length of unstopped pipe required to produce a pitch written as C2. Praetorius noted that the Doppel-Quint-Fagott was at 'the twelve-foot organ pitch', or F1. Kilbey 2002:116.
3. Williams 2001.
4. Kilbey 2002:124.
5. Ibid. 131.
6. Ibid. 176. The scoring also included *fagotto commune* and *fagotto piccolo*.
7. Praetorius 1618–20, transl. Crookes, 48, my revision.
8. Kilbey 2002:107.
9. Wiemken 2007:31. Kilbey 2002:113 translated much of the Praetorian discussion of transposition by wind consorts. For further details, see Van Heyghen 2005.
10. Kilby 2002:107.
11. Wiemken 2007:32.
12. The quartbass at Linz (Mu 217) is an exception, with a configuration of 7 + 3. See Young 1997:188; Lyndon-Jones 1994:45–7. Angerhöfer 1990:47 gave measurements for the Augsburg instrument.
13. Kilbey 2002:240.
14. In 1668–71, these were called 'Octave Bombart'. One was in the church inventory in 1789 as 'large bombard, not in use', and still later as 'serpent'. Heyde 1987b:26.
15. Weber 1991 compared the Sonderhausen and Augsburg instruments; Lyndon-Jones 1994 compared these three plus the Pillnitz contrabass.
16. Lyndon-Jones 1994:4; Angerhöfer 1990:48. Praetorius 2005 gives detailed measurements.
17. Kilbey 2002:137.
18. Hubmann 2002:414.
19. Selfridge-Field 2001.
20. Paris, Bibliothèque Nationale, Rés. 921, pp. 60–1, no. 48.
21. Baines 1948:15.
22. Haynes 2001b:146.
23. Fuhrmann 1706, transl. in Snyder 1987:378.
24. Heyde 1987:30.
25. Heyde 1987:32.
26. Psalm 118, TWV 7:5, ed. Theis; cited by Koch 1980:233.
27. Heyde 1987:32, citing Koch 1980:136.
28. Selfridge-Feld 1979:332–8.
29. Museum für Kunst und Kulturgeschichte der Hansestadt Lübeck, no. 1893/63.
30. Dreyfus 1990:127.
31. Heyde 1987:32.
32. Carreras 2008:4.

33. The bell diameter increases from 59 to 100 mm. See Birsak 2007:165.
34. A second newspaper report from 1739 attributed two contrabassoons to Thomas Stanesby Senior (d.1734), obviously confusing the son with his late father. Clouding the issue further was Charles Burney's unsupported claim, published in 1785, that Stanesby Senior made one contrabassoon for use in 1727. See Langwill 1965:114–15.
35. The oboist W. T. Parke, quoted in Langwill 1965:116; see Burney 1785: plate VIII.
36. `It is significant that Handel avoids the notes below F, which it may be assumed were uncertain or of bad quality.' Langwill 1965:116. The part descends to written D2, as Chatterton pointed out in a personal communication, 22 March 2008.
37. Mahillon 1909:271–2, no. 1000.
38. Heyde 1993:599.
39. On a Rorarius contra in the Waterhouse collection, these vents have depths of 26 mm and 16 mm, respectively.
40. *Wiener Zeitung*, 7 September 1785, p. 2109. Thanks to Melanie Piddocke for this citation.
41. Szórádová 2000:372.
42. Maunder 1998:187; 189.
43. Waterhouse 1993:218; 232–3; 334; 92; 256; 361; 404; 181.
44. Brussels 1002, Linz Mu 37.
45. Brussels 1001. On the last page of Almenräder 1823, a list of instruments offered by B. Schott Söhne includes 'an octave contrabassoon with seven keys'.
46. Biebrich: Heckel KF1, marked Schott, Mainz; estimated date 1834.
47. Caecilia 22 (1826):19.
48. Langwill 1965:117; Mahillon 1912:363.
49. *Catalogue des produits de l'industrie nationale à la trosième exposition générale à Bruxelles* (Brussels: Fonderie et imprimerie normale, 1830):19.
50. Waterhouse 1993:300; 23, s.v. 'Baumann, Joseph'.
51. Paris Exhibition 1844:564.
52. Jensen 1992:203. At the Danish royal theater between 1779 and 1792, three bassoonists and one oboist were also described as contra players. Ibid. 197.
53. Waterhouse 1993:369.
54. Hubmann 1994:49.
55. Langwill 1965:116–17.
56. 'In Harmoniemusik one uses, instead of the contraviolone, a size of this instrument a fourth lower, therefore named Quartfagott.' Koch 1807:96–7. Koch possibly mistook the common Viennese contra to D (6 + 3) for a Quartfagott. Jansen 1978 frequently succumbed to this misleading usage.
57. See *AmZ* 1813:665–8 (reference supplied by Roger Hellyer). 'The trombone, serpent, double bass and double bassoon were variously employed [after the 1780s] to give a sixteen-foot quality; the instrument used depended upon availability, and such parts were often optional.' Hellyer 2001.
58. H. C. Robbins Landon, foreword to the Bärenreiter edition, no. 4709. See Rice 2009:203–4 for details of the additions.
59. Maunder 1998:187. Lotz also played contrabassoon in a wind sextet by Anton Stadler in a concert at the lodge on 15 December 1785. Ibid.
60. Apparently Haydn gained convenient access to a contrabassoon and player at Esterházy only in 1805, when one of the existing bassoonists, Johann Michl, bought himself one. Hellyer 1985:54–5.
61. Langwill 1965:119–20.
62. Thayer 1970:502. The others are WoO 18 and 24.
63. The contra was not included in the duet in the first performance (1805); Beethoven added it for later performances. Hess 1981:101–2.
64. Sehnal 1973:132; 137–42.
65. Letellier and Flament 1927:1563.
66. Quoted in Langwill 1965:121.
67. Pierre 1890:30.
68. Bartenstein 1974:114.
69. Waterhouse 1993:300; 181; 350; 213; 208–9; 422; 223.
70. Florence 1980:104 (n.139); Leipzig 1402.
71. Munich 16794.

72. Biebrich KF-3 and Ann Arbor 683.
73. Ehrle 1983:50.
74. Travis 1956: 45.
75. Ibid.
76. Sawerthal 1846:317, quoted in Habla 1990:317.
77. Habla 1990:320 gives score citations.
78. Ibid. 317.
79. Letellier and Flament 1927:1563.
80. Kastner 1836, reprinted in Saint-Arroman 2005:ii:162.
81. Page 2001, 1:629; 630.
82. Page 2001, 2:631.
83. Habla 1990:324.
84. Travis 1956:45. These marches, apparently lost, are not listed in *NGDMM 2*.
85. Pierre called unsuccessfully for a modern semi-contra, to be used on second-bassoon parts. This would circumvent the sometimes awkward LT technique of the bassoon, which makes legato difficult in the range from B♭1 to E2. Pierre 1890:28–9.
86. Ridley 1984:32–3, no.91; to F1; eight keys; 1.63 m.
87. This was the property of a bassoonist at the Opéra, according to Pierre 1890:29. He mentioned as 'German' an early nineteenth century contra by G. Schuster, reportedly a Viennese maker, which had been retired to the Conservatoire museum by 1890. Gétreau 1996:657, nos. E. 478, C.512.
88. Waterhouse 1993:142.
89. Pierre 1890:30.
90. Haynes 2001a:800.
91. Jancourt 1885.
92. Pierre 1890:31.
93. Pierre 1890:32. A contra by Martin frères roughly matches this brief description (Metropolitan Museum of Art, New York; dated c.1900). Virtually all of the lead pipe is made of wood, including a *petite culasse* (small boot joint) at the top.
94. *Larigot* 21 (September 2010):158–9, no. 769.
95. Geoffrey Rendall, letter to L. G. Langwill, c.14 September 1942. Rendall also mentioned a 'Bohemian-made French model' (later in the Stutfield collection, in simple 6 + 5 upright format with a petite culasse in the lead pipe). In surviving pictures, the contra appears similar to the contra by Martin frères mentioned in note 93.
96. Hodges 1980:625; International Inventions Exhibition 1885: Official Catalogue, third ed. (London: Clowes, 1885):55.
97. Heckel 1931:20–1.
98. *Grifftabelle für Kontrafagott (System F. Stritter)*. Leipzig: Carl Merseburger, n.d. Altenburg 1899:341 still referred to the Heckel contra models of 1897 and 1898 as 'after the Stritter System'.
99. This paragraph is adapted from Waterhouse 1993:390, with my own substantive additions. See Joppig 2012 for further details.
100. Heckel 1931a:21.
101. Langwill 1965:130; Jansen 1978, 2:610.
102. Illustrated in *ZfI* 1898:169.
103. Altenburg 1899:340–1.
104. Heckel 1899:17; Altenburg 1898:341.
105. *Nachtrag 1901 zu Der Fagott* (Biebrich: Heckel, 1901):[5].
106. Altenburg 1899:340–1.
107. Heckel 1931:20. Martin Bernstein, in a letter to Lyndesay G. Langwill dated 9 November 1965, pointed out that Wagner's autograph of the prelude, dated 23 August 1879, predates the October 1879 meeting described by Heckel; Waterhouse archive. On Richter, see 'Richard Wagner und Mainz', *Biebricher Tagespost* 13 March 1933:2–3.
108. Corder 1896:50.
109. Widor 1906:47–50.
110. Letellier and Flament 1927:1564; 1562 showed both a C bell and a tall but down-turned B♭ bell for the Evette & Schaeffer.
111. Unlike the interchangeable Heckel bells for C and B♭, the Evette B♭ 'bonnet' could be taken in half to leave a C bell; a small finial could then be added to the upright cylinder. Evette & Schaeffer catalogue (Paris: self-published, 1912):34.

112. The F# spatula for RT was coupled to the F key, so that R4 was free to operate the G# spatula.
113. Heckel 1931:21; *Grifftabelle für den Heckel-Kontrafagott*, post-1931.
114. Joppig 1985:24 noted several further developments of the Heckel-type contrabassoon during the twentieth century.
115. Reed contrabasses offered by Boosey & Co. in 1902 and by Besson in 1911 under the names 'contra-fagott' and 'contrabassoon' are discussed in chapter 10.
116. Robert Anderson, review of Elgar's own recording of his Symphony no. 2 (1925), as reissued on Pearl, *Musical Times* 117, no. 1605 (November 1976):913–14.
117. Widor 1906 (1945):204. Gordon Jacob, appendix to 1945 edition.
118. Authorities disagreed, for example, on the venting and fingering for G3, some favoring a register key and others an open L1.
119. Allard and Öhlberger 1984:38.
120. Bushell 1988:175–6.
121. Schulze 1985:31–3.
122. Koenigsbeck 1994:591; Bulling 1989:391–405.

Chapter 10. *The bassoon idea: relatives after mechanization*

1. Berlioz 1844:120.
2. Kiefer 2010:49–53.
3. Čížek 1992:75.
4. Kiefer 2010:58–60.
5. Ibid. 61.
6. Ibid. 56–66.
7. Extant Harmonie-Bass specimens by Stehle are in Leipzig (1404), Nuremberg (MIR 59), Paris (E 1175/C 1124), Toronto (909.17.15), and Budapest. An eight-key contrabassoon by Stehle, of traditional hairpin design with metal bell, is preserved in Salzburg, no. 210.
8. Nemetz 1846:53.
9. Eppelsheim 1979:104–6.
10. *Allgemeine Zeitung München*, 5 May 1839. Thanks to Thomas Kiefer for this information.
11. Szórádová 2000:376–7; 398. See also Hrabussay 1961:226. Thanks to Václac Vonášek for translating portions of this text.
12. Kiefer 2010:69–70.
13. Ibid. 61.
14. Hrabussay 1961:207.
15. Claudius 585, Danish Music Museum, Copenhagen. Kiefer 2010:70.
16. Kiefer 2010:73–4.
17. *Gazzetta di Firenze*, 15 September 1842, quoted in Onerati 1994/5:68–9.
18. Tosoroni 1850:29, quoted in Onerati 1995:79, note 56.
19. Tosoroni 1850:29.
20. Ann Arbor, Stearns Collection 0913.
21. Waterhouse 1993:296.
22. Kiefer 2010:76.
23. Meucci 1994:305; Čížek 1992:75; Joppig 1992:216; Kiefer 2010:70.
24. Waterhouse 1993:163–4.
25. Dibley 2000:69.
26. Inches are given in Langwill 1965:129.
27. Paul Blackman, unpublished conference paper, 2004.
28. Baines 1977:337.
29. Pierre 1890:27.
30. Pierre 1890:37–8. The patent is transcribed and translated in Dibley 2000.
31. Berdahl 1986:698.
32. Langwill 1965:128.
33. Baines 1948:191.
34. Kiefer 2010:79.
35. Dullat 1984:101–2. This was an adaptation of Lampferhoff's brasswind 'contrahorn' of 1844.

36. Ibid. 105. This was partly due to the high cost of developing the idea. Makers declining to collaborate with Wieprecht apparently included Halary (1847) and J. A. Heckel (1852); see Kiefer 2010:81.
37. Comaš 1990:7.
38. Dullat 1984:105.
39. Mendel 1873:607; Kiefer 2010:81.
40. Mendel 1879:349.
41. Prague 1357E; see Kiefer 2010:94.
42. Schafhäutl 1882:1872; Kiefer 2010:89.
43. Kiefer 2010:89.
44. Čížek 1992:75–6. Fingerings are given in Eppelsheim 1974:263–4.
45. Assertions that the Universal-kontrabass of 1839 was 'folded on itself five times' confuse the early form with Červený's revised model of 1856, and include the folded lead pipe in the count. See, for example, Langwill 1965:123.
46. Mendel 1873:607; Schafhäutl 1882:872.
47. Čížek 1992:75–6.
48. Prague 1357 E, 85 cm. This may be identifiable with a 'kleines Metallfagott' shown at the London Exhibition of 1862, noted for its construction 'after the principles of Boehm'; see Kiefer 2010:93.
49. Pierre 1890:35; Eppelsheim 1979:108–10.
50. Eppelsheim 1979:110; see Rice and Bukalski 1985 for a general introduction.
51. Mahillon 1874:173.
52. *Mahillon: Manufacturers of Orchestral and Military Musical Instruments*. London: self-published, c.1908.
53. 'Metodo completo per Contrabasso ad Ancia ovvero Controfagotto d'ottone', 139 pages. Cited in G. Angerhöfer Ms, dated 29 x 1999; Waterhouse archive.
54. Eppelsheim 1979:112 described this as uncatalogued.
55. Blaikley 2001:297.
56. Ibid.; *Larigot* I bis (December 1986):58; *Larigot* IX (September 1998):70–1.
57. Jolivet 1985:76.
58. Jolivet 1985:85.
59. Heckel 1899:14.
60. Corder 1896:50.
61. Widor 1906:47–50.
62. Kiefer 1990:120.
63. Jolivet 1985:73.
64. Ibid. 77
65. Blaikley 2001:298. Schulze 1992 discusses repertory.
66. Hough 1998:128.
67. 'Sousa', *WINDS* (Spring 1994):15.
68. *DR* 28/1:41–2.
69. Blaikley 2001:297.
70. 'Mandy, Make up your Mind', with the Clarence Williams Blue Five, 1924. 'Sarrusophone', *NGDJ*.
71. Kernfeld 2002.
72. Waterhouse 2001c:784.
73. Wolf 2002:60–2.

Chapter 11. Smaller bassoons

1. Pierre 1890:26 accused Evette & Schaeffer of 'pure coquetry' in having produced a bassoon pitched a minor third higher than normal.
2. Kilbey 2002:119.
3. See Kilbey 2002:259–61 for detailed descriptions of surviving small dulcians
4. Kilbey 2002:28.
5. Ibid. 94–5; 97; 100–1.
6. Kenyon de Pascual 1995a:67.

7. Borràs i Roca 2008, Annexo, 3.
8. Kilbey 2002:73.
9. Borràs i Roca 2008:360.
10. Kilbey 2002:96.
11. Waterhouse 1993:85; 146; 219; Mahillon 1909:265; Waterhouse 1993:353; 362. References to pitches of small bassoons here are based on received descriptions. Further research may reveal a great variety.
12. Waterhouse 1993:228.
13. Jeltsch 1997:131, n. 12.
14. Ibid. 151.
15. Sittard 1886:10; see also Jensen 1992:190.
16. Sittard 1886:10.
17. Owens 2005:238.
18. Ahrens 2009:42; 46; 50.
19. Published in *Denkmäler der deutsche Tonkunst* 21/22 (Leipzig, 1905):236–59.
20. Koch 1980:134.
21. Hodges 1980:419.
22. Waterhouse 1993:48; 69; 77; 84; 146; 191; 242; 337; 354; 3; 14; 35; 55; 104; 133; 146; 177; 215; 294; 349; 395; 401; 405; 438.
23. Lasocki 2010:111; Waterhouse 1993:69; Wilson 1889:71, quoting *The Georgia Gazette*, 10 February 1785, on 'Mr. Hewill'.
24. Waterhouse 2001:893.
25. Waterhouse 1993:405; Langwill 1965:118.
26. Maunder 1998:181–90.
27. Waterhouse 1993:361.
28. Waterhouse 2001:893.
29. Hubmann 2011:79–84. An analogous practice, not always remarked, is use of the violoncello piccolo, tuned a fifth above the conventional cello. See Wijsman 2001.
30. Hubmann 2011:79–82; Hubmann 2002:414; Weidauer 1994:158.
31. British Library, Add. Ms 29801, folios 74–80. Completed and edited by Willy Hess as *Romance cantabile für Klavier, Flöte und Fagott* (Wiesbaden: Breitkopf & Härtel, 1952; no. 3704).
32. Hodges 1980:659.
33. Moore 1992:37. See Kinsky and Halm 1955:479–80, WoO 37.
34. Hedlund 1958:78–84.
35. Ventzke 1977:151–3.
36. Heyde 1993:596.
37. Shive 1992:159
38. Maunder 1998:181.
39. Hodges 1980:190.
40. Waterhouse 1993:98; 165; 231; 311; 347; 384; 435.
41. Pierre 1890:26; Waterhouse 1993:129; 165; 218; 255; 264; 273; 334; 347.
42. John B. Taylor Instrument Collection, Williamstown, MA; typescript catalogue received by Lyndesay G. Langwill on 29 April 1975; Waterhouse archive.
43. Bizzi and Girodo 1991:130, no. MTS-FA/12.
44. Bernardini 1989:60.
45. Finkelman 2001b:282. Fahrbach 1840:397 spoke of 'the two piccolo fagotti being adopted as the corni da caccia'.
46. Waterhouse 1983, no. 33.
47. Pierre 1890:26–9.
48. Almenräder 1843:1.
49. Waterhouse 2001:893.
50. Satzenhofer 1900:3–4.
51. Waterhouse 1993:334.
52. Pierre 1890:25–6. Pierre used the same terminology for the *basson tierce* made by Evette & Schaeffer in 1889.
53. Tosoroni c.1850:26.
54. A. Orefici, 'Storia del fagotto'. Ms dated Turin, May 1926. Turin, Conservatory Library.
55. Langwill 1965:174.

56. Waterhouse 1993:222.
57. Weissenborn 1887:ix.
58. *Verzeichnis über Künstler-Instrumente: Ausgabe 204* (Biebrich: Heckel, c.1907):7.
59. Moore 1992:37. An example is reported to be at the Abbey House Museum in Kirkstall, Leeds.
60. John B. Taylor Instrument Collection, Williamstown, MA; typescript catalogue received by Lyndesay G. Langwill on 29 April 1975; Waterhouse archive.
61. Moore 1992:37.
62. Vonk 2007:101.
63. Ibid. 101.
64. Ring 2001:14–15.
65. Vonk 2007:102.
66. Loewe 2004:82–3.
67. Ter Voert 1992; Müller 1995; Rüdiger 1999.

Epilogue

1. Backus 1977:238–9.

Bibliography

Writings about the bassoon: Encyclopedic sources

The universe of the bassoon and its makers, players, and repertory is accessible in rich detail through certain reference works of broad scope. William Waterhouse, *The New Langwill Index* (1993), contains short articles about hundreds of bassoon makers up to about World War II, including further bibliographical references. Hundreds of surviving bassoons by major makers up until the mid-nineenth century are catalogued in Phillip T. Young, *4900 Historical Woodwind Instruments* (1993). Information includes external measurements, number of keys, and locations of specimens. Werr 2011 offers illustrations and similar data for 75 selected bassoons, dating from c.1700 to c.1945. Among the most detailed catalogues of bassoons in museum collections are those of Linz and Nuremberg, cited below as Young 1997 and Kirnbauer 1993. Detailed catalogues of private bassoon collections include Langeveld 1992 (de Wit collection) and Waterhouse 1983. Many of the bassoons discussed in this book are pictured in the searchable database of the Musical Instrument Museum Online: http://www.mimo-db.en/MIMO/Infodoc/

Bodo Koenigsbeck's *Bassoon Bibliography* (1994) embraces solo and chamber works for bassoon up to the date of publication, naming both modern editions and, in many instances, original manuscript or printed sources. One significant category absent from Koenigsbeck is arias with obligato bassoon(s), a repertory surveyed in Stockigt 2008; an expanded online version is cited below. Daniel G. Lipori, *A Researcher's Guide to the Bassoon* (2002), lists several annotated bibliographies covering narrow segments of the bassoon's repertory. Kilbey 2002 described all the dulcians then known to survive, and gave extensive information on makers, players, and repertory. A long-lived web site maintained by Hans Mons contains many images of dulcians and early bassoons: http://www.dulcians.org

Hodges 1980 gives biographical sketches of more than 800 bassoonists born before 1825. Both *NGDMM 2* and *MGG 2* contain much information on individual composers, makers, and players of interest to bassoonists. I have attempted in my text to provide the spellings and forenames that will make consultation easy. Beginning in the 1970s, the activities of living bassoonists are covered in publications of the various double-reed associations named in chapter 8.

There are times when a reader wants opinion and selectivity, rather than universal coverage. William Waterhouse's *Bassoon* (2003) contains 'Recommended Repertoire' (pp. 231–42) and 'Recommended Pedagogical Material' (pp. 242–3), among much other valuable information and advice.

Works cited

Omitted from this listing are a small number of works that are short or ephemeral, sometimes lacking in title or author. These include web sites, trade catalogues, exhibition catalogues, letters, and short items from periodicals. Full citations are given in the endnotes.

Adlung, Jacob (1758). *Anleitung zu der musicalischen Gelartheit.* Erfurt: Jungnicol.

Ahrens, Christian (2009). *'Zu Gotha ist eine gute Kapelle ...'. Aus dem Innenleben einer thüringischen Hofkapelle des 18. Jahrhunderts.* Stuttgart: Franz Steiner.

Aksdal, Bjørn (1982). *Med Piver og Basuner, Skalmeye og Fiol.* Trondheim: Tapir.

Albrecht, Theodore (1999). 'E. C. Lewy and Beethoven's Ninth Symphony Premiere', *The Horn Call* 29/3 (May):27–33.

—— (2006). 'Beethoven's Brass Players', *HBSJ* 18 (2006):47–72.

—— (2008). 'Valentin Czejka im Theater an der Wien', *Wiener Oboe Journal* 40 (December):12–15.

Alexander, Meyrick (1993). 'Le Basson en France aujourd'hui', *DRN* 24 (August):12–16.

Allard, Maurice, and Karl Öhlberger (1984). 'Outlines of Bassoon Study at the Conservatoire National Supérieur de Musique, Paris, and the Hochschule für Musik, Vienna', *JIDRS* 12:35–9.

Almanach musicale (1781).

Almenräder, Carl (1823). *Abhandlung über die Verbesserung des Fagotts.* Mainz: Schott. Dated by Waterhouse.

—— (1837). 'Bemerkungen über Blasinstrumente mit Tonlöchern', *Cäcilia* 19:77–87. Signed November 1835.

—— (1843). *Die Kunst des Fagottblasens oder Vollständige theoretisch praktische Fagottschule.* Mainz: Schott. Dated by Ventzke/Waterhouse.

Alta Musica: Eine Publikation der Gesellschaft zur Erforschung und Förderung der Blasmusik. (1976–present). Tutzing: Schneider.

Altenburg, Wilhelm (1899). 'Zur Geschichte und Statistik des Heckel-Fagotts', *ZfI* 19/12:340–41.

Ambrogio degli Albonesi, Theseo (1539). *Introductio in Chaldaicam linguam, Syriacam atque Armeniacam at decem alias linguas.* Pavia: Simoneta.

Angerhöfer, Gunther (1990). 'Das Contrafagott: Seine Entwicklung und seine Verwendung im Orchester bis 1800'. *Oboe Klarinette Fagott* 5/1:43–56.

Ashman, Gordon (1998). 'West Gallery Music', *DRN* 43 (Summer):9–10.

Atanasov, Svetoslav (2006). 'The Austrian School of Bassoon Practice and Pedagogy', *DR* 29/4:77–82.

Baade, Colleen Ruth (2001). 'Music and Music-Making in Female Monasteries in Seventeenth-Century Castile'. PhD dissertation, Duke University.

Backus, John. (1977). *The Acoustical Foundations of Music,* second edition. New York: Norton.

Bärmann, Carl (1820). Über die Natur und Eigentümlichkeit des Fagotts', *AmZ* 22:601–7.

Bailleux (1775). Jacques-Martin Hotteterre le romain. *Méthode pour apprendre à jouer en très peu de temps de la flute traversière ... augmentée ... des tablatures de la clarinette et du basson. Réédition de Bailleux.* Paris, c.1775. *R* Lescat and Saint-Arroman 1999:42.

Baines, Anthony (1948a). 'Some Aspects of English Orchestral Playing', *London Musical Digest* 8:189–93.

—— (1948b). 'James Talbot's Manuscript (Christ Church Library Music Ms 1187)', *GSJ* 1: 9–26.

—— (1950). 'Fifteenth–century Instruments in Tinctoris's De Inventione et Usu Musicae', *GSJ* 3:19–25.

—— (1951). 'Two Cassel Inventories', *GSJ* 4:30–38.

—— (1977). *Woodwind Instruments and their History,* third edition. New York: Dover.

—— (1984). 'Shawm', *NGDMI* 3:364–71.

Baker, Geoffrey (2004). 'Music at Corpus Christi in Colonial Cuzco', *EM* (August):355–80.

Balthasar, S. L. (2001). 'Mayr, Simon', *NGDMM* 16:178–83.

Bartenstein, Hans (1974). *Hector Berlioz' Instrumentationskunst und ihre geschichtliche Grundlagen,* second edition. Baden-Baden: Koerner.

Bartholomäus, Helge (1992). *Das Fagottenensemble: Kleines Handbuch für Musikpraxis*. Berlin: Werner Feja.

—— (1999). ' "Victor, fang mit kleinen Sachen an!": Der Fagottist und Komponist Victor Bruns wurde 87', *Oboe Klarinette Fagott, Schorndorf* 6/4:186–93.

Bashford, Christina (2001). 'Cambert, Robert', *NGDMM 2* 4:855–8.

Bate, Philip (1969). *The Flute: A Study of its History, Development and Construction*. London: Benn.

Bate, Philip, and Ludwig Böhm (2001). 'Theobald Boehm', *NGDMM 2* 3:777–8.

Bate, Philip, and Jerry Voorhees (2001). 'Keywork', *NGDMM 2* 13:352–6.

Bate, Philip, and Wally Horwood (2001). 'Sax', *NGDMM 2* 22:346–8.

Beebe, Jon (2009). 'Rays of Light: Conversations with Ray Pizzi', *DR* 32/3:91–7.

Béhague, Gerard (2001a). 'Argentina: I. Art Music', *NGDMM 2* 1:873–5.

—— (2001b). 'Colombia, Republic of: I, Art Music', *NGDMM 2* 4:134–6.

Berdahl, Susan (1986). 'The First Hundred years of the Boehm Flute in the United States, 1845–1945'. Ph.D dissertation, University of Minnesota.

Bélis, Annie (2001). 'Aulos', *NGDMM 2* 2:178–84.

Benoit, Marcelle (1971a). *Musiques de cour: Chapelle, chamber, écurie, 1661–1733*. Paris: Picard.

—— (1971b). *Versailles et les musiciens du roi, 1661–1733*. Paris: Picard.

—— (1992), *Dictionnaire de la musique en France aux XVIIe et XVIIIe siècles*. Paris: Fayard.

Berlioz, Hector (1844). *Voyage musical en Allemagne et en Italie*. Paris: Labitte.

—— (1969). *Memoirs of Hector Berlioz*, ed. David Cairns. New York: Knopf. First published 1870.

—— (2009). *Critique musicale 1823–1863*, 6. Paris: Buchet-Castel.

Bermúdez, Egberto (1999). 'The Ministriles Tradition in Latin America. Part One: South America. 1. The Cases of Santafé (Colombia) and La Plata (Bolivia) in the Seventeenth Century', *HBSJ* 11:149–62.

Bernardini, Alfredo (1989). 'Woodwind Makers in Venice, 1790–1900', *JAMIS* 15:52–73.

Berr, Frédéric (1836). *Méthode complète de basson*. Paris: J. Meissonier. *R* Saint–Arroman 2005:ii:7–128.

Bertement, Philippe (1981). 'Quinze "Buffet" pour un congrès', *Le Basson* 7 (March):4.

Béthisy, Jean-Laurent de (1754). *Exposition de la Musique*. Paris: Lambert. *R* (excerpt) Lescat and Saint-Arroman 1999:25.

Bhosys, Waldemar (1949). 'The Reed Problem', *Woodwind Magazine* 1/3 (January):7–8.

Biggers, Cornelia Anderson (1977). *Contra-Bassoon: A Guide to Performance*. Bryn Mawr, Pennsylvania: Elkan-Vogel.

Birnstingl, Roger (1981). 'Ce qu'ils en pensent', *Le basson* 7 (March):11–12.

Birsak, Kurt (2007). 'Contrabassoon in BBB flat', in Falletti 2007:165.

Bizzi, Guido, and Lorenzo Girodo, editors (1991). *La Collezione di strumenti musicali del Museo Teatrale alla Scala*. Milan: Il Laboratorio.

Blaikley, D. J., Anthony Baines, and William Waterhouse (2001). 'Sarrusophone', *NGDMM 2* 22:296–8.

Blomhert, Bastiaan (1996). 'The Harmonie Version of Beethoven's Seventh Symphony', in Wolfgang Suppan, ed., *Kongressbericht Abony/Ungarn 1994. Alta Musica* 18:91–102.

Boehm, Theobald (1847). *Über den Flötenbau und die neusten Verbesserungen desselben*. Mainz: Schott.

—— (1922). *The Flute and Flute–Playing in Acoustical, Technical, and Artistic Aspects*, second English edition by Dayton C. Miller. Cleveland: self-published. Originally published 1871.

Bonomo, Gabriele (1992). 'Le *Compositioni musicali fatte per sonare col fagotto solo* (1645) di Giovanni Antonio Bertoli', in R. Cafiero et al., eds., *Liuteria e musica strumentale a Brescia tra cinque e seicento*. Brescia: Fondazione Civiltà Bresciana, 91–161.

Bonta, Stephen (1989). 'L'impiego di instrumenti nella musica sacra in Italia (1560)–1700', in A. Colzani et al., eds., *Tradizione e stile*. Como: A.M.I.S., 9–28.

[Borjon de Scellery, Pierre] (1672). *Traité de la musette*. Lyons: Girin and Rivière.

Borràs i Roca, Josep (2001). 'Constructors d'instruments de vent-fusta a Barcelona', *Revista Catalana de Musicologia* 1:93–156.

—— (2008). 'El baixó a la peninsula ibèrica'. Doctoral thesis, Barcelona.

Borràs, Josep, and Antonio Ezquerro (1999). 'Chirimías en Catalayud', *Revista de Musicología* 22/2:1–74.

Botwinick, Sara (2005). 'Fear not the Zippel Fagottist! A Tale of Avoidance and Prejudice', *Bach Notes: Newsletter of the American Bach Society* (Fall 2005/4):8–9.

Bouterse, Jan (1997). 'The Selhof Auction (1759)', *FoMRHI Quarterly* 89 (October):23–6.

—— (2000). 'Communication', *JAMIS* 26:243–50. On the Haka invoice of 1685.

—— (2005). *Dutch Woodwind Instruments and their Makers, 1660–1760*. Utrecht: KVNM. Book and CD–ROM.

Bowles, Edmund (2001). 'Festival 2: Court Festivals of State, c.1350–c.1800', *NGDMM 2* 8:734–5.

Boydell, Barra (1982). *The Crumhorn and other Renaissance Windcap Instruments*. Buren: Frits Knuf.

—— (2001). 'Cromorne', *NGDMM 2* 6:717.

Brindley, Giles (1968). 'The Logical Bassoon', *GSJ* 21:152–61.

Brixel, Eugen (1996). 'Zur Frage des Blasorchester-Stimmung im k.(u.)k, Militärmusikwesen Österreich-Ungarns', in W. Suppan, ed., *Kongressbericht Abony/Ungarn 1994. Alta Musica* 18:127–48.

Brook, Barry S., et al. (2001). 'Gossec, François–Joseph', *NGDMM 2* 10:186–90.

Brossard, Sebastian de (1703). *Dictionnaire de musique*. Paris: Ballard; R Geneva: Minkoff, 1992.

Brown, Edgar (1998). 'Another Look at the Bassoon', *DRN* 42:8–10.

Brown, Howard Mayer (1973). *Sixteenth-Century Instrumentation: The Music for the Florentine Intermedii*. [Rome]: American Institute of Musicology.

—— (1975). 'A Cook's Tour of Ferrara in 1529', *Rivista italiana di musica* 10:216–41.

Bukoff, Ronald N. (1985). 'Boismortier, Corrette, and Le Phénix: Music for the French Baroque bassoon', *JIDRS* 13:48–56.

Bula, Karol (1976). 'Blasinstrumente in der polnischen Musikpraxis der ersten Hälfte des 18. Jahrhunderts', *Die Blasinstrumente und ihre Verwendung*. Konferenzbericht der 4. Wissenschaftlichen Arbeitstagung Blankenburg/Harz, 26–32.

Bulling, Burchard (1989). *Fagott-Bibliographie*. Wilhelshaven: Florian Noetzel.

Burgess, Geoffrey, and Bruce Haynes (2004). *The Oboe*. New Haven and London: Yale University Press.

Burgess, Geoffrey (2012). 'New Triebert Discoveries', GSJ 65:(forthcoming).

Burney, Charles (1771). The Present State of Music in France and Italy. London: Becket.

—— (1785). *An Account of the Musical Performances . . . in Commemoration of Handel*. London: Payne and Robinson.

Burton, James Lee (1975). 'Bassoon Bore Dimensions'. DMA dissertation, Eastman School of Music of the University of Rochester.

Bushell, Garvin (1988). *Jazz from the Beginning*. New York: Da Capo Press.

Camden Archie (1982). *Blow by Blow: The Memories of a Musical Rogue and Vagabond*. London: Thames.

Cardoze, Nicolas (1999). 'Le Sarrusophone, un instrument moderne', *Larigot* 14 (August). (unpaginated)

Carreras, Francesco (2008). 'The Identity of Ioannes Maria Anciuti finally Disclosed', *Galpin Society Newsletter* (October):4.

Carroll, Paul (1998). *Baroque Woodwind Instruments: A Guide to their History, Repertoire and Basic Technique*. Aldershot: Ashgate.

Carry, François (1978). 'Le Naissance d'un basson', *Le Basson* 4 (March):19.

—— (1982). 'Ils nous ont quittés: Robert Carrée', *Le Basson* 8 (March): 17.

Carse, Adam (1939). *Musical Wind Instruments*. London: Macmillan. R New York: Da Capo.

—— (1948). *The Orchestra from Beethoven to Berlioz*. Cambridge: CUP.

Carter, Stewart (2001). 'The Gütter Family: Wind Instrument Makers and Dealers to the Moravian Brethren in America', *JAMIS* 27:48–83.

Castagna, Paulo (1999). 'The Use of Music by the Jesuits in the Conversion of the Indigenous Peoples of Brazil', in John W. O'Malley et al., eds., *The Jesuits: Cultures, Sciences, and the Arts, 1540–1773*. Toronto: University of Toronto Press, 641–58.

Castil-Blaze, François Henri Joseph (1825). *Dictionnaire de musique moderne*, second edition. Paris: Magasin de musique de la lyre moderne. First published 1821; R (excerpt) in Saint-Arroman 2005, 1:163–6.

Cavicchi, Camilla (2002). 'Afranio, phagotista virtuoso', *Ferrara: Voce di una cittá* (17 December):43–6.

Červenka, František (1992). 'Fagottkonzerte tschechischer Meister des 18. Jahrhunderts', in Sallagar and Nagy 1992:21–7.

Cessac, Catherine (1988). *Marc-Antoine Charpentier*. Portland, Oregon: Amadeus.

Chantauraud, Alain (1995). 'Le Basson: "Ni fleurs ni couronnes"', *JIDRS* 23:83–4; transl. David Rachor, ibid., 85–6.

Cheape, Hugh (2008). *Bagpipes: A National Collection of a National Instrument*. Edinburgh: National Museums Scotland.

Christlieb, Don (1945). *Notes on the Bassoon Reed: Machinery, Measurement, Analysis*. Los Angeles: self–published.

—— (1996). *Recollections of a First-Chair Bassoonist*. Los Angeles: self-published.

Chouquet, Gustave (1875). *La Musée du Conservatoire national de musique: Catalogue raisonné de cette collection*. Paris: Didot.

Chybiński, Adolf (1949). *Słownik muzkow dawnej Polskido roku 1800*. Krakow: Polskie wydawnictwo muzyczne.

Čížek, Bohuslav (1992). 'Václav František Červený und seine Musikinstrumente im Prager Nationalmuseum', *MI* 4/11 (November):73–8.

Clarke, Christopher (1999). 'Le Pianoforte en France 1780–1820', *MIM* 11:98–126.

Cocks, William A. (1959). 'The Phagotum: An Attempt at Reconstruction', *GSJ* 12:57–9.

Cokken, Jean François Barthélemy (c.1860). *Méthode de basson: nouvelle édition de la méthode de F. Beer revue et augmentée*. Paris: Gerard.

Colas, Damien (2007). 'Halévy and his Contribution to the Evolution of the Orchestra in the Mid-Nineteenth Century', in Niels Martin Jensen and Franco Piperno., eds., *The Impact of Composers and Works on the Orchestra*, 143–84. Online publication at http://halshs.archives-ouvertes.fr/halshs-00461727/.

Collver, Michael, and Bruce Dickey (1996). *A Catalog of Music for the Cornett*. Bloomington: Indiana University Press.

Comaš, Thomaš (1990). 'Vom Kontrahorn zum Klaviatur-Kontrafagott', *Clarino* 8:4–7.

Comstock, Allan Dale (1999). 'The Bajón at Palencia, 1553–1700'. DMA dissertation, University of Memphis.

Cooper, Hugh, and Howard Toplansky (1968). *Essentials of Bassoon Technique (German System)*. Union, New Jersey: Toplansky.

Corder, Frederick (1896). *The Orchestra and How to Write for It*. London: Cocks.

Corey, Gerald (1975). 'Bassoon Viewpoint', *JIDRS* 3:28.

—— (1977). 'Remembrances of Muccetti', *TWB* 7/1:5–6.

Cotte, Roger (1979). 'Blasinstrumente bei freimaurerischen Riten', *Tibia* 79/2:315–17.

Cox, Jeffrey (2000). 'Bassonicus – Twentieth Century Concertos', *DRN* 52 (Autumn):14–15.

Cucuel, Georges (1913). *Études sur un orchestre au 18e siècle*. Paris: Fischbacher.

Cuçiureanu, Gheorge (1985). 'The Future of the Cuçiureanu System Bassoon', *DR* 8/2:26–9.

[Cugnier, Pierre] (1780). [Bassoon method] in J.-B. de Laborde, *Essai sur la musique*. Paris: Pierres, 323–43. *R* Lescat and Saint-Arroman 1999:43–67.

Curwen, Spencer (1897). 'The Old Village Musicians', *Strand Musical Magazine* 6/10 (September):137–9.

Dann, Lewis (1993). 'Back? The Buffet Was Never Away', *DRN* 24 (August):14.

Dart, Mathew (2011). 'The Baroque Bassoon: Its Design, Construction and Development'. PhD dissertation, London Metropolitan University.

David, Hans T., and Arthur Mendel, eds. (1945). *The Bach Reader: A Life of Johann Sebastian Bach in Letters and Documents*. New York: Norton.

Day, Timothy (2002). *A Century of Recorded Music*. New Haven and London: Yale University Press.

Decobert, Laurence (2001). 'Du Mont, Henry', *NGDMM* 2 7:699–702.

Del Mar, Norman (1969). *Richard Strauss: A Critical Commentary on his Life and Works*, 2. London: Barrie & Rockliff.

Dibley, Tom (2000). 'A Contrabassophone by Alfred Morton', *GSJ* 53:60–77.

Diderot, Dénis, and J. d'Alembert (1751–65). 'Basson de hautbois', in *Encyclopédie ou dictionnaire raisonné des sciences, des arts et des métiers*, 2. Paris: Le Breton. *R* in Framery and Ginguené 1788; *R* in Lescat and Saint-Arroman 1999:69–73.

Diepen, Lex van (2007). 'Recording the Bassoon for CD', in Vonk 2007:111–112.

Dietz, William (1987). 'A Conversation with Sol Schoenbach', *DR* 10/3:48–51.

Dreyfus, Laurence (1990). *Bach's Continuo Group*. Cambridge: Harvard University Press.

Duffin, Ross (2007). 'Shawm and Curtal', in Jeffrey Kite-Powell, ed., *A Performer's Guide to Renaissance Music*, second edition. Bloomington: Indiana University Press, 69–75.

Dullat, Gunter (1984). 'Vom Contrahorn über den 16füßigen Orgelbaß und den Contra–Bassophon zum Claviatur-Contrafagott', *Tibia* 9/2:99–105.

—— (1990a). *Metallblasinstrumentenbau: Entwicklungsstufen und Technologie*. Bergkirchen: Bochinsky.

—— (1990b). 'Die Holzblasinstrumentenbauer Berthold in Speyer', *Tibia* 4/90: 273–7.

—— (1990c). *Holzblasinstrumentenbau: Entwicklungsstufen und Technologien*. Celle: Moeck.

Durran, Darryl (2005). 'Gioacchino Rossini: Concerto a Fagotto Principale', *DR* 28/2:107–8.

Edwards, Constance (2010). 'Czech and Slovak Music for Bassoon and Piano in the Twentieth Century', *DR* 33/2:77–80.

Edwards, Warwick (2001). 'Sources of Instrumental Ensemble Music to 1630', *NGDMM 2* 24:1–19.

Ehrle, Thomas (1983). 'Die Instrumentation in den Symphonien von Felix Mendelssohn Bartholdy'. Dissertation, Goethe University, Frankfurt an Main.

Eifert, Otto (1982). 'Basson Camp Korea', *DR* 5/2:22.

Eisel, J. P. (1738). *Musicus Autodidaktos*. Erfurt: Funck. *R* Leipzig, 1976.

Eisen, Cliff (2001). 'Mozart: (1) Leopold Mozart', *NGDMM 2* 17:270–75.

Eliason, Robert (2001). 'Charles G. Christman, Musical Instrument Maker in Nineteenth-Century New York', *JAMIS* 27:84–119.

Emery, Walter, and Christoph Wolff (2001). 'Bach, J. S., 3. 'Arnstadt', *NGDMM 2* 2:312–13.

Eppelsheim, Jürgen (1976). 'Das Subkontrafagott', in W. Suppan and E. Brixel, eds., *Bericht über die erste internationale Fachtagung zur Erforschung der Blasmusik, Graz 1974. Alta Musica* 1:233–72.

—— (1979). 'More Facts about the "Subkontrafagott" ', *GSJ* 32:104–14.

—— (1986). 'Garsaults Notionaire (Paris 1761) als Zeugnis für den Stand des französischen Holzblasinstrumentariums um 1760', in Eitelfriedrich Thom, ed., *Bericht über das sechste Symposium zu Fragen des Musikinstrumentenbaus in Michaelstein*. Michaelstein/Blankenburg: [Institut für Aufführungspraxis], 56–77.

—— (1995). 'Tradition und Veränderung: Beobachtungen an den Fagottparteien von Joseph Haydn's Schöpfung', in B. Edelmann and M. H. Schmid, eds., *Das Altes im Neuen* [Festschrift Theodore Göllner]. Tutzing: Schneider, 257–67.

Euting, Ernst (1899). 'Zur Geschichte der Blasinstrumente im 16. und 17. Jahrhundert', dissertation: Friedrich-Wilhelms-Universität, Berlin.

Ewell, Terry (1992). 'A Bassoonist's Expansions upon Marcel Tabuteau's "Drive" ', *JIDRS* 20:27–30.

—— (2005). 'Interview with Joanne Cameron of the Bent Leather Band', *DR* 28/2:115–20.

——, ed. (2009). *Celebrating Double Reeds: A Festschrift for William Waterhouse and Philip Bate*. Baltimore: IDRS.

Fahrbach, Joseph (1840). *Neueste Wiener Fagottschule*. Vienna: Diabelli.

Falletti, Franco, et al. (2007). *Marvels of Sound and Beauty: Italian Baroque Musical Instruments*. Milan: Giunti.

Farmer, Judith (2001). 'Karl Öhlberger (1912–2001)', *DR* 24/4:35.

Fauquet, Joël-Marie (2003). *Dictionnaire de la musique en France au XIXe siècle*. Paris: Fayard.

Federhofer, Helmut, and Steven Saunders (2001). 'Sansoni', *NGDMM 2* 22:249–50.

Feicht, Hieronim (1966). ' "Liber Chamorum" jako źródło do historii muzyki polskiej', *Muzyka* 2:84–93.

Fertonani, Cesare (1998). *La Musica strumentale di Antonio Vivaldi*. Florence: Olschki.

Fétis, François Joseph (1856). 'Fabrication des Instruments de Musique', *Exposition universelle, 1855: Rapports du jury mixte international*. Paris: Imprimerie impériale.

Finkelman, Michael (2001a). 'Hautbois d'église', *NGDMM 2* 11:151–2.

—— (2001b). 'Oboe III (4) (iv): English horn', *NGDMM 2* 18:282–4.

Finscher, Ludwig (1997). 'The Old in the New', in Gottfried Böhm et al., eds., *Canto d'amore: Classicism in Modern Art and Music 1913–1935*. Basel: Paul Sacher Stiftung, 63–6.

Fiske, Roger, and Richard G. King (2001). 'Galliard, John Ernest', *NGDMM 2* 10:451–3.

Fleming, Hans Friedrich von (1726). *Der vollkommene Teutsche Soldat*. Leipzig.

Fletcher, Kristine Klopfenstein (1998). *The Paris Conservatoire and the Contest Solos for Bassoon*. Bloomington: Indiana University Press.

Forsyth, Cecil (1914). *Orchestration*. London: Macmillan.

Foster, Charles (2005). 'Tinctoris's Imperfect Dulcina Perfected – the Mary Rose Still Shawm', *GSJ* 58:46–50.

Florence (1980). *Antichi strumenti: Dalla racolta dei Medici et dei Lorena*. Florence: Palazzo Pitti.

Framery, N. E., and P.-L. Ginguené (1788). 'Basson de hautbois ou simplement Basson', *Encyclopédie méthodique: Musique*. Paris: Pankoucke. *R* Lescat and Saint-Arroman 1999: 69–74. Reprints portions of Diderot and d'Alembert, *Encyclopédie des arts et métiers* (Paris, 1751–80).

Francoeur, Louis-Joseph (c.1772). *Diapason général de tous les instrumens à vent*. Paris: Le Marchand. *R* (bassoon portion) in Lescat and Saint-Arroman 1999:29–40.

Frandsen, Mary E. (2006). *Crossing Confessional Boundaries: The Patronage of Italian Sacred Music in Seventeenth-Century Dresden*. Oxford: OUP.

Fröhlich, Joseph (1810/11). *'Fagott-schule', Vollständige theoretisch-praktische Musiklehre für alle bei dem Orchestergebräuchliche Instrumente.* Bonn: Simrock.

—— (1829). *Systematischer Unterricht in den vorzüglichsten orchester Instrumenten.* Würzburg: Franz Bauer.

Fucci, Monica (1992). *El fagot en la Argentina.* Buenos Aires: Ediciones Dafne.

Fuhrmann, Martin Heinrich (1706). *Musicalischer-Trichter.* Frankfurt. Excerpt transl. in Snyder 1987.

Fusenig, Thomas, ed. (2006). *Suermondt-Ludwig-Museum Aachen: Bestandkatalog der Gemäldegalerie.* N.p: Hirmer-Verlag.

Galle, Philipp (c.1590). *Encomium musices.* Antwerp: self-published.

Gallino, Nicola (1993). 'Lo «Scuolaro» Rossini e la musica strumentale al liceo di Bologna: Nuovi documenti', *Bollettino del «Centro Rossiniano di Studi* 33/1–3:5–41.

Galpin, Francis (1940–41). 'The Romance of the Phagotum', *Proceedings of the Musical Association* 67:57–72.

Garsault, F. A. P. de (1761). *Notionaire ou mémorial raisonné.* Paris: Desprez.

Gärtner, Heinz, and Reinhard G. Pauly (1994). *John Christian Bach: Mozart's Friend and Mentor.* N. p.: Hal Leonard.

Gerber, Ernst Ludwig (1812–14). *Neues historisch-biographisches Lexikon der Tonkünstler* (4 vols.). Leipzig: Kühnel. *R* Graz: Olms, 1966–77.

Gerhard, Anselm, (2001). 'Spontini, Gaspare', *NGDMM* 24:212–19.

Gesualdo, Vicente (1961). *Historia de la música en la Argentina.* Buenos Aires: Editorial Beta S. R. L.

Gétreau, Florence (1996). *Aux Origines du Musée de la Musique: Les Collections du Conservatoire de Paris, 1793–1993.* Paris: Klincksieck.

Giannini, Tula (1987). 'A Letter from Louis Rousselet, 18th-Century French Oboist at the Royal Opera in England', *NAMIS* 16/2 (June):10–11.

—— (1993). 'Jacques Hotterre le Romain and his Father, Martin', *EM* 21:377–95.

—— (1998). 'A French Dynasty of Master Woodwind Makers Revealed, Bizey, Prudent and Porthaux, Their Workshop in Paris, rue Dauphine, St. André des Arts, ca. 1745–1812: New Archival Documents', *NAMIS* (Winter):xiii.

Gilbert, Adam Knight (2005). 'The Improvising Alta Capella, ca. 1500: Paradigms and Procedures', *BJHM* 29:109–23.

—— (2008). 'Quattrocento Consorts', *EM* 36/4:626–8.

Gillessen, Klaus (1998). 'Friedrich Kulow (1853–1939), a Less Known Maker of Woodwinds'. *JIDRS* 26:109–12.

Girard, Alain (2001) 'Les Hautbois d'église et leur enigma I.IR', *Glareana* 2:67–129.

Girdlestone, Cuthbert. *Jean Philippe Rameau: His Life and Works*, rev. ed. New York: Dover, 1969.

Giron, Caroline (2006). 'Une collection perdue: les instruments de l'ospedale des Mendicanti, à Venise', *MII* 8:105–21.

Gjerdingen, Robert (2007). *Music in the Galant Style.* Oxford and New York: OUP.

Gontershausen, Heinrich Welcker von (1855). *Neu eröffnetes Magazin musikalischer Tonwerkezeuge.* Frankfurt am Main: self-published.

Gray, W. F. (1933). 'The Musical Society of Edinburgh and St Cecilia's Hall', *Book of the Old Edinburgh Club* 19:189–246.

Gregoir, E. (1862). *Galerie biographique des Artistes Musiciens Belges du XVIII et XIXe Siècle.* Brussels: Schott.

Griswold, Harold E. (1979). 'Etienne Ozi (1754–1813): Bassoonist, Teacher, and Composer', D.M.A. dissertation, Peabody Institute of Johns Hopkins University.

—— (1985). 'Fundamentals of Bassoon Playing as Described in Late Eighteenth-Century Tutors', *JIDRS* 13:13–42.

—— (1988). 'Changes in the Tonal Character of the Eighteenth-Century French Bassoon', *JAMIS* 14:114–25.

—— (1996). 'Mozart's "Good Wood-Biter": Georg Wenzel Ritter (1748–1808)', *GSJ* 49:103–12.

—— (2001). 'Ozi, Etienne', *NGDMM* 2 18:835–6.

Grossman, Arthur (1981). 'Ce qu'ils en pensent', *Le basson* 7 (March):12.

Habla, Bernard (1990). *Besetzung und Instrumentation des Blasorchesters seit der Erfindung der Ventile für Blechblasinstrumente.* Tutzing: Schneider.

—— (1998). 'Doppelrohrblattinstrumente in der deutschen und österreichischen Blasmusik vom 19. Jahrhundert bis zum Zweiten Weltkrieg'. *Rohrblatt* 13/4:154–63.

Hähnchen, Dieter (2008). 'Die neue Fagottbassröhre', *Das Orchester* 4 (April):36–9.

Halfpenny, Eric (1957). 'The Evolution of the Bassoon in England, 1750–1800', *GSJ* 10:30–39.

Haine, Malou (1995). 'Participation des facteurs d'instruments de musique aux expositions nationales et universelles du 19e siècle', *MII* 1:76–83.

—— and Ignace de Keyser (1980). *Catalogue des instruments Sax au Musée instrumental de Bruxelles.* Brussels: Musée instrumental.

Hansche, Michael (2000). 'Der Fagottist Mordechai Rechtman, Tel Aviv', *Rohrblatt* 15/3:120–1.

Haynes, Bruce (1997). 'New Light on Some French Relatives of the Hautboy in the 17th and Early 18th Centuries: The Cromorne, Hautbois de Poitou and Chalumeau Simple', in Nikolaus Delius., ed., *Sine musica nulla vita: Festschrift Hermann Moeck.* Celle: Moeck, 257–70.

—— (2001a). 'Pitch, I: Western Pitch Standards', *NGDMM 2* 19:793–802.

—— (2001b). *The Eloquent Oboe.* Oxford: OUP.

—— (2007). *The End of Early Music.* Oxford: OUP.

Heckel, Wilhelm (1899). *Der Fagott.* Biebrich: self-published.

Heckel, Wilhelm (1931). *Der Fagott. R* of Heckel 1899, extensively revised by Wilhelm Hermann Heckel. Leipzig: Merseburger.

Hedlund, H. Jean (1958). 'Ensemble Music for Small Bassoons', *GSJ* 11:78–84.

Heller, Karl (1997). *Antonio Vivaldi: The Red Priest of Venice.* Portland, OR: Amadeus.

Hellyer, Roger (1973). ' "Harmoniemusik": Music for Small Wind Band in the Late Eighteenth and Ninteenth Centuries'. Dissertation, Oxford University.

—— (1975). 'Some Documents Relating to Viennese Wind-Instrument Purchases, 1779–1837', *GSJ* 28:50–59.

—— (1985). 'The Wind Ensembles of the Esterházy Princes, 1761–1813', *The Haydn Yearbook* 15:5–192.

—— (2001). 'Harmoniemusik', *NGDMM 2* 10:856–8.

Herbert, Trevor (2006). *The Trombone.* New Haven and London: Yale University Press.

Herman, František (1992). 'Die Prager Fagottschule', in Sallagar and Nagy (1992):95–8.

Hess, Ernst (1957). 'Ist das Fagottkonzert KV Anhang 230a von Mozart?', *Mozart Jahrbuch*, 223–32.

Hess, Willy (1981). 'Das Kontrafagott im Schaffen Beethovens', *Beethoven: Studien zu seinem Werk.* Winterthur: Amadeus-Verlag.

Heyde, Herbert (1972). 'Carl Almenräders Verdienst um das Fagott', *BzMw* 14:225–30.

—— (1977). 'Die Instrumentenbauer Jehring (Adorf) und Heckel (Adorf, Dresden, Biebrich)', *BzMw* 17/2:121–4.

—— (1987a). 'Der Holzblasinstrumentenbau in Leipzig in der 2. Hälfte des 18. Jahrhunderts', *Tibia* 3/87:481–6.

—— (1987b). 'Contrabassoons in the 17th and Early 18th Century', *GSJ* 40:24–36.

—— (1993). 'Die Werkstatt von Augustin Grenser d. Ä. und Heinrich Grenser in Dresden', *Tibia* 4/93: 593–602.

—— (2007a). 'Entrepreneurship in Pre-Industrial Instrument Making', *Musikalische Aufführungspraxis in nationalen Dialogen des 16. Jahrhunderts, teil 2: Musikinsrumentenbauzentren im 16. Jahrhundert.* Michaelstein and Augsburg: Stiftung Kloster Michaelstein, 25–63.

—— (2007b). 'Zoomorphic and Theatrical Musical Instruments in the Late Italian Renaissance and Baroque Eras', in Falletti 2007:80–93.

Hicks, Anthony (2001). 'Handel: Works: Music for Wind Ensembles', *NGDMM 2* 10:801.

Hilkenbach, Dieter (1989). 'Le modèle RC – le nouveau basson Buffet-Crampon – das "andere" Fagott', *Oboe, Fagott* 18 (December):13–16.

Hodges, Woodrow Joe (1980). 'A Biographical Dictionary of Bassoonists Born Before 1825', PhD dissertation, University of Iowa.

Hofer, Achim (1992a). *Blasmusikforschung: Eine kritische Einführung.* Darmstadt: Wissenschaftliche Buchgesellschaft.

—— (1992b). ' ". . . ich dien auf beede recht in Krieg und Freidens Zeit": Zu den Märschen des 18. Jahrhunderts unter besonderer Berücksichtigung ihrer Besetzung'. *Tibia* 17/3:182–91.

—— (2006). 'Harmoniemusik-Forschung: Aktuell dituert – Kritisch unterfragt', in Bernhard Schrammek, ed., *Zur Geschichte und Aufführungspraxis der Harmoniemusik.* Michaelstein: Institut für Aufführungspraxis, 26–31.

Holman, Peter (2005). 'From Violin Band to Orchestra', in Wainwright and Holman 2005:241–58.

Holman, Peter, and Todd Gilman (2001). 'Arne, Thomas Augustine', *NGDMM 2* 2:36–46.

Hough, James D. (1998). 'The Evolution of Double Reed Playing in Spain', *DR* 21/3:123–9.

—— (1999). 'My Experience in the Far East', *DR* 22/1:75–8.

Howey, Henry (1991). 'The Lives of Hoftrompeter and Stadtpfeiffer as Portrayed in Three Novels of Daniel Speer', *HBSJ* 3:65–78.

Hrabussay, Zoltán (1961). 'Výroba a Výrobcovia hudobných nástrojov v Bratislave', *Hudobnovdné stúdie v SAV*, 197–238.

Huber, Alfons (1999). 'Vom Fagott im Klavier', in Eszter Fontana, ed., *Festschrift Rainer Weber*. Leipzig, Universität Leipzig, 85–90.

Hubmann, Klaus (1990). 'Untersuchungen zur Authentizität der Mozartschen Fagottsonate KV 292 (196c)', *Oboe Klarinette Fagott; Schorndorf* 5/2:99–106.

—— (1992). 'Wolfgang Freiherr von Dürniz und seine Kompositionen für Fagott', in Sallagar and Nagy (1992):29–37.

—— (1994). 'Beiträge zur Frühgeschichte des Fagotts in Österreich', in Monika Lustig, ed., *Flöten, Oboen und Fagotte des 17. und 18. Jahrhunderts*. Michaelstein: Institut für Aufführungspraxis, 47–51.

—— (2002). 'Fagott', in Rudolf Flotzinger, ed., *Österreichisches Musiklexikon*. Vienna: Österreichischen Akademie der Wissenschaften, 1:412–15.

—— (2011). 'Hoch gestimmte Fagotte (Tenorfagotte) in der Musik vom späten 16. bis zum späten 18. Jahrhundert', in Christian Ahrens and Gregor Klinke, eds., *Flöte, Oboe, Klarinette und Fagott Holzblasinstrumente bis zum Ende des 18. Jahrhunderts*. Munich and Salzburg: Katzbichler, 71–84.

Humblot, Émile (1909). *François Devienne (1759–1803)*. Saint-Dizier: Brulliard. R Geneva: Minkoff, 1984.

Hutchings, Arthur (1961). *The Baroque Concerto*. London: Faber & Faber.

Ibisch, Larry (1978). 'A French Bassoonist in the United States, Auguste Mesnard', *DR* 1/2:5–6.

Irving, D. R. M. (2010). *Colonial Counterpoint: Music in Early Modern Manila*. Oxford: OUP.

Jackson, Myles W. (2006). *Harmonious Triads: Physicists, Musicians, and Instrument Makers in Nineteenth–Century Germany*. Cambridge and London: MIT Press.

James, Cecil (1990). 'Life as a "Buffet" Player', *DRN* 11:4–5.

—— (1999). 'Life with the French Bassoon', *DRN* 48:28. First published 1987.

Jameson, James A. (1933). 'Social Assemblies of the Eighteenth Century', *Book of the Old Edinburgh Club* 19:48–9.

Jancourt, Eugène (1847). *Méthode théorique et pratique pour le basson en 3 parties*. Paris: Richault. R Saint-Arroman 2005:iv.

—— (1876). *Étude du basson perfectionné*, op. 58. Paris: Evette & Schaeffer.

—— (1885). 'Perfectionnements apportés au basson', op. 98. Paris: Evette & Schaeffer (unpaginated).

Jansen, Will (1978). *The Bassoon*, five vols. Buren: Knuf.

Jeltsch, Jean (1997). ' "Prudent à Paris": vie et carrière d'un maître faiseur d'instruments à vent', *MII* 3:129–52.

Jensen, Werner (1992). 'Dulcianen og fagotten i Danmark i 1600–og 1700–tallet', *Musa–Årbog*, 182–209. Arhus: MUSA-Print.

Jirka, Rudolf R. (2003). 'Die Georg-Rieger-GmbH: Präzisionsmaschinen für den Doppelrohrbau aus dem Nordschwarzwald', *Rohrblatt, Schorndorf* 18/3:144–7.

Johnson, David (1972). *Music and Society in Lowland Scotland in the Eighteenth Century*. Oxford: OUP.

Jolivet, Michel R. (1985). 'An English Translation of a Monograph on the Sarrusophone Written by Roger Leruste', *DR* 8/2:73–88.

Jones, David Wyn (2009). *The Life of Haydn*. Cambridge: CUP.

Joppig, Gunther (1981). '150 Jahre Heckelinstrumente', *Tibia* 81/2:345–50.

—— (1982). 'Musikmesse Frankfurt 1982', *Tibia* 82/2:119–23.

—— (1985). 'Zur Entwicklung des Kontrafagottes im 19. und 20. Jahrhundert', *MI* 34/11:20–24.

—— (1986). 'Gebrüder Mönnig – ein Begriff im Musikinstrumentenbau', *MI* 35/3:48–51.

—— (1987). 'Zur Entwicklung des deutschen Fagotts', in F. Hellwig, ed., *Studia organologica: Festschrift für John Henry van der Meer*. Tutzing: Schneider, 253–76.

—— (1991). 'Basson und Fagott: Vergleich am konkreten Beispiel', *MI* 11:42–4.

—— (1992). 'Václav František Červený: Leading European Inventor and Manufacturer', *HBSJ* 4:210–28.

—— (1997a). 'Auf Holz gebaut: 100 Jahre Püchner', *MI* 8:36–7.

—— (1997b). *100 Jahre Püchner*. Wiesbaden: J. Püchner.

_____ (2012) 'Zur Geschichte des Kontrafagotts', in Sebastian Werr, ed., *Tradition und Innovation im Holzblasinstrumentenbau des 19. Jahrhunderts*. Augsburg: Wißner, 225–38.

Jurgens, Madeleine (1974). *Documents du Minutier central concernant l'histoire de la musique (1600–1650)*, 2. Paris: La Documentation française.

Justi, Vicente de Paulo (1995). 'O Fagote e as valsas solo de Francisco Mignone'. Dissertaçào de Mestradto, Universidade de Sào Paulo.

Kastner, George (1836), *Traité général d'instrumentation*. Paris: Philipp. *R* (excerpt) in Saint-Arroman (2005):159–62.

—— (1848). *Manuel générale de musique militaire à l'usage des armées françaises*. Paris: Didot; *R* Geneva: Minkoff, 1973.

Keeß, Stephan Ritter von, and W. C. W. Blumenbach (1830). *Systematische Darstellung der neuesten Fortschritte in den Gewerben und Manufacturen*. Vienna: Carl Gerold.

Kelly, Thomas Forrest (2001). *First Nights: Five Musical Premieres*. New Haven and London: Yale University Press.

Kenyon de Pascual, Beryl (1984). 'A Brief Survey of the Late Spanish Bajón', *GSJ* 37, 72–9.

—— (1994). 'Ventes d'instruments à vent à Madrid au 2e moitié du 18e siècle', *Larigot* 15 (June):24–27.

—— (1995a). 'The Recorder Revival in Late Seventeenth–Century Spain', in David Lasocki, ed., *The Recorder in the Seventeenth Century. Proceedings of the International Recorder Symposium 1993*. Utrecht: STIMU, 65–74.

—— (1995b). 'The Ophecleide in Spain', *HBSJ* 7:142–8.

—— (2001). 'Pla', *NGDMM 2* 19:823–4.

Kernfeld, Barry (2002). 'Mitchell, Roscoe', *NGDJ*.

Kiefer, Thomas (1990). 'Anmerkungen zur Produktion von Sarrusophonen bei der Firma Buffet-Crampon', *Tibia* 2/90:113–20.

—— (2010). 'Tiefstimmige Doppelrohrblattinstrumente von der Harmoniemusik bis in das Blasorchester des 19. Jahrhunderts', in Wolfgang Meighörner, ed., *Wissenschaftlicher Jahrbuch der Tirolischer Landesmuseens 2010*. Innsbruck: Studien-Verlag, 47–99.

Kiefer, Thomas, and William Waterhouse (1994). 'Hochverehrter Freund! Eine Anweisung zum Fagottspiel aus dem Jahre 1823', *Tibia* 2/94:104–9.

Kilbey, Maggie (2002). *Curtal Dulcian Bajón: A History of the Precursor to the Bassoon*. St. Alban's: self-published.

Kinsky, G., and H. Halm (1955). *Das Werk Beethovens: Thematisch-bibliographisches Verzeichnis seiner sämtlichen vollendeten Kompositionen*. Munich: Henle.

Kirnbauer, Martin (1989). 'Historische Holzblasinstrumente in der Sammlung des Germanischen Nationalmuseums in Nürnberg', *Tibia* 2/89:424–9.

_____ (1993). *Verzeichnis der Europäischen Musikinstrumente im Germanischen Nationalmuseum Nürnberg*, 2: *Flöten- und Rohrblattinstrumente bis 1750: Beschreibender Katalog*. Wilhelmshaven: Noetzel.

Kleefeld, Wilhelm (1899/90). 'Das Orchester der Hamburger Oper 1678–1738', *Sammelbände der Internationalen Musik-Gesellschaft* 1:219–89.

Klimko, Ron (1979). 'The C. Kruspe Bassoon and the World's Columbia Exposition of Chicago, 1893', *JIDRS* 7: 9–16.

Klimko, Ronald J. (1983). 'The Boehm-System Bassoon and the Wilhelm Heckel Firm', *JIDRS* 11:20–2.

—— (2009). '"Verfehltes System": A History of the Adolph Sax, Cornelius Ward, and Triebert-Marzoli-Boehm Reform-System Bassoons', in Terry B. Ewell, ed., *Celebrating Double Reeds: A Festschrift for William Waterhouse and Philip Bate*. Baltimore: IDRS, 213–39.

Klitz, Brian (1971). 'A Composition for Dolzaina', *JAMS* 24:113–18.

Knebel, Konrad (1899). 'Die Mal- und Zeichenkunst in Freiberg', *Freiburger Altertumsverein: Mitteilungen* 36:7–114.

Koblitz, Wolfgang (2001). 'Wiener Fagott?', *Wiener Oboe* 9:10–11.

Koch, H. C. (1802). *Musikalisches Lexikon*, 2. Frankfurt am Main: Hermann.

—— (1807). *Kurzgefaßtes Handwörterbuch der Musik*. Leipzig: Hartknoch.

Koch, Hans Oskar (1980). 'Sonderformen der Blasinstrumente in der deutschen Musik vom späten 17. bis zur mitte des 18. Jahrhunderts'. Dissertation: Heidelberg.

Koegel, John (2001). 'Spanish and French Mission Music in Colonial North America', *Journal of the Royal Music Association*.

Köhler, Wolfgang (1987). *Die Blasinstrumente aus der 'Harmonie Universelle' des Marin Mersenne*. Celle: Moeck.

Koenigsbeck, Bodo (1994). *Bassoon Bibliography*. Monteux: Musica Rara.

Kohon, Benjamin (1932). 'A Few Notes on the Bassoon', *The Metronome* 48/7 (July):12.

Kolneder, Walter (1954). 'Fagott', *MGG* 1, 3:1717–31.

Kopp, James B. (1999). 'The Emergence of the Late-Baroque Bassoon', *DR* 22/4:73–87.

—— (2002). 'Precursors of the Basson in France before Louis XIV', *JAMIS* 28:63–117.

—— (2004). 'The Musette de Poitou in 17th-Century France', *GSJ* 57:127–45.

—— (2007). 'The Not-Quite-Harmonic Overblowing of the Bassoon', *DR* 29/2:61–75.

—— (2010). 'Juilliard's President Joseph W. Polisi Talks about the Future, the Past, and the Bassoon', *DR* 33/3:51–6.

—— (2011). 'The French Court Musette to 1672: Further Notes', *GSJ* 64:243–7.

—— (2012). ' "The Stradivari of the Bassoon" – Zur Instrumenten der Savary jeune', in Sebastian Werr, ed., *Tradition und Innovation in Holzblasinstrumente des 19. Jahrhunderts*. Augsburg: Wissner-Verlag, 199–212.

Kott, Tama I., and Olga Haldey (2005). 'Contemporary Russian Music for Bassoon: Sonatas for Solo and Accompanied Bassoon', *DR* 28/2:27–40.

—— (2008). 'Contemporary Russian Music for Bassoon, Part 2: Short Works for Solo and Accompanied Bassoon', *DR* 28/2:27–40.

—— (2009). 'Russian Music for Bassoon and Large Ensemble after World War II', *DR* 32/4:85–96.

—— (2010a). 'Russian Music for Bassoon and Large Ensemble after World War II (continued)', *DR* 33/1:66–78.

—— (2010b). 'Russian Music for Bassoon and Large Ensemble after World War II, part 3', *DR* 333/3:65–77.

Kreitner, Kenneth (1992). 'Minstrels in Spanish Churches: 1400–1600', *EM* 20:532–46.

Krieger, Irene (1991). 'Fagott–ogott! Die Tokyo-Fagottiade', *Oboe Karinette Fagott, Schorndorf* 6/1:10–14.

Kroll, Oskar (1937). 'Der Werdegang eines Holzblasinstruments', *Die Musik-Woche* 5/10 (6 March):1–3.

Krüger, Walther (1991). 'Entwicklungswege im Fagottbau', in Monika Lustig, ed., *Flöten, Oboen und Fagotte des 17. und 18. Jahrhunderts*. Michaelstein: Institut für Aufführungspraxis, 57–66.

—— (2005). 'Fagott VII. Akustische Grundlagen des Fagotts under der Oboe', *MGG* 2, Sachteil 3:299–306.

Küffner, Joseph (1828/9). *Principes élémentaires de la musique et gamme de basson*. Mainz: Schott.

Kurtzmann, Jeffrey, and Linda Maria Koldau (2002). 'Trombe, Trombe d'argento, Trombe squarciate, Tromboni, and Pifferi in Venetian Processions and Ceremonies of the Sixteenth and Seventeenth Centuries', *Journal of Seventeenth-Century Music* 8/1. Online publication at http://sscm–jscm.press.illinois.edu/v8no1.html.

Kurz, Roland (1981). 'Récital de basson (français) à Londres', *Le Basson* 7 (March):9.

Kuttner, Wolfgang (2002). 'Hommage zum 90. Geburtstag von Prof. Karl Öhlberger (30. April 2002)', *Wiener Oboe* 13:9.

La Barre, Michel de (c.1740). 'Mémoire sur les musettes', Ms Paris, Archives Nationales O1 878, no. 240. Transl. in Kopp 2004:140.

Laborde, J.-B. de (1780). *Essai sur la musique*. Paris: Pierres. Contains bassoon method by Cugnier.

La Granville, Frédéric (2009). 'La coexistence du clavecin et du piano au Conservatoire de musique de Paris de 1796 à 1802', *MIM* 11:151–61.

Landon, H. C. Robbins (1978). *Haydn: Chronicle and Works: Haydn at Esterháza 1766– 90*. Bloomington: Indiana University Press.

Landsmann, Ortrud (1989). 'The Dresden Hofkapelle during the Lifetime of Johann Sebastian Bach', *EM* 17/1 (February):17–30.

Langeveld, Erik (1992). *Tentoonstelling van Fagotten, Prenten, Boeken en Manuscripten uit de Collectie van Henk de Wit*. Amsterdam: Muziekcentrum De Ijsbreker

Langwill, Lyndesay G. (1965). *The Bassoon and Contrabassoon*. London: Ernest Benn; New York: W. W. Norton.

Lasocki, David (1983). 'Professional Recorder Players in England, 1540–1740'. Ph.D dissertation, University of Iowa.

—— (1988). 'The French Hautboy in England, 1673–1730', *EM* 16/3:339–58.

—— (2009). 'New Light on the Recorder and Flageolet in Colonial North America and the United States, 1700–1840, From Newspaper Advertisements'. *JAMIS* 35:5–80.

—— (2010). 'New Light on Eighteenth-Century English Woodwind Makers from Newspaper Advertisements', *GSJ* 63:73–142.

La Touche, Wendy Digges (2000). 'The Heckel Factory – Interview with Ralf Reiter', *DR* 23/2: 11–15.

Lavoix, Henri (1878). *Histoire de l'instrumentation*. Paris: Firmin–Didot.

Layton, Robert, and D. M. Grimley (2001). 'Berwald: (3) Georg Johann Abraham Berwald', *NGDMM* 2 3:376.

Lein, Janet (1999). 'Bassoon Makers of the Vogtland: Adler, Hüller, Mönnig', *DR* 22/2:11–22.

—— (2003). 'The Mollenhauer Bassoon: An Achievement by Two Families', *DR* 26/3:79–82.

—— (2010). 'Living Life for Music: The Story of the Schreiber Bassoon', *DR* 33/1:79– 85.

Lein, Janet, and Paul Lein (1990). 'Whatever Happened to the Kohlerts?', *DR* 13/1:16– 18.

—— (1997). 'The Püchner Family: 100 Years of Craftsmanship', *DR* 20/2:23–8.

Lescat, Philippe, and Jean Saint-Arroman (1999). *Méthodes et Traités 4: Basson*. Courlay: J. M. Fuzeau.

Letellier, Léon, and Edouard Flament (1927). 'Basson', *Dictionnaire de la musique et Encyclopédie du Conservatoire*, part 3, vol. 3. Paris: Delagrave, 1556–96.

Levin, Robert (1988). *Who Wrote the Mozart Four-Wind Concertante?* Stuyvesant, NY: Pendragon.

Lindorff, Joyce (2004). 'Missionaries, Keyboards and Musical Exchange in the Ming and Qing Courts', *EM* 32/3 (August):403–14.

Lipori, Daniel G. (2002). *A Researcher's Guide to the Bassoon*. Lewiston, NY: Edwin Mellen.

Lockwood, Lewis (1995). 'Adrian Willaert and Cardinal Ippolito d'Este', *Early Music History* 5:85–112.

Loewe, Barbara (2004). 'Ein Projeckt der Universität der Musik und darstellende Kunst in Wien: Neue Musik für junge Fagottisten', *Rohrblatt* 19/2:82–3.

Lorente, Andrés (1672). *El porqué de la musica*. Alcalá de Henares: Xamares.

Lunn, Henry C. (1871). 'Distant Music', *Dwight's Journal of Music* 32:226–7.

Lyndon-Jones, Graham (1994). 'Four Great Curtals,' *FoMRHI* (October):45–47.

Mackey, Melissa (2001). 'An Interview with Stephen Maxym', *DR* 24/4:31–5.

Macnutt, Richard (2001). 'Magasin de musique (i)', *NGDMM* 2 15:579.

Mahillon, Victor Charles (1874). *Éléments d'acoustique musicale & instrumentale*. Brussels: Mahillon.

—— (1909, 1912). *Catalogue descriptif & analytique du Musée instrumental du Conservatoire Royal de Musique de Bruxelles*, vols. 2 (1909); 4 (1912). Ghent: Hoste.

Maillard, Jean–François (1987). 'L'Esprit pastoral et populaire dans la musique française baroque pour instruments à vent'. Doctoral thesis, Université de Paris Sorbonne.

Majer, F. J. B. C. (1732). *Museum musicum theoretico practicum*. Nuremberg.

Marucini, Lorenzo. (1577). *Il Bassano*. Venice: Perchacino.

Masel, Andreas (1995). 'Doppelrohrblattinstrumenten', *MGG* 2, Sachteil 2:1349–1404.

Masier, Miloslav (1995). 'The History of the Bassoon School at the Conservatory of Prague Czech Republic', *DR* 18/3: 46.

Mattheson, Johann (1713). *Das neu-eröffnete Orchester*. Hamburg.

Mauleón Rodriguez, Gustavo. 'Juan Gutiérrez de Padilla desde el ámbto civil: un *corpus* documental', in Gustavo Mauleón Rodriguez, ed., *Juan Gutiérrez de Padilla y la época palafoxiana*. Puebla: Gobierno del Estado de Puebla, 179–240.

Maunder, Richard (1998). Viennese Wind-Instrument Makers, 1700–1800, *GSJ* 51:170–91.

McCredie, A. D. (1964). 'Instrumentarium and Instrumentation in the North German Baroque Opera'. Doctoral thesis, University of Hamburg.

McGee, Timothy (2005). 'Florentine Instrumentalists and their Repertory Circa 1500', *BJHM* 29:145–59.

McGill, David (2007). 'Milde Has a Face!', *DR* 30/3:71–5.

—— (2008). *Sound in Motion*. Bloomington: Indiana University Press.

Meer, John Henry van der (1999). 'Das Buttafuoco', in Eszter Fontana, ed., *Festschrift Rainer Weber*. Halle: J. Stenkovics, 47–56.

Mellers, Wilfrid (1987). *François Couperin and the French Classical Tradition*, second edition. London: Faber & Faber.

Mendel, Hermann, and A. Reissmann (1873; 1879). *Musikalisches Conversations-Lexikon: Eine Encyklopädie der gesammten musikalischen Wissenschaften*, vols. 2 (1873); 11 (1879). Berlin: Oppenheim.

Méndez, Jorge Garcia del Valle (2003). 'Mehrklänge auf dem Fagott: Eine Computeranalyse', *Rohrblatt* 18/2:72–9.

Mendoza de Arce, Daniel (2006). *Music in North America and the West Indies from the Discovery to 1850*. Lanham, MD: Scarecrow.

Mersenne, Marin (1635). *Harmonicorum libri xii*. Paris: Ballard; *R* Geneva: Minkoff, 1972.

Mersenne, Marin, (1636). *Harmonie universelle*. Paris: Cramoisy; *R* Paris: CNRS, 1963.

Meucci, Renato (1994). 'The Pelitti Firm: Makers of Brass Instruments in Nineteenth-Century Milan', *HBSJ* 6:304–33.

Mongrédien, Jean (1996). *French Music from the Enlightenment to Romanticism: 1789–1830*. Portland, Oregon: Amadeus.

Montgomery, William (1975). 'The Life and Works of François Devienne 1759–1803'. Dissertation, Catholic University.

—— (2001). 'Devienne, François', *NGDMM 2* 7:266–8.

Moore, Richard (1992). 'The Renaissance of the Tenor Bassoon', *DRN* 19:37–9.

Mooser, R. Aloys (1948). *Annales de la musique et des musiciens en Russie au XVIIIme siècle*, 1. Geneva: Mont–Blanc.

Morgan, Ralph (1998). 'A Look at the Raw Beginnings of the Lesher Woodwind Co.', *TechniCom* (March–April):15–16.

Morley-Pegge, Reginald (2001). 'Serpent', *NGDMM 2* 23:140–6.

Moser, Hans Joachim (1966). *Paul Hofhaimer*, second edition. Hildesheim: Olms.

Moutier, M. du (1766). 'Faiseur d'instrumens à vent', in *Dictionnaire portatif des arts et métiers*, 1:438–439. Paris: Lacombe.

Müller, Ralf (1995). *Quintfagottschule in zwei Bänden*. Regensburg: Molinari.

Müller-Logemann, Ingeborg, and Hans-Jurgen Müller (1992). 'Im Musikzentrum "De Ijsbreker" in Amsterdam: Gelungene dreitägige Veranstaltung', *Oboe Klarinette Fagott* 7/2:131–40.

Myers, Herbert (1983). 'The Mary Rose "Shawm"', *EM* 11/3:358–60.

—— (1989). 'Slide Trumpet Madness: Fact or Fiction?,' *EM* 17/3:383–4.

—— (2000). 'Reeds and Brass', in Jeffrey Kite-Powell, ed., *The Performer's Guide to Medieval Music*. Bloomington: Indiana University Press, 384–98.

Nagy, Michael (1983). 'Theobald Hürth und seine Fagottschule', *Tibia* 83/1:258–64.

—— (1984). 'Zum Fagottbau in Wien', in E. Brixel, ed., *Bericht über die vierte Konferenz der IGEB, Uster 1981. Alta Musica* 7:25–76.

—— (1987). 'Holzblasinstrumente der tiefen Lage im Schaffen von Johann Joseph Fux', in B. Habla., ed., *Johann Joseph Fux und die barocke Bläsertradition: Kongreßbericht Graz 1985, Alta Musica* 9:95–6.

Narusawa, Ryoichi (2004). 'A History of Oboe Playing in Japan', *DR* 27/4:117–20.

Nassare, Pablo (1723). *Escuela música*. Zaragoza: Larumbre.

Nemetz, Andreas (1844). *Allgemeine Musikschule für Militärmusik*. Vienna: Diabelli. English transl. by Arnold Merrrick as *Niemitz's Method for Musical Instruments Used in a Military Band with Complete Scales* (London: Cocks).

Ness, Arthur J., and C. A. Kolczynski (2001). 'Sources of Lute Music', *NGDMM 2* 24:39–63.

Neuls-Bates, Carol, ed. (1982). *Women in Music: An Anthology of Source Readings from the Middle Ages to the Present*. New York: Harper & Row.

Newman, William S. (1972). *The Sonata in the Baroque Era*, third edition. New York: Norton.

Nicholson, William (1821). 'Musical Instruments', *American ed. of the British Encycl: or Dictionary of Arts and Sciences*, 8 (unpaginated).

Nickel, Ekkehard (1971). *Der Holzblasinstrumentenbau in der freien Reichsstadt Nürnberg*. Munich: Katzbichler.

Nimetz, Daniel (1967). 'The Wind Music of Carlo Besozzi'. Dissertation, University of Rochester.

Nösselt, Hans-Joachim (1980). *Ein ältest Orchester 1530–1980. 450 Jahre Bayerisches Hof- und Staatsorchester*. Munich: Bruckmann.

Nutly, Léon (1858). 'Willent-Bordogni', *Mémoires de la Société impériale d'agriculture, sciences et arts, deuxième série*. Douai: Adam, 4:321–40.

Onerati, Alessandro (1995). 'Strumenti a fiato nella vita musicale fiorentina dell'ottocento'. Thesis, Università degli studi di Urbino.

Ongaro, Giulio (1985). 'Sixteenth-Century Wind Instrument Makers and their Clients', *EM* 13/3:391–7.

Orselli, Luigi (1874). *Metodo completo per fagotto*. Turin: Giudici e Strada.

Ottenbourgs, Stefaan (1989). 'Die Familie Rottenburgh [...] Teil 2: Die Instrumente', *Tibia* 89/4:557–67.

Owens, Samantha K. (1995). 'The Württemberg Hofkapelle c.1680–1721'. PhD dissertation, Victoria University of Wellington, New Zealand.

—— (2005). 'Upgrading from Consort to Orchestra at the Württemberg Court', in Wainwright and Holman 2005:227–40.

Ozi, Etienne (1787). *Méthode nouvelle et raisonée pour le basson*. Paris: Boyer (the edition was advertised 13 November 1787). R Lescat and Saint-Arroman 1999:109– 36.

—— (1803). *Nouvelle méthode de basson*. Paris: Imprimerie du Conservatoire de Musique. R Saint-Arroman 2005:7–159.

—— (1805) *Nouvelle méthode de basson par Ozi, membre du conservatoire de musique à Paris: français & allemande*. Offenbach: Jean André.

—— (1806). *Neue Fagot-Schule von Ozi, Mitglied des Conservatorium der Musik in Paris: beym Unterricht in diesem Institute eingeführt*. Leipzig: Breitkopf & Härtel.

Page, Janet K. (2001). 'Band: II:2:I, Military', *NGDMM 2* 2:623–8.

Paradin, Claude (1551). *Devises héroïques*. Lyons: de Tourne and Gazeau.

Parkinson, John A. (1992). 'Artaxerxes', *NGDO*.

Penazzi, Sergio (1971). *Metodo per fagotto*. Milan: Zerboni.

—— (1982). *Il fagotto: Altre tecniche; Nuove fonti di espressione musicale*. Milan: Ricordi.

Perfetti, Franco (1989). *Il Fagotto: Origine ed evoluzione*. Bologna: Rodi.

Philidor, Jean-François, and Nicolas Dupont-Danican Philidor (1995). *Les Philidor: Une dynastie de musiciens*. Paris: Zurfluh.

Philidor, Nicolas Dupont-Danican (1997). *Les Philidor: Répertoire des œuvres, généalogie, bibliographie*. Paris: Zurfluh.

Philip, Robert F. (1992). *Early Recordings and Musical Style: Changing Tastes in Instrumental Performance, 1900–1950*. Cambridge: CUP.

Piard, Marius (1952). *Enseignement du contrebasson*. Paris: Leduc.

Pierre, Constant (1890). *La facture instrumentale à l'Exposition universelle de 1889: Notes d'un musicien sur les instruments à souffle humain*. Paris: Librairie de l'art indépendant.

——— (1895a). *B. Sarrette et les origines du conservatoire national de musique et de déclamation*. Paris: Delalain.

——— (1895b). *Le Magasin de musique à l'usage des fêtes nationales et du conservatoire*. Paris: Fischbacher.

—— (1900). *Le Conservatoire national de musique et de déclamation*. Paris: Imprimerie nationale.

Pillaut, Léon. (1894). *Le Musée du Conservatoire national de musique; 1er supplément au catalogue de 1884*. Paris: Fischbacher.

Pirro, André (1907). *L'Esthétique de Jean-Sébastien Bach*. Paris: Fischbacher.

Piwkowski, Kazimierz (1970). 'Sztort i Krzywuła w Tradycji Staropolskiej'. Habilitationschrift, Warsaw.

Polk, Keith (2005). 'Instrumental Music c.1500: Players, Makers and Musical Contexts', *BJHP* 29:21–34.

Pontécoulant, Adolphe le Doulcet, comte de (1861). *Organographie: Essai sur la facture instrumentale*, 2. Paris: Castel.

Porter, Lewis (2002). 'Bassoon', *NGDJ*.

Powell, Ardal (1996). 'The Hotteterre Flute: Six Replicas in Search of a Myth', *JAMS* 49:225–63.

Praetorius, Martin, H. Mons, and K. Bickhardt. (2005). 'Der Kontrabass-Dulzian Mö. 36 in Kunstgewerbemuseum Dresden Pillnitz', *Glareana* 54:23–49.

Praetorius, Michael (1618–20). *Syntagma Musicum II: De Organographia Parts I and II*. Wolfenbüttel, 1618–19; 1620. Transl. David Z. Crookes. Oxford: Clarendon Press, 1986.

——— (1619). *Syntagma Musicum III: Termini musici*. Wolfenbüttel. Transl. Jeffrey Kite-Powell. Oxford and New York: OUP, 2004.

Price, John (2006). 'My Collections of Gwydion Brooke', *DRN* 76 (Autumn):7.

Prizer, William F. (1982). 'Isabella d'Este and Lorenzo da Pavia, "Master Instrument-Maker" ', *Early Music History* 2:87–127.

Prunières, Henry (1911). 'La musique de la chambre et de l'écurie sous le règne de François Ier', *L'année musicale* 1:215–51.

Pyron, Nona (2001), 'Ferro, Marco Antonio', *NGDMM 2* 8:726.

Rabinowitz, Michael (2007). 'Bassoon Amplification in Jazz and Popular Music', in Vonk 2007:108–10

Radant, Else, and H. C. Robbins Landon (1994). 'Documents from the Esterházy Archives in Eisenstadt and Forchtenstein, edited by János Harich II', *Haydn Jahrbuch* 19:1–38.

Rampley, Nick (2004). 'Berio's Sequenza XII for Solo Bassoon', *DRN* 68:13–14.

Rapoport, Ricardo (2009). 'The Six Bassoon Sonatas by M. Dard', *DR* 32/1: 67–94.

Raumberger, Claus, and Karl Ventzke (2001). 'Saxophone', *NGDMM 2* 22:352–8.

Reissinger, Marianne (2001). 'Eichner, Ernst (Dieterich Adolph)', *NGDMM 2* 8:23–4.

Rhodes, David J. (1983). 'Franz Anton Pfeiffer and the Bassoon', *GSJ* 36:97–103.

—— (1995). 'Harmonie Music at the Mecklenburg-Schwerin Court in the 18th–19th Centuries', *JIDRS* 23:21–34.

—— (2000). 'Carl Stamitz and Ludwigslust', in Karl Heller et al., eds., *Musik in Mecklenburg*. Hildesheim: Olms, 489–510.

Rice, Albert R. (2009). *From the Clarinet d'Amour to the Contra Bass: A History of Large Size Clarinets 1740–1860*. Oxford: OUP.

Rice, Albert R., and P. J. Bukalski (1985). 'Two Reed Contrabasses (Contrabassi ad ancia) at Claremont', *JAMIS* 11:115–22.

Ridley, E. A. K. (1984). *Royal College of Music Museum of Instruments Catalogue, I: European Wind Instruments*. London: Royal College of Music.

Riedelbach, Heinz (1988). *Systematik moderner Fagott- und Bassontechnik*. Celle: Moeck.

Rifkin, Joshua, et al. (2001). 'Schütz', *NGDMM 2* 22:826–60.

Ring, William (2001). 'The 2nd Mini-Bassoon Festival Leipzig 2001', *DRN* 57 (Winter): 14–15.

Ritzarev, Marina (2006). *Eighteenth-Century Russian Music*. Aldershot and Burlington, VT: Ashgate.

Robin, Vincent (2004). 'Hautbois et cromorne en France aux XVIIe et XVIII siècles. Essai de clarification terminologique', *BJHM* 28:23–36.

Rosand, Ellen (1993). 'Venice, 1580–1680', in Curtis Price, ed., *Music and Society: The Early Baroque Era*. Englewood Cliffs: Prentice Hall, 1993, 75–102.

Rosemeyer, Julia (2002). 'Carl Almenräder (1786–1843): Untersuchungen zu Leben und Schaffen', MA thesis, Johannes-Guttenberg-Universität Mainz.

—— (2003). 'Carl Almenräder (1786–1843): Biografie und Vokalwerke eines mittelrheinsichen Musikers', *Mitteilungen der Arbeitgemeinschaft für mittelrheinische Musikgeschichte* 76/77 (February): 317–58.

Rostagno, Antonio (2001). 'Rolla, Alessandro', *NGDMM 2* 21:529–30.

Rüdiger, Beate von (1999). *Das Zauberbündel*, 2 vols. Remscheid: self-published.

Ruffati, A. (1998). 'La Famiglia Piva-Bassano nei documenti degli archivi di Bassano del Grappa', *Musica e storia* 6/2 (December):349–67.

Sadie, Stanley (1972). *Handel Concertos*. London: BBC Music Guides.

—— (1983). *The New Grove Mozart*. New York: Norton.

Sadler, Graham (1981–2). 'Rameau and the Orchestra', *Proceedings of the Royal Musical Association* 108:47–68.

—— (1992a), 'Castor et Pollux', *NGDO*.

—— (1992b), 'Daradanus', *NGDO*.

—— (1992c). 'Zoroaster', *NGDO*.

Saint-Arroman, Jean, ed. (2005). *Méthodes & Traités: Basson: France 1800–1860*, 4 vols. Courlay: Fuzeau.

Sallagar, W. H. (1978). 'Wiener Holzblasinstrumente', *Tibia* 3/1:1–6.

Sallagar, W. H., and Michael Nagy, eds. (1992). *Fagott Forever: Eine Festgabe für Karl Öhlberger zum achzigsten Geburtstag*. Wilhering: Hilaria.

—— (1993). 'Imre-Weidinger-Fagott-festival und -Wettbewerb in Pécs', *Rohrblatt* 8/2:81–2.

Salvetti, Guido, and T. H. Keahey (2001). 'Besozzi', *NGDMM 2* 3:487–8.

Sanders, Ernest H. (2001). 'Motet, §III: Baroque', *NGDMM 2* 17:215–22.

Satzenhofer, Julius (1900). *Fagottschule*. Leipzig: Zimmermann.

Sawerthal, Joseph (1846). 'Über einige Regimentskapellen in Ungarn und Österreich: Reisebericht', *Allgemeine Wiener Musik-Zeitung*, 6. Excerpts quoted in Habla 1990:317–25.

Schafhäutl, Karl von (1882). 'V. F. Červený und sein Reich von Blechblasinstrumenten', *AmZ* 52:841–79.

Schilling, Gustav (1835–8). *Universal Lexikon der Tonkunst*, 6 vols. Stuttgart: Köhler.

Schlosser, Julius (1920). *Die Sammlung alter Musikinstrumente*. Vienna: Schroll.

Schmid, Manfred Hermann (1994). 'Kontrabaß-Oboe und Großbaß-Pommer zu Traditionsüberlagerung im 18. Jahrhundert', *Musik in Baden-Württemberg* 1:95–121.

Schmidt, Carl B. (1995). *The Music of Francis Poulenc*. Oxford: OUP.

Schoenbaum, Camillo, and J. Backus (2001). 'Komorous, Rudolf', *NGDMM 2* 13:767–8.

Schönemann, Karl (1937). 'Besuch in der Kasseler Instrumentenbauanstalt Mollenhauer', *Die Musik– Woche* 5/27 (3 July):1–3.

Schreiber, Ottmar (1938). *Orchester und Orchesterpraxis in Deutschland zwischen 1780 und 1850*. Berlin: Triltsch & Zuther.

Schuller, Gunther (1968). *Early Jazz*. Oxford: OUP.

——— (1989). *The Swing Era: The Development of Jazz, 1930–1945*. New York and Oxford: OUP.

Schultze-Florey, Andreas (2002). 'Auswahl des Rohrholzes mit der AuftriebSummenFormen', *Rohrblatt* 17/1:6–9.

Schulze, Werner (1985). 'Sololiteratur für Kontrafagott: Versuch einer Bibliographie', *Oboe-Fagott* 5:30–33.

——— (1992). 'Kontra Streich: Versuch einer Neubewertung der "Neben"-Instrumente des Fagottisten', in Sallagar and Nagy 1992:177–213.

Sehnal, Jiří (1973). 'Die Bläserharmonie des Augustinerklosters in Altbrünn', *Studia minora facultatis philosphicae universitatis brunensis* 8:125–42.

Selfridge-Field, Eleanor (1976). 'Bassano and the Orchestra of St Mark's', *EM* 4:152–8.

——— (1979). 'Vivaldi's Esoteric Instruments', *EM* 7/3:332–8. Response by Michael Talbot in *EM* 7/4:561.

——— (1994). *Venetian Instrumental Music from Gabrieli to Vivaldi*, third edition. New York: Dover.

——— (2001). 'Fedeli', *NGDMM 2* 8:636–8.

Sherwood, Thomas (1998). *Starting on an Early Bassoon*. Cambridge: self-published.

Shive, Clyde A. Jr. (1992). 'The Wind Band in the United States 1800 to 1825', in B. Habla, ed., *Kongressberichte Oberschützen/Burgenland 1988, Toblach/Südtirol 1990. Alta Musica* 14:159–191.

——— (1996). 'Harmoniemusik and the Early Wind Band in the United States', in W. Suppan, ed., *Kongressbericht Abony/Ungarn 1994. Alta Musica* 18:405–21.

Silbiger, Alexander (2001), 'Weckmann', *NGDMM 2* 27:199–202.

Sirker, Udo (1968). *Die Entwicklung des Bläserquintetts in der ersten Hälfte des 19. Jahrhunderts*. Regensburg: Bosse.

Sittard, Josef (1886). 'Reinhard Keiser in Württemberg', *Monatshefte für Musikgeschichte* 18:7–44.

Smith, Anthea (2010). 'Charpentier's Music at Court: The Singers and Instrumentalists of the Chapelle Royale, 1663–1683 and Beyond', in Shirley Thompson, ed., *New Perspectives on Marc-Antoine Charpentier*. Burlington and Aldershot: Ashgate, 133–59.

Snyder, Kerala (1987). *Dieterich Buxtehude*. New York: Schirmer.

——— (2001). 'Buxtehude', *NGDMM 2* 4:695–710.

Sonneck, Oscar G. (1907). *Early Concert-Life in America (1731–1800)*. Leipzig: Breitkopf.

Spagnoli, Gina (1993). 'Dresden at the Time of Heinrich Schütz', in Curtis Price, ed., *The Early Baroque Era: From the Late 16th Century to the 1660s*. Englewood Cliffs, NJ: Prentice–Hall, 164–184.

Spaniol, Doug (2009). 'A History of the Weissenborn Practical Method for Bassoon', in Ewell 2009:87–118.

Speer, Daniel (1697). *Grund-richtiger Kurtz- Leicht- und Nöthiger jetzt Wol-vermehrter Unterricht der Musicalischen Kunst oder Vierfaches Musicalisches Kleeblatt*. Ulm: Georg Wilhelm Kühn; *R* Leipzig, 1974.

Spencer, Jennifer (2001). 'Kalinnikov, Vasily Sergeyevich', *NGDMM 2* 13:325–6.

Spiessens, Godelieve (1998). 'De Antwerpse Speellieden, 1415–1794', *Musica Antiqua* 15/4 (November):170–79.

——— (2000). 'Jan Meulepas (vóór 1567–1620?): Van Antwerps speelman en fagotbouwer tot Brussels hofmuzikant', *Musica Antiqua* 17/1:12–18.

Spitzer, John, and Neal Zaslaw (2004). *The Birth of the Orchestra: History of an Institution, 1650–1815*. Oxford: OUP.

Spohr, Arne (2004). 'Wind Instruments in the Anglo-German Consort Repertoire, ca. 1630–40: A Survey of Music by Johann Schop and Nicolaus Bleyer', *HBSJ* 16:43–65.

Stadio, Ciro (1908). *Grande metodo per fagotto*. Naples: Rocco.

Stanley, Barbara, and Graham Lyndon-Jones (1983). *The Curtal*. St. Albans, Hertfordshire: self–published.

Starner, Robert (2000). 'The Introduction of Double Reeds to New Mexico 1624–33', *DR* 23/2:73–7.

———. (2006) 'Two Mexican Bajones: Images of a Double Reed Instrument in Rural Michoacán', *Music in Art* 31/1–2:118.

Steblin, Rita (2008). 'Woodwind Makers in the Classical Era, with Emphasis on Friedrich Lempp's Request for Protection in 1768', *JAMIS* 34:26–73.

Stevenson, Robert (1968). *Music in the Aztec and Inca Territory*. Berkeley and Los Angeles: University of California Press.

Stilz, Bernhard (1995). 'Von "Stadtpfeiffern" und "Hoboiste": Holzbläser als Berufsmusiker in der frühen Neuzeit. Teil 2', *Rohrblatt* 10/3:101–6.

Stock, Jonathan P. J. (2001). 'Shanghai', *NGDMM 2* 23:201–2.

Stockigt, Jim (2008). 'The Bassoon in Vocal Works 1700–1850', *DR* 31/1:86–109. Expanded version online at http://www.jimstockigtinfo.com/arias_with_obbligato_bassoon/

Stone, W. H. (1879). 'Bassoon', in George Grove, ed., *A Dictionary of Music and Musicians*, 1:151–4. London: Macmillan.

Storch, Leila (2008). *Marcel Tabuteau*. Bloomington: Indiana University Press.

Stradner, Gerhard (1987). 'Die Blasinstrumente in einem Inventar der Wiener Hofkapelle von 1706', *Studien zur Musikwissenschaft* 38 (1987):53–63.

Sundelin, A. (1828). *Die Instrumentirung für sämmtliche Militär-Musik-Chöre*. Berlin: Wagenführ.

Swiney, Alvin (1999). 'Hans Moennig's Water Tube', *Woodwind Quarterly* 17:71–3.

Szórádová, Eva (2000). 'Blasinstrumentenbau in Bratislava', in A. Suppan, ed., *Kongressbericht Banská Bystrica 1998. Alta Musica* 22:365–98.

Talbot, Michael (1979). 'Comment on "Vivaldi's Esoteric Instruments"', *EM* 7/4:561.

—— (1993). *Vivaldi*. New York: OUP.

—— (2003/4). 'The Pietà as Viewed by Johann Christoph Maier (1795)', *Studi Vivaldiani* 3/4:75–111.

—— (2005). 'Vivaldi and the Violino in Tromba Marina', *The Consort* 62 (Summer):5–17.

Tamplini, Giuseppe (1888). *Brevi cenni sul sistema Boehm e della sua applicazione al fagotto*. Bologna: Andreoli.

Tarr, Edward H. (2003). *East Meets West: The Russian Trumpet Tradition*. Hillsdale, NY: Pendragon.

Taruskin, Richard (1996). *Stravinsky and the Russian Tradition*. Berkeley: University of California Press.

Ten Bokum, Jan (2001). 'Coenen, Johannes Meinardus', *NGDMM 2* 6:85.

Térey-Smith, Mary (2001). 'Instrumentation and Orchestration: Baroque', *NGDMM 2* 12:406–9.

Ter Voert, Georg (1992). *Fagottino, Band 1: Schule für Kinder*. Markgröningen, Germany: self-published.

Terry, Charles Sanford (1972). *Bach's Orchestra*. London: OUP. Originally published 1932.

Tevo, Zaccaria (1706). *Il Musico testore*. Venice

Thayer, Henry (1970). *Thayer's Life of Beethoven*, revised and edited by Eliot Forbes. Princeton: PUP.

Tilmouth, Michael (2001). 'Farewell', *NGDMM 2* 8:562–3.

Tosca i Mascó, Tomàs Vicent (1707). *Compendio mathemático*. València: Garcia.

Toschi, Andrea (1998). 'Antonio Torriani and the XIX Century Milanese Bassoon School: A First Survey', *JIDRS* 26:93–7.

Tosoroni, Antonio (c.1850). *Trattato prattico di strumentazione*. Florence: Guidi.

Travis, Francis Irving (1956). *Verdi's Orchestration*. Zurich: Juris-Verlag.

Tremmel, Erich (1993). 'Musikinstrumenten im Hause Fugger', in Renate Eikelmann, ed., *Die Fugger und die Musik: 'lautenschlagen lernen und lieben': Anton Fugger zum 500. Geburtstag*. Augsburg: Städtische Kunstsammlungen, 61–70.

Trichet, Pierre (c.1640). *Traité des Instruments de musique (vers 1640)*, ed. François Lesure. Neuilly-sur-Seine: Société de Musique d'Autrefois, 1957; *R* Geneva: Minkoff, 1978.

Turkovic, Milan (2001). 'Basson und Fagott', *Wiener Oboe* 11 (September):3–4.

Valdrighi, L. F. (1881). 'Il Phagotus di Afranio', *Musurgiana* 5. Milan: S. Giuseppe.

Valls, Francesc (1742). 'Mapa armónico práctico'. Ms, Barcelona, Biblioteca de la Universitat. Facsimile edition by Josep Pavio i Simó. Barcelona: CSIC, 2002.

Van Heyghen, Peter (2005). 'The Recorder Consort in the Sixteenth Century', in David Lasocki, ed., *Musicque de Joye: Proceedings of the International Symposium on the Renaissance Flute and Recorder Consort Utrecht 2003*. Utrecht: STIMU, 227–322.

Vasconcellos, Joaquim (1870). *Os Musicos portuguezes: Biografia-bibliografia*. Imprensa Portugueza.

Vasconcellos, Simão de (1663). *Chronica da Companhia de Jesu do Estado do Brasil*. Lisbon.

Veazey, Charles O. (1988). 'Observations of Laryngeal Activity of Woodwind Instruments During Performance Using a Fiberoptic Laryngoscope', *Flutist Quarterly* 13 (Spring):44–8.

Ventzke, Karl (1976). 'Boehm–System Fagotte im 19 Jahrhundert', *Tibia* 1/1:13–18.

—— (1977). 'Ensemble Music for Small Bassoons', *GSJ* 30:151–3.

—— (1991). 'Deutsche Reichsgebrauchsmuster für Oboen und Fagotte', *Tibia* 3/91:541–2.

—— (1995). 'Über die Wiesbadener Fagottbauer Reinhold Lange (1854–1905) und Hermann Ficker (1862–1945)', *Tibia* 4/94:601–2.

—— (1996). 'Zum "Stuttgarter" Fagott des 19.Jahrhunderts', *Musik in Baden-Württemberg* 3:102–13.

—— (2001). 'Über den Koblenzer Instrumentenbauer Heinrich Joseph Haseneier (1798–1890)', *Oboe-Fagott* 62/1:11–14.

Ventzke, Karl, and Enrico Weller (2005). 'Deutsche Reichs-Gebrauchsmuster (DRGM) für Holzblasinstrumente 1892–1940', *Instrumentenbau-Zeitschrift* 11–12:13–16.

Volkmann, Hans (1942). *Beethoven und seine Beziehungen zu Dresden.* Dresden: Melchert. Excerpt transl. by John G. Cole in *DR* 14/3 (1991):61–3.

Vonk, Maarten (2007). *A Bundle of Joy: A Practical Handbook for the Bassoonist.* Amersfoort, Netherlands: self–published.

Voorhees, Jerry L. (2003). *The Development of Woodwind Fingering Systems in the Nineteenth and Twentieth Centuries.* Hammond, LA: self-published. Contains schematic diagrams of key work of twenty–three French and German bassoons.

Wagner, Käthe (1976). 'Die Fagott-Instrumente des 17. Jahrhunderts: Untersuchung zu ihrer Entwicklung und zu ihrer Verwendung', Diplomarbeit, Schola Cantorum, Basel.

Wainwright, Jonathan, and Peter Holman, eds. (2005). *From Renaissance to Baroque: Change in Instruments and Instrumental Music in the Seventeenth Century.* Aldershot: Ashgate.

Walther, J. G. (1732). *Musikalisches Lexikon.* Leipzig.

Ward. Martha Kingdon (1949). 'Mozart and the Bassoon', *Music & Letters* 30/1:8–25.

Warrack, John (1976). *Carl Maria von Weber.* Cambridge: CUP.

Wasielewski, Wilhelm Joseph von (1878). *Geschichte der Instrumentenmusik im XVI. Jahrhundert.* Berlin: Guttentag.

Waterhouse, William (1983). *The Proud Bassoon: An Exhibition Showing the Development of the Bassoon over the Centuries.* Edinburgh University Collection of Historic Musical Instruments. Unpaginated.

—— (1992) 'A Critical Bibliography of Historical Teaching Material for Bassoon 1700–1900: Tutor, Chart and Etude', in Sallagar and Nagy 1992:39–62.

—— (1993). *The New Langwill Index: A Dictionary of Musical Wind-Instrument Makers and Inventors.* London: Tony Bingham.

—— et al. (1999a). 'Cecil James' [obituaries], *DRN* 47 (Summer):12–16.

—— (1999b). 'Obituary: Sol Schoenbach (1915–99)', *DRN* 48 (Autumn):35.

—— (2001a). 'Bassoon', *NGDMM 2* 2:873–95.

—— (2001b). 'Racket', *NGDMM 2* 20:719–23.

—— (2001c). 'Rothophone', *NGDMM 2* 21:784.

—— (2003). *Bassoon.* Yehudi Menuhin Music Guides. London: Kahn & Averill.

—— (2007). 'New Light on the Weissenborn Family', *DR* 30.2:35–44.

Weait, Christopher (1979). 'A Visit to the People's Republic of China', *DR* 2/1:5–7.

Weaver, Robert (1961). 'Sixteenth-century Instrumentation', *Musical Quarterly* 57:363–78.

Weber, Gottfried (1816a). 'Versuch einer praktischen Akustik der Blasinstrumente', *AmZ* 18:65–73.

—— (1816b). 'Vervollkommnung der Blasinstrumente', *AmZ* 18: 697–700; 729; 749, 763.

—— (1817). 'Praktische Resultate aus des Verfassers Akustik der Blasinstrumente', *AmZ* 19: [809, 825].

—— (1828). 'Wesentliche Verbesserungen des Fagottes', *Cäcilia* 2/6:123–40.

Weber, Rainer (1991). 'Kontrabass-Dulciane, die Vorläufer des Kontrafagottes', *Oboe Klarinette Fagott*, 6 (1991), 97–105.

—— (2006). 'Das Rackett-Fagott des Barock', *Tibia* 31/4:259–63.

Weber, Rainer, and J. H. van der Meer (1972). 'Some Facts and Guesses Concerning Doppioni', *GSJ* 25:22–9.

Weidauer, Stephan (1989). 'Versuch einer kurzen Einführung für angehende Barockfagottisten', *Oboe-Fagott* 19 (April):3–12.

—— (1992). 'Probespielstellen für Oboe, Klarinette, Fagott und Nebeninstrumente', *Oboe Klarinette Fagott* 7/1:1–4.

—— (1994). 'Musik für ein Stiefkind: Literatur für Fagott, dargestellt am Concertino D-Fur von Johann E. Brandl', *Rohrblatt* 9:152–9.

—— [as Wei Dao Er] (2006). 'In drei Wochen mit vier Fagottisten durch fünf Städte Chinas: Eines gab es nie: Reis', *Rohrblatt* 22/33:141–6.

—— (2007). 'Zweite China-Tour "United Sounds of Püchner": Mit Blaulicht durch Chonqing', *Rohrblatt* 23/3:177–80.

Weisberg, Arthur (1998). 'Bringing the Bassoon into the 21st Century', *DR* 21/2:85–7.

—— (2001). 'A Double Automatic Octave Key System for the Bassoon', *DR* 24/3:93–4.

Weissenborn, Julius (1887). *Praktische Fagott-Schule.* Leipzig: Forberg.

Weller, Enrico (1997). 'Plexiglas im Holzblasinstrumentenbau', *Instrumentenbau-Zeitschrift* 1–2:85–91.

Werba, Michael (1995). 'Wiener Bläserstil', *WWV Blätter* (11 April):8–11.

Werba, Michael, and Michael Nagy (1993). 'Wiener Klang auf Doppelrohrblattinstrumenten', *Vom Pasqualatihaus* 1:12–20.

Werr, Sebastian (2011). *Geschichte des Fagotts.* Augsburg: Wißner.

Weston, Steven (1997). 'Double-Reed Instruments in the English Church Choir-Band', *DRN* 40 (Autumn):44–7.

White, Kelly, and Arnold Myers (2004). 'Woodwind Instruments of Boosey & Company', *GSJ* 57:62–80.

White, Mickey (2000). 'Biographical Notes on the "Figlie di coro" of the Pietà Contemporary with Vivaldi', *Informazioni e studi Vivaldiani* 21:75–97.

White, Chappell, et al. (2001). 'Cambini, Giuseppe', *NGDMM 2* 4:858–61.

Widor, Charles-Marie (1906). *Technique de l'orchestre moderne.* Paris: Lemoine, 1904; transl. Edward Suddard as *The Technique of the Modern Orchestra.* London: Williams, 1906. *R* with appendix by Gordon Jacob; London: Williams, 1945.

Wiemken, Robert (2007). 'Dulcians Great and Small: An Octavebass Dulcian on the U.S. Mainland', *Early Music America* (Spring):27–32.

Wijsman, Suzanne (2001). 'Violoncello: II (1) ii. Five-string and Piccolo Cellos', *NGDMM 2* 26:750–1.

Willent-Bordogni, J. B. (1844). *Méthode complète pour le basson.* Paris: Troupenas. *R* Saint-Arroman 2005, 3:33–138.

Williams, Peter (2001). 'Sixteen-foot', *NGDMM 2* 23:462.

—— and David Ledbetter (2001). 'Continuo', *NGDMM 2* 6:345–67.

Wilmer, Val, and Gary W. Kennedy (2001). 'Cooper, Lindsay (Charlotte)', *NGDJ.*

Wilson, Adelaide (1889). *Picturesque Savannah.* Boston: Boston Photogravure Co.

Wolf, Guntram (2002). 'The Contrabassoon in 2002 – A New Design', *DRN* 60 (Autumn):60–2.

Wolff, Christoph (2001). 'Bach, Carl Philipp Emanuel: Works', *NGDMM 2* 2:398–408.

Woodley, Ronald (2001). 'Tinctoris, Johannes', *NGDMM 2* 25:497–501.

Young, Phillip T. (1993). *4900 Historical Woodwind Instruments.* London: Bingham.

—— (1997). *Woodwind Instruments of the Oberösterreichisches Landesmuseum.* Linz: Oberösterreichisches Landesmuseum.

Zohn, Steven (2001). 'Telemann', *NGDMM 2* 25:199–232.

—— (2009). 'The Overture-Suite, Concerto Grosso, Ripieno Concerto, and *Harmoniemusik* in the Eighteenth Century', in Simon Keefe, ed., *Cambridge History of Eighteenth-Century Music.* Cambridge: CUP, 556–82.

Index

DATE DUE

DEMCO 38-296